한 권에 끝내는
Level 2
G-TELP
실전모의고사

이현아 취향저격
G - T E L P

이현아 취향저격

지텔프코리아
공식
지정

한 권에 끝내는
Level 2
G-TELP
실전모의고사

5회

Preface
머리말

Real 실전이다!
G-TELP 취향저격 실전모의고사

지텔프(G-TELP) 공부를 하는 수험생들은 대부분 7급 공무원, 세무사, 노무사와 같은 시험 준비 과정에서 지텔프를 접하게 됩니다. 영어인증점수요건은 준비하는 시험의 전제 자격과 같아서 최대한 적은 시간과 노력으로 최단기간 목표점수를 획득하는 것이 관건입니다.

최단기간 & 최고효율의 학습법. 누구나 바라는 바이지만, 쉬운 길은 아닙니다. 더욱이 지텔프 시험은 공무원이나 수능처럼 기출문제가 공개되지도 않습니다. 제대로 된 실전문제를 한 번도 접하지 않은 상태에서 시험장에 들어가는 수험생들은 당황할 수밖에 없습니다.

전국의 수많은 수험생들에게 지텔프를 강의하는 강사로서 제대로 된 가이드를 드리는 것이 임무라고 생각했습니다. 그게 가능할까..? 깊은 고민 후에 지텔프 '진짜' 문제를 정확한 해설로 제공하자는 결정을 내렸고, 이 책이 출간될 수 있었던 이유입니다.

이현아 [한 권에 끝내는 취향저격 지텔프 실전모의고사 5회]에 담긴 실전모의고사 5회분(400문항)은 지텔프시험 주관사인 [지텔프코리아]가 직접 출제했습니다. 각 문항에 대한 해설은 지텔프 국내 최고 전문가인 제가 맡았습니다. 이 교재를 독학으로 활용하는 수험생들도 학습에 어려움이 없도록 간단하면서도 명료한 해설을 담으려고 노력했습니다.

실전서인만큼 기본 개념이론을 이 책에 정리해 두지는 않았습니다. 지텔프 시험 범위와 방향성에 대해 익숙하지 않은 분들은 이현아 [한 권에 끝내는 취향저격 지텔프] 점수 시리즈 교재 (32점/ 50점/ 65점)를 선택해서 학습하실 것을 권해드립니다. 목표하는 점수와 가장 가까운 점수대의 책을 한 권 선택해서 학습하신다면 훨씬 높은 시너지 효과를 얻으실 수 있습니다.

방대한 영어문법 학습이나 한 문장씩 뜯어보는 번역식 독해공부법에서 벗어나세요. Real 지텔프 실전시험문제로 전략적으로! 현명하게! 준비하신다면 목표하시는 바를 어렵지 않게 이루실 수 있을 겁니다.

여러분들의 꿈과 도전을 응원합니다!

신림동에서
저자 이현아

G-TELP에 대한 소개

■ G-TELP 평가영역

구술능력평가	종합능력평가	작문능력평가	특수목적형 평가
G-TELP Speaking Test	G-TELP Grammar, Listening, Reading	G-TELP Writing Test	

정규시험
- 평가 영역별 시험을 통한 분야별 능력평가

- 기업 및 단체의 목적과 수준에 맞는 맞춤형 평가

GRAMMAR   **Listening**   **Reading**

    4지 선다형 질문으로 구성되어 있으며 문법, 청취, 독해 및 어휘를 평가합니다.
    G-TELP는 문법(Grammar), 청취(Listening), 독해 및 어휘(Reading & Vocabulary) 모두 75%이상 획득한 경우, Mastery 한 것으로 인정됨으로 영어 능력을 종합적으로 평가하여 수험자의 정확한 영어 활용 수준을 판단할 수 있습니다.

구분	출제방식	시간	평가 기준	합격자의 영어 구사 능력
Level1	청취 30문항	약 30분	Native Speaker에 준하는 영어 능력 : 상담, 토론 가능	일상 생활은 물론 상담, 토론 등에서 영어를 모국어로 하는 외국인과 거의 대등한 의사 소통이 가능하며 국제회의 통역도 가능한 수준입니다.
	독해 60문항	70분		
	전체 90문항	약 100분		
Level2	문법 26문항	20분	다양한 상황에서 대화 가능: 업무상담 및 해외 연수 등이 가능한 수준	일상 생활 및 업무 상담 등에서 어려움 없이 의사소통 할 수 있으며 외국인과의 회의 및 세미나 참석, 해외 연수 등이 가능한 수준입니다.
	청취 26문항	약 30분		
	독해 28문항	40분		
	전체 80문항	약 90분		
Level3	문법 22문항	20분	간단한 의사소통과 친숙한 상태에서의 단순 대화 가능	간단한 의사 소통과 친숙한 상태에서의 단순한 대화가 가능하며 해외 여행과 단순한 업무 출장을 할 수 있는 수준입니다.
	청취 24문항	약 20분		
	독해 24문항	40분		
	전체 70문항	80분		
Level4	문법 20문항	20분	기본적인 문장을 통해 최소한의 의사소통이 가능한 수준	기본적인 어휘의 짧은 문장을 통해 최소한의 의사 소통이 가능한 수준으로 외국인이 자주 반복하거나 부연설명을 해주어야 이해할 수 있는 수준입니다.
	청취 20문항	약 15분		
	독해 20문항	25분		
	전체 60문항	약 60분		
Level5	문법 16문항	15분	극히 초보적인 수준의 의사소통 가능	영어 초보자로서 일상의 인사, 소개 등을 듣고, 이해할 수 있으나 말 또는 글을 통한 자기표현은 거의 불가능한 수준입니다.
	청취 16문항	약 15분		
	독해 18문항	25분		
	전체 50문항	약 55분		

※ G-TELP 시험에서는 1등급에만 응시자격 제한 (2등급 Mastery)이 있습니다.
* 모든 시험은 청취시간에 따라 시험소요 시간이 변동될 수 있습니다.

■ Mastery 기준
- 각 Section별 (문법·청취·독해 및 어휘) 75% 이상 획득해야 해당 등급 Mastery
- 한개 Section이 75% 미만인 경우 Near Mastery

Section	점수비율
문법 (Grammar)	100점만점
청취 (Listening)	100점만점
독해 및 어휘 (Reading &Vocabulary)	100점만점
총점	총 300점만점
평균	100점 (성적표 상 You have answered 00% of all the question on the test correctly 부분)

G-TELP Speaking Test

"글로벌 시대의 개막과 함께 영어 말하기의 중요성"이 부각되고 있습니다.

국가 차원에서뿐만 아니라, 국내 유수 기업들이 관심을 갖고 영어 말하기를 적극 장려하고 있으며 이 추세는 앞으로 더욱 확대되어질 것입니다. 하지만 영어 말하기 능력을 측정하는 데에 기존 면대면 인터뷰 방식이나 말하기 능력을 간접적으로 평가하는 Written Test만으로는 많은 어려움이 있었습니다.

G-TELP Speaking Test는 국내에서 가장 오래된 최고의 신뢰받는 영어 말하기평가 전문시험으로서 "Simulated Oral Proficiency Interview"방식을 통해 이러한 문제점을 해소하고, 과학적이고 신뢰성 있는 평가기준으로 수험자의 말하기 능력을 객관적으로 평가합니다.

G-TELP Speaking Test는 ITSC(국제테스트연구원)의 평가 전문가들에 의해 개발된 구술시험으로 표준화된 기준에 의하여 Native Speaker가 녹음한 테이프를 통하여 질문하고 수험자가 답을 녹음하는 "Simulated Oral Proficiency Interview" 방식의 시험입니다.

수험자는 40분 동안 11개 Parts의 약 30여개의 질문들에 대해 답변하게 됩니다. 수험자의 답변은 Contents(내용), Grammar(문법), Fluency(유창도), Vocabulary(어휘), Pronunciation(발음), Interaction(상호응대) 의 다섯 가지 기능 분야에 대해 훈련된 2인의 Rater에 의해 교차채점 과정을 거칩니다.

시험방식	Simulated Oral Proficiency Interview
시험시간	약 40분
성적통보	약 3주 (정기시험기준)
전체문항	11개 Parts 30여개 질문
평가기준	Contents(내용), Grammar(문법), Fluency(유창도), Vocabulary(어휘), Pronunciation (발음)
평가등급	하위 No Mastery(11) 등급부터 상위 Level1까지 11단계 등급시험
평가점수	100점 평균

G-TELP에 Writing Test

"G-TELP Writing Test는 영어를 모국어로 사용하지 않는 사람의 쓰기능력을 평가"

G-TELP Writing Test의 작문주제들은 '실생활'에 기반을 둔 것으로, 편지에 응답 또는 문의, 레포트 작성, 저널작성 등 일상생활에서 흔히 일어날 수 있는 문제들로 구성되어 있습니다. G-TELP Writing Test는 수험자들이 영어쓰기에 있어서 올바른 구성과 표현, 문체를 향상시킬 수 있도록 작문주제 및 질문들을 구성하였습니다.

G-TELP Writing Test는 총 5개의 파트로 구성되어 있으며 60분에 걸쳐 수험자의 영어쓰기능력을 평가합니다.

평가내용	Part 1. Constructing a Paragraph (주어진 단어를 이용하여 작문하기)	6분
	Part 2. Composing a Personal Letter (개인적인 편지쓰기)	12분
	Part 3. Composing a Formal Letter (비즈니스영역에서의 편지 쓰기)	12분
	Part 4. Describing a Situation (주어진 상황에 대해 설명하기)	14분
	Part 5. Writing an Essay (특정한 주제에 대한 의견 진술하기)	16분
평가시간	약 60분	
평가영역	Grammar, Vocabulary, Organization, Substance, and Style (문법, 어휘, 구성, 내용, 스타일)	
평가등급	11등급 (최상위 레벨1~최하위 레벨11)	
시험방식	CBT(Computer Based Test)	
채점기간	2 주	
성적유효	2 년	

* 2017년 지텔프 시험센터에서 매일 시행됩니다.

G-TELP Level Test의 특징

1. 다섯 단계의 등급으로 나누어져 있어 수준별로 평가합니다.

영어실력이 낮은 사람이 높은 수준의 문제를 푸는 것과 영어실력이 높은 사람이 낮은 수준의 문제를 푸는 것은 무의미합니다. 단일 등급시험의 경우 영어수준이 낮은 사람이 높은 수준의 문제를 풀었을 때 소위 "찍기"가 되어 수험자의 실력에 대한 정확한 평가가 어렵습니다. 따라서 등급별로 수준이 정의된 테스트는 해당 등급에 가장 적절한 문제가 나옴으로써 영어사용능력을 정확하게 평가할 수 있습니다.

2. 절대평가방식(Criterion-Referenced Method)으로 영어능력을 종합적으로 평가합니다.

타 시험의 경우 단순히 총점에 의한 계산으로 인하여 청취력이 취약하더라도 문법이나 독해능력이 뛰어나면 해당 수준에 도달하였다고 인정합니다. G-TELP는 문법, 청취, 독해 및 어휘 등 세 가지 영역에서 모두 75%이상 획득해야만 해당 등급에 합격된 것으로 인정됨으로써 영어능력을 종합적으로 평가할 수 있으며 정확한 영어 활용 수준을 판단할 수 있습니다.

3. 세밀한 성적분석을 통한 개인이 강·약점을 분석 진단함으로써 학습방법을 제시합니다.

각 Structure 별, Question Information Type 별로 성적을 분석함으로써 개인이 강·약점을 세밀하게 분석·진단합니다. 이후 수험자의 학습방향을 제시함으로써 평가의 궁극적 목적인 교육효과를 극대화 할 수 있습니다.

4. 교육적 효과가 큰 시험입니다.

평가의 목적은 평가, 진단, 분석, 그리고 학습동기를 제공하는 것입니다. G-TELP는 초급부터 고급까지 수준별, 단계별로 구성되어 낮은 등급부터 합격하여 실력이 향상됨에 따라 상위 등급으로 도전하고자 하는 교육적 동기를 유발시킵니다. 또한 수험자 개개인의 강·약점을 세밀하게 분석 진단하여 수험자의 부족부분을 보충하게 함으로써 교육적 효과까지 기대할 수 있습니다.

5. 변별력이 높은 시험입니다.

G-TELP는 실제 영어 활용능력을 측정할 수 있도록 절대평가방식으로 개발한 시험으로 문법, 청취, 독해 및 어휘 등 세 가지 영역에서 모두 75% 이상 득점해야만 해당 등급에 합격됨으로써 취득점수와 실제 언어능력간의 변별력이 상실되는 문제점을 극복할 수 있는 과학적인 시험입니다.

G-TELP Level 2 출제범위

■ 문법(Grammar)

이 등급에 해당되는 수험자는 다음과 같은 기본적인 문법구조와 아울러 어느 정도 복잡한 문장구조를 이해하는 사람입니다.
- 가정법: 가정법 과거, 가정법 과거완료 등
- 시제: 진행형, 완료형, 완료진행형 등
- 조동사: 다양한 조동사의 쓰임 및 요구/제안/명령 동사와 should 생략 등
- To 부정사와 동명사: 역할 및 목적어로 취하는 동사들 등
- 접속사: 종속접속사, 등위접속사, 접속부사
- 관계사: 관계대명사, 관계부사 등

■ 청취(Listening)

이 등급의 수험자는 영어를 모국어로 사용하는 사람이 정상속도로 말하지만, 다소 쉽게 변형하여 부연 설명해서 말하는 아래의 내용과 같은 것을 이해합니다.
- 개인적인 이야기
- 어떤 결정에 이르고자 하는 비공식적인 협상등의 대화
- 어떤 특정한 행동의 진행상황을 설명하거나 특정한 상품을 추천하는 공식적인 담화
- 일반적인 어떤 일의 진행이나 과정에 대한 설명

■ 독해와 어휘(Reading&Vocabulary)

이 등급에 해당되는 수험자는 실제 혹은 다소 쉽게 변형된 일반적인 아래와 같은 내용의 글을 읽고 이해합니다.
- 과거 역사속의 사건이나 현시대의 이야기
- 최근의 사회적이고 기술적인 묘사에 초점을 맞춘 잡지나 신문의 기사
- 전문적인 것이 아닌 일반적인 내용의 백과사전
- 어떤 것을 설명하거나 설득하는 상업서신

■ 성적표

G-TELP의 개인성적표는 그 등급의 Mastery (합격) 여부를 표시하는 Overall Proficiency (전체 등급 능숙도)와 Skill area Score (문법, 청취, 독해 및 어휘 점수) 그리고 Task/Structure Score (각 기능의 세분화된 부분의 점수 및 문제형태)에 대한 정보를 알려줍니다.

[기존 성적표 양식]   [변경된 성적표 양식]

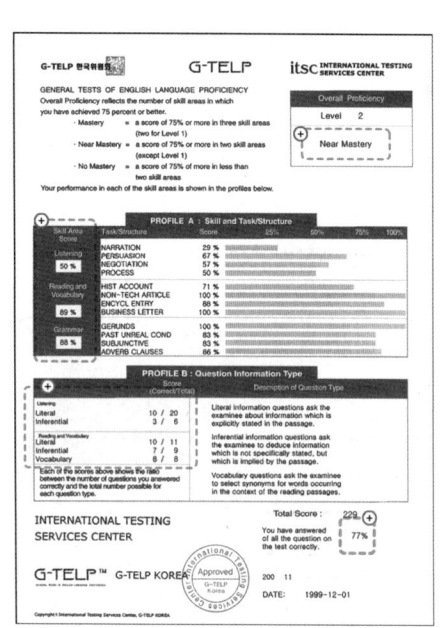 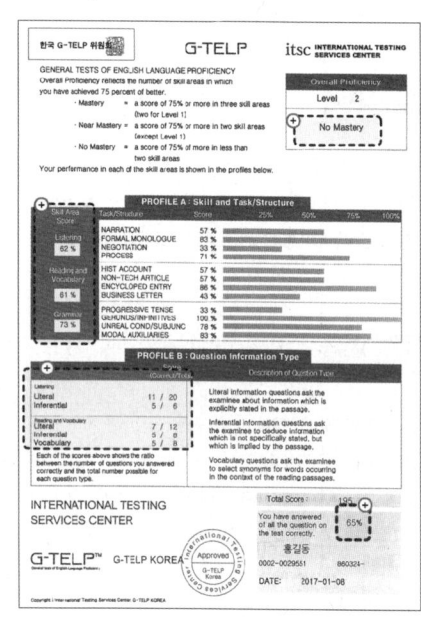

* 2017년 12월 31일까지는 기존 성적표 양식과 변경된 성적표 양식 2가지 다 사용가능

■ 성적보고

등급시험의 성적인 시험일로부터 5일 후 온라인으로 확인 가능하며, 원본 성적표는 온라인 성적표를 바로 인쇄하거나, 시험일로부터 2주 이내에 기재하신 주소로 우편 발송됩니다.

Contents
목차

문제편 모의고사 1회

GRAMMAR SECTION ··· 15
LISTENING SECTION ·· 23
READING AND VOCABULARY SECTION ··· 29

문제편 모의고사 2회

GRAMMAR SECTION ··· 41
LISTENING SECTION ·· 49
READING AND VOCABULARY SECTION ··· 55

문제편 모의고사 3회

GRAMMAR SECTION ··· 67
LISTENING SECTION ·· 75
READING AND VOCABULARY SECTION ··· 81

문제편 모의고사 4회

GRAMMAR SECTION ··· 93
LISTENING SECTION ·· 101
READING AND VOCABULARY SECTION ··· 107

문제편 모의고사 5회

GRAMMAR SECTION ··· 119
LISTENING SECTION ·· 127
READING AND VOCABULARY SECTION ··· 133

해설편　모의고사 1회

GRAMMAR SECTION ··· 144
LISTENING SECTION ·· 146
READING AND VOCABULARY SECTION ·· 158

해설편　모의고사 2회

GRAMMAR SECTION ··· 170
LISTENING SECTION ·· 173
READING AND VOCABULARY SECTION ·· 184

해설편　모의고사 3회

GRAMMAR SECTION ··· 196
LISTENING SECTION ·· 199
READING AND VOCABULARY SECTION ·· 211

해설편　모의고사 4회

GRAMMAR SECTION ··· 222
LISTENING SECTION ·· 225
READING AND VOCABULARY SECTION ·· 236

해설편　모의고사 5회

GRAMMAR SECTION ··· 248
LISTENING SECTION ·· 251
READING AND VOCABULARY SECTION ·· 262

지텔프코리아 공식지정

G-TELP
LEVEL 2

이현아 취향저격 지텔프 실전모의고사

TEST 1

한 권에 끝내는 G-TELP 실전모의고사 5회

SECTION 01 GRAMMAR

SECTION 02 LISTENING

SECTION 03 READING & VOCABULARY

GRAMMAR

문법

GRAMMAR SECTION

DIRCECTIONS:

The following items need a word or words to complete the sentence. From the four choices which follow each item, choose the best answer. Tnen blacken in the correct circle on your answer sheet.

Example:

> The boys _____ in the car.
>
> (a) be
> (b) is
> (c) am
> (d) are

The correct answer is (d), so the circle with che letter (d) has been blackened.

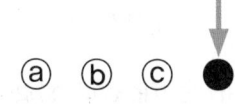

NOW TURN THE PAGE AND BEGIN

Grammar Test

1. To recognize his productive career in architecture, Arthur Daniel will soon be inducted into the California Building Industry Hall of Fame. Daniel's architectural firm _____ impressive buildings in the US for 35 years now.

    (a) will design
    (b) designs
    (c) has been designing
    (d) is designing

2. Finding a cure for autism hasn't been easy for the medical community. Because the disability has a genetic basis, doctors _____ first locate the exact gene that causes autism before any drug can be developed.

    (a) will
    (b) can
    (c) may
    (d) must

3. In my youth, the Triumph GD-87 mobile phone was already a top-of-the-line model. It was the first to have WAP capability, polyphonic ringtones, and a built-in camera. I really enjoyed _____ the phone.

    (a) using
    (b) to use
    (c) to be using
    (d) uses

4. James wants to join his school's basketball team. Because of his lack of height, he'll try out for the volleyball team instead. If he were tall, he _____ his chance with the basketball tryouts.

    (a) has taken
    (b) will be taking
    (c) would take
    (d) takes

5. Digital technology is revolutionizing music education. Many music instructors are now recommending that their students _____ the latest computer software to learn how to read musical scales and play musical instruments.

    (a) will use
    (b) use
    (c) used
    (d) are using

6. The Department of Health is actively pursuing its anti-smoking drive. The Health Secretary, _____, has ordered all government offices to strictly enforce the anti-smoking policy.

    (a) who started the campaign
    (b) whom started the campaign
    (c) that the campaign started
    (d) when the campaign started

7. A photography and archaeology enthusiast, Carol is happy with her new job. She was recently hired by National Geographic to shoot images of historical sites. She _____ pictures of the ancient ruins of Greece right now.

(a) will take
(b) takes
(c) took
(d) is taking

8. Some coffee shop owners in Europe have stopped buying genetically-modified coffee beans. They believe that the beans don't taste as good as natural coffee beans. _____, natural coffee beans cost less.

(a) Besides
(b) However
(c) Naturally
(d) Therefore

9. In Zurich, there is a zoo that recreates the environment of the Madagascar rainforest. The zoo's management intends _____ exactly how animals live in their natural habitat rather than in mere cages.

(a) to show
(b) having showed
(c) showing
(d) to be showing

10. Marco Pantani, the Italian cycling champion, died at the age of 34. His untimely death upset many sports fans. If he had not died so soon, he_____ a sports legend.

(a) had become
(b) would have become
(c) is becoming
(d) became

11. Patty had invited some of her friends to her house for dinner. She left the office early to prepare but met heavy traffic on her way home. She _____ when her friends arrived.

(a) was still cooking
(b) still cooked
(c) still cooks
(d) will still cook

12. White whales used to be seen often swimming along the coasts of Alaska. Recently, however, there are fewer sightings of these creatures. It is urgent that the public _____ in saving the whales from extinction.

(a) participates
(b) participate
(c) will participate
(d) participated

Grammar Test

13. The HR department is planning the company's annual teambuilding activity. They have yet to find a venue. The HR clerk _____ resorts starting tomorrow to see which has the best facilities and rates.

(a) is calling
(b) will be calling
(c) will call
(d) calls

14. An earthquake killed many people in Morocco last month. Many journalists criticized the Moroccan government, saying that if government officials had enforced stricter building regulations, they _____ the impact of the disaster.

(a) had lessened
(b) lessened
(c) will have been lessening
(d) would have lessened

15. The New York Philharmonic Orchestra is known for its masterful interpretation of classical pieces. Classical music fans don't mind _____ "full-series" to their concerts for a higher fee just to get the best seats.

(a) to subscribe
(b) subscribing
(c) subscribed
(d) subscribe

16. The Doctors Without Borders, a volunteer group that provides free medical aid to people in disaster areas, is known for its efficiency. The doctors _____ fly to any location at a moment's notice.

(a) might
(b) shall
(c) can
(d) would

17. Sally's pet poodle was caught by an animal control officer when it ran across the street. Sally had to claim her dog from the pound. If she had put the dog on leash, it _____ near her.

(a) will be staying
(b) would have stayed
(c) had stayed
(d) stayed

18. Lynn earned her postgraduate degree in African Studies at the University of California. After graduating, she joined a non-profit organization that supports Africa. She wants _____ in improving the lives of women and children in the region.

(a) having helped
(b) to be helping
(c) helping
(d) to help

19. Jason began using free video chat services for business only six months ago. He _____ his clients by traditional phone service for years before he discovered he could do voice and video calls using the Internet.

    (a) had been calling
    (b) was calling
    (c) would have called
    (d) called

20. Some amateur athletes have launched a website to promote outdoor sports in Canada. However, lack of financing is forcing them to shut it down. If the site were attracting more advertisers, it _____ for a long time.

    (a) would survive
    (b) has survived
    (c) will survive
    (d) survives

21. In January, 32 cases of physical injury and verbal abuse were recorded in Lima, Peru. The victims were mostly traffic policewomen. A bill _____ for attacks on female police officers is being drafted to address the problem.

    (a) who will raise penalties
    (b) which penalties will raise
    (c) where will raise penalties
    (d) that will raise penalties

22. My sister is an avid collector of Asian art. She travels throughout Asia to look for antique furniture and rare paintings. She desires that she _____ as many Asian art collectibles as she can.

    (a) is acquiring
    (b) acquires
    (c) will acquire
    (d) acquire

23. Whenever the Atherton Water District detects coliform bacteria in the town's water supply, it conducts further _____ to check if more dangerous bacteria are present. Fortunately, the result in its latest water analysis was negative.

    (a) tested
    (b) to test
    (c) testing
    (d) test

24. Carl's friend, Mary, is inviting him to attend her birthday party on Saturday. Unfortunately, Carl already said yes to another friend's invitation. If the parties _____ on different dates, he would gladly accept Mary's invitation.

    (a) are
    (b) were
    (c) will be
    (d) have been

Grammar Test

25. A team of engineers have won a grant from NASA to design a satellite that could operate beyond the moon. By the time it is finished in 2018, the team _____ on it for three years.

(a) will be working
(b) could have worked
(c) has been working
(d) will have been working

26. Martina wants to join this year's Chicago Marathon. However, she needs to inform the organizers about her recent hospitalization due to influenza. She must present a certificate of fitness _____ she can participate in the sports event.

(a) so that
(b) after
(c) since
(d) but

*THIS IS THE END OF THE GRAMMAR SECTION
DO NOT GO ON UNTIL TOLD TO DO SO*

LISTENING
듣기

LISTENING SECTION

DIRCECTIONS:

The Listening Section has four parts. In each part you will hear a spoken passage and a number of questions about the passage. First you will hear the questions. Then you will hear the passage. From the four choices for each question, choose the best answer. Then blacken in the correct circle on your answer sheet.

Now you will hear an example question. Then you will hear an example passage

Now listen to the example question.

Example:

> (a) one
> (b) two
> (c) three
> (d) four

Bill Johnson has four brothers, so the best answer is (d). The circle with the letter (d) has been blackened.

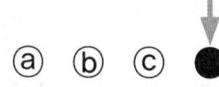

NOW TURN THE PAGE AND BEGIN

Listening Test

PART 1. You will hear two people talking. First you will hear questions 27 through 33. Then you will hear the conversation. Choose the best answer to each question in the time provided.

27. (a) because he just came back from a vacation
    (b) because he went shopping
    (c) because he will be going to Europe
    (d) because he is on leave from school

28. (a) an environmental group
    (b) a local government office
    (c) a university
    (d) a private tourism firm

29. (a) It protects the environment while giving the locals jobs.
    (b) It doesn't have any commercial interests.
    (c) It causes damage to the environment.
    (d) It lets tourists explore the sites by themselves.

30. (a) He is a full-time tour guide.
    (b) He is from Costa Rica.
    (c) He is the founder of the lodge.
    (d) He is actually a scientist.

31. (a) to be able to catch a glimpse of the shy animals
    (b) to avoid being attacked by the wild animals
    (c) to prevent waking up the sleeping animals
    (d) to keep the forest empty and peaceful

32. (a) a small poisonous beak
    (b) a huge but light beak
    (c) its inability to fly
    (d) its being endangered

33. (a) food that the visitors cook themselves
    (b) food that's grown somewhere else
    (c) food that is always fresh
    (d) food that is cooked with milk

PART 2. *You will hear a woman talking about an anti-shoplifting system. First you will hear questions 34 through 39. Then you will hear the talk. Choose the best answer to each question in the time provided.*

34. (a) The store's goods were being stolen.
    (b) The store didn't have enough stockholders.
    (c) The store gave its employees too many benefits.
    (d) The store lacked customers.

35. (a) offer fewer employee benefits
    (b) increase the inventory of products
    (c) invite more potential investors
    (d) make the products harder to access

36. (a) because the sales staff refused to follow it
    (b) because it led to other similarly pressing problems
    (c) because it wasn't helpful in reducing the theft
    (d) bcause it banned the touching of the goods

37. (a) to make the display cases more secure
    (b) to force the sales staff to accept the extra work
    (c) to replace the system with a new one
    (d) to watch out for shoplifters more closely

38. (a) by preventing products from being lifted
    (b) by making stolen products more difficult to carry out
    (c) by helping to identify potential shoplifters
    (d) by forcing customers to pay for any product they handle

39. (a) It will allow them to concentrate on their work.
    (b) It will make their products more attractive.
    (c) It will help them deal easily with thieves.
    (d) It will increase their sales by 60%.

Listening Test

PART 3. *You will hear a conversation between two people. First you will hear questions 40 through 46. Then you will hear the conversation. Choose the best answer to each question in the time provided.*

40. (a) how to manage a new project
    (b) where to find a lost document
    (c) how to organize her time better
    (d) what type of computer to buy

41. (a) because it serves his purposes well
    (b) because it has better software
    (c) because he loves carrying it in a backpack
    (d) because it sets his schedules

42. (a) calculating figures
    (b) editing videos
    (c) creating games
    (d) sending email

43. (a) a handwriting recognition program
    (b) an operating system
    (c) instructions on how to operate
    (d) a handheld pen-like device

44. (a) by adding a flash drive
    (b) by writing on its screen
    (c) by installing a stylus
    (d) by adding a keyboard to it

45. (a) It has unlimited storage space.
    (b) It automatically answers emails.
    (c) One can work with it anywhere.
    (d) One can call a taxi with it.

46. (a) read magazine reviews about tablets
    (b) buy a tablet right away
    (c) ask Julian to choose a tablet for her
    (d) find out how much tablets cost

PART 4. *You will hear an explanation of a process. First you will hear questions 47 through 52. Then you will hear the explanation. Choose the best answer to each question in the time provided.*

47. (a) establishing new preschools
    (b) promoting quality education for children
    (c) designing academic programs
    (d) teaching preschool children

48. (a) Both are focused on childcare.
    (b) They both offer well-prepared learning programs.
    (c) Both teach elementary school students.
    (d) They both cater to preschoolers.

49. (a) because the children have the same age-related skills
    (b) because the children are of different ages
    (c) because preschools have better facilities
    (d) because preschools offer full-day programs

50. (a) It follows all popular educational systems.
    (b) It takes care of the child's safety and welfare
    (c) It encourages a child to adopt a foreign language
    (d) It prepares children in dealing with emergencies.

51. (a) by supplying details about the best daycare centers
    (b) by accrediting only competent preschools
    (c) by giving details on accredited local preschools
    (d) by giving parents free childcare services

52. (a) visiting the preschool with the children
    (b) considering daycare center services first
    (c) asking their children if they're ready for preschool
    (d) inquiring about the other children's age

THIS IS THE END OF THE GRAMMAR SECTION
DO NOT GO ON UNTIL TOLD TO DO SO

READING AND VOCABULARY
독해 · 어휘

READING AND VOCABULARY SECTION

DIRCECTIONS:

You will now read four different passages. Each passage is followed by comprehension and vocabulary questions. From the four choices for each item, choose the best answer. Then blacken in the correct circle on your answer sheet.

Read the following example passage and example question.

Example:

> Bill Johnson lives in New York. He is 25 years old. He has four brothers and two sisters.
>
> How many brothers does Bill Johnson have?
>
> (a) one
> (b) two
> (c) three
> (d) four

The correct answer is (d), so the circle with che letter (d) has been blackened.

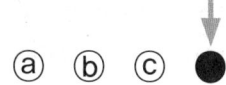

NOW TURN THE PAGE AND BEGIN

Reading and Vocabulary Test

PART 1. Read the following biographical narrative and answer the questions. The underlined words in the article are for vocabulary questions.

ANDRES SEGOVIA

Andres Segovia was an influential Spanish guitarist of the 20th century. He was the most important figure in making the guitar a concert instrument. Considered one of the greatest guitarists of all time, he is regarded as the "father of modern classical guitar."

Andres Segovia Torres was born on February 21, 1893 in Linares, Spain, and was raised in Granada. He took piano and violin lessons at an early age, but became more interested in the guitar. Despite the objections of his family and music teachers, young Andres taught himself to play what was considered a lowly instrument and developed his own technique. At the age of 16, he made his musical debut in Granada. Minor performances followed in Madrid and Barcelona.

Segovia gradually became known outside Spain as his artistry matured. He was ready for a major tour by 1919, and performed in South America and Europe, winning over even those who doubted the significance of classical guitar. His most important early performance was his Paris debut in 1924. Arranged at the insistence of the famed Spanish cellist, Pablo Casals, the concert was attended by international celebrities. This and his successful Berlin debut greatly enhanced Segovia's global reputation. In 1928, after his show in New York City, Segovia gained a devoted following in the United States.

Through constant performances, Segovia elevated the guitar from being a minor musical instrument to one with a distinguished place on the concert stage. He also widened the guitar's musical range by adopting the works of famous classical composers, such as Sylvius Leopold Weiss and Johann Sebastian Bach. Segovia's efforts inspired many modern composers to write music especially for the guitar. They usually did so under Segovia's guidance. Despite his busy schedule, the maestro managed to share his talent with a younger generation of guitarists by establishing and teaching at music schools in different parts of Europe. Classical guitar became an important part of these schools' academic programs due to his influence.

Segovia continued to play his music well into his 90s. He also established competitions and scholarships for young guitarists, and even performed at the 75th anniversary of his debut concert. Later in life, he was conferred the title Marques de Salobreña by the king of Spain. He died in Madrid on June 2, 1987.

53. What is Andres Segovia famous for?

(a) being the father of a guitarist
(b) designing classical guitars
(c) being a classical guitarist
(d) composing guitar music

54. What would establish Segovia's worldwide reputation early in his career?

(a) his performances in Paris and Berlin
(b) his friendships with international celebrities
(c) his concerts in Madrid and Barcelona
(d) his musical debut in Granada

55. How did Segovia's music influence the composers of his time?

(a) It made them go back to classical traditions.
(b) It challenged them to perform the guitar in concerts.
(c) It inspired them to copy the classical composers.
(d) It encouraged them to compose guitar music.

56. How was Segovia able to share his skills with young guitarists?

(a) through musical performances
(b) through music school tutorials
(c) by training classical teachers
(d) by designing school programs

57. Based on the article, what could be Segovia's greatest contribution to music?

(a) He improved the guitar's status.
(b) He revived classical music.
(c) He performed great concerts.
(d) He supported many scholars.

58. In the context of the passage, doubted means _____.

(a) trusted
(b) hesitated
(c) questioned
(d) ignored

59. In the context of the passage, elevated means _____.

(a) performed
(b) redesigned
(c) devalued
(d) promoted

PART 2. *Read the following article and answer the questions. The underlined words in the article are for vocabulary questions.*

TRACKING MARINE ANIMALS CAN HELP IN PROTECTING THEM

There has been a continuing decline in the population of fish and other marine species. In the past 20 years, for example, 90% of leatherback turtles and large predatory fish, such as sharks, have disappeared. The reason has been hard to identify because the oceans are difficult to monitor. However, the situation is improving according to research presented to the American Association for Marine Science.

Marine biologists can now keep track of their research subjects, thanks to advances in underwater electronic tagging. This system employs electronic tags that are implanted in the bodies of marine animals. The tags then either send location data to satellites or store it on memory chips that can be retrieved when the fish are caught. Either way, the devices can now tell scientists exactly where the animals travel.

Barbara Block of Hopkins Marine Station in California and her team have already tagged around 700 bluefin tuna, a commercially valuable fish. With the help of fishermen, they were able to chart the migration of over 200 bluefin across the Atlantic. All of these fish are born in the Caribbean, and then travel as far as the coast of Southern Spain before returning to breed in their birthplace.

Meanwhile, Andrew Read, a marine biologist at Duke University in North Carolina, is monitoring 45 tagged loggerhead turtles. When these animals come to the surface to breathe, the electronic tags glued to their shells send messages to the nearest satellite. Together, all this work is beginning to fill in the map of marine "highways" used by particular species. It is showing where particular animals prefer to stay close to the water surface and where they prefer deeper waters.

The tracking will be helpful in "ocean zoning," a concept being promoted by conservationists. Through zoning, parts of the sea, such as "turtle highways," would be declared sensitive and subject to restrictions against industries that exploit natural resources. Ultimately, scientists like Dr. Read will be able to devise better ways of protecting rare species without interfering too much with the trading of common ones.

60. What is true about the current condition of marine species?

(a) Their populations are increasing.
(b) They are showing previously unobserved behavior.
(c) They are becoming fewer and fewer in number.
(d) They are following new migratory routes.

61. What do the electronic tags do?

(a) prevent the fish from being caught
(b) monitor the animals' location
(c) track the fish's activities
(d) record the animals' diet

62. What isn't known about bluefin tuna?

(a) where they breed
(b) how they live
(c) what they eat
(d) where they head to

63. Why do loggerhead turtles come to the surface of the water?

(a) because they need to breathe air
(b) because they are showing their location
(c) because the electronic tags force them to do so
(d) because they have to locate the highway

64. How will electronic tagging likely help protect endangered marine animals?

(a) by making them difficult to catch
(b) by helping agencies control the areas that they frequent
(c) by marking them as protected species
(d) by allowing scientists to follow and control them

65. In the context of the passage, retrieved means _____.

(a) improved
(b) replaced
(c) emitted
(d) recovered

66. In the context of the passage, rare means _____.

(a) uncommon
(b) standard
(c) unique
(d) attractive

PART 3. Read the following encyclopedia article and answer the questions. The underlined words in the article are for vocabulary questions.

WINDMILL

A windmill is a machine that converts wind into useful energy. This energy is derived from the force of wind acting on slanted blades or sails which are attached to a device called a "windshaft." When used with a water pump, grain mill, or any machine that performs simple tasks, the whole mechanism is called a "windmill." When used to generate electricity, it is called a "wind turbine generator."

As early as the 7th century AD, simple windmills were probably already being used in Persia (now Iran) for irrigating farmlands and milling grain. Although these windmills were somewhat inefficient, their use spread throughout the Middle East and China. In Europe, the first windmills appeared in England and France during the 12th century and eventually became popular in other parts of the continent. By the 19th century, the Dutch were using around 9,000 windmills.

The use of wind turbines for generating electricity was pioneered in Denmark late in the 1890s. In the US, small wind turbine generators supplied electricity to many rural communities until the 1930s. During that decade, power lines were extended across the nation and the first large wind turbines were built. Modern wind turbines are propelled in either of two ways: the "drag," wherein wind pushes the blades; and the "lift," where the blades move in the same way an airplane's wing rises on an air current.

Used in large-scale power generation, the most successful wind turbine generators can produce 100 to 400 kilowatts of electricity. These generators are sometimes installed in groups called "wind farms." The world's largest wind farms are in California, where the wind turbines can collectively generate up to 1,120 megawatts, a little more than the capacity of a typical nuclear plant.

Wind turbine generators could provide as much as 10% of the world's electricity by the middle of the 21st century. Wind energy creates very little pollution and few greenhouse gases, and is an environment-friendly alternative to non-renewable fuels such as oil. However, countries that have low wind speed and space limitations must come up with specially-designed wind turbines.

67. What is a windmill used for?

(a) generating wind
(b) controlling the flow of wind
(c) converting into wind
(d) turning wind into power

68. What is not true about the early windmills?

(a) They were used to generate electricity.
(b) They were mainly used in farms.
(c) They had flaws.
(d) Persians were among the very first to use them.

69. How does the wind propel a wind turbine by means of the "drag"?

(a) by pushing the blades backward
(b) by pressing on the blades
(c) by raising the blades into the air
(c) by moving the blades upward

70. Based on the article, what could be an advantage of electricity produced by wind turbines?

(a) It is produced more cheaply.
(b) It is much simpler to use.
(c) Its source will never run out.
(d) It can be produced anywhere in the world.

71. Why couldn't wind turbines be used to provide all the world's energy requirements?

(a) because lawmakers haven't learned of its benefits
(b) because they need certain climatic conditions
(c) because people prefer non-renewable sources energy
(d) because most countries have space limitations

72. In the context of the passage, mechanism means _____.

(a) system
(b) idea
(c) device
(d) force

73. In the context of the passage, alternative means _____.

(a) difference
(b) alteration
(c) option
(d) interest

Reading and Vocabulary Test

PART 4. Read the following business letter and answer the questions. The underlined words in the article are for vocabulary questions.

January 15, 2016

Mr. David Gagnon
Director of Operations
Organic Trade Association
Greenfield, MA 01302

Dear Mr. Gagnon:

The United States Department of Agriculture (USDA) is <u>soliciting</u> nominations for membership in the Advisory Committee on Meat and Poultry Inspection. Under the authority of the USDA Food Safety and Inspection Service, the Committee serves as an advice-giving body on product quality and labeling standards for the meat and poultry industries. It also serves as a forum for the sharing of ideas on how our regulatory system can best serve consumers and the industries.

In recent years, membership in the Committee was opened up to represent the interests of various sectors. Nominees for membership are generally persons who have shown ability to represent the producers and processors, academe, government, and consumers. Due to the sudden resignation of Mr. Donald Smith, my office is now in need of a representative from the producers' group. The individual who will fill this vacancy is expected to work with the Committee until March 31, 2018.

If your association would like to nominate someone, please send his or her application form, a detailed résumé, and three letters of reference to me at the address indicated below. All nomination materials should be postmarked not later than April 1, 2016. Application forms may be downloaded from www.fsis.usda.gov. Please note that incomplete documents will not be <u>entertained</u>.

For further details, please contact my assistant, Ms. Sonya West, by telephone at (202) 720-2561 or e-mail at sonya.west@fsis.usda.gov. Thank you very much.

Sincerely,

Garry McKee

Garry L. McKee, M.D.
Administrator

Food Safety and Inspection Service, USDA
300 12th Street SW
Washington, DC

74. What is the main task of the Committee?

(a) doing safety inspections of meat products
(b) providing capital to meat-processing businesses
(c) developing trade regulations on meat products
(d) promoting the US meat industry in foreign markets

75. Why does the Committee have a vacancy?

(a) It has just been established.
(b) A representative has left.
(c) It was recently opened to producers.
(d) Gary McKee is resigning.

76. Who is the Committee most likely to accept as a nominee for the vacancy?

(a) one who can represent all the concerned sectors
(b) one who is commercially successful
(c) one who can speak on behalf of a represented sector
(d) one who can work full-time

77. What was not mentioned as a nomination requirement?

(a) work history
(b) a letter of nomination
(c) recommendation letters
(d) an application form

78. If they want to nominate someone, what will the association likely do after reading McKee's letter?

(a) They will apply through the Committee's website.
(b) They will send Sonya West an email.
(c) They will mail the required documents to McKee.
(d) They will visit the USDA office.

79. In the context of the passage, soliciting means _____.

(a) granting
(b) rejecting
(c) opening
(d) seeking

80. In the context of the passage, entertained means _____.

(a) supported
(b) accepted
(c) amused
(d) used

THIS IS THE END OF THE TEST

지텔프코리아 공식지정

G-TELP
LEVEL 2

이현아 취향저격 지텔프 실전모의고사

TEST 2

한 권에 끝내는 G-TELP 실전모의고사 5회

SECTION 01 GRAMMAR
SECTION 02 LISTENING
SECTION 03 READING & VOCABULARY

GRAMMAR
문법

GRAMMAR SECTION

DIRCECTIONS:

The following items need a word or words to complete the sentence. From the four choices which follow each item, choose the best answer. Tnen blacken in the correct circle on your answer sheet.

Example:

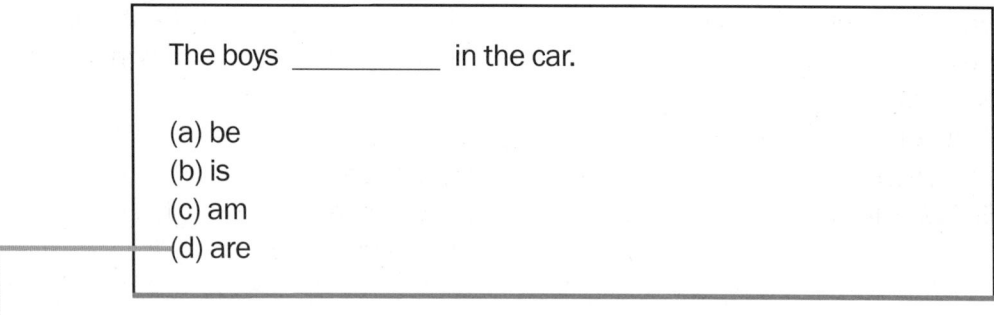

The correct answer is (d), so the circle with che letter (d) has been blackened.

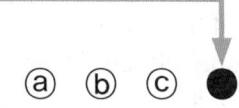

NOW TURN THE PAGE AND BEGIN

Grammar Test

1. Despite the recent attack of scale insects on his farm, Mr. Barlow has been harvesting a good supply of lemons and oranges. _____, what surprised him most was that the sickly trees actually yielded tasty and juicy fruits.

   (a) However
   (b) Therefore
   (c) Likewise
   (d) Besides

2. A hot air balloon caught fire and crashed in Texas yesterday. The balloon had passengers at the time of the accident. At this time, investigators _____ the number and identities of the victims.

   (a) still determine
   (b) will still determine
   (c) still determined
   (d) are still determining

3. In 1965, Fred DeLuca made a $1,000 loan from Peter Buck to build the highly successful Subway sandwich store. DeLuca and Buck later entered into partnership _____ Franchise Brands, a company that helps entrepreneurs in the franchising industry.

   (a) to have formed
   (b) forming
   (c) to form
   (d) having formed

4. Bert and Sara hadn't anticipated the large amount of money needed for the renovation of their beach house. That's why since last month, they _____ for a bank loan to help finance the renovation.

   (a) will be looking
   (b) have been looking
   (c) were looking
   (d) had looked

5. The UCLA Downtown Center can be rented for social activities but needs enough time to prepare the place. Hence, its management advises that clients _____ the Center of bookings at least four days in advance.

   (a) notify
   (b) notified
   (c) will notify
   (d) to notify

6. Despite being a well-made film, The Spy Who Came in from the Actively Cold didn't generate much profit in the box office. If the movie had featured exciting visual effects, more moviegoers _____ it.

   (a) would watch
   (b) would have watched
   (c) were watching
   (d) watched

7. "Mystery shoppers" are amateur detectives hired by business firms to observe their service staff secretly. _____ upscale stores to examine the efficiency of sales clerks and the overall quality of service is part of their job.

(a) Having visited
(b) To be visiting
(c) Visiting
(d) Visits

8. The British rock star, Robert Chalmers, was 54 years old when he died of a heart attack. According to reports, Chalmers _____ in France for just a week when he suffered the attack.

(a) traveled
(b) had been traveling
(c) would travel
(d) was traveling

9. The department manager _____ a conference tomorrow. She told her assistant that if anyone wants to see her, she will be spending the whole day at Lakeview Hotel's Grand Hall.

(a) is attending
(b) will have attended
(c) attends
(d) will be attending

10. The Senate rejected Senator Dayton's proposal to fund the education of disabled American children. If the senators had approved the proposal, Senate _____ about $22 billion to the country's special education programs.

(a) granted
(b) is granting
(c) would have granted
(d) had granted

11. The growing number of Internet users is continuously bringing good prospects to electronic commerce. In fact, most retailers _____ e-commerce are satisfied with the growth of their business.

(a) whom are positively adopting
(b) who are positively adopting
(c) which are positively responding
(d) how they positively respond

12. Having no visual aids, a radio advertisement should grab and hold the listeners' attention. That's why the best radio commercials use comedy as a selling technique. Most consumers will remember a radio ad _____ it is funny.

(a) and
(b) so
(c) but
(d) if

Grammar Test

13. When I started living alone, I would normally eat at an expensive restaurant instead of cook. However, I later realized that if I had made an effort to prepare my own meals, I _____ a lot of money.

(a) was saving
(b) would have saved
(c) saved
(d) had saved

14. The Hong Kong Design Center will hold a high-profile design contest this year. A panel of judges will review hundreds of nominations from various design institutes _____ the winners at the fair.

(a) decided
(b) deciding
(c) will decide
(d) to decide

15. Leila is determined to achieve a weight of 55 kilos. At her current weight, these may not be easy to do. She _____ nothing but fruits and vegetables for two years before she reaches her ideal weight.

(a) has been eating
(b) has eaten
(c) will have been eating
(d) would eat

16. For Dell, the technology company, profitability depends on selecting the right customers. These customers are large firms and well-to-do individuals who replace their computers regularly and _____ provide the company with a predictable revenue stream.

(a) would
(b) may
(c) should
(d) can

17. My friend is encouraging me to accept a consultancy job at the Department of Education. However, I tell her that if I were to work for the government, I _____ a more challenging job with the Department of Defense.

(a) would take
(b) had been taking
(c) will take
(d) am taking

18. The luxury cruise liner, Crystal Cruises, received the highest score in the 2015 Readers' Choice survey of Traveler magazine. Tourists and travel writers recommend _____ its cruises because of its outstanding service and well-maintained facilities.

(a) to be booking
(b) booking
(c) having booked
(d) to book

19. The Federal Aviation Administration warned the public about using devices that might interfere with the aircraft's electronic system during flights. The FAA urged that passengers _____ from using gadgets that may put the aircraft at risk.

(a) refrain
(b) are refraining
(c) to refrain
(d) will refrain

20. A recent survey showed that venture capital is vital to many European firms. Majority of the companies _____ were young and medium-sized. Most of them believed that their companies wouldn't have grown without outside funding.

(a) whom they surveyed
(b) who were surveyed
(c) that were surveyed
(d) when they were surveyed

21. Music critic, Ernest Hooper, thinks that The Florida Orchestra's financial problem can be solved easily by attracting audiences to its shows. He says that if the orchestra played popular musical compositions, more people _____ to their performances.

(a) are going
(b) will go
(c) go
(d) would go

22. Two months ago, Chicago reported strong sales of electronic appliances. However, the figures were still lower than those posted in previous months. Revenues were also weak in Boston, New York, and Atlanta, but _____ in Cleveland.

(a) would have improved
(b) will be improving
(c) were improving
(d) could be improved

23. Anne lost her credit card, but she hasn't informed the credit card company about it yet. If I were her, I _____ the incident as soon as possible to prevent other people from using the credit card.

(a) would report
(b) will be reporting
(c) report
(d) am reporting

24. Eastern University is eager to increase its world university ranking in the next few years. To do this, it is reorganizing its departments. The president proposes that they _____ research-oriented faculty to help increase the university's ranking.

(a) recruited
(b) will recruit
(c) recruit
(d) to recruit

Grammar Test

25. Donny, my 15 year-old cousin, was disappointed when he couldn't contribute to Red Cross's blood donation drive in our town. Volunteers allow _____ blood only from donors who are at least 17 years old.

(a) to be receiving
(b) receiving
(c) having received
(d) receive

26. Gordon Fisheries, Inc. will be implementing ways to lessen the wastewater emissions from its factory. It's also cutting down its water and power consumption. Management is confident that the company _____ save $50,000 yearly as a result.

(a) should
(b) might
(c) must
(d) will

THIS IS THE END OF THE GRAMMAR SECTION
DO NOT GO ON UNTIL TOLD TO DO SO

LISTENING

듣기

LISTENING SECTION

DIRCECTIONS:

The Listening Section has four parts. In each part you will hear a spoken passage and a number of questions about the passage. First you will hear the questions. Then you will hear the passage. From the four choices for each question, choose the best answer. Then blacken in the correct circle on your answer sheet.

Now you will hear an example question. Then you will hear an example passage

Now listen to the example question.

Example:

> (a) one
> (b) two
> (c) three
> (d) four

Bill Johnson has four brothers, so the best answer is (d). The circle with the letter (d) has been blackened.

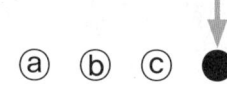

NOW TURN THE PAGE AND BEGIN

Listening Test

PART 1. *You will hear a conversation between two people. First you will hear questions 27 through 33. Then you will hear the conversation. Choose the best answer to each question in the time provided.*

27. (a) to a skiing competition
    (b) to the beach
    (c) to a friend's house
    (d) to a ski resort

28. (a) by learning it from Ted
    (b) by watching an exhibition
    (c) by being introduced to it by Mark
    (d) by watching Mark join a competition

29. (a) the ability to turn quickly
    (b) flexibility and strength
    (c) speed and coordination
    (d) the ability to jump high

30. (a) bunny slope
    (b) steep slope
    (c) practice slope
    (d) basic slope

31. (a) to join the Winter Olympics
    (b) to learn some ski stunts
    (c) to see the snow-covered mountains
    (d) to practice downhill skiing

32. (a) freestyle skiing
    (b) cross-country skiing
    (c) downhill ski racing
    (d) ski jumping

33. (a) learn how to ski with his wife and children
    (b) go to Colorado with Emily's family
    (c) watch a professional skiing contest
    (d) enroll his children at a ski academy

PART 2. *You will hear a woman talking about a company program. First you will hear questions 34 through 39. Then you will hear the talk. Choose the best answer to each question in the time provided.*

34. (a) to promote a department store
    (b) to launch a new product
    (c) to train new employees
    (d) to inform employees about a new marketing strategy

35. (a) at all Milton department stores
    (b) at only one branch of Milton
    (c) anywhere customer loyalty cards are honored
    (d) at all department stores nationwide

36. (a) priority checkout lines
    (b) rebates on their purchases
    (c) discounts during holidays
    (d) after-hours shopping privileges

37. (a) getting income tax breaks
    (b) promotion of merchandise
    (c) immediate increase in the number of customers
    (d) valuable data on customers' spending habits

38. (a) by filling-out an application form
    (b) by being a Milton shopper long enough
    (c) by paying a membership fee
    (d) by being interviewed at a Milton store

39. (a) It will erase all customer data from the system.
    (b) It will keep back-up files of important information.
    (c) It will protect the information from being stolen by others.
    (d) Only customers will have access to the data.

Listening Test

PART 3. You will hear a conversation between two people. First you will hear questions 40 through 46. Then you will hear the conversation. Choose the best answer to each question in the time provided.

40. (a) buying a good printer
    (b) choosing a printing company
    (c) starting a printing business
    (d) working for a magazine

41. (a) She needed the most affordable printing service.
    (b) She wanted a printer with modern facilities.
    (c) She needed a printer with highly-skilled technicians.
    (d) She needed a good printer in the city where she works.

42. (a) a marketing specialist
    (b) a publication designer
    (c) an account executive
    (d) an editorial assistant

43. (a) design and layout
    (b) distribution
    (c) large-format printing
    (d) direct mail

44. (a) excited
    (b) annoyed
    (c) confident
    (d) anxious

45. (a) They are eager to please their new clients.
    (b) They can offer a wider range of services.
    (c) They are considered a practical choice by reputable clients.
    (d) They offer lower prices than famous printing firms.

46. (a) because the man will be doing her job for her
    (b) because she already found a printing company
    (c) because she became more informed about her task
    (d) because she has accepted that the project would fail

PART 4. *You will hear an explanation of a process. First you will hear questions 47 through 52. Then you will hear the explanation. Choose the best answer to each question in the time provided.*

47. (a) to students who want to practice their skills in the arts
    (b) to people who want to earn from a home-based craft
    (c) to workers who are learning new jobs in a factory
    (d) to volunteers who wish to preserve the environment

48. (a) white glue
    (b) an old cotton shirt
    (c) an old wire hanger
    (d) an electric iron

49. (a) thick and grayish
    (b) unevenly textured
    (c) completely white
    (d) extremely sticky

50. (a) The frame should be laid on a flat surface.
    (b) The paper should be cut into smaller pieces.
    (c) The frame should be exposed to direct heat.
    (d) The paper should be peeled off carefully.

51. (a) to put patterns onto it
    (b) to smoothen its surface
    (c) to dry it more quickly
    (d) to increase its durability

52. (a) colors
    (b) glue
    (c) blending agents
    (d) water

THIS IS THE END OF THE GRAMMAR SECTION
DO NOT GO ON UNTIL TOLD TO DO SO

READING AND VOCABULARY
독해 · 어휘

READING AND VOCABULARY SECTION

DIRCECTIONS:

You will now read four different passages. Each passage is followed by comprehension and vocabulary questions. From the four choices for each item, choose the best answer. Then blacken in the correct circle on your answer sheet.

Read the following example passage and example question.

Example:

> Bill Johnson lives in New York. He is 25 years old. He has four brothers and two sisters.
>
> How many brothers does Bill Johnson have?
>
> (a) one
> (b) two
> (c) three
> (d) four

The correct answer is (d), so the circle with che letter (d) has been blackened.

NOW TURN THE PAGE AND BEGIN

Reading and Vocabulary Test

PART 1. *Read the following biographical narrative and answer the questions. The underlined words in the article are for vocabulary questions.*

ISADORA DUNCAN

Isadora Duncan was an American dancer who developed less traditional, freer forms of movement that influenced modern dance techniques. She is widely known as the "Mother of Modern Dance."

Isadora Duncan was born Dora Angela Duncan on May 27, 1878 in San Francisco, California. She was the youngest of the four children of Joseph Charles Duncan, a bank employee and art lover, and Mary Gray, a pianist and music teacher. Dora and her siblings lived with their mother after her parents divorced. At the age of six, Dora helped support her family by teaching local children how to dance. As a teenager, Duncan joined Augustin Daly's theater company and performed in stage productions in Chicago and New York. Although she studied ballet, the young dancer experimented with freer, more natural ballet movements that were less traditional.

In 1899, Duncan moved to London with her family. There, she observed the ancient Greek sculptures at the British Museum and started associating her own dance movements with the free-flowing classical movements found in the artworks. Later on, she would dance barefoot and wear flowing costumes patterned after classical Greek designs. As ballet became a less popular art form in the early 20th century, Duncan's choreography was increasingly admired for its "natural movement," which included skipping, jumping, and running. Her performances in Europe were eagerly received.

Duncan's bohemian attitude applied not only to her profession but also to her personal life. She would have a number of rich male partners and illegitimate children, and was strongly criticized in conservative circles. As an artist, however, she sought to promote among audiences a new awareness of human emotions and social realities. Ultimately, her liberating approach to movement made her known as the pioneer of modern dance.

Duncan established dance schools in Europe to share her art. The first opened in 1904 in Grunewald, Germany, where she welcomed students from poor families. Duncan's career would be disrupted when her two children died in an accident in 1913. She was able to recover only when she returned to teaching and holding dance tours. She was eventually forced to close her school in Germany, and later, another school in Moscow, due to lack of funds. She then spent her time performing mostly in Europe.

In 1922, Isadora Duncan married the Russian poet Sergei Yesenin, but their marriage failed after three years. She spent the rest of her sad life in Nice, France. She died in a car accident on September 14, 1927. Her autobiography, My Life, was published in 1928.

53. What did the young Isadora Duncan do to help support her family?

(a) perform in ballet productions
(b) teach other children music
(c) develop new dance moves
(d) teach other children dancing

54. What did Isadora Duncan use as a basis for her dance movements and costumes?

(a) classical Greek art
(b) modern British dance
(c) popular American music
(d) traditional German ballet

55. Based on the passage, what can be said about modern dance?

(a) It never replaced traditional ballet in the 20th century.
(b) It was a welcome change from an outdated dance style.
(c) It made the audience more emotional.
(d) It is a financially stable art form.

56. Why did Duncan receive criticisms in traditional circles?

(a) because of her unusual costumes
(b) because of her fast dance moves
(c) because of her wealthy dance partners
(d) because of her unchecked lifestyle

57. How did Duncan get over the untimely death of her children?

(a) by building her first school
(b) by marrying a literary artist
(c) by pursuing her career
(d) by closing her schools

58. In the context of the passage, associating means _____.

(a) connecting
(b) developing
(c) separating
(d) combining

59. In the context of the passage, disrupted means _____.

(a) offended
(b) stopped
(c) disjointed
(d) promoted

PART 2. Read the following article and answer the questions. The underlined words in the article are for vocabulary questions.

RESEARCH SHOWS THAT FIRSTBORNS GAIN HIGHER I.Q.

A study found that the eldest children in families are more likely to have a higher "intelligence quotient" (I.Q., or a person's intelligence as compared to those of other people of their age) than their younger siblings. The results, which were published in two journals, *Science* and *Intelligence*, are solely due to family dynamics, and are independent of biological factors such as a person's genes and development before birth.

In the study, Norwegian scientists analyzed the birth order, health status, and I.Q. scores of 241,000 men, using their military records. The men were aged 18 to 19 and born from 1967 to 1976. The study excluded other factors including the mother's age, parents' education, and family size. The results showed that the average I.Q. score of firstborns was 103.2: almost 3% higher than that of second children (100.3), and over 4% higher than that of thirdborns (99.0).

Although a discrepancy of three IQ points seems small, it is significant: The difference between "gifted" and "above average" intelligence may mean the distinction between admission to an elite school and a common public school, which could open up more opportunities for the firstborn.

The study eliminated the biological factor by analyzing the scores of "accidental firstborns," or those who became the eldest after an older sibling died. Their scores were generally the same as those of biological firstborns.

Different theories explain why the eldest children have higher I.Q. One theory is that firstborns had their parents' undivided attention for a longer time than their younger siblings, giving them an early edge in developing their language and reasoning abilities. Another cites the tendency of elder children to teach their younger siblings, giving them more practice at organizing information, which builds their I.Q.

Another theory involves the siblings' inclination to find their place in the family. Firstborns are usually regarded as more responsible and achievement-oriented, so younger siblings distinguish themselves by developing other skills such as high sociability and musical talent. However, these skills are not measured by I.Q. tests.

The results would lead to more in-depth research about family dynamics. Since gender has little effect on I.Q., the results could also apply to females.

60. Which was a finding of the study?

(a) Firstborns had an average I.Q.
(b) Secondborns had the lowest intelligence scores.
(c) Firstborns outscored their younger siblings in I.Q.
(d) Most firstborns go to prestigious schools.

61. How did the researchers gather information for the study?

(a) by administering I.Q. tests to siblings
(b) by looking at past records of intelligence
(c) by following babies from birth until adulthood
(d) by analyzing the personal records of siblings

62. What did the results among non-biological firstborns show?

(a) that biological firstborns are more intelligent
(b) that the results only apply to natural firstborns
(c) that I.Q. is a purely biological trait
(d) that the difference in I.Q. isn't inborn

63. According to a theory, why most likely do younger siblings have lower I.Q.s?

(a) They only rely on firstborns to gain knowledge.
(b) They are born lacking in intelligence.
(c) They don't pursue what the firstborns are already good at.
(d) Parents give unequal attention to their children.

64. What significant conclusion could be inferred from the study?

(a) that intelligence and birth order are related
(b) that firstborns are more successful
(c) that birth order determines school performance
(d) that female firstborns have higher I.Q.s than male ones

65. In the context of the passage, solely means _____.

(a) clearly
(b) only
(c) simply
(d) also

66. In the context of the passage, edge means _____.

(a) advantage
(b) boundary
(c) start
(d) border

PART 3. Read the following encyclopedia article and answer the questions. The underlined words in the article are for vocabulary questions.

DOMINOES

Dominoes are small, flat, rectangular tiles used to play a variety of games. They were probably introduced in Europe from China in the 1300s. Most sets of dominoes are made of bone, ivory, plastic, or wood. A regular set consists of 28 domino tiles, or "bones," each of which is two inches long. Tiles are one-inch wide and 3/8-inch thick. A line divides each domino into two square "sections." Twenty-one of the dominoes have one to six dots, or "pips," on each section. One domino's two sections are both blank, and the six remaining dominoes have one blank section and one section with pips. No two dominoes are alike.

The game was invented in China in the 14th century. Its first recorded reference in Europe is from Italy, where the royalty of Venice and Naples played the game. The tiles were made by gluing two sheets of ebony on either side of the tile. This prevented cheating by allowing a player to see the pip from the back of the tile in certain lights. In the 18th century, the domino game arrived in Britain from France and quickly became popular in inns and taverns. The word "domino" is French for a black and white hood worn by Christian priests in winter.

The most commonly played domino games are "blocking games." In these games, one domino is connected to either end of the first domino if the number of its dots matches the number of dots of one (or both) section of the first tile. If, for example, the first tile has a section with four dots, a player can connect to it a tile with one end also marked with a four. A player's goal is to play all his seven tiles (his "hand") while blocking the other player's attempt to do the same. A score may be determined by counting the total pips of the losers remaining tiles.

Dominoes or variants of it are played in almost all countries of the world, but it is most popular in Latin America. The National English Domino and Cribbage Championships have been organized by Keith Masters annually in Stoke on Trent since 1985.

67. Which is not a characteristic of dominoes?

    (a) They are composed of 28 tiles.
    (b) They can be made from different materials.
    (c) They first came from Europe.
    (d) Most tile sections have dots.

68. Why were ebony sheets glued on each side of a domino tile?

    (a) to make the tile last longer
    (b) to indicate what country the set was made
    (c) to make the tile more attractive
    (d) to prevent dishonest play during a game

69. How is a "blocking game" played?

    (a) by linking a tile to one with a smaller number of dots
    (b) by being the first to play all tiles with a blank end
    (c) by linking tile sections with the same number of dots
    (d) by trying to draw the highest total of pips

70. Who wins in a blocking game?

    (a) the first player to play all his dominoes
    (b) the player with more remaining tiles after the game
    (c) the player with the highest total of dots after the game
    (d) the last player to play a tile

71. Based on the article, what can be said about the domino game?

    (a) One type of dominoes is used worldwide.
    (b) It retains its popularity worldwide.
    (c) It is exclusively played by Latin Americans today.
    (d) It remains an unorganized game.

72. In the context of the passage, divides means _____.

    (a) separates
    (b) decorates
    (c) indicates
    (d) combines

73. In the context of the passage, matches means _____.

    (a) exceeds
    (b) increases
    (c) equals
    (d) reduces

Reading and Vocabulary Test

PART 4. *Read the following business letter and answer the questions. The underlined words in the article are for vocabulary questions.*

January 26, 2016

Mr. Christopher D. Gibson
Manager
Hamlin Garden Park
2000 Hamlin Boulevard
Tampa, Florida 33612

Dear Mr. Gibson:

I would like to relate to you my family's terrible experience at Hamlin Garden Park. We went to visit your park last Saturday, January 24, to celebrate my birthday. My 1½ years old son, Jeff, loved going to Hamlin Garden Park, but that time had not been pleasant for us.

Jeff was enjoying the kiddie rides in your Dinosaur Land until we made the mistake of putting him on one of your little cars that run separately on tracks. He was the last kid to get off a car, and there was an empty toy car behind him. The ride attendant pushed that toy car which hit the back of my son. He sustained a whiplash and started to cry. He was <u>traumatized</u> after that and didn't want to take any more rides.

You must be fully aware of what those rides can do without proper supervision. A fellow park visitor told me a similar accident had happened before. If the cars can possibly hurt kids, why haven't you taken safety measures against it? Obviously, the cars should be operated all together-not independently-to prevent accidents like this from happening.

My husband and I thought that our son's injury wasn't serious until we came home to watch our home video of the incident. We saw how our boy had also been struck on the back of the head by the toy car. If a medical examination shows that something serious happened to our son, I will definitely hold your company responsible and pursue legal actions.

I demand that you thoroughly review the safety of all your rides in Dinosaur Land, <u>particularly</u> those for the smaller kids. You have to do this immediately before similar accidents happen. I expect to hear from you soonest about this matter.

Katrina Pitman
Katrina S. Pitman
Ft. Lauderdale, Florida

74. Why did Katrina Pitman and her family visit the park?

(a) to report about an accident
(b) to try the new rides
(c) to teach her son how to drive
(d) to celebrate a special event

75. What happened to Katrina Pitman's son?

(a) His toy car hit another boy.
(b) He wasn't allowed to ride a toy car.
(c) He got hit by an empty toy car.
(d) A ride attendant scolded him.

76. According to Pitman, how can the toy cars be made safer to ride?

(a) by having the kids accompanied
(b) by making the cars run in a series
(c) by having the kids wear safety gear
(d) by making the cars run individually

77. Based on the letter, what will Pitman most likely do if her son sustained worse injury?

(a) She won't take him to the park anymore.
(b) She will take him to the hospital.
(c) She will scold the ride attendant.
(d) She will sue Hamlin Garden Park.

78. What did Ms. Pitman want Mr. Gibson to do?

(a) to check the safety of the park rides
(b) to retrain the park employees
(c) to stop operating the toy cars
(d) to refund their park entrance fees

79. In the context of the passage, traumatized means _____.

(a) pleased
(b) warned
(c) distressed
(d) injured

80. In the context of the passage, particularly means _____.

(a) remarkably
(b) exceptionally
(c) unusually
(d) specifically

THIS IS THE END OF THE TEST

지텔프코리아 공식지정

G-TELP
LEVEL 2

이현아 취향저격 지텔프 실전모의고사

TEST 3

한 권에 끝내는 G-TELP 실전모의고사 5회

SECTION 01 GRAMMAR
SECTION 02 LISTENING
SECTION 03 READING & VOCABULARY

GRAMMAR
문법

GRAMMAR SECTION

DIRCECTIONS:

The following items need a word or words to complete the sentence. From the four choices which follow each item, choose the best answer. Tnen blacken in the correct circle on your answer sheet.

Example:

> The boys _____ in the car.
>
> (a) be
> (b) is
> (c) am
> (d) are

The correct answer is (d), so the circle with che letter (d) has been blackened.

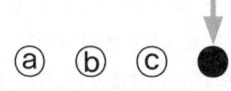

NOW TURN THE PAGE AND BEGIN

Grammar Test

1. Medieval manuscripts used to be locked up inside monasteries and royal libraries. Today, copies of them are widely available on the Internet. In fact, if I were given a chance to research about them, I _____ by the quantity of available data.

   (a) would be overwhelmed
   (b) will be overwhelmed
   (c) was overwhelmed
   (d) am being overwhelmed

2. A drought has been causing many deaths in Ethiopia. In response to this emergency, international organizations have begun relief operations for the victims. Right now, Red Cross workers _____ food rations to the affected communities.

   (a) distribute
   (b) has been distributing
   (c) have distributed
   (d) are distributing

3. Greenwood's Grocery had been extremely profitable until three new grocery stores began competing for its market two years ago. The new pricing scheme it adopted, _____, aimed at winning back former customers.

   (a) how reduced its prices significantly
   (b) when it significantly reduced prices
   (c) which reduced its prices significantly
   (d) that reduced its significant prices

4. Arnold bought a new smart phone yesterday. He used to be a technophobe who was suspicious of developments in communications technology. He _____ getting a mobile phone until he realized how useful they were.

   (a) has been resisting
   (b) had been resisting
   (c) will be resisting
   (d) would have resisted

5. Tony and Alice were delighted to hear that their 18-year-old daughter would join an educational tour in Cambodia. However, they got worried when they discovered that the trip would involve _____ on foot to wild places.

   (a) traveling
   (b) having traveled
   (c) to be traveling
   (d) to travel

6. To become a licensed optometrist, one must go through a six-month internship under a licensed optometrist. When the internship is completed, the supervisor _____ submit an evaluation of the intern's performance to the Board of Examiners in Optometry.

   (a) may
   (b) could
   (c) will
   (d) can

7. My cousin Dorothy is a chef for an upscale Italian restaurant. She was asked _____ dinner for our family reunion next month. She said she will be preparing for us a full-course, sumptuous meal.

(a) hosting
(b) to host
(c) having hosted
(d) to have hosted

8. Dr. Abigail Morton is a physiotherapist who studies the connection between good posture and musculoskeletal disorders. For her current research, she is observing the posture of 150 corporate employees _____ they perform various office tasks.

(a) so
(b) because
(c) and
(d) while

9. Last Wednesday, Uncle Joseph experienced chest pains. When he was brought to the hospital for a checkup, his doctor told him it was necessary that he _____ a heart bypass surgery at once.

(a) had undergone
(b) undergoes
(c) undergo
(d) will undergo

10. Peter Darwin has always seemed to be a talented tennis player who has had several winning streaks. However, some critics are suspecting that he _____ be using banned substances to improve his sports performance.

(a) will
(b) could
(c) shall
(d) would

11. After working as an unknown model for eight years, Bettina Humphrey decided to shift careers. It turned out to be a wise decision. By August this year, she _____ award-winning documentary films for three years.

(a) has been making
(b) will be making
(c) would have made
(d) will have been making

12. The Heritage Alliance is a successful non-government organization that promotes the rights of cultural minorities in Southeast Asia. It receives big donations from private citizens. If there were no such support, the agency _____ to protect the region's indigenous communities.

(a) would fail
(b) is failing
(c) fails
(d) failed

Grammar Test

13. Edgar had promised his dad that he wouldn't take alcohol at the party because he had to drive home afterwards. However, he could not resist drinking five shots of tequila, _____ he knew it was dangerous to do so.

(a) since
(b) although
(c) while
(d) that

14. Some residents of Wilmington were against the construction of an overpass near the town park. They _____ a strike when officials suddenly announced that the town council is looking for an alternative site for the structure.

(a) already plan
(b) are already planning
(c) will already plan
(d) were already planning

15. Travis and Georgia are the hosts of a television talk show. Recently, they have been receiving viewer feedback that the show is becoming uninteresting. If only the producers revised its format, the program _____ much more entertaining.

(a) was
(b) will be
(c) would be
(d) is being

16. The new CEO of Schiller Pharmaceuticals is eager to save the company from bankruptcy. She decided to expand its product lines. She and her team of chemists have already begun _____ a new line of high-profit cosmetics.

(a) to have developed
(b) developing
(c) to be developing
(d) having developed

17. Daniel had been rushing to finish a series of paintings for an exhibit. However, the stress had triggered severe back pains that caused him to be bedridden. If he had not put too much pressure on himself, he _____ such trouble.

(a) will avoid
(b) had been avoiding
(c) would have avoided
(d) avoided

18. In his book The Disappearance of Childhood, Neil Postman suggests that the print media has helped promote the distinction between children and adults. He argues that this important distinction _____ since the arrival of the television.

(a) is being eroded
(b) would have eroded
(c) have been eroding
(d) has been eroding

19. My friend Bart uses unusual methods in taking pictures of high-profile subjects. When he photographed Georgina Brown, _____, he made her sit on a large dictionary.

(a) who is a popular writer
(b) to whom writing is popular
(c) whose is a popular writer
(d) that is a popular writer

20. When Anne took her usual route when she drove to work this morning, her car was caught in a traffic jam. If she had listened to the traffic report, she _____ a different route.

(a) took
(b) is taking
(c) would have taken
(d) had taken

21. JKNY's president announced a plan to reduce the firm's expenditures. He ordered that all managers _____ cost-cutting measures in all their stores nationwide. This action can lower overhead costs by as much as 12%.

(a) will implement
(b) implement
(c) implemented
(d) are implementing

22. Many executives have been awaiting world-famous management expert Benjamin Spade to conduct the workshop next month. You must call the event organizers immediately _____ a slot.

(a) to be reserving
(b) having reserved
(c) to reserve
(d) reserving

23. Sonia's book collection is growing rapidly. Her books are practically pouring out of the two shelves in her tiny apartment. It is best that she _____ from buying more books until she has found a bigger space.

(a) refrain
(b) refrains
(c) will refrain
(d) refrained

24. Some psychiatrists are convinced that "narcissism" is a serious personality disorder. They say that although the disorder can be treated by psychotherapy, _____ the patient acknowledge his or her own flaw is the toughest part of the treatment.

(a) to be making
(b) having made
(c) making
(d) makes

Grammar Test

25. I enrolled in a German language course five years ago. However, I never really learned to speak the language. If only I had used German regularly in my conversations with friends, I _____ it.

(a) had mastered
(b) would have mastered
(c) am mastering
(d) would master

26. Fatherhood, a film adaptation of Shakespeare's King Lear, took three years to produce because of the director's high standards. To the delight of Shakespeare fans, cinemas _____ the much-awaited film starting next month.

(a) finally show
(b) are finally showing
(c) have finally shown
(d) will finally be showing

THIS IS THE END OF THE GRAMMAR SECTION
DO NOT GO ON UNTIL TOLD TO DO SO

LISTENING
듣기

LISTENING SECTION

DIRCECTIONS:

The Listening Section has four parts. In each part you will hear a spoken passage and a number of questions about the passage. First you will hear the questions. Then you will hear the passage. From the four choices for each question, choose the best answer. Then blacken in the correct circle on your answer sheet.

Now you will hear an example question. Then you will hear an example passage

Now listen to the example question.

Example:

> (a) one
> (b) two
> (c) three
> (d) four

Bill Johnson has four brothers, so the best answer is (d). The circle with the letter (d) has been blackened.

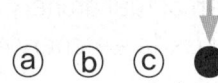

NOW TURN THE PAGE AND BEGIN

Listening Test

PART 1. You will hear two people talking. First you will hear questions 27 through 33. Then you will hear the conversation. Choose the best answer to each question in the time provided.

27. (a) an archery class
    (b) a badminton game
    (c) a company outing
    (d) a game of archery

28. (a) that it was exciting
    (b) that it was dangerous
    (c) that it was difficult
    (d) that it was entertaining

29. (a) because the target is outlined on the ground
    (b) because it is almost similar to hunting
    (c) because it requires target shooting
    (d) because it requires long distance shooting

30. (a) 10 meters
    (b) 30 meters
    (c) 70 meters
    (d) 90 meters

31. (a) her physical energy
    (b) her aiming position
    (c) her mental focus
    (d) her handling of archery gear

32. (a) One must be interested in hunting to learn archery.
    (b) It can be played only by people who have strong arms.
    (c) One must expect to accidentally hit people to learn archery.
    (d) It can be enjoyed by people of almost all ages.

33. (a) enroll his whole family in archery classes
    (b) purchase the basic archery gear
    (c) watch an actual archery competition
    (d) contact Carla's archery instructor

PART 2. You will hear a chief librarian talking about a library services for the save person. First you will hear questions 34 through 39. Then you will hear the talk. Choose the best answer to each question in the time provided.

34. (a) providing free library services to the disabled
    (b) making public buildings easier to reach for the disabled
    (c) hiring disabled persons to work in public agencies
    (d) publishing a regular newsletter for the disabled

35. (a) wheelchair-accessible elevators
    (b) electrically powered doors
    (c) access ramps for wheelchairs
    (d) special furniture for the disabled

36. (a) by providing voice and sound oriented services
    (b) by making the software available on a wheelchair
    (c) by helping the client hear better
    (d) by making the databases easier to read

37. (a) a government agency
    (b) a civic association
    (c) a multinational firm
    (d) a private foundation

38. (a) by hiring more library workers
    (b) by holding workshops on library services
    (c) by buying more library materials
    (d) by publicizing the project

39. (a) give them time alone
    (b) approach them all the time
    (c) require another person to accompany them
    (d) expect them to be more demanding

Listening Test

PART 3. You will hear a conversation between two people. First you will hear questions 40 through 46. Then you will hear the conversation. Choose the best answer to each question in the time provided.

40. (a) It is a popular magazine.
    (b) It is very accessible.
    (c) It is his favorite magazine.
    (d) It is easy to understand.

41. (a) He is sometimes unable to buy a copy of the latest issue.
    (b) He frequently misplaces his copy of it.
    (c) He often can't access its online edition.
    (d) He is usually too busy to read it.

42. (a) to borrowing magazines from a library
    (b) to ordering artwork over the Internet
    (c) to buying grocery items wholesale
    (d) to buying old magazine issues

43. (a) by resolving the complaints immediately
    (b) by ignoring the complaints indefinitely
    (c) by blaming the publishers
    (d) by giving away free copies

44. (a) more updated information
    (b) articles that are better written
    (c) more humorous writers
    (d) special printed contents

45. (a) because it can be hand-carried
    (b) because it is more relaxing to read
    (c) because it is released much earlier
    (d) because it has a more attractive design

46. (a) He will buy cheaper ink and paper.
    (b) He will just read the magazine's online version.
    (c) He will subscribe to Enterprise magazine.
    (d) He will get a subscription to Art Review.

PART 4. *You will hear an explanation of a process. First you will hear questions 47 through 52. Then you will hear the explanation. Choose the best answer to each question in the time provided.*

47. (a) It is very relaxed.
    (b) It is very disturbing.
    (c) It is very boring.
    (d) It is very hectic.

48. (a) those whose vital sign readings are more critical
    (b) those whose vital sign readings are most stable
    (c) those who have records of their medical history
    (d) those who arrived at the ER first

49. (a) because they refused to give information the first time
    (b) because they have never been to any hospital before
    (c) because they are usually minor cases
    (d) because it is usually their first ER admission

50. (a) emergency response
    (b) differential diagnosis
    (c) laboratory examination
    (d) surgical procedure

51. (a) She performs the required laboratory tests.
    (b) Only she can determine the patients' condition.
    (c) She confirms the findings of the emergency doctor.
    (d) Only she can explain to the patients their condition.

52. (a) refer them to a specialist at once
    (b) give them proper medical attention nonetheless
    (c) send them away as soon as possible
    (d) give them priority over other patients

THIS IS THE END OF THE GRAMMAR SECTION
DO NOT GO ON UNTIL TOLD TO DO SO

READING AND VOCABULARY
독해 · 어휘

READING AND VOCABULARY SECTION

DIRCECTIONS:

You will now read four different passages. Each passage is followed by comprehension and vocabulary questions. From the four choices for each item, choose the best answer. Then blacken in the correct circle on your answer sheet.

Read the following example passage and example question.

Example:

> Bill Johnson lives in New York. He is 25 years old. He has four brothers and two sisters.
>
> How many brothers does Bill Johnson have?
>
> (a) one
> (b) two
> (c) three
> (d) four

The correct answer is (d), so the circle with che letter (d) has been blackened.

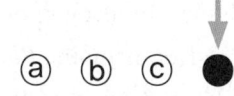

NOW TURN THE PAGE AND BEGIN

Reading and Vocabulary Test

PART 1. Read the following biographical narrative and answer the questions. The underlined words in the article are for vocabulary questions.

MARGARET MEAD

Margaret Mead was an American anthropologist who was famous for her research on cultural anthropology and her insights on how the world functioned. Through her writings and interviews in mass media, she has made anthropology <u>accessible</u> to many people.

Margaret Mead was born in 1901 in Philadelphia, Pennsylvania. She was the eldest of the four children of Edward Sherwood Mead, a professor of economics at the University of Pennsylvania, and Emily Fogg, a sociologist. <u>She was studying sociology at Barnard College in New York when she became keenly interested in anthropology</u>. There, she met the anthropologist Franz Boas who would later become her mentor at Columbia University graduate school.

At age 23, Mead traveled to the South Pacific to do research for her doctoral dissertation. The resulting book, *Coming of Age in Samoa*, became a bestseller. She continued studying the cultures of North America and Southeast Asia after earning her PhD. In Bali, Indonesia, she pioneered the use of photography in anthropological research, taking more than 30,000 pictures of the Balinese.

In the course of her career, Mead had important insights about childrearing, women's roles, and gender relations in many cultures. She was one of the first to introduce the idea that society expected individuals to behave in certain "acceptable" ways, and that these ways varied greatly between cultures. She further proposed that masculine and feminine behavior were not all caused by biological differences but by "cultural conditioning" or "socialization."

Mead taught at the New School for Social Research, Yale University, and Emory University. She was also the first woman anthropologist to become president of the American Association for the Advancement of Science. During her lifetime, she produced more than 40 books and 1,000 scholarly articles. Although Mead was controversial, it is widely acknowledged that her research and numerous documentary films promoted a greater understanding of cultures that had been ignored by mainstream American society.

From 1926 until her retirement, Mead worked at the American Museum of Natural History. A committed activist, she often commented on social and environmental issues. In recognition of her achievements, *Time* magazine named her "Mother of the World" in 1969. Her memoirs, *Blackberry Winter*, were published in 1972. She died in New York in 1978. A year later, she was posthumously <u>awarded</u> the Presidential Medal of Freedom.

53. What field of study did Margaret Mead pursue before becoming an anthropologist?

(a) journalism
(b) economics
(c) filmmaking
(d) sociology

54. What was probably Mead's major contribution while studying Balinese society?

(a) building a large collection of Balinese artifacts
(b) writing a bestselling book about Bali
(c) founding a center for women's studies in Indonesia
(d) making photography a part of field research

55. How did Mead explain gender behavior?

(a) It is determined at birth.
(b) It is similar across all cultures.
(c) It is shaped by one's society.
(d) It can only be explained by biology.

56. Which was a result of Mead's work in the US?

(a) an interest in modern societies
(b) an increased awareness of other cultures
(c) a sudden growth in research
(d) a preference for more primitive research subjects

57. Based on the passage, why most probably was Mead named "Mother of the World"?

(a) for her efforts in promoting the understanding of cultures
(b) for her work in modernizing ancient cultures
(c) because she has raised the status of women
(d) because she acted like a mother to her research subjects

58. In the context of the passage, accessible means _____.

(a) handy
(b) restricted
(c) available
(d) nearby

59. In the context of the passage, awarded means _____.

(a) donated
(b) allowed
(c) paid
(d) given

Reading and Vocabulary Test

PART 2. *Read the following article and answer the questions. The underlined words in the article are for vocabulary questions.*

ITALIAN SUPERVOLCANO IS GETTING ACTIVE

Located near a densely populated area and inactive for more than 400 years, the "supervolcano" Campi Flegrei is starting to show signs of becoming active. Named "burning fields" in Italian, and also known as the Phlegraean Fields, the volcano is near the Bay of Naples in Italy. Recent monitoring has shown that it is heating up and getting active, and scientists are saying that it may erupt in the near future.

Like all supervolcanoes, Campi Flegrei is characterized by a large depression, called "caldera," that spans more than six miles. The volcano is not a single volcanic cone, but a large <u>complex</u> of 24 craters and geysers that release hot gases. A large portion of the volcano is submerged in the Mediterranean Sea.

The volcano is believed to have formed hundreds of thousands of years ago. Its first eruption, which occurred 200,000 years ago, <u>spewed</u> so much ash that it blocked sunlight from reaching the earth's surface, triggering a "volcanic winter" or global cooling. The volcano erupted again 40,000 years ago, and scientific evidence suggests it might be one of the reasons why Neanderthals have become extinct. The volcano's most recent eruption in 1538 lasted for eight straight days, spreading ash all over Europe and forming a new mountain. Since its last eruption, Campi Flegrei has been inactive.

Recently, there have been signs that Campi Flegrei is approaching a critical pressure point that can trigger another eruption. The location of the volcano is quite problematic. It is near the metropolitan area of Naples, Italy: one of the densely populated areas of the world. Most of the increasing rock deformation and heating have been observed in the area.

Despite these findings, it is very hard to determine the volcano's "tipping point" or the time it will erupt. The eruption may not even happen for the next 100 years. However, as a precautionary measure, the government has already raised the threat level from green ("quiet") to yellow ("requires scientific monitoring"). The Italian National Institute of Geophysics is monitoring the situation and analyzing real-time findings.

60. What does not describe Campi Flegrei?

(a) It is the largest volcano in the world.
(b) It is in close proximity to a bay.
(c) Its name suggests its deadly effects.
(d) It might erupt in the coming years.

61. What makes Campi Flegrei a supervolcano?

(a) It has erupted many times in the past.
(b) It was formed hundreds of thousands of years ago.
(c) It was an inactive volcano that is now becoming active.
(d) Its depression is very big.

62. How most likely did Campi Flegrei cause the "volcanic winter"?

(a) by covering the atmosphere with ash
(b) by forming another volcano nearby
(c) by spreading ash across European lands
(d) by forming a snow-like terrain around the world

63. According to the article, when did the volcano last erupt?

(a) 200,000 years ago
(b) during the 16th century
(c) when the Neanderthals were wiped out
(d) 500 years ago

64. What is the likely reason why the location of the volcano is problematic?

(a) It makes the volcano difficult to access.
(b) It makes its eruption hard to predict.
(c) Many people could die if it erupts.
(d) It generates rock deformation and heat.

65. In the context of the passage, complex means _____.

(a) cone
(b) union
(c) building
(d) group

66. In the context of the passage, spewed means _____.

(a) dripped
(b) ejected
(c) absorbed
(d) increased

Reading and Vocabulary Test

PART 3. *Read the following encyclopedia article and answer the questions. The underlined words in the article are for vocabulary questions.*

MEDITERRANEAN SEA

The Mediterranean Sea is a body of water bordered by three continents: Europe, Asia, and Africa. The sea served as a major route for merchants and travelers during ancient times. This was due to the many opportunities for trade and cultural exchange the Mediterranean provided the peoples of the region. Often called the "cradle of civilization," the region around the Mediterranean Sea was home to many early cultures and civilizations.

The sea covers an area of 2,509,000 square kilometers and has an average depth of 1,500 meters. Due to its limited tidal range and high rate of evaporation, the Mediterranean is much saltier than the Atlantic Ocean to which it is connected through a narrow channel called The Strait of Gibraltar.

The Mediterranean Sea is believed to be a remnant of Tethys, the vast ancient sea that has been shrinking since the tectonic plates carrying Africa and Eurasia began to collide 30 million years ago. Slight movements of these plates cause the eruption of volcanoes such as Etna, Vesuvius, and Stromboli in Italy, and trigger earthquakes in parts of Europe and Africa.

Some of the world's first civilizations flourished around the Mediterranean. The sea was used as a thoroughfare by merchants trading from Phoenicia. Carthage, Greece, Sicily, and Rome all rivaled for commercial and political control of the Mediterranean region. Under the Roman Empire, the citizens referred to the Mediterranean as *Mare Nostrum*, meaning "our sea." Later, the Byzantine Empire and the Arabs gained supremacy in the area. Between the 11th and 14th centuries, trading states such as Genoa, Venice, and Barcelona dominated the region. These states struggled with the Turkish territories for naval dominance. Commodities from Asia passed to Europe over Mediterranean routes until the late 15th century when a new passage was established around the Cape of Good Hope.

At present, the Mediterranean Sea facilitates European and American access to the petroleum of Libya, Algeria, and the Persian Gulf region via the Suez Canal. The Mediterranean region has also become a popular tourist destination because of its beautiful beaches and warm climate. To protect the sea, countries bordering the Mediterranean agreed in 1995 to eliminate toxic waste disposal.

67. What is true about the Mediterranean Sea?

   (a) It has been used for economic trade for centuries.
   (b) It lies between four continents.
   (c) It has fewer salt deposits than the Atlantic Ocean.
   (d) Its surrounding areas had been unlivable.

68. Which disaster remains a threat to the Mediterranean region?

   (a) droughts
   (b) wars
   (c) earthquakes
   (d) tsunamis

69. How did the early Romans consider the Mediterranean Sea?

   (a) as the remains of an older sea
   (b) as a property of the empire
   (c) as the cradle of civilization
   (d) as the source of Roman culture

70. What probably happened to the Mediterranean Sea after the 15th century?

   (a) It was acquired by the Turks.
   (b) It became useless to European traders.
   (c) It became even more crowded.
   (d) It became a less important trade route to Asia.

71. In the 1990s, what did the countries in the region decide to do?

   (a) stop dumping poisonous waste into the sea
   (b) promote the region as a tourist destination
   (c) increase their trade of petroleum
   (d) open the Suez Canal

72. In the context of the passage, major means _____.

   (a) serious
   (b) important
   (c) heavy
   (d) old

73. In the context of the passage, rivaled means _____.

   (a) cooperated
   (b) played
   (c) competed
   (d) shared

Reading and Vocabulary Test

PART 4. Read the following business letter and answer the questions. The underlined words in the article are for vocabulary questions.

April 22, 2016

Dr. Michael Smith
Dean, College of Engineering
California Polytechnic State University
San Luis Obispo, CA 93407

Dear Dr. Smith:

Colby Systems, Inc., a global leader in the production of consumer technology devices, announces its "Create the Future" Design Contest for 2016. The contest is open to all full-time designers, college professors, and students currently living in the United States.

Design ideas may be submitted in any of the following categories:

(1) *Everyday product*: an original design of a functional product that enhances consumers' quality of life.
(2) *Safety device*: an original design of a mechanical or electronic device that ensures people's safety at home, in the office, or outdoors.
(3) *Transportation equipment*: an original design of a mechanical or electromechanical tool that improves the quality of cars, trains, and other modes of transport.

We emphasize that all design entries should be original and have never been patented before. Contestants are required to submit an essay that focuses on how the product works; how it would be manufactured; where it could be used; and how it would benefit both its intended market and the world as a whole. They must also include an illustration of the product in one of the formats listed on the entry form.

Entry forms are available at www.colbycontest.com. For guidelines, prizes, and other details about the contest, please refer to the attached brochure. Kindly share this information with the California Polytechnic community. Thank you.

Sincerely,

Geraldine Klein
Head, Industrial Division
Colby Systems, Inc.

87 Shelton Technology Center
P.O. Box 598

74. What kind of organization is sponsoring the contest?

(a) a state university
(b) a transportation agency
(c) a research institute
(d) a manufacturing firm

75. Who may join the contest?

(a) only those who are employees of an academic institution
(b) only those who are working as professional designers
(c) only those who are US residents at the time of the contest
(d) only those who have advanced degrees in engineering

76. How can the design ideas required for the contest be described?

(a) as solely for household use
(b) as beneficial to the consumers
(c) as adaptations of earlier designs
(d) as hi-tech digital products

77. Which doesn't need to be described in the essay about the proposed product?

(a) how it would be profitable
(b) how it would be produced
(c) how it would be used
(d) how it would be helpful

78. Why most likely is Colby Systems, Inc. sponsoring the contest?

(a) They want more publicity.
(b) They are looking for new products to make.
(c) They would like to support the designers.
(d) They are seeking to promote their products.

79. In the context of the passage, announces means _____.

(a) hides
(b) reveals
(c) declares
(d) shows

80. In the context of the passage, modes means _____.

(a) objects
(b) trends
(c) processes
(d) ways

THIS IS THE END OF THE TEST

지텔프코리아 공식지정

G-TELP
LEVEL 2

이현아 취향저격 지텔프 실전모의고사

TEST 4

한 권에 끝내는 G-TELP 실전모의고사 5회

SECTION 01 GRAMMAR
SECTION 02 LISTENING
SECTION 03 READING & VOCABULARY

GRAMMAR
문법

GRAMMAR SECTION

DIRCECTIONS:

The following items need a word or words to complete the sentence. From the four choices which follow each item, choose the best answer. Tnen blacken in the correct circle on your answer sheet.

Example:

> The boys _____ in the car.
>
> (a) be
> (b) is
> (c) am
> (d) are

The correct answer is (d), so the circle with che letter (d) has been blackened.

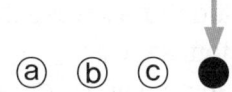

NOW TURN THE PAGE AND BEGIN

Grammar Test

1. Neal Livingston is a well-respected independent filmmaker. He produces documentary films for television on a wide variety of topics. Considered a genius by many, he _____ award-winning films for more than 35 years since he was twelve.

   (a) had been produced
   (b) was producing
   (c) has been producing
   (d) has produced

2. With the Internet, students can now tailor-fit their learning based on their individual study needs and schedules. If Internet-based schooling were not available today, working people _____ a hard time obtaining graduate degrees.

   (a) would have
   (b) will have
   (c) are having
   (d) have

3. Bruce knew that his fees would be substantial if Nexar Films would hire his company's advertising services. He _____ to manage Nexar's advertising needs for three years before its president finally agreed a month ago.

   (a) would have offered
   (b) had been offering
   (c) would offer
   (d) was offering

4. A new computer game is seriously distracting students from their studies, resulting in poor attendance and poor performance in class. School officials urged that parents _____ more vigilant of their children's after-school activities.

   (a) are
   (b) will be
   (c) be
   (d) have been

5. My cousin Jeff joined a national photography competition for the first time and won the first prize. Little did we know that he has been perfecting his craft _____ he got his first professional camera at age 18.

   (a) at last
   (b) ever since
   (c) and yet
   (d) until

6. Type 2 diabetes mellitus is a costly and serious disease that afflicts 8% of adults in the United States. Despite its threat, many doctors say that _____ this disease can actually be done through regular physical exercise.

   (a) preventing
   (b) having prevented
   (c) to prevent
   (d) prevents

7. Joanne is fond of playing jokes on people. Yesterday, she pulled a cruel joke on Greg. She _____ have thought that Greg would not retaliate, but he will file a lawsuit against her for mischief.

   (a) would
   (b) may
   (c) must
   (d) should

8. Agnes, an interior decorator and writer for a lifestyle magazine, always misses the monthly deadlines set by her editor. This _____ if she weren't busy renovating houses.

   (a) wouldn't happen
   (b) won't happen
   (c) isn't happening
   (d) didn't happen

9. After working as a professional pilot for over 20 years, Mark decided to quit flying and go into business on his own. Next month, he _____ travel souvenirs through a chain of curio shops in international airports.

   (a) would sell
   (b) sells
   (c) is selling
   (d) will be selling

10. My friends and I had agreed to meet at Tater's for lunch. However, I had a flat tire on the way there, and was running late. I didn't want them _____ for me so I said I'd just join them for dessert.

    (a) wait
    (b) to wait
    (c) waiting
    (d) will wait

11. Martin has been suffering severe migraines for no obvious causes since two months ago. For fear that his condition might be serious, he has been delaying _____ an appointment with his doctor.

    (a) to be making
    (b) having made
    (c) to make
    (d) making

12. The Junior Jaycees International is a youth organization that trains its members to become effective leaders. Many of its former members now hold high-ranking positions. If it hadn't been for the organization, they _____ as successful as they are now.

    (a) would not have been
    (b) have not been
    (c) were not being
    (d) not having been

Grammar Test

13. Many citizens have been looking forward to having a truly good and competent president. Thus, when Robert Powell, _____, announced his candidacy, the people were jubilant.

(a) whose a good governance advocate
(b) who is a good governance advocate
(c) why he's a good governance advocate
(d) that's a good governance advocate

14. The Arkansas Geriatric Education Center provides free training to professionals who take care of older people. Several times a year, the Center sponsors free seminars _____ individuals about caring for the elderly.

(a) will educate
(b) educating
(c) to educate
(d) to be educating

15. Mr. Greeley should have left at least an hour earlier to drive to the new Greek restaurant, Ethos-Gallery. Traffic was so heavy that the restaurant _____ when he arrived at 10:00 p.m.

(a) already closes
(b) would already close
(c) already closed
(d) was already closing

16. I was not interested in science and technology until I first read a copy of Discover magazine. It has easy-to-understand articles and impressive pictures. If I _____ to subscribe to a science-oriented publication, my first choice would be Discover.

(a) was
(b) were
(c) will be
(d) am

17. After four years in college and four years in medical school, Greta entered a three-year residency training. By the time she obtains her specialization in pediatrics, she _____ for eleven straight years!

(a) will have been studying
(b) will be studying
(c) has been studying
(d) would study

18. The police chief reported that about $2,000 worth of cash and merchandise was stolen from Garfield Department Store last Friday. He says it is important that department store owners _____ the security of their buildings.

(a) improved
(b) are improving
(c) will improve
(d) improve

19. A theater in Istanbul was named after the 20th-century Turkish actress Afife Jale. She is remembered for her persistence in performing in stage plays _____ the Turkish government forbade women from having acting careers that time.

(a) although
(b) therefore
(c) because
(d) while

20. Louie's business trip to Oregon was only two days. His packed schedule of meetings and presentations left him no free time. If only his trip had been longer, he _____ his aunt in Hillsboro.

(a) would visit
(b) visited
(c) is visiting
(d) would have visited

21. Several universities and federal agencies in Canada are doing research on climate change and its harmful effects on animal life. At present, environmental scientists _____ forest changes and their impact on insect and bird populations.

(a) are examining
(b) were examined
(c) will be examining
(d) examine

22. During World War 1, many American businessmen entered the aviation industry due to the huge demand for war aircraft engines. After the war, most of the companies _____ immediately went back to their original business.

(a) who had been making plane engines
(b) that had been making plane engines
(c) where plane engines had been making
(d) which the plane engines had been making

23. Flu viruses are evolving so quickly that last year's flu vaccine may no longer be effective. This is why new flu vaccines are released every year. Health experts also advise that everyone _____ a flu vaccine yearly.

(a) get
(b) to get
(c) will get
(d) gets

24. Many observers were disappointed that the senate postponed the approval of an energy bill. Many are saying that if the bill had been passed, it _____ new job opportunities in all sectors, including agriculture and technology.

(a) had created
(b) created
(c) will be creating
(d) would have created

Grammar Test

25. Marina began experiencing headaches and diarrhea after taking a diet pill for losing weight. She immediately realized that she must stop _____ the pill because it was doing her more harm than good.

(a) to use
(b) having used
(c) using
(d) to be using

26. Damian resigned from his post as vice president for research at Brown University because he missed lecturing in the classroom. That is why next spring, he _____ return to the Brown faculty as professor of applied physics.

(a) could
(b) will
(c) can
(d) shall

THIS IS THE END OF THE GRAMMAR SECTION
DO NOT GO ON UNTIL TOLD TO DO SO

LISTENING
듣기

LISTENING SECTION

DIRCECTIONS:

The Listening Section has four parts. In each part you will hear a spoken passage and a number of questions about the passage. First you will hear the questions. Then you will hear the passage. From the four choices for each question, choose the best answer. Then blacken in the correct circle on your answer sheet.

Now you will hear an example question. Then you will hear an example passage

Now listen to the example question.

Example:

> (a) one
> (b) two
> (c) three
> (d) four

Bill Johnson has four brothers, so the best answer is (d). The circle with the letter (d) has been blackened.

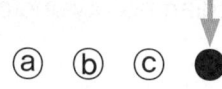

NOW TURN THE PAGE AND BEGIN

Listening Test

PART 1. You will hear two people talking. First you will hear questions 27 through 33. Then you will hear the conversation. Choose the best answer to each question in the time provided.

27. (a) Carol's out-of-country trip
    (b) the history of Cambodia
    (c) where to spend a vacation
    (d) James' business trip

28. (a) It employs people from different parts of Cambodia.
    (b) It receives donations from charitable groups.
    (c) It exports expensive crafts.
    (d) It provides assistance to poor Cambodians.

29. (a) antique works of art
    (b) a Buddhist temple
    (c) historical documents
    (d) a souvenir shop

30. (a) gloomy
    (b) complicated
    (c) touching
    (d) intimidating

31. (a) beautiful beaches
    (b) historical sites
    (c) magic shows
    (d) seafood markets

32. (a) She was shocked.
    (b) She was scared.
    (c) She was amazed.
    (d) She was amused.

33. (a) he should consult a travel agency about trips to Cambodia
    (b) he should assist in making a documentary about Cambodia
    (c) he should go with her family the next time they visit Cambodia
    (d) he should read materials about Cambodian history and culture

PART 2. *You will hear a woman talking about a policy proposal. First you will hear questions 34 through 39. Then you will hear the talk. Choose the best answer to each question in the time provided.*

34. (a) a revised company policy
    (b) a new energy-saving strategy
    (c) a new information systems design
    (d) a detailed expense report

35. (a) in summer
    (b) in autumn
    (c) in winter
    (d) in spring

36. (a) The heating system in each work area can be switched on and off as needed.
    (b) Each department's power use can be recorded.
    (c) The heating system can function at all times.
    (d) The maintenance department can repair heating vents easily.

37. (a) by blocking the air vents
    (b) by using as few furniture as possible
    (c) by not lowering the thermostat
    (d) by ensuring that the heat outlets are not blocked

38. (a) so they can plan the company's energy use
    (b) so they can eat together and become friends
    (c) because they know the company the most
    (d) because they have better energy-saving ideas

39. (a) They will be sharing their opinions.
    (b) They will be listening to another speaker.
    (c) They will go back to their work.
    (d) They will go home.

Listening Test

PART 3. You will hear a conversation between two people. First you will hear questions 40 through 46. Then you will hear the conversation. Choose the best answer to each question in the time provided.

40. (a) He wants to take up a short course in gardening.
    (b) He plans to join an organization of amateur gardeners.
    (c) He wants to have a garden at his new home.
    (d) He and his wife want to put up a flower business.

41. (a) character
    (b) health
    (c) personality
    (d) climate

42. (a) Morning light makes a garden both healthy and attractive.
    (b) Different plants need varying amounts of light to survive.
    (c) Gardens that face north tend to be damp due to very little light.
    (d) Plants need more artificial light than sunlight to survive.

43. (a) study and record the features of the garden site
    (b) consult a horticulturist about the garden's look
    (c) prepare the soil for planting by applying fertilizer
    (d) buy gardening equipment and outdoor furniture

44. (a) It helps plants survive during winter.
    (b) It can nourish more trees.
    (c) It is highly resistant to weeds.
    (d) It means big savings in gardening costs.

45. (a) They sell only expensive and unusual plant varieties.
    (b) They charge high for assistance.
    (c) They can usually supply the basic gardening materials.
    (d) They promote the exclusive use of organic fertilizers.

46. (a) show Clarissa his plans for the garden
    (b) start recording the conditions of his backyard
    (c) buy seedlings from a nursery
    (d) gather organic matter to be used as fertilizer

PART 4. *You will hear an explanation of a process. First you will hear questions 47 through 52. Then you will hear the explanation. Choose the best answer to each question in the time provided.*

47. (a) to launch a non-government organization
    (b) to encourage people to donate blood
    (c) to collect funds for a health center
    (d) to educate about the need for blood donors

48. (a) It should be promoted in more American communities.
    (b) It can be a profitable activity for health agencies.
    (c) It requires the use of complex medical equipment.
    (d) It is simpler than many prospective donors think.

49. (a) at temporary collection centers
    (b) at the local health center
    (c) at university clinics
    (d) at all hospitals nationwide

50. (a) to diagnose the donor's illness right away
    (b) to ensure that the donor can produce enough blood samples
    (c) to check if the donor is honest about his medical history
    (d) to make sure that the donor's blood is safe for donation

51. (a) have a blood test done
    (b) eat some food and drink some water
    (c) get three hours of sleep
    (d) take a multivitamin pill

52. (a) the schedule of blood drive
    (b) the medical personnel involved
    (c) the other requirements for donors
    (d) the intended recipients of the donation

THIS IS THE END OF THE GRAMMAR SECTION
DO NOT GO ON UNTIL TOLD TO DO SO

READING AND VOCABULARY
독해 · 어휘

READING AND VOCABULARY SECTION

DIRCECTIONS:

You will now read four different passages. Each passage is followed by comprehension and vocabulary questions. From the four choices for each item, choose the best answer. Then blacken in the correct circle on your answer sheet.

Read the following example passage and example question.

Example:

> Bill Johnson lives in New York. He is 25 years old. He has four brothers and two sisters.
>
> How many brothers does Bill Johnson have?
>
> (a) one
> (b) two
> (c) three
> (d) four

The correct answer is (d), so the circle with che letter (d) has been blackened.

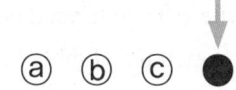

NOW TURN THE PAGE AND BEGIN

Reading and Vocabulary Test

PART 1. *Read the following biographical narrative and answer the questions. The underlined words in the article are for vocabulary questions.*

EDWIN HUBBLE

Edwin Hubble was an American astronomer who was the first to show that there are other galaxies in the universe besides the Milky Way. He created a classification system for galaxies that is still in use today. One of the leading astronomers of the 20th century, he is also the namesake of the Hubble Space Telescope.

Edwin Powell Hubble was born in Marshfield, Missouri on November 20, 1889. As a young man, Hubble was a fine student and athlete, and was fond of reading science fiction novels. He received a degree in mathematics and astronomy from the University of Chicago. His athletic and academic excellence would later earn him a Rhodes scholarship at Oxford University in England, where he studied law.

Upon returning to the US in 1913, he worked halfheartedly as a lawyer. He eventually quit law and pursued advanced studies in astronomy at the Yerkes Observatory in Wisconsin, and received his PhD in 1917. Two years later, he began working at Mount Wilson Observatory in California.

Most astronomers of Hubble's time believed that the Milky Way galaxy made up the whole universe and that the spots of light called "nebulae" were simply clouds of glowing gas that were quite near to Earth. In 1924, however, Hubble found proof that negated this claim. He showed that the Andromeda nebula was nearly a million light-years away, far beyond the bounds of the Milky Way. Thereafter, Hubble established the presence of other galaxies. He also proved that the universe is expanding – a discovery that confirmed Albert Einstein's earlier theory that the universe is able to expand or contract.

In 1929, Hubble formulated what is now known as Hubble's Law, which states that the farther a galaxy is from another point in space, the faster it appears to move away. This scientific law helped astronomers estimate the age of the universe. His reputation as an astronomer was strengthened by his publication of such papers as *The Velocity-Distance Relation among Extra-Galactic Nebulae (1931)*, *The Realm of Nebulae (1936)*, and *The Problem of the Expanding Universe (1942)*, among others.

Hubble later transferred to the Palomar Observatory in California, where he continued doing space research until his death in 1953. Besides his many awards, NASA also named the Hubble Space Telescope after him for his groundbreaking discoveries in modern astronomy.

53. What was Edwin Hubble most famous for?

(a) his work in science fiction
(b) his discoveries about outer space
(c) his discovery of the Milky Way
(d) his invention of a telescope

54. Why most likely did Hubble give up his job as a lawyer?

(a) because he wanted to return to Chicago
(b) because he preferred studying to working
(c) because it wasn't really his interest
(d) because law was too difficult

55. How was Hubble able to prove that the entire universe wasn't just made up of the Milky Way?

(a) by establishing that Earth was within the Milky Way
(b) by showing that a nebula was far outside the Milky Way
(c) by discovering the universe is expanding
(d) by learning that the universe is getting smaller

56. What is the basic principle of Hubble's Law?

(a) The farther a galaxy is, the faster it seems to move away.
(b) There are other galaxies in the universe besides the Milky Way.
(c) The size of the universe is not changing.
(d) Nebulae are clouds of gas that are very close to Earth.

57. Based on the passage, what can be said about Edwin Hubble?

(a) He always supported the accepted theories of his time.
(b) His scientific discoveries are no longer relevant today.
(c) He was the best astronomer who ever lived.
(d) His discoveries led to a better understanding of the universe.

58. In the context of the passage, excellence means _____.

(a) image
(b) appeal
(c) ability
(d) interest

59. In the context of the passage, negated means _____.

(a) approved
(b) enriched
(c) fought
(d) contradicted

Reading and Vocabulary Test

PART 2. *Read the following article and answer the questions. The underlined words in the article are for vocabulary questions.*

STUDY SHOWS THAT SOME ASTHMA PATIENTS ACTUALLY DON'T HAVE ASTHMA

A study shows that adults who have been diagnosed with asthma may not have the disease after all. According to the study, which was held at the Ottawa Hospital Research Institute in Canada, about a third of more than 600 asthma patients did not suffer from asthma, a condition wherein a person's airway swells and breathing becomes difficult when exposed to external causes.

Researchers tested 613 Canadian adults who had been diagnosed with asthma in the past five years, 45 percent of whom were taking asthma medications daily. The participants were first asked to go through a lung-function test to measure how much air they could blow out of their lungs. If the test proved that a patient was negative of asthma, he was made to inhale methacholine, a chemical that commonly <u>triggers</u> an asthma attack.

The tests showed that 203 of the participants did not test positive for asthma. They were then asked to lower, and eventually, stop their medication during weeks of observation. When their condition did not worsen after stopping asthma medication, they were observed for another year to see if the disease might return. Over 90 percent remained asthma-free even without any medication. The researchers concluded that the subjects may have been cured of the disease or incorrectly diagnosed.

Many of the asthma-free participants were proven to be completely healthy all the while. Most weren't surprised with the finding, suspecting all along that their medications weren't really working. Others were diagnosed with different diseases that had been improperly identified as asthma, including obesity-related breathing difficulties and allergies, and even more serious conditions such as heart disease and lung infection. The participants went on to receive proper treatment for their illnesses.

According to Dr. Shawn Aaron, the study head and professor at the University of Ottawa in Ontario, the results show that some adult asthma patients may need to have their diagnosis <u>reassessed</u>. They may be undergoing asthma medication when they don't need to, and are putting themselves at risk of harmful side effects from the drugs. Moreover, they continue paying for the costs of treatment without any real benefit.

60. What did the study find out about some asthma patients?

(a) that they could be easily cured of asthma
(b) that their disease is non-existent
(c) that they could get rid of asthma themselves
(d) that they didn't know they had the disease

61. How most likely did a participant pass the lung-function test?

(a) by being immune to a chemical
(b) by blowing air as loudly as they could
(c) by having an asthma attack
(d) by blowing a sufficient amount of air

62. What was the study able to learn about a third of the participants?

(a) that they needed less asthma medication
(b) that their drugs were working
(c) that their asthma would return
(d) that their medication was useless

63. Why most likely were the patients misdiagnosed as having asthma?

(a) Their real diseases were cured by asthma drugs.
(b) Their real diseases always lead to asthma.
(c) Their real diseases showed the same symptoms.
(d) They claimed that they had asthma during diagnosis.

64. According to the study, what is a cause of harmful side effects?

(a) taking an asthma drug when it isn't necessary
(b) taking the wrong drug for asthma
(c) taking more than the prescribed dosage for asthma
(d) not taking asthma drugs daily

65. In the context of the passage, <u>triggers</u> means _____.

(a) fires
(b) starts
(c) prevents
(d) cures

66. In the context of the passage, <u>reassessed</u> means _____.

(a) renewed
(b) changed
(c) reviewed
(d) maintained

PART 3. *Read the following encyclopedia article and answer the questions. The underlined words in the article are for vocabulary questions.*

STONEHENGE

Stonehenge is a prehistoric monument that consists of large standing stones, or "megaliths," located on the Salisbury Plain in Wiltshire, southern England. Constructed 5,000 years ago, both who built it and why it was built remain a mystery.

The stones are enclosed in a circular ditch about 300 feet in diameter. The ditch has an earth bank on the inner side and is approached through a wide pathway called the Avenue. The monument's outer part is a circle of sandstones about 13.5 feet high and connected by stone beams. Within it is a circle of bluestone megaliths, a horseshoe-shaped group, and in the innermost part, an oval group.

Archaeological research shows that the stones were made somewhere else before they were installed on the site, and that building Stonehenge required careful planning and advanced knowledge of geometry and symmetry.

Most archaeologists think that Stonehenge was constructed between 3000 BC and 2000 BC. The older circular earth bank and ditch have been dated to about 3100 BC. However, the existing stones are only the ruins of what is believed to have been a bigger structure.

The creation of Stonehenge has been credited to many ancient peoples from throughout thousands of years. The most believable theory is that the construction was begun by the people of the late Neolithic period, around 3000 BC, and continued by the so-called Beaker Folk who lived in a more advanced economy and were more closely knit way than their ancestors.

The purpose of Stonehenge has also been the subject of much debate. Some have assumed that the structure was a temple used for worshipping the gods. Others have regarded it as an astronomical observatory for marking significant events on the prehistoric calendar. Still others believe it was a sacred burial site for high-ranking citizens of ancient times. Regardless of its purpose, there is agreement that Stonehenge had played a key role in the lives of those who invested considerable effort in its creation.

Today, Stonehenge is regarded as a British national icon that represents mystery, power, and endurance. It was designated as a UNESCO World Heritage Site in 1986.

67. What is Stonehenge?

(a) a rock formation
(b) a group of stones
(c) a prehistoric house
(d) a religious monument

68. Which is true about Stonehenge's formation?

(a) It is believed to be added to the structure later on.
(b) It was only discovered recently.
(c) It is composed of three layers of stone structures.
(d) It was constructed in 3000 BC.

69. What is said about the Beaker Folk?

(a) Their social system was more advanced than their ancestors.
(b) They most likely started building of Stonehenge.
(c) They rebuilt Stonehenge into a more modern structure.
(d) Stonehenge was damaged during their time.

70. Why has there been much discussion about Stonehenge?

(a) because it is regarded as sacred
(b) because it has high academic significance
(c) because it has great economic value
(d) because its purpose is still unknown

71. Why most likely do experts believe that Stonehenge served an important purpose to its builders?

(a) because it was well preserved
(b) because it is now a heritage site
(c) because it was difficult to make
(d) because remains have been found around it

72. In the context of the passage, existing means _____.

(a) fresh
(b) present
(c) past
(d) missing

73. In the context of the passage, subject means _____.

(a) topic
(b) result
(c) course
(d) belief

Reading and Vocabulary Test

PART 4. Read the following business letter and answer the questions. The underlined words in the article are for vocabulary questions.

January 10, 2004

Mr. Thomas Dillon
Vice President for Operations
Beckman Associates, Inc.
4102 Pine Ridge Road
Abington, PA 19001

Dear Mr. Dillon:

I know that your organization is very much concerned about efficiency and productivity. We at the People Company can help you achieve those goals by organizing a team-building program to help make your employees more efficient and your entire company more productive.

Our industrial psychologists at the People Company have developed the Team Survival Program, a two-day team-building <u>session</u> that will teach participants how to cope with a fast-paced business environment. On the first day, the participants will attend a seminar that focuses on strategic planning, time management, and work process improvement. On the second day, the participants will undergo outdoor search-and-rescue exercises designed to improve communication and teamwork among them.

The Team Survival Program will be an effective learning experience because it is based on the following principles:

(1) Alignment – to bridge the gap between corporate goals and current performance;
(2) Engagement – to standardize the different working styles of team members;
(3) Commitment – to open communication lines between management and staff; and
(4) Action – to enable team members to work on shared values and goals.

The People Company would <u>welcome</u> the opportunity to assist Beckman Associates in building a unified team. Please feel free to contact me anytime to discuss the Team Survival Program in detail.

Sincerely,

Miranda S. Barnett
Accounts Manager
The People Company
Tel: (215) 884-4887

74. Why did Miranda Barnett write Thomas Dillon the letter?

(a) to inquire about the services of his company
(b) to ask what goals his company wants to achieve
(c) to apply for as a manager at his company
(d) to offer a program suited to his company's need

75. How does the Team Survival Program aim to improve teamwork among participants?

(a) through pretend search-and-rescue activities
(b) by undergoing psychology tests
(c) through a seminar on time management
(d) by planning strategies together

76. What does the principle of Alignment most likely say?

(a) Team members should have the same goals.
(b) Managers should communicate with their staff.
(c) Various working styles should be standardized.
(d) Employee performance should meet management goals.

77. What did Barnett request Dillon to do?

(a) to inform his employees about the program
(b) to set a schedule for the team-building session
(c) to contact her if he is interested in the program
(d) to prepare a budget for the team-building session

78. What business is Miranda Barnett most probably involved in?

(a) an employee-training company
(b) an account management firm
(c) an emergency response team
(d) a recruitment company

79. In the context of the passage, session means _____.

(a) plan
(b) subject
(c) council
(d) activity

80. In the context of the passage, welcome means _____.

(a) secure
(b) appreciate
(c) admit
(d) disallow

THIS IS THE END OF THE TEST

지텔프코리아 공식지정

G-TELP
LEVEL 2

이현아 취향저격 지텔프 실전모의고사

TEST 5

한 권에 끝내는 G-TELP 실전모의고사 5회

SECTION 01 GRAMMAR
SECTION 02 LISTENING
SECTION 03 READING & VOCABULARY

GRAMMAR
문법

GRAMMAR SECTION

DIRCECTIONS:

The following items need a word or words to complete the sentence. From the four choices which follow each item, choose the best answer. Tnen blacken in the correct circle on your answer sheet.

Example:

> The boys _____ in the car.
>
> (a) be
> (b) is
> (c) am
> (d) are

The correct answer is (d), so the circle with che letter (d) has been blackened.

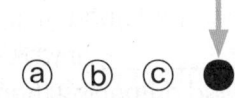

NOW TURN THE PAGE AND BEGIN

Grammar Test

1. Researchers have found that people who consume less than 20 grams of fat per day have fewer and less severe migraine attacks. On this basis, some doctors _____ their migraine-suffering patients to reduce their fat intake.

   (a) have now been advising
   (b) now advised
   (c) will now advise
   (d) are now advising

2. Sarah was only five years old when her father, an army lieutenant, was assigned to Africa. Now in her 20s, Sarah remembers _____ to the savanna to watch the wild animals roam.

   (a) going
   (b) goes
   (c) go
   (d) to go

3. Some people believe that caffeine causes acne. However, UCLA dermatology professor Joshua Wieder says that acne is caused by physical stress and hormonal problems. He advises that coffee drinkers not _____ about their coffee intake.

   (a) will worry
   (b) worried
   (c) worry
   (d) to worry

4. A friend recently gave me a hard-bound collection of beautiful poems. Because the book is heavy, I cannot carry it around to read outside my home. However, if I were to go out of town on vacation, I _____ the book with me.

   (a) am definitely taking
   (b) would definitely take
   (c) will definitely take
   (d) have definitely taken

5. Jerome isn't an art-history graduate and has never been employed full-time by an art institution. Nevertheless, he was hired as museum curator by an experimental art museum and _____ as its co-director for several months now.

   (a) would be working
   (b) was working
   (c) has been working
   (d) had been worked

6. Jake often forgets to remove his discs from the CD-ROM drive after playing them. When his brother, a computer engineer, learned about this, he said that Jake _____ always remove the discs to avoid damaging them and the CD-ROM.

   (a) should
   (b) will
   (c) may
   (d) could

7. Susanna Moore has written several novels with intriguing female characters. Among these novels are In the Cut, _____, and One Last Look. In her next work, Moore will be telling the story a mother who commits a heinous crime.

(a) who has been adapted into a film
(b) that has been adapted into a film
(c) where a film has been adapted
(d) which has been adapted into a film

8. Mr. Gibson was diagnosed with Alzheimer's disease last year. His wife realized that the best way _____ him cope with the disease was to learn about it. This is why they've been participating in awareness campaigns about Alzheimer's.

(a) to help
(b) will help
(c) to be helping
(d) helping

9. My cousin Denise is an amusement park designer for some of the world's biggest theme parks. Her love for design was evident from childhood. While we all played outdoors, she _____ LEGO houses in her room.

(a) will always play
(b) always plays
(c) had always played
(d) was always building

10. Technology company, Constellation Corp., is eager to release its new-generation disc that has 20 times more storage room than the average DVD. However, the marketing department is against _____ the product too early this year.

(a) having released
(b) to have released
(c) releasing
(d) to release

11. In 1998, California's governor didn't allow a legislative bill that proposed a statewide system for monitoring HIV cases. Health officials were disappointed, saying the bill _____ as an effective means of preventing HIV if it had been passed.

(a) would serve
(b) would have served
(c) has served
(d) was serving

12. Andre went to Moscow to start writing about the fashion trends during the Romanov Dynasty. After seeing the magnificent costumes at the Armory Museum, he became so inspired that he finished the article _____ he was still in Moscow.

(a) and
(b) but
(c) so
(d) while

Grammar Test

13. Leo Fender's interest in electronics began at an early age. After graduating from high school in 1928, he has already made public address systems and amplifiers _____ to organizers of social functions.

(a) when he rented out
(b) what he rents out
(c) that he rented out
(d) who rented him out

14. Some film critics criticized Woody Allen's Mighty Aphrodite for its not-so interesting scenes. They said that if the director and editor had given the script more thought, they _____ several boring dialogues and scenes.

(a) would have eliminated
(b) will be eliminating
(c) eliminated
(d) had eliminated

15. Dr. William Magee is a plastic surgeon and his wife is a nurse and social worker. In 1982, they founded Operation Smile _____ free reconstructive surgery to poor children with facial deformities.

(a) providing
(b) to be providing
(c) to provide
(d) having provided

16. The Ospreys was a 1950s band that only achieved moderate success. It could be _____ the band didn't develop a unique sound and merely copied the hit-making groups of its time instead.

(a) although
(b) because
(c) that
(d) when

17. Louise wants to give her parents a bottle of champagne for their wedding anniversary. Tomorrow, she _____ Rafael's Winery to choose from its large collection of vintage wines.

(a) will be visiting
(b) visits
(c) is visiting
(d) would visit

18. A group of African-American women in Alabama have been making quilts for many generations now. If the older generation had failed to pass the craft to their children, their means of livelihood _____ to this day.

(a) hasn't been lasting
(b) wouldn't have lasted
(c) is not lasting
(d) hadn't lasted

19. In just a year, the River Dogs has become a promising team in Oregon's amateur baseball league. Its manager says that the team would truly succeed if only it _____ a bigger fan base and a few more sponsorships.

    (a) is generating
    (b) will generate
    (c) generated
    (d) generates

20. Car mechanics say that a car won't run smoothly if one of its four tires is not balanced. Thus, they advise that car owners _____ that one section of their vehicle isn't heavier than the others.

    (a) ensure
    (b) ensures
    (c) are ensuring
    (d) will ensure

21. Irene has a creative way of teaching earth science. She makes sure her classes learn not just from lectures but also from practical applications. Next week, she _____ require her students to build miniature earthquake-proof buildings for the science fair.

    (a) should
    (b) can
    (c) may
    (d) will

22. Puerto Vallarta is a beautiful town on the Mexican Riviera. It is a popular tourist spot with charming beach resorts, gardens, and souvenir shops. Tourists also enjoy _____ in the town's lively nightlife scene.

    (a) to be participating
    (b) participating
    (c) to participate
    (d) having participated

23. Almost 50% of new teachers who graduated from the University of Iowa are now teaching in neighboring states. These teachers would have stayed in Iowa if only good opportunities _____ to them.

    (a) has been available
    (b) were available
    (c) would be available
    (d) had been available

24. David searches for out-of-print titles at BookFinder.com where he pays only $4 to $16 per book. To save money, he _____ for interesting books at bargain bookstores for years before he discovered the website.

    (a) had been looking
    (b) was looking
    (c) looks
    (d) looked

Grammar Test

25. Xanana Gusmão, the first president of East Timor, led the young republic's efforts to build its legal, economic, and education systems. Even today, he urges that politicians _____ the good governance expected by the East Timorese.

(a) are delivering
(b) delivered
(c) deliver
(d) to deliver

26. Julia is an IT specialist who has been tasked to evaluate the usability of her company's website. By the time the site goes "live" next month, she _____ with its various users for three months.

(a) would have coordinated
(b) will have been coordinating
(c) is coordinating
(d) will coordinate

THIS IS THE END OF THE GRAMMAR SECTION
DO NOT GO ON UNTIL TOLD TO DO SO

LISTENING
듣기

LISTENING SECTION

DIRCECTIONS:

The Listening Section has four parts. In each part you will hear a spoken passage and a number of questions about the passage. First you will hear the questions. Then you will hear the passage. From the four choices for each question, choose the best answer. Then blacken in the correct circle on your answer sheet.

Now you will hear an example question. Then you will hear an example passage

Now listen to the example question.

Example:

(a) one
(b) two
(c) three
(d) four

Bill Johnson has four brothers, so the best answer is (d). The circle with the letter (d) has been blackened.

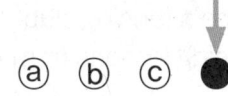

NOW TURN THE PAGE AND BEGIN

Listening Test

PART 1. You will hear two people talking. First you will hear questions 27 through 33. Then you will hear the conversation. Choose the best answer to each question in the time provided.

27. (a) teach a sports class
    (b) organize a sports event
    (c) enroll in a sports class
    (d) join a sports competition

28. (a) because the foil sword is light
    (b) because the foil sword's blade is wide
    (c) because the foil sword's blade is Y-shaped
    (d) because the foil sword doesn't bend easily

29. (a) using both hands at the same time
    (b) hitting the opponent's chest
    (c) bending the sword the farthest
    (d) hitting the opponent's arm

30. (a) Her brother introduced her to the sport.
    (b) She had practice bouts with her father.
    (c) Her father pushed her to learn about the sport.
    (d) She wrote a book about the sport.

31. (a) the advice of her instructors
    (b) her participation in her first competition
    (c) watching her father win an amateur bout
    (d) her training as a high school student

32. (a) being ready to deal with any of the opponent's attacks
    (b) being able to use both hands during a bout
    (c) being able to beat the opponent simply through strength
    (d) being good at planning an attack strategy

33. (a) watch some professional fencing sessions
    (b) read a book about fencing
    (c) join Anne's fencing club
    (d) get fencing lessons from Anne

PART 2. *You will hear a woman talking about a company program. First you will hear questions 34 through 39. Then you will hear the talk. Choose the best answer to each question in the time provided.*

34. (a) company manager
    (b) human resources head
    (c) network administrator
    (d) information technology chief

35. (a) to gather ideas needed for a proposed policy
    (b) to ask questions about a recent memorandum
    (c) to introduce the development of a new policy
    (d) to emphasize the salient points of a new policy

36. (a) It will be erased immediately from the delivery system.
    (b) It will be saved in a remote server for further analysis.
    (c) It will be delivered after the virus has been removed.
    (d) It will be returned to the sender within 24 hours.

37. (a) through an Internet-based service provider
    (b) using a third-party e-mail address
    (c) through the company's local area network
    (d) using a secure corporate website

38. (a) Its volume is limited to half of the employee's mailbox space.
    (b) It may be sent and received only on a limited basis.
    (c) It must be erased as soon as the recipient has read it.
    (d) It may be only sent and received using an unofficial address.

39. (a) for improving the reputation of the company
    (b) for evaluating the performance of the IT department
    (c) as basis for giving a worker a promotion
    (d) as basis for disciplining a worker

Listening Test

PART 3. You will hear a conversation between two people. First you will hear questions 40 through 46. Then you will hear the conversation. Choose the best answer to each question in the time provided.

40. (a) She needs to buy a product that is sold only on the web.
(b) She does not have time to shop at regular stores.
(c) She thinks online stores charge lower than regular stores.
(d) She wants to try out her new credit card.

41. (a) on an electronic shopping cart
(b) on a special network server
(c) on a Web-based product catalog
(d) on an electronic message board

42. (a) the price of the item bought
(b) the shipping fee
(c) the Internet service charge
(d) the tax rate

43. (a) pay additional charges in cash
(b) contact the online store by phone
(c) verify her credit card account balance
(d) review the information in the form

44. (a) a receipt sent by mail
(b) the store's printed catalog
(c) a printout of the confirmation form
(d) the customer's credit card bill

45. (a) It is the fastest way of transmitting data.
(b) It ensures that only the store will see the customer's data.
(c) It is used by all online stores at all times.
(d) It checks whether customers gave accurate information.

46. (a) confused
(b) nervous
(c) hesitant
(d) relieved

PART 4. *You will hear an explanation of a process. First you will hear questions 47 through 52. Then you will hear the explanation. Choose the best answer to each question in the time provided.*

47. (a) the ideal type of child to adopt
    (b) the best countries to apply for an adoption
    (c) the best time to adopt a child
    (d) the steps in adopting a child

48. (a) to determine if one is fit to adopt a child
    (b) to confirm the validity of one's documents
    (c) to help one find a suitable child to adopt
    (d) to help one complete the documents

49. (a) the high cost of legal services involved in adoption
    (b) the difficulty of obtaining required documents
    (c) the lack of social workers to help in the process
    (d) the different family laws of the various U.S. states

50. (a) during the pre-placement stage
    (b) once the home study process begins
    (c) during the placement stage
    (d) once all the papers are completed

51. (a) through court appearances
    (b) through visits by the social worker
    (c) through legal investigations
    (d) through visits by the child's true parents

52. (a) everything the child demands the new parents
    (b) what the child used to get from his former parents
    (c) everything the law entitles them to
    (d) only what the new parents decide to give the child

THIS IS THE END OF THE GRAMMAR SECTION
DO NOT GO ON UNTIL TOLD TO DO SO

READING AND VOCABULARY
독해 · 어휘

READING AND VOCABULARY SECTION

DIRCECTIONS:

You will now read four different passages. Each passage is followed by comprehension and vocabulary questions. From the four choices for each item, choose the best answer. Then blacken in the correct circle on your answer sheet.

Read the following example passage and example question.

Example:

> Bill Johnson lives in New York. He is 25 years old. He has four brothers and two sisters.
>
> How many brothers does Bill Johnson have?
>
> (a) one
> (b) two
> (c) three
> (d) four

The correct answer is (d), so the circle with che letter (d) has been blackened.

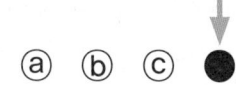

NOW TURN THE PAGE AND BEGIN

Reading and Vocabulary Test

PART 1. *Read the following biographical narrative and answer the questions. The underlined words in the article are for vocabulary questions.*

Bertrand Russell

Bertrand Arthur William Russell was a British philosopher, mathematician, and political activist. He was a Nobel Prize recipient for his influential literary work on improving people's lives.

Bertrand Arthur William Russell was born in Trelleck, Wales on May 18, 1872. His parents were John Russell, Viscount Amberley, and Katherine. He was also the grandson of John Russell, a British prime minister. Russell was orphaned at age three, and was raised by his grandparents. Early in life, he learned French and German. He was eleven years old when he was introduced to the work of the Greek mathematician Euclid, an event that changed his life

After obtaining a first-class degree from Trinity College, Cambridge, Russell worked as an assistant at the British embassy in Paris. In 1903, he published his *Principles of Mathematics*, which argued that mathematics could be derived from logic. The ideas in this book were further developed in the influential *Principia Mathematica*, which he co-wrote with Alfred North Whitehead in 1913.

Russell was appointed lecturer at Trinity College in 1910. However, when World War I broke out, his refusal to bear arms brought him in conflict with the British government. He lost his teaching position in 1916 and was sent to jail two years later. His bad experiences due to his anti-war beliefs, and his three marriages and two divorces in less than 20 years, <u>resulted</u> in his highly controversial 1932 book, *Marriage and Morals*.

In 1938, Russell went to the United States to teach. However, his lectureship at City College, New York was <u>terminated</u> in 1940 due to complaints that he was an enemy of religion and traditional morality. He abandoned his pacifist stand in 1939, and supported the allied cause in World War II. After the war, he was granted an Order of Merit. He was then awarded the Nobel Prize for Literature in 1950 and was cited as "the champion of humanity and freedom of thought." Russell had published many important works in his life, including the best-selling *History of Western Philosophy* and various papers on social, moral, and religious issues.

Russell became a supporter of nuclear disarmament. At the age of 89, he was again imprisoned after an antinuclear demonstration. His last major publication was his three-volume autobiography (1967-1969). Today, Russell is considered as a major philosopher and a leading social reformer of the 20th century. Bertrand died in Wales on February 2, 1970.

53. What attribute did Bertrand Russell show as a young child?

(a) being politically ambitious
(b) being deeply religious
(c) an inclination for learning
(d) a talent for literary writing

54. What statement did Russell make in his book, Principles of Mathematics?

(a) that logic can be translated into mathematics
(b) that Euclid's mathematical principles are timeless
(c) that mathematics doesn't agree with logic
(d) that life could be improved through mathematics

55. Why most likely was Russell sent to jail in 1918?

(a) He was lecturing at Trinity College illegally.
(b) He opposed his government's war activities.
(c) He couldn't make his marriages last.
(d) His divorces were not approved by the government.

56. What can be said about Russell's views on the two world wars?

(a) They were consistent.
(b) They didn't affect his teaching career.
(c) They were opposing.
(d) They both earned him awards.

57. How did Bertrand Russell spend his last days?

(a) by supporting the use of nuclear weapons
(b) by writing a book about his life
(c) by writing a book about Western philosophy
(d) by staying away from politics

58. In the context of the passage, resulted means _____.

(a) stopped
(b) produced
(c) affected
(d) printed

59. In the context of the passage, terminated means _____.

(a) promoted
(b) delayed
(c) continued
(d) ended

PART 2. *Read the following article and answer the questions. The underlined words in the article are for vocabulary questions.*

THE GENDER GAP IN SCIENCE SHOULD BE BRIDGED

When Austrian sociologist, Helga Nowotny, began a graduate fellowship at Berlin's Institute for Advanced Study in 1981, only one of her 19 fellow graduates was also female. Today, Nowotny is back at the Institute as a visiting professor, and things have changed. Over half of the current group of students are female.

Researchers across the European Union agree that things are now better for women in science, but say that there is still a lot to be done. Europe has a growing need for scientific talent, but many of its female scientists still don't enjoy equal opportunities. While roughly 40% of recent doctoral degrees awarded in Europe were earned by women, they make up only 15% of researchers in the private sector. Scientific laboratories are still a male-dominated work place despite the fact that women are "as talented as men." She suggests that there must be a mechanism to encourage women to compete.

The E.U. is trying to bridge the gender gap by funding programs to support women scientists and requiring gender-based hiring plans. However, many researchers say that the scientific community tends to suffer when factors such as gender are used to determine funding. They suggest that longer-term solutions that encourage both young men and women to pursue science are a better option. Hannele Kurki, an adviser at the Academy of Finland, says that an early introduction to science may help break down gender stereotypes.

Jürgen Hambrecht, the chief executive of German chemicals giant BASF, agrees. He says that women are important because of the differences in character between men and women. Hambrecht also states that women scientists are exactly the bridge needed in the workplace. BASF runs a laboratory where children of both genders get hands-on exposure to chemistry.

Scientific institutions are also realizing that the best way to inspire young scientists, female or male, is by example. Nowotny recalls how, 20 years ago, the fellows at the Berlin Institute were incredulous that the only other female fellow was pregnant. Today, fellows are encouraged to bring their families to work. By promoting a family-friendly environment, institutions can make science a fulfilling career for more women.

60. What is the article about?

(a) new opportunities for female scientists in Germany
(b) the career of Helga Nowotny
(c) the restructuring of a graduate program in Berlin
(d) the lack of opportunities for female scientists in Europe

61. How can the status of European female scientists with doctoral degrees be described?

(a) Only a few of them earn doctor's degrees.
(b) Only a few of them are hired by the industries.
(c) Europe needs more of them.
(d) Most of them join the private sector.

62. Why does Hannele Kurki suggest that people be introduced to science early?

(a) to produce female science graduates in the future
(b) to prevent male scientists from advancing
(c) to save female scientists from unfair labeling.
(d) to give female science students better training

63. What is Jürgen Hambrecht most likely suggesting?

(a) that women scientist's work can balance those of men
(b) that girls make better scientists
(c) that men should bridge the workplace
(d) that girls are good at chemistry

64. How can institutions make women have a satisfying scientific career?

(a) by encouraging them to have families
(b) by accepting only women
(c) by making favorable work environments for women
(d) by accepting male associates who tolerate women

65. In the context of the passage, growing means _____.

(a) producing
(b) increasing
(c) raising
(d) shrinking

66. In the context of the passage, promoting means _____.

(a) upholding
(b) marketing
(c) upgrading
(d) assisting

Reading and Vocabulary Test

PART 3. *Read the following encyclopedia article and answer the questions. The underlined words in the article are for vocabulary questions.*

PLASTIC

Plastic is a manmade or natural material that is used in a variety of products. Plastics are made of long chains of carbon molecules called "polymers" that give them their many unique and highly useful properties.

The word "plastic" is derived from the Greek word *plastikos* which means "to mold." Plastic can be made as strong as steel, as transparent as glass, as light as wood, and as elastic as rubber. They can also be produced in almost any color. Different types of plastic can be alloyed into more useful varieties. More than 50 families of plastics have already been produced through combinations, and new types are currently being developed.

Although synthetic plastics are relatively new, natural plastics have been in use for thousands of years. The ancient Egyptians wrapped their mummies in burial cloths that were soaked in gum-like and semisolid substances called "resins." Many cultures also used natural resin-bearing animal horns and turtle shells to make spoons, combs, and buttons. During the mid-19th century, "shellac," a substance secreted by an insect called "lac," was used in molding small cases, phonograph records, and mirror frames.

In the late 19th century, scientists began to develop many more types of plastics in the laboratory and more efficient ways of producing them. Among the inventors who contributed to the development of plastics was Leo Baekeland, who created what is known today as "phenolic resin," also called Bakelite. It has been used to make telephones, pot handles, and many other products. By the 1930s, water-soluble, flexible, and durable polymers, called "acrylics," were already being produced by German, British, and American companies.

Plastics are very important to modern life. They are widely used in automobile and aircraft manufacturing, food packaging, and health care. Although plastics are extremely useful, they also have some disadvantages. When burned, some plastics produce noxious fumes that cause health risks. Their use has also resulted in a growing garbage problem in many parts of the world. To address the problem, consumers are being encouraged to reduce their use of plastics and recycle used plastic products.

67. Which property of plastic does the origin of its name suggest?

(a) its flexibility
(b) its lightness
(c) its durability
(d) its transparency

68. How were phonographs made in the 19th century?

(a) by using the horns of animals
(b) by using a material from an insect
(c) by employing the shells of a turtle
(d) by harvesting gum from a tree

69. What major development in the history of plastics occurred in the late 19th century?

(a) the development of better ways of making plastic
(b) the discovery of natural plastic
(c) the invention of more durable types of plastic
(d) the promotion of plastic waste recycling

70. Which type of plastic is used for the manufacture of telephone?

(a) acrylics
(b) natural resin
(c) phenolic resin
(d) shellac

71. Based on the passage, why most likely are people being asked to lessen their use of plastic?

(a) It will conserve the animals plastics are made from.
(b) It will reduce the health dangers the material can cause.
(c) It will slow down society's rapid industrialization.
(d) It will control the consumers' dependence of plastic.

72. In the context of the passage, alloyed means _____.

(a) divided
(b) consumed
(c) hardened
(d) blended

73. In the context of the passage, noxious means _____.

(a) smelly
(b) harmful
(c) widespread
(d) powerful

Reading and Vocabulary Test

PART 4. *Read the following business letter and answer the questions. The underlined words in the article are for vocabulary questions.*

February 17, 2016

Ms. Adriana Kelly
General Manager
Kelly Design Studio
52 Sherman Avenue
Evanston, IL 60208

Dear Ms. Kelly:

The Chicago Architecture Foundation (CAF) is offering adult education classes for Spring 2016. We invite you and the staff of Kelly Design Studio to enroll in any of the following courses:

Historic Western Architecture and Modern Chicago: Students will discover how medieval France and Renaissance Italy influenced the design of Chicago's civic commercial buildings, university campuses, and residential structures. The instructor is Prof. Nancy Cook from DePaul University's Art and Architecture Department.

Introduction to City Planning: Students will explore issues of urbanism or city dwellers' lifestyles, including theories of city design and the history of city design in Rome, Paris, and Washington. The course will also examine recent trends in American and international city design. The instructor is Prof. Brent D. Ryan of the City Design Center, University of Illinois at Chicago.

Architectural Geology of the Chicago Region: Students will learn the connection between natural elements and architecture and find out how city planners altered the Chicago coastline. This course includes two walking tours of Chicago's architectural landmarks. The instructor is Mr. Raymond Wiggers, an environmental geologist of the State of Illinois.

For course schedules, venues, and registration fees, please refer to the attached sheet. Your CAF membership entitles you and your employees to a 20% discount. You may register in person at the CAF offices or online at www.architecture.org.

I hope to see you at the CAF soon. Thank you very much.

Sincerely,

Grant Moseley
Program Coordinator
Chicago Architecture Foundation
224 South Michigan Avenue, Chicago IL 60604
Tel: (312) 922-3432

74. Why did Grant Moseley write Adriana Kelly the letter?

(a) to ask her to deliver a lecture on city planning
(b) to convince her to join an organization of architects
(c) to offer courses to her design company's workers
(d) to invite her to the inaugural of a building in Chicago

75. What will the first course of the adult classes be about?

(a) the history of Western architecture
(b) how Chicago's architecture was improved
(c) how Italy influenced French architecture
(d) European architecture's influence on Chicago

76. What is said about the Introduction to City Planning course?

(a) It will show how nature influences building design.
(b) It will discuss developments in worldwide city design.
(c) It will include a tour of major European and American cities.
(d) It will be handled by a well-known geologist.

77. Based on the letter, what is most likely the purpose of the walking tours during the last course?

(a) to know how Chicago's architecture can be improved
(b) to see how architecture will change Chicago coastline
(c) to give the students a break from the lessons
(d) to see how city planning influenced natural elements in Chicago

78. What was not mentioned in the letter?

(a) the number of sessions for each course
(b) the ways for interested parties to register
(c) the official designation of the letter sender
(d) the discount being offered to ACF members

79. In the context of the passage, influenced means _____.

(a) destroyed
(b) convinced
(c) designed
(d) affected

80. In the context of the passage, refer means _____.

(a) notice
(b) study
(c) ignore
(d) see

THIS IS THE END OF THE TEST

한 권에 끝내는
Level 2
G-TELP
실전모의고사

회

초 판 1쇄 발행 2019년 1월 7일
2쇄 발행 2020년 3월 20일

출제 G-TELP KOREA 영어연구소 **해설** 이현아
발행인 이항준 **발행처** (주)법률저널
등록일자 2008년 9월 26일 **등록번호** 제15-605호
주소 151-862 서울 관악구 복은4길 50 (서림동 120-32)
대표전화 02)874-1144 **팩스** 02)876-4312
홈페이지 www.lec.co.kr
ISBN 978-89-6336-365-3

정가 22,000원

한 권에 끝내는
G-TELP Level 2
실전모의고사

5회

이현아 취향저격
G-TELP

이현아 취향저격

G-TELP
PG-TEL
TELP-G
G-TELP
TELP G-
PG-TEL
G-TELP
ELPG-T
G-TELP
TELP-G
G-TELP
ELPG-T

지텔프코리아
공식
지정

한 권에 끝내는
Level 2
G-TELP
실전모의고사

5 회

이현아 취향저격

지텔프코리아
공식
지정

한 권에 끝내는
Level 2
G-TELP
실전모의고사

5회

해설편

출제 G-TELP KOREA 영어연구소
해설 이현아

음원 다운로드
1타 에듀   http:gtelp.1taedu.com
법률저널   http://www.lec.co.kr

법률저널

저자소개

이현아

한국외국어대학교 졸업
현) 1타에듀 지텔프 강의
현) 아모르이그잼 영어 전임교수
현) 에듀윌 공무원 영어교수
전) YBM 토익강의
　　동국대학교, 인하대학교 토익강의
　　현대건설, 인터콘티넨탈호텔 비즈니스 영어강의
　　중앙일보 일간스포츠 공채 기자

저서
이현아 Real 쌩기초영어 문법
이현아 Real 쌩기초영어 독해
이현아 콤팩트 문법 핵심이론
이현아 콤팩트 문법 문제풀이
이현아 콤팩트 구문독해
이현아 콤팩트 기출문제풀이
이현아 콤팩트 공무원어휘 500제
이현아 콤팩트 문법 500제
이현아 Real 공무원 필수어휘 2000
이현아 취향저격 G-TELP 어휘 900
이현아 한 권에 끝내는 취향저격 G-TELP 32점
이현아 한 권에 끝내는 취향저격 G-TELP 50점
이현아 한 권에 끝내는 취향저격 G-TELP 65점
[지텔프코리아 공식지정]
이현아 한 권에 끝내는 취향저격 G-TELP 모의고사

음원 다운로드
1타 에듀　http:gtelp.1taedu.com
법률저널　http://www.lec.co.kr

이현아 취향저격

지텔프코리아
공식
지정

한 권에 끝내는
Level 2
G-TELP
실전모의고사

5회

지텔프코리아 공식지정

G-TELP
LEVEL 2

이현아 취향저격 지텔프 실전모의고사

해설편 1

Answers and Explanations

한 권에 끝내는 G-TELP 실전모의고사 5회

SECTION 01 GRAMMAR
SECTION 02 LISTENING
SECTION 03 READING & VOCABULARY

Grammar Test 01회
Question 1-26

ANSWER KEY　　　　　　　　　　p.15

01	ⓒ	02	ⓓ	03	ⓐ	04	ⓒ
05	ⓑ	06	ⓐ	07	ⓓ	08	ⓐ
09	ⓐ	10	ⓑ	11	ⓐ	12	ⓑ
13	ⓑ	14	ⓓ	15	ⓑ	16	ⓒ
17	ⓑ	18	ⓓ	19	ⓐ	20	ⓐ
21	ⓓ	22	ⓓ	23	ⓒ	24	ⓑ
25	ⓓ	26	ⓐ				

01　▶ 정답 ⓒ

해석 Arthur Daniel의 성공적인 건축분야 경력을 인정하기 위해, 그는 곧 캘리포니아 빌딩산업 명예의 전당에 입회하게 될 것이다. Daniel의 건축사무소는 현재 35년 동안 미국에서 인상적인 건물들을 설계해오고 있다.

해설 기간을 표현하는 for 35 years가 왔으므로 완료시제가 들어가야 한다는 것을 알 수 있다. 시간 부사 now가 있으므로 현재완료(진행)시제의 쓰임이 적절하다.

02　▶ 정답 ⓓ

해석 의료계에서 자폐증 치료제를 찾는 것은 쉽지 않다. 장애는 유전적인 원인이 있기 때문에, 의사는 어떤 약품을 개발하기 전, 먼저 자폐증을 유발하는 정확한 유전자를 찾아야 한다.

해설 해석을 통해 풀어야 하는 조동사문제이다. 자폐증을 유발하는 유전자를 찾아야 한다는 의무 표현이 들어가야 문맥상 자연스럽다. '~해야 한다'를 의미하는 must가 정답이다.

03　▶ 정답 ⓐ

해석 내가 젊었을 때, Triumph GD-87 핸드폰은 이미 최신 모델이었다. 그것은 WAP기능, 화음 벨소리 및 내장 카메라가 있는 최초의 것이었다. 나는 그 전화기 사용을 정말로 즐겼다.

해설 enjoy는 목적어 자리에 동명사를 취하는 3형식 타동사이다.

04　▶ 정답 ⓒ

해석 James는 학교의 농구 팀에 들어가고 싶어 한다. 그의 작은 키 때문에, 대신 그는 배구팀으로 시도할 것이다. 키가 크다면, 그는 농구 평가전에서 기회를 잡을 수 있을 텐데.

해설 if절의 동사가 were이므로 가정법 과거임을 알 수 있다. 「조동사 과거형 + 동사원형」이 주절에 들어가야 한다.

05　▶ 정답 ⓑ

해석 디지털 기술은 음악 교육에 혁명을 일으키고 있다. 많은 음악 강사들은 현재 학생들이 최신 컴퓨터 소프트웨어를 사용하여 음정을 읽는 법과 악기를 연주하는 법을 배울 것을 권장하고 있다.

해설 명령, 동의, 제안, 주장, 요구, 충고 동사의 목적어 자리에 that절이 와서 당위성을 나타내는 경우 동사는 「(should) 동사원형」이 되어야 한다.

06　▶ 정답 ⓐ

해석 보건부는 금연 운동을 적극적으로 추진하고 있다. 캠페인을 시작한 보건부 장관은 모든 정부 기관이 금연 정책을 엄격하게 시행할 것을 명령했다.

해설 관계사 문제이다. 선행사가 The Health Secretary로 사람이 선행사이며 보기에 동사가 바로 오므로 주격 관계대명사 who의 쓰임이 적절하다. 관계대명사 that은 콤마(,)뒤에 쓸 수 없다.

07　▶ 정답 ⓓ

해석 사진과 고고학 애호가인 캐롤은 새로운 일에 만족하고 있다. 그녀는 최근에 National Geographic에 채용되어 유적지 이미지를 촬영했다. 그녀는 지금 그리스의 고대 유적지 사진을 찍고 있다.

해설 시간부사 right now가 있으므로 현재진행시제가 가장 적절하다.

08　▶ 정답 ⓐ

해석 유럽의 일부 카페 주인들은 유전적으로 변형된 커피 원두 구매를 중단했다. 그들은 그 원두가 천연커피원두만큼 맛있지 않다고 생각한다. 게다가 천연커피원두는 가격이 덜 든다.

해설 빈칸 앞 문장에서 유전적으로 변형된 커피 원두가 천연 커피 원두보다 맛이 없다는 부정적인 내용이 언급되어 있다. 빈칸 뒤의 내용도 천연 커피 원두보다 비싸다는 내용이므로 순접 관계의 첨가를 표현하는 접속부사 Besides가 가장 적절하다.

09　▶ 정답 ⓐ

해석 취리히에는 Madagascar 열대우림 환경을 재현하는 동물원이 있다. 동물원의 경영진은 동물이 그저 우리 속에서가 아니라 그들의 자연 서식지에서 정확히 어떻게 살아가는지를 보여주려는 의도이다.

해설 intend는 목적어 자리에 to 부정사를 취하는 3형식 타동사이다.

10　▶ 정답 ⓑ

해석 이탈리아 사이클 챔피언 Marco Pantani는 34세의 나이로 생을 마감했다. 만약 그가 그렇게 빨리 죽지 않았다면, 그는 스포츠의 전설이 되었을 텐데.

해설 If절의 시제가 had p.p.이므로 가정법 과거완료임을 알 수 있다. 주절에는 「조동사 과거형 + have p.p.」가 들어가야 한다.

11 ▶ 정답 ⓐ

해석 Patty는 친구 몇 명을 집으로 저녁 식사 초대했다. 그녀는 준비를 하기 위해 사무실을 일찍 나섰지만, 집으로 가는 길에 차가 많이 막혔다. 친구들이 도착했을 때 그녀는 여전히 요리 중이었다.

해설 when이 이끈 시간부사절의 동사가 arrived로 과거시제이므로 주절에는 과거진행 시제가 가장 적절하다.

12 ▶ 정답 ⓑ

해석 종종 흰 고래가 알래스카 연안을 따라 수영하는 것이 목격되곤 했다. 그러나 최근에는 이들을 목격하는 경우가 줄어들었다. 대중들이 고래를 멸종 위기로부터 구하는데 참여하는 것이 시급하다.

해설 당위성·이성적 판단의 형용사의 목적어 자리에 that이 오면 동사는「(should) + 동사원형」이 되어야 한다.

13 ▶ 정답 ⓑ

해석 인사과에서는 회사의 연간 팀워크 활동을 계획하고 있다. 그들은 아직 장소를 찾지 못했다. 인사과 직원은 어떤 곳이 가장 좋은 요금과 시설을 갖추고 있는지 알아보기 위해 내일부터 리조트에 연락을 취할 것이다.

해설 시간부사 starting tomorrow(내일부터)가 있으므로 미래를 표현하는 것임을 알 수 있다. 내일부터 시작하는 것을 강조하고 있으므로 단순 미래시제보다 진행을 포함하고 있는 미래진행시제가 더 적절하다.

14 ▶ 정답 ⓓ

해석 지난 달 모로코에서 지진으로 많은 사람들이 사망했다. 많은 언론인들은 만약 모로코 정부가 더 엄격한 건축 규제를 시행했다면, 재난의 충격을 줄일 수 있었을 것이라고 비난했다.

해설 If절의 동사가 had p.p로 가정법 과거완료임을 알 수 있다. 주절에는「조동사 과거형 + have p.p」가 쓰여야 하므로 (d)가 올바르다.

15 ▶ 정답 ⓑ

해석 New York Philharmonic Orchestra는 고전 작품에 대한 탁월한 해석으로 유명하다. 클래식 음악팬들은 제일 좋은 좌석을 차지하기 위해, 더 높은 비용을 내고 콘서트 전 시리즈를 예약하는 것을 개의치 않는다.

해설 mind는 목적어 자리에 동명사를 취하는 3형식 타동사이다.

16 ▶ 정답 ⓒ

해석 재해 지역 사람들에게 무료의료혜택을 제공하는 자원 봉사단체인 Doctors Without Borders (국경없는 의사회)는 그 효율성으로 유명하다. 그 단체의 의사들은 언제든지 어디로든 갈 수 있다.

해설 문맥상 그 단체 의사들은 어디로든 갈 수 있다는 '능력/가능'을 표현하는 것이 가장 적절하므로 조동사 can이 들어가야 한다.

17 ▶ 정답 ⓑ

해석 동물 통제관은 도로를 건너가는 Sally의 애완용 푸들을 붙잡았다. Sally는 보호소에서 그녀의 애완견을 찾아야 한다. 만약 그녀가 애완견을 끈으로 매어놨더라면, 개는 그녀 옆에 머물러 있었을 텐데.

해설 If절의 시제가 had p.p이므로 주절에는「조동사 과거형 + have p.p」가 들어가야 하는 가정법 과거완료문제이다.

18 ▶ 정답 ⓓ

해석 Lynn은 University of California에서 아프리카학 석사 학위를 받았다. 졸업 후, 그녀는 아프리카를 후원하는 비영리단체에 합류했다. 그녀는 이 지역 여성과 어린이들의 삶을 개선하는 데 도움주기를 원한다.

해설 want의 목적어 자리가 빈칸으로 나왔다. to 부정사를 목적어로 취하므로 정답은 (d)이다.

19 ▶ 정답 ⓐ

해석 Jason은 불과 6개월 전에 비즈니스용 무료 화상채팅 서비스를 사용하기 시작했다. 그는 인터넷을 이용해 음성 및 화상 통화를 할 수 있다는 사실을 알기 전, 몇 년 동안 기존의 전화 서비스로 고객들에게 전화를 걸었었다.

해설 기간을 나타내는 시간부사 for years(몇 년 동안)가 나왔으므로 완료시제가 들어가야 하는 것을 알 수 있다. before 부사절의 시제가 과거이므로 과거완료진행이 주절에 쓰이는 것은 문맥상 자연스럽다.

20 ▶ 정답 ⓐ

해석 일부 아마추어 운동선수들은 캐나다에서 야외 스포츠를 홍보하기 위해, 웹 사이트를 개설했다. 그러나 자금 조달이 충분하지 않아 사이트를 중단해야 한다. 만약 더 많은 광고주를 끌어 들인다면, 그 사이트는 오래 지속될 텐데.

해설 If절의 시제가 과거(were attracting)인 것으로 보아 가정법 과거임을 알 수 있다. 주절에는「조동사 과거형 + 동사원형」이 쓰여야 한다.

21 ▶ 정답 ⓓ

해석 1월에 Peru의 Lima에서 32건의 신체상해 및 언어폭력이 기록되었다. 피해자는 대부분 여성 교통경찰이었다. 이 문제를 해결하기 위해 여성 경찰관 폭행에 대한 처벌을 올리는(=강화하는) 법안 초안이 작성되고 있다.

해설 보기를 통해 관계사 문제임을 알 수 있다. 선행사에 A bill(법안)이 나왔으므로 사람 선행사를 수식하는 who는 들어갈 수 없다. 관계부사 where은 완벽한 문장을 이끌어야 한다. 문맥상 법안이 처벌을 올리는 것이 되어야 하므로 (b)는 문맥상 올바르지 않다. 주격 관계대명사 that이 이끈 절이 가장 문법적으로, 문맥상 적절하다.

22
▶ 정답 ⓓ

해석 | 내 여동생은 아시아 예술의 열렬한 수집가이다. 그녀는 골동품 가구와 희귀한 그림을 찾기 위해 아시아 곳곳을 여행한다. 그녀는 가능한 많은 아시아 미술품을 구입할 것을 원한다.

해설 | 명령, 동의, 제안, 주장, 요구, 충고 동사의 목적어 자리에 that절이 오는 경우 동사는 「(should) 동사원형」이 되어야 한다.

23
▶ 정답 ⓒ

해석 | Atherton Water District는 도시 상수도에서 대장균 박테리아를 발견할 때마다, 더 위험한 박테리아가 존재하는지 확인하기 위해 추가 테스트를 실시한다. 다행히도 가장 최근의 수질검사 결과는 음성이었다.

해설 | conduct는 목적어 자리에 동명사를 취하는 3형식 동사이다.

24
▶ 정답 ⓑ

해석 | Carl의 친구인 Mary는 그를 토요일에 하는 자신의 생일 파티에 초대한다. 유감스럽게도, Carl은 이미 다른 친구의 초대에 응했다. 만약 파티가 다른 날짜라면, 그는 기꺼이 Mary의 초대를 받아들일 텐데.

해설 | 가정법 문제로 주절의 시제가 「조동사 과거형 + 동사원형」인 것으로 보아 가정법 과거임을 알 수 있다. 과거동사는 (b)의 were밖에 없다.

25
▶ 정답 ⓓ

해석 | 한 엔지니어 팀이 달을 넘어서도 작동할 수 있는 인공위성을 설계하기 위해 NASA로부터 보조금을 받았다. 2018년에 그 설계가 끝날 쯤에는, 그 팀은 3년 동안 작업을 해온 것이 될 것이다.

해설 | 시간 부사절 접속사 by the time의 시제가 현재시제인 것으로 보아 주절에는 미래시제가 들어가야 함을 알 수 있다. 또한 '~할 때쯤'에 의미하므로 문맥상 지속성을 표현하는 미래완료시제가 더욱 적절하다.

26
▶ 정답 ⓐ

해석 | Martina는 올해 시카고마라톤에 참가하는 것을 원한다. 그러나 그녀는 최근 인플루엔자로 인해 입원한 사실을 주최측에 알릴 필요가 있다. 그녀는 운동경기에 참여할 수 있도록 건강진단서를 제출해야 한다.

해설 | 해석을 통해 문맥상 가장 적절한 것을 찾는 접속사 문제이다. '~하기 위해서'라는 목적을 표현하는 so that이 글의 흐름상 가장 적절하다.

Listening Test 01회
Question 27-52

ANSWER KEY p.23

27	ⓐ	28	ⓒ	29	ⓐ	30	ⓓ
31	ⓐ	32	ⓑ	33	ⓒ	34	ⓐ
35	ⓓ	36	ⓑ	37	ⓒ	38	ⓑ
39	ⓐ	40	ⓒ	41	ⓐ	42	ⓒ
43	ⓑ	44	ⓓ	45	ⓒ	46	ⓑ
47	ⓑ	48	ⓓ	49	ⓐ	50	ⓑ
51	ⓒ	52	ⓐ				

[Part 1]

Now listen to the questions.

27: Why does Robert look so well rested?
28: What kind of organization manages the San Luis Ecolodge?
29: How can "sustainable tourism" be described best?
30: What can be said about Steve, the tour guide?
31: Why does one have to be very quiet when exploring the forest?
32: Which feature characterizes the toucan?
33: Based on the conversation, what kind of food is probably served at the ecolodge?

해석

27: 로버트가 굉장히 휴식을 잘 취한 것처럼 보이는 이유는 무엇인가요?
28: San Luis Ecolodge를 경영하는 단체의 종류는 무엇인가요?
29: 어떻게 '지속 가능한 관광'을 가장 잘 설명할 수 있나요?
30: 여행 가이드 스티브에 관해 말할 수 있는 것은 무엇인가요?
31: 왜 숲을 탐험할 때 굉장히 조용히 해야 하나요?
32: 큰부리새는 어떤 특징이 있나요?
33: 대화를 토대로, ecolodge에서 어떤 종류의 음식이 제공되나요?

Now you will hear the conversation.
[conversation]

F 27) Hello, Robert! You look so relaxed and refreshed. Did you just come from a vacation?

M 27) Yes, Maggie. I stayed in Costa Rica for a week, and I went hiking in a forest reserve there. It was great!

F Costa Rica? You? What a surprise! I always thought your ideal holiday would be shopping in Europe.

M Yes, that was true. But when a friend told me about her visit to Costa Rica, I changed my mind. 28) She told me that the University of Georgia is now managing an ecotourism site and research center in Costa Rica called Ecolodge San Luis.

F What did your friend say about it?

M She found the place simply beautiful. That made me so curious that I decided to see for myself.

F Mmmm…That sounds interesting! But did you say "ecotourism site"? What makes that different from other tourist spots?

M 29) Well, an ecotourism site is a business like any other tourist attraction, but it's operated under the principle of "sustainable tourism." That means the management protects the natural surroundings while supporting the local communities through tourism. So staying at the Ecolodge is both a holiday and a learning experience.

F Interesting! Was the place as beautiful as your friend had said?

M Oh, it was truly amazing! I stayed in a cottage surrounded by trees. The atmosphere was very peaceful. When I wasn't reading or writing my journal, I would hike with the other tourists on the Monteverde Forest Reserve.

F It's good that you were able to get around by yourselves.

M Oh, we weren't alone! 30) We had a tour guide named Steve who was an American biologist. He has been studying Costa Rica's natural resources for years, and he taught us about the plant and animal species in that rainforest.

F How are things in a forest?

M 31) Well, even though it looks empty and quiet, there are actually many animals that hide in the bush and avoid human contact. You have to be very quiet and stay still for a long time to see them. At least once each hike, I would sit on a rock and wait to see what animal would appear.

F That sounds wonderful! What animals did you actually see?

M I caught a glimpse of the famous "poison arrow frog," which Steve said was an endangered species. I also saw a raccoon, and some colorful birds called "toucans" and "tanagers."

F Oh, I've read about them. 32) Toucans have huge beaks, right?

M 32) Yes, and apparently the beaks are very light so they don't affect their ability to fly.

F I see… Did you take any pictures of them?

M No, I couldn't because I had to be quiet. But I was able to take beautiful pictures of some orchids native to Costa Rica.

F Now that seems like my kind of place to visit. But tell me, how was the food?

M The food was simply great! The Ecolodge had such meticulous cooks. 33) They used only ingredients that came straight from the surrounding farms. When I asked for fresh milk, they even challenged me to milk a cow myself at a nearby dairy farm. And I did!

F What a remarkable experience! I hope I can find time to visit that Costa Rican ecolodge myself soon!

Words

forest reserve 산림보호구역 tourist spot 관광지
tourist attraction 관광 명소 principle 원칙
cottage 오두막 rainforest 열대우림
bush 덤불 glimpse 얼핏 보임
endangered 멸종 위기에 처한 orchid 난초
meticulous 세심한 cook 요리사
ingredient 재료, 성분 dairy farm 낙농장

해석

F 27) 안녕, 로버트! 너 여유 있고 생기 있어 보인다. 휴가에서 막 돌아왔어?

M 27) 응, 매기. 일주일 정도 Costa Rica에 머무르면서, 거기 있는 산림보호구역 도보 여행을 했어. 진짜 멋졌어!

F Costa Rica? 네가? 진짜 놀랍다! 나는 너의 이상적인 휴가는 유럽에서의 쇼핑일 거라고 항상 생각했거든.

M 응, 맞아. 그런데 친구 한 명이 내게 Costa Rica를 방문했던 얘기를 했을 때, 마음을 바꿨어. 28) 그녀가 말하기를 Georgia대학이 요즘 Costa Rica에 Ecolodge San Luis라는 생태관광지역과 연구센터를 운영하고 있대.

F 네 친구가 그것에 관해 뭐라고 이야기했어?

M 그녀가 정말로 아름다운 장소를 발견했대. 그 말이 내 호기심을 유발시켜서 직접 가봐야겠다고 결심했어.

F 음…흥미롭게 들린다! 그런데 '생태관광지'이라고 했지? 다른 관광지랑 뭐가 달라?

M 29) 음, 생태관광지역이라는 건 다른 관광명소들과 같은 관광사업이긴 하지만, '지속가능한 관광' 원칙에 따라 운영돼. 이는 관광산업을 통해 지역사회를 지원하면서 자연환경을 보호한다는 것을 의미해. 그래서 Ecolodge에 머무는 것은 휴가이기도 하면서 학습 경험이기도 하지.

F 흥미롭다! 네 친구가 말한 것처럼 아름다운 장소였어?

M 오, 진짜 놀라웠어! 나는 나무로 둘러싸인 오두막에 머물렀어. 분위기가 정말 평화로웠어. 기사를 읽거나 쓰지 않을 때는, 다른 여행객들과 함께 Monteverde Forest Reserve로 도보 여행을 갔어.

F   너희들만 따로 다닐 수 있었다니 좋았겠다.

M   아, 우리만 있었던 건 아니야! 30) 우리는 미국인 생물학자 스티브라는 여행 가이드를 구했어. 그는 몇 년째 Costa Rica의 천연자원에 대해 연구하고 있는데, 그 열대 우림에 있는 식물 및 동물 종에 관해 가르쳐 줬어.

F   숲 속에서는 어땠어?

M   31) 음, 비어있고 조용한 것처럼 보이지만, 실제로는 덤불 속에 숨어서 인간의 접촉을 피하는 동물들이 많이 있어. 그들을 보려면 오랫동안 조용히 움직이지 않고 기다려야 해. 하이킹 할 때마다 적어도 한 번은, 바위에 앉아서 어떤 동물이 나타나는지 보려고 기다리곤 했어.

F   멋지다! 실제로 어떤 동물들을 봤어?

M   유명한 '독화살 개구리'를 얼핏 봤는데, 스티브가 멸종 위기에 처한 종이라고 하더라. 라쿤도 봤고, '큰부리새'와 '풍금조'라는 화려한 색의 새들도 봤지.

F   오, 그것들에 관해 읽어본 적 있어. 32) 큰부리새는 거대한 부리를 가지고 있지, 그렇지?

M   32) 응, 실제로 부리가 아주 가벼워서 날아다니는 데 영향을 주지 않는대.

F   그렇구나... 그 새들 사진은 좀 찍었어?

M   아니, 조용히 있어야 해서 못 찍었어. 그래도 Costa Rica의 몇몇 야생 난초들의 아름다운 사진은 찍어올 수 있었어.

F   이제 방문하게 될 장소처럼 여겨져. 그런데 음식은 어땠는지 말해줄래?

M   음식도 정말 좋았어! 그 Ecolodge에는 굉장히 세심한 요리사들이 있었어. 33) 그들은 근처 농장에서 직접 나온 재료들만 사용했어. 내가 신선한 우유를 요청했을 때, 요리사들이 나에게 근처 낙농장에서 직접 우유를 짜보라고 했어. 그래서 직접 해봤지!

F   진짜 놀라운 경험이었겠다! 나도 곧 Costa Rica의 ecolodge에 방문할 수 있으면 좋겠다.

27 ▶ 정답 ⓐ

Why does Robert look so well rested?
(a) because he just came back from a vacation
(b) because he went shopping
(c) because he will be going to Europe
(d) because he is on leave from school

해석
로버트가 굉장히 휴식을 잘 취한 것처럼 보이는 이유는 무엇인가요?
(a) 그가 휴가에서 돌아왔기 때문에
(b) 그가 쇼핑하러 갔기 때문에
(c) 그가 유럽에 갈 것이기 때문에
(d) 그는 휴학 중이기 때문에

해설
대화 도입부에 '휴가에서 막 돌아왔고 Costa Rica에서 일주일 정도 머물렀다'는 로버트의 말이 나온다.

28 ▶ 정답 ⓒ

What kind of organization manages the San Luis Ecolodge?
(a) an environmental group
(b) a local government office
(c) a university
(d) a private tourism firm

해석
San Luis Ecolodge를 경영하는 단체의 종류는 무엇인가요?
(a) 환경 단체
(b) 지방 정부 관청
(c) 대학
(d) 민간 관광 회사

해설 "the University of Georgia is now managing an ecotourism site and research center in Costa Rica called Ecolodge San Luis."을 통해 대학임을 확인할 수 있다.

29 ▶ 정답 ⓐ

How can "sustainable tourism" be described best?
(a) It protects the environment while giving the locals jobs.
(b) It doesn't have any commercial interests.
(c) It causes damage to the environment.
(d) It lets tourists explore the sites by themselves.

해석
어떻게 '지속 가능한 관광'을 가장 잘 설명할 수 있나요?
(a) 지역 주민들에게 일자리를 제공하면서 환경을 보호한다.
(b) 어떠한 상업적 이익도 갖지 않는다.
(c) 환경에 피해를 야기 시킨다.
(d) 관광객들이 스스로 지역을 탐험할 수 있게 한다.

해설 "That means the management protects the natural surroundings while supporting the local communities through tourism."에서 환경을 보호하며, 관광을 통해 지역 주민들에게 일자리를 제공한다는 것을 알 수 있다.

30 ▶ 정답 ⓓ

What can be said about Steve, the tour guide?
(a) He is a full-time tour guide.
(b) He is from Costa Rica.
(c) He is the founder of the lodge.
(d) He is actually a scientist.

해석

여행 가이드 스티브에 관해 말할 수 있는 것은 무엇인가요?

(a) 그는 풀타임 투어 가이드이다.
(b) 그는 코스타리카 출신이다.
(c) 그는 오두막 설립자이다.
(d) 그는 실제로 과학자이다.

해설 "We had a tour guide named Steve who was an American biologist."를 통해 스티브가 생물학자임을 확인할 수 있다.

31 ▶ 정답 ⓐ

Why does one have to be very quiet when exploring the forest?

(a) to be able to catch a glimpse of the shy animals
(b) to avoid being attacked by the wild animals
(c) to prevent waking up the sleeping animals
(d) to keep the forest empty and peaceful

해석

왜 숲을 탐험할 때 굉장히 조용히 해야 하나요?

(a) 겁이 많은 동물을 엿볼 수 있기 위해
(b) 야생 동물들의 공격을 피하기 위해
(c) 잠자는 동물을 깨우지 않기 위해
(d) 숲을 비고 평화로운 상태로 유지하기 위해서

해설 "Well, even though it looks empty and quiet, there are actually many animals that hide in the bush and avoid human contact. You have to be very quiet and stay still for a long time to see them."을 통해 사람을 피하는 야생동물이 숨어 있다는 것은 겁이 많다는 (a)의 내용으로 추론할 수 있다.

32 ▶ 정답 ⓑ

Which feature characterizes the toucan?

(a) a small poisonous beak
(b) a huge but light beak
(c) its inability to fly
(d) its being endangered

해석

큰부리새는 어떤 특징이 있나요?

(a) 작은 독성이 있는 부리
(b) 크고 가벼운 부리
(c) 날지 못함
(d) 멸종 위기

해설 "Toucans have huge beaks, right?" "Yes, and apparently the beaks are very light so they don't affect their ability to fly."의 대화를 통해, 큰부리새의 부리는 크지만 가볍다는 것을 알 수 있다.

33 ▶ 정답 ⓒ

Based on the conversation, what kind of food is probably served at the ecolodge?

(a) food that the visitors cook themselves
(b) food that's grown somewhere else
(c) food that is always fresh
(d) food that is cooked with milk

해석

대화를 토대로, ecolodge에서 어떤 종류의 음식이 제공되나요?

(a) 방문자가 스스로 요리하는 음식
(b) 다른 곳에서 재배된 음식
(c) 항상 신선한 음식
(d) 우유로 조리 된 음식

해설 "The ecolodge had such meticulous cooks. They used only ingredients that came straight from the surrounding farms. When I asked for fresh milk, they even challenged me to milk a cow myself at a nearby dairy farm."를 통해, 근처에서 바로 조달 가능한 신선한 음식을 제공한다는 것을 알 수 있다.

[Part 2]

Now listen to the questions.

34: Why did Trumble's Department Store lose profits the previous year?
35: What did management do to solve the problem?
36: Why was the first solution not practical?
37: What was decided to correct the limitations of the first security system?
38: Based on the talk, how most likely does the "electronic article surveillance" work?
39: According to the speaker, which is an advantage of EAS to the salespeople?

해석

34: 작년에 왜 Trumble 백화점은 수익이 떨어졌나요?
35: 경영진이 문제를 해결하기 위해 한 일은 무엇인가요?
36: 왜 첫 번째 해결책이 실용적이지 않았나요?
37: 첫 번째 보안 시스템의 한계를 바로잡기 위해서 결정한 것은 무엇인가요?
38: 연설을 바탕으로, 어떻게 '전자식 물품 감시'가 작동하는 거 같나요?
39: 화자에 따르면, 판매 직원들에게 EAS의 어떤 것이 장점인가요?

Now you will hear the talk.

Good morning, everyone, and thank you for attending this meeting. As you know, last year, Trumble's Department Store enforced new security measures to prevent shoplifting. 34) Our losses from customer theft in the Men's and the Women's Clothing Departments alone had reached a point where they were among our highest operating expenses. In fact, we were losing more profits that way than we were spending on either your vacation pay or your medical insurance.

Because of complaints from the company's stockholders, corporate management agreed that tighter security was needed. 35) They decided to put our high-end clothes and fashion accessories inside locked display cases made of steel and glass. 36) And although that strategy did reduce our problem with theft by customers, it created other problems.

Now, I know that none of our sales staff liked that system, and I appreciate your patience with the extra work it created for you. First, you had to unlock the display case every time a customer wanted to hold an item or try it on. Then, you had to stand there and watch the customer until they were finished. Then, you had to either ring up the sale or return the item to the display case and lock it again.

36) It was not only discouraging for you, it also discouraged our customers from examining and trying on the items that we sell. As a result, many potential shoppers simply went to other stores where the merchandise was more accessible. We simply didn't create a pleasant retail experience for either our staff or our customers. Today we would like to propose a new solution.

37) With the help of Jack Ellison, a retail security specialist from Checkpoint Systems, management decided to have a new anti-shoplifting system installed in our five store branches. It's called the "electronic article surveillance" or EAS system. This anti-theft system is very popular among firms that operate globally, especially in retailing. In fact, more than 800,000 such systems have already been installed worldwide.

Now, you may ask: How does the EAS system work? Basically, plastic tags with identification codes are attached to each piece of apparel. These tags, which are also called "hard tags," are sturdy and reusable. 38) Imagine that a person is carrying a stolen item. When he passes through the detection devices, or "pedestals," installed by the exit, the hard tag attached to the item will send a radio frequency signal to the pedestal, and an alarm will sound. However, if an item has been paid for, the store clerk will remove the hard tag attached to the merchandise. In that case, the alarm will not emit the sound as the shopper passes through the pedestals.

Although we have yet to discover if the EAS system will totally eliminate shoplifting, we believe that it can cut instances of theft by 60% without creating extra work for you.

Also, it won't discourage our customers from browsing and buying. 39) It will also smoothen store operations because our sales personnel can focus on assisting shoppers rather than constantly watching out for shoplifters. Now, let me call on Mr. Ellison, our security consultant, to demonstrate the proper use of the EAS system to our store clerks.

Words

enforce 시행하다
shoplifting 절도, 도둑질
corporate management 경영진
appreciate 감사하다
identification code 식별 코드
sturdy 견고한
browse 살펴보다
security measure 보안 조치
operating expense 영업비용
high-end 고가의, 고급의
merchandise 상품
apparel 의류
detection 탐지, 감지

해석

여러분, 안녕하세요. 본 회의에 참석해주셔서 감사합니다. 아시다시피, 작년 Trumble 백화점은 절도 방지를 위해 새로운 보안조치를 시행했습니다. 34) 남성 및 여성 의류 매장에서 고객 절도로 인한 손실은 우리 영업비용에서 가장 큰 부분을 차지하기에 이르렀습니다. 사실, 여러분의 휴가 수당이나 의료보험에 지출하는 비용보다 절도로 인한 손실이 더 큽니다.

회사 주주들의 불만으로 인하여, 경영진은 더 엄격한 보안이 필요하다는 것에 동의했습니다. 35) 고가의 의류나 패션 액세서리를 강철과 유리로 만든 잠금 장치가 되어있는 진열대에 보관하기로 결정했습니다. 36) 그러한 전략은 고객 절도로 인한 문제는 감소시켰지만, 다른 문제들을 만들었습니다.

자, 영업직원 중 누구도 그런 시스템을 좋아하지 않는다는 것을 잘 알고 있고, 그로 인해 발생되는 추가적 업무에 관해 여러분의 인내에 감사하고 있습니다. 먼저, 여러분은 고객들이 상품을 만져보거나 입어보길 원할 때마다 매번 진열대를 열어야 했습니다. 그런 다음 그 곳에 서서 고객이 끝날 때까지 지켜보고 있어야 했습니다. 그 후, 여러분은 판매를 하거나, 그 상품을 진열대에 넣고 다시 잠가 두어야 합니다.

36) 그것은 여러분의 사기를 꺾을 뿐 아니라, 우리가 판매하는 상품을 고객들이 살펴보고 착용해보려는 시도를 방해했습니다. 그 결과, 많은 잠재고객들이 좀 더 쉽게 상품에 접근 할 수 있는 다른 가게로 갔습니다. 우리는 우리 직원이나 고객들에게 즐거운 쇼핑경험을 만들어 주지 못했습니다. 오늘 우리는 새로운 해결 방안을 제시하고자 합니다. 37) Checkpoint System의 소매보안전문가인 Jack Ellison의 도움으로, 경영진은 우리 회사 5개 매장에 새로운 도난방지시스템을 설치하기로 결정했습니다. 이는 '전자 물품 감시' 또는 EAS 시스템이라고 합니다. 세계적으로 이 도난 방지 시스템은 운영하고 있는 회사들 사이에서, 특히 소매업에서 매우 인기가 있습니다. 사실, 전 세계적으로 80만개 이상 이러한 시스템이 이미 설치되어 있습니다.

이제, 여러분은 궁금해 하실 지도 모릅니다 : EAS 시스템은 어떻게 작동하나요? 기본적으로 각 의류마다 식별 코드가 있는 플라스틱 태그가 부착되어 있습니다. '하드 태그'라고도 불리는 이 태그는 견고하고 재사용이 가능합니다. 38) 어떤 사람이 훔친 물건을 가지고 나간다고 가정해 봅시다. 그가 출구에 설치된 탐지장치, 즉 '검색대'를 통과할 때 상품에 붙어 있는 하드태그가 무선 주파수 신호를 검색대로 보내고, 경보음이 울립니다. 그런데, 만약 상품이 지불 되었다면, 점원은 상품에 부착된 하드 태그를 제거합니다. 이런 경우, 고객이 검색대를 통과할 때 경보음이 나지 않습니다. EAS 시스템이 전적으로 절도를 방지해 줄지는 아직 모르지만, 여러분에게 추가 작업을 발생시키지 않고 절도 사례를 60%까지 줄일 수 있다고 생각합니다. 또한, 우리의 고객들이 물건을 살펴보고 구매하는 것을 방해하지 않을 것입니다. 39) 우리 영업사원들은 지속적으로 절도범들을 경계하는 대신 고객들을 돕는 데 주력할 수 있으므로 매장운영이 한층 원활해 질 것입니다. 자, 우리 점원들에게 EAS 시스템을 올바르게 사용하는 방법을 보여주실 것을 보안 컨설턴트인 Mr.Ellison에게 요청드립니다.

34 ▶정답 ⓐ

Why did Trumble's Department Store lose profits the previous year?

(a) The store's goods were being stolen.
(b) The store didn't have enough stockholders.
(c) The store gave its employees too many benefits.
(d) The store lacked customers.

해석
작년에 왜 Trumble 백화점은 수익이 떨어졌나요?
(a) 상점의 물품이 도난당하고 있었다.
(b) 상점에는 충분한 주주가 없었다.
(c) 가게가 직원들에게 너무 많은 혜택을 주었다.
(d) 상점에는 고객이 없었다.

해설 "Our losses from customer theft in the Men's and the Women's Clothing Departments alone had reached a point where they were among our highest operating expenses."를 토대로 고객들의 절도가 백화점 수익의 가장 큰 원인임을 알 수 있다.

35 ▶정답 ⓓ

What did management do to solve the problem?

(a) offer fewer employee benefits
(b) increase the inventory of products
(c) invite more potential investors
(d) make the products harder to access

해석
경영진이 문제를 해결하기 위해 한 일은 무엇인가요?
(a) 직원 복지혜택을 줄였다.
(b) 제품 재고를 높였다.
(c) 더 많은 잠재 투자자들을 유치했다.
(d) 제품에 접근하기 어렵게 만들었다.

해설 "They decided to put our high-end clothes and fashion accessories inside locked display cases made of steel and glass."에서 강철과 유리로 만든 잠금 장치가 있는 진열대에 보관함으로써 고객들의 상품 접근을 어렵게 만들었다.

36 ▶정답 ⓑ

Why was the first solution not practical?

(a) because the sales staff refused to follow it
(b) because it led to other similarly pressing problems
(c) because it wasn't helpful in reducing the theft
(d) because it banned the touching of the goods

해석
왜 첫 번째 해결책이 실용적이지 않았나요?
(a) 영업직원이 그것을 따르기를 거부했기 때문
(b) 다른 비슷하게 시급한 문제를 만들 수 있기 때문
(c) 도난을 줄이는데 도움 되지 않았기 때문
(d) 물건을 만지지 못하게 했기 때문

해설 "It was not only discouraging for you, it also discouraged our customers from examining and trying on the items that we sell. As a result, many potential shoppers simply went to other stores where the merchandise was more accessible."에서 직원과 고객들에게 모두 불편을 느끼게 함으로써 다른 상점으로 고객이 빼앗겼다는 내용이 나온다. 첫 번째 문제를 해결하는 과정에서 다른 문제가 발생했다는 (b)가 가장 적절하다.

37 ▶정답 ⓒ

What was decided to correct the limitations of the first security system?

(a) to make the display cases more secure
(b) to force the sales staff to accept the extra work
(c) to replace the system with a new one
(d) to watch out for shoplifters more closely

해석
첫 번째 보안 시스템의 한계를 바로잡기 위해 결정한 것은 무엇인가요?
(a) 전시 케이스를 더 안전하게 만드는 것
(b) 영업직원이 추가 작업을 받아들이도록 강요하는 것
(c) 시스템을 새로운 것으로 교체하는 것
(d) 도둑을 좀 더 신중하게 지켜보는 것

해설 "With the help of Jack Ellison, a retail security specialist from Checkpoint Systems, management decided to have a new anti-shoplifting system installed in our five store branches."에서 새로운 도난 방지 시스템으로 교체한다는 내용이 언급되었다.

38 ▶정답 ⓑ

Based on the talk, how most likely does the "electronic article surveillance" work?

(a) by preventing products from being lifted
(b) by making stolen products more difficult to carry out
(c) by helping to identify potential shoplifters
(d) by forcing customers to pay for any product they handle

해석
연설을 바탕으로, 어떻게 '전자식 물품 감시'가 작동하는 거 같나요?
(a) 제품을 들어 올리지 못하게 함으로써
(b) 도난당한 제품을 들고 나가는 것을 어렵게 함으로써
(c) 잠재 도둑을 알아낼 수 있도록 도와줌으로써
(d) 그들이 만지는 모든 제품에 대해 비용을 지불하도록 강요함으로써

해설
"Imagine that a person is carrying a stolen item. When he passes through the detection devices, or "pedestals," installed by the exit, the hard tag attached to the item will send a radio frequency signal to the pedestal, and an alarm will sound."에서 검색대를 통과할 때 계산하지 않은 물건은 경보음이 울리게 된다고 언급하고 있다. 도난 물품을 상점 밖으로 가지고 나가는 것을 어렵게 시스템이 바뀐다는 것을 알 수 있다.

39 ▶ 정답 ⓐ

According to the speaker, which is an advantage of EAS to the salespeople?
(a) It will allow them to concentrate on their work.
(b) It will make their products more attractive.
(c) It will help them deal easily with thieves.
(d) It will increase their sales by 60%.

해석
화자에 따르면, 판매 직원들에게 EAS의 어떤 것이 장점인가요?
(a) 그들이 자신들의 업무에 집중할 수 있게 해줄 것이다.
(b) 제품을 더욱 매력적으로 만들 것이다.
(c) 그들이 도둑에 쉽게 대처할 수 있도록 도와줄 것이다.
(d) 판매를 60% 증가시킬 것이다.

해설
"It will also smoothen store operations because our sales personnel can focus on assisting shoppers rather than constantly watching out for shoplifters."에서 절도범들에 쏟을 에너지를 고객들을 돕는데 주력할 수 있다고 언급했다. 이는 판매 사원의 본업에 더욱 충실할 수 있게 된다는 내용의 (a)로 정리할 수 있다.

[Part 3]
Now listen to the questions.

40: What kind of advice does Vicky need?
41: Why does Julian prefer using a tablet computer over other computers?
42: Which is not mentioned as a task that the gadget could do?
43: What does a tablet have in common with desktop and laptop computers?
44: How does Julian manage to write long documents on a tablet?
45: What makes tablet computers convenient to work with?
46: Based on the conversation, what will Vicky most likely do about her problem?

해석
40: 어떤 종류의 조언을 비키는 필요로 하나요?
41: 왜 줄리안은 다른 컴퓨터보다 태블릿 컴퓨터 사용을 선호하나요?
42: 태블릿으로 할 수 있는 일로 언급되지 않은 것은 무엇인가요?
43: 태블릿은 데스크 탑 및 노트북 컴퓨터와 어떤 공통점을 갖고 있나요?
44: 어떻게 줄리안은 태블릿으로 긴 문서를 작성하나요?
45: 무엇이 태블릿 컴퓨터 작업을 편리하게 하나요?
46: 대화에 따르면, 어떻게 비키는 그녀의 문제를 해결할 것 같나요?

Now you will hear the conversation.
[conversation]

F Hi, Julian, Thanks for meeting me for coffee.
M Hi, Vicky, No problem. What's on your mind?
F 40) <u>I was hoping you could give me advice on how to better manage my time</u>. You're one of the few people I know whose life seems very well organized. Even though you're always busy, you don't seem overwhelmed by all the things you're doing.
M Thanks. That's quite a compliment, but to be honest, I was pretty disorganized myself until I got a tablet computer and started using the software on it to keep track of my time and tasks.
F Really? Can't you do all of that on a computer instead?
M I tried to do that, 41) <u>but even carrying a laptop around in a backpack made it difficult for me to write everything down</u>. So I never kept my schedule up to date.
F So, what makes a tablet better?
M 41) <u>Well, a handheld tablet is bigger than my smart</u>

phone, so it's easier to read but small enough that I just put it in my pocket when I go out. 42-a) I can use it as a calendar, a notebook, and a calculator. 42-d) I can even answer email with it, so I'm always on top of my schedule and project deadlines.

F I thought tablets were just for games, but now I understand why they are so popular these days. But is a tablet really that effective in managing your appointments and finances?

M Yes, and that is only one of its most basic functions. It can also do complex tasks like editing pictures. 42-b) I even edit videos and music on it.

F That's very interesting! How can such a small device do so many things?

M Well, 43) like a standard desktop computer or laptop, a tablet has an "operating system." That system contains instructions that tell the device what to do.

F Just like a typical computer, huh?

M That's right. What's more, my tablet also has what's called a "handwriting recognition program." This feature enables me to write information directly on the gadget's screen by using a pen-like device called a "stylus." 44) And when I want to write long documents and emails, I simply attach a keyboard to the tablet.

F But how does such a small machine store all the data you encode?

M My tablet has 32 gigabytes of storage capacity, and I can add a flash drive to it if I need more space. So, I keep all my schedules and email contacts, along with whatever books I am reading, as files inside the machine.

F I see… Is there enough space for all your other files?

M Not always. I keep the video and music projects I am doing on a flash drive. 45) 42-d) Tablets are really convenient. I can deal with clients' and friends' emails when I am in a taxi or on the subway and work on projects when I have a few minutes to spare. 42-b) I edited most of the last video production I did while waiting for a friend to show up for lunch.

F Wonderful! Now I really want to buy a tablet. But do you think I can afford one?

M I'm sure you can, Vicky. They cost between $100 and $400 and above. I bought mine for $200.

F 46) I can afford that! Thanks for the information, Julian! I'll be getting one as soon as possible.

Words

overwhelm 압도하다, 제압하다
laptop 노트북
gadget 도구, 장치
spare 할애하다, 내주다
compliment 칭찬
handheld 휴대용의, 손에 쥘 만한 크기의
storage capacity 저장 용량

해석

F 안녕, 줄리안, 커피 마시러 만나줘서 고마워.

M 안녕, 비키, 천만에. 무슨 일 있어?

F 40) 내 시간을 더 잘 관리할 수 있는 방법에 대해 너에게 조언을 구하고 싶어서. 너는 내가 아는 계획적으로 생활하는 몇 안 되는 사람 중 한 명이거든. 너는 항상 바쁘지만, 네가 하는 모든 일에 압도당하는 것처럼 보이지 않아.

M 고마워. 대단한 칭찬이지만, 솔직히 말하면, 나도 태블릿 컴퓨터를 가지고, 내 시간과 업무를 기록하는 소프트웨어를 사용하기 전까지는 매우 체계적이지 못했어.

F 정말? 그 모든 작업을 컴퓨터로 대신 할 수는 없을까?

M 나도 그렇게 하려고 해봤는데, 41) 노트북을 배낭에 넣고 다니는 것 때문에 모든 것을 적는 것이 힘들어. 그래서 내 스케줄을 업데이트하지 못했지.

F 그러면, 태블릿은 어떤 점이 더 좋아?

M 41) 음, 휴대용 태블릿은 내 스마트 폰보다 커서 읽기가 훨씬 편하지만, 외출할 때는 주머니에 넣을 수 있을 만큼 충분히 작아. 42-a) 달력이나 노트북, 계산기로도 쓸 수 있어. 42-d) 심지어 이메일 답변을 할 수도 있어서, 나는 항상 내 스케줄과 업무 마감일을 파악하고 있어.

F 나는 태블릿은 단지 게임용이라 생각했는데, 이제는 요즘 왜 그렇게 인기 있는지 알겠어. 근데 태블릿이 네 약속이나 재정 관리에 실제로 그렇게 효과적이야?

M 응, 그건 태블릿의 가장 기본 기능 중 하나에 불과해. 사진 편집과 같은 복잡한 작업도 할 수 있어. 42-b) 나는 심지어 비디오와 음악을 편집하기도 하거든.

F 그거 정말 흥미롭다! 어떻게 그렇게 작은 기계가 그렇게 많은 일들을 할 수 있지?

M 음, 43) 일반 데스크탑 컴퓨터나 노트북처럼 태블릿도 '운영 체제(OS)'가 있어. 이 시스템은 장치에 무엇을 할지 알려주는 지시사항을 포함하고 있어.

F 전형적인 컴퓨터처럼?

M 맞아. 게다가 태블릿에는 '필기인식 프로그램'이라는 것이 있어. 이 기능은 펜처럼 생긴 '스타일러스(stylus)'라는 도구를 이용해서 기기 화면에 직접 정보를 쓸 수 있도록 해줘. 44) 그리고 내가 긴 문서나 이메일을 작성하려고 할 때 키보드를 태블릿에 연결하기만 하면 돼.

F 그런데 그렇게 작은 기계가 어떻게 네가 인코딩하는 모든 데이터를 저장하지?

M 내 태블릿은 저장 용량이 32 기가바이트인데, 더 많은 공간이 필요하면 플래쉬 드라이브를 추가할 수 있어. 따라서, 나는 모든 일정과 이메일 연락처를 내가 읽고 있는 어떤 책과도 함께 컴퓨터 안에 파일로 보관하고 있어.

F 그렇구나… 다른 모든 파일들에 충분한 공간이 있어?

M 늘 그런 건 아니야. 나는 비디오 및 음악 작업은 플래시 드라이브에 보관하고 있어. 45) 42-d) 태블릿은 정말 편리해. 택시나 지하철에서도 고객이나 친구의 이메일을 처리할 수 있고, 잠깐 시간이 날 때 업무를 볼 수도 있어. 42-b) 점심식사에 친구가 오기를 기다리는 동안 나는 최

근의 비디오 작품 대부분을 편집했어.
F 멋지군! 나도 정말 태블릿 사고 싶다. 내가 살 수 있는 여유가 될까?
M 살 수 있을 거야, 비키. 비용이 100달러에서 400달러 사이와 그 이상도 있어. 나는 200달러에 샀어.
F 46) 그 정도면 살 수 있겠다. 정보 고마워, 줄리안! 가능한 빨리 하나 장만해야겠어.

40 ▶정답 ⓒ

What kind of advice does Vicky need?
(a) how to manage a new project
(b) where to find a lost document
(c) how to organize her time better
(d) what type of computer to buy

해석 어떤 종류의 조언을 비키는 필요로 하나요?
(a) 새 프로젝트를 어떻게 관리하는지
(b) 분실된 문서를 어디에서 찾는지
(c) 그녀의 시간을 어떻게 잘 관리하는지
(d) 어떤 종류의 컴퓨터를 살지

해설 인사를 나눈 후 대화 초반에 비키는 "시간을 더 잘 관리할 수 있는 방법에 대해 조언을 구하고 싶다"고 말한다.

41 ▶정답 ⓐ

Why does Julian prefer using a tablet computer over other computers?
(a) because it serves his purposes well
(b) because it has better software
(c) because he loves carrying it in a backpack
(d) because it sets his schedules

해석 왜 줄리안은 다른 컴퓨터보다 태블릿 컴퓨터 사용을 선호하나요?
(a) 그것이 그의 목적에 잘 부합하기 때문에
(b) 그것이 더 좋은 소프트웨어를 갖고 있기 때문에
(c) 그는 그것을 배낭에 넣고 다니는 것을 좋아하기 때문에
(d) 그것이 그의 스케줄을 정하기 때문에

해설 "Well, a handheld tablet is bigger than my smart phone, so it's easier to read but small enough that I just put it in my pocket when I go out. I can use it as a calendar, a notebook, and a calculator. I can even answer email with it, so I'm always on top of my schedule and project deadlines."에서 노트북으로는 스케줄을 관리하기 힘들었으나, 태블릿은 휴대가 편하고 스케줄 관리와 다양한 기능을 활용할 수 있다고 말한다. 줄리안의 목적에 더 잘 맞는다는 (a)의 내용이 적절하다.

42 ▶정답 ⓒ

Which is not mentioned as a task that the gadget could do?
(a) calculating figures
(b) editing videos
(c) creating games
(d) sending email

해석 태블릿으로 할 수 있는 일로 언급되지 않은 것은 무엇인가요?
(a) 숫자 계산
(b) 비디오 편집
(c) 게임 만들기
(d) 이메일 전송

해설 "I can use it as a calendar, a notebook, and a calculator. (달력이나 노트북, 계산기로도 쓸 수 있어)", "I even edit videos and music on it. (나는 심지어 비디오와 음악을 편집하기도 하거든.)", "I can deal with clients' and friends' emails when I am in a taxi or on the subway (택시나 지하철에서도 고객이나 친구의 이메일을 처리할 수 있고)"를 언급을 통해 a), b), d)는 언급된 것임을 확인할 수 있다.

43 ▶정답 ⓑ

What does a tablet have in common with desktop and laptop computers?
(a) a handwriting recognition program
(b) an operating system
(c) instructions on how to operate
(d) a handheld pen-like device

해석 태블릿은 데스크 탑 및 노트북 컴퓨터와 어떤 공통점을 갖고 있나요?
(a) 필기인식 프로그램
(b) 운영체제
(c) 작동방법에 관한 지시사항
(d) 휴대용 펜과 같은 장치

해설 일반 데스크탑 컴퓨터나 노트북처럼 태블릿도 운영체제(OS)가 있다고 언급했으므로, 공통사항은 운영체제라고 할 수 있다.

44 ▶정답 ⓓ

How does Julian manage to write long documents on a tablet?
(a) by adding a flash drive
(b) by writing on its screen
(c) by installing a stylus
(d) by adding a keyboard to it

해석 어떻게 줄리안은 태블릿으로 긴 문서를 작성하나요?
(a) 플래시 드라이브를 연결함으로써
(b) 화면에 글쓰기를 함으로써

(c) 스타일러스를 설치함으로써
(d) 키보드를 태블릿에 연결함으로써

해설 "And when I want to write long documents and emails, I simply attach a keyboard to the tablet."에서 태블릿에 키보드를 연결해 긴 문서를 작성할 수 있다고 말한다.

45 ▶ 정답 ⓒ

What makes tablet computers convenient to work with?

(a) It has unlimited storage space.
(b) It automatically answers emails.
(c) One can work with it anywhere.
(d) One can call a taxi with it.

해석
무엇이 태블릿 컴퓨터 작업을 편리하게 하나요?
(a) 무제한 저장 공간이 있다.
(b) 이메일에 자동적으로 응답한다.
(c) 어느 곳에서나 작업할 수 있다.
(d) 택시를 부를 수 있다.

해설 "Tablets are really convenient. I can deal with clients' and friends' emails when I am in a taxi or on the subway and work on projects when I have a few minutes to spare."에서 장소에 상관없이 작업할 수 있다는 점이 언급되어 있다.

46 ▶ 정답 ⓑ

Based on the conversation, what will Vicky most likely do about her problem?

(a) read magazine reviews about tablets
(b) buy a tablet right away
(c) ask Julian to choose a tablet for her
(d) find out how much tablets cost

해석
대화에 따르면, 어떻게 비키는 그녀의 문제를 해결할 것 같나요?
(a) 태블릿에 관한 잡지 후기들을 읽는다.
(b) 즉시 태블릿을 구입한다.
(c) 줄리안에게 그녀를 위해 태블릿을 선택해 달라고 요청한다.
(d) 태블릿의 비용을 알아본다.

해설 대화 마지막에 "I can afford that! Thanks for the information, Julian! I'll be getting one as soon as possible."를 토대로 비키는 태블릿을 바로 구매할 것임을 추측할 수 있다.

[Part 4]

Now listen to the questions.

47: What is the task of the Association for the Education of Young Children?
48: What is a similarity of preschools and daycare centers?
49: Why most likely can preschools offer activities that are appropriate for the children?
50: Which is one of the signs that a preschool is right for a child?
51: How can the Childcare Aware hotline help parents?
52: What final step should parents take before enrolling their children in a preschool?

해석
47: 아동교육협회(the Association for the Education of Young Children)가 하는 일은 무엇인가요?
48: 유치원과 어린이집은 무엇이 유사한가요?
49: 유치원이 어린이들에게 적합한 활동을 제공할 수 있을 것 같은 이유는 무엇일 것 같나요?
50: 유치원이 아이에게 적합한지 알 수 있는 신호 중 하나는 무엇인가요?
51: 어떻게 Childcare Aware의 직통 전화가 부모들을 도울 수 있나요?
52: 유치원에 자녀들을 등록시키기 전에 부모들은 마지막 단계로 무엇을 해야 하나요?

Now you will hear the talk.

Good morning, ladies and gentlemen. I'm from the Association for the Education of Young Children. I'm glad to be at this seminar on effective parenting. 47) As part of the association's task of promoting excellence in early childhood education, I would like to share some ideas on how to choose a good preschool for your child.

A lot of parents have asked me: "What's the difference between a preschool and a daycare center?" 48) Well, both are schools that accept young children who don't attend elementary school yet. They're also both regulated by certain agencies and have learning programs. The difference is that preschools are more concerned with child learning than daycare centers are. Preschools also typically offer half-day programs that are more structured than those offered by daycare centers. That means if you want to enroll your child in a full-time preschool program, you may have to pay more.

49) There are advantages to preschools, however. One of these is, unlike daycare centers, they only accept pupils of similar ages. Your child would then be surrounded

by kids his or her own age and abilities. This is why preschools are able to offer activities that are better suited to their students. This feature can be a real advantage for your child because it can better prepare him or her for the school environment that will follow.

While I'm obviously suggesting that you consider sending your child to preschool rather than daycare, I'm sure you're wondering how to choose the right preschool for your child. First of all, you should do a lot of research about how the school is run. Be careful not to base your choice just on a school's reputation. 50) Always look for the following signs of a good preschool: clean and safe facilities; caring and qualified teachers; and clear rules on handling sicknesses or emergencies.

Next, you should study both the curriculum and the educational system of the school. Ask yourself: Do you prefer a specific approach to learning, such as a Waldorf or Montessori program? Do you want a program that includes sports and field trips? Would you prefer that your child be introduced to creative activities such as painting or dance or music lessons? Perhaps you would like your child to be exposed to a foreign language?

Once you've answered those questions, make sure that the school has a current license and is fully accredited by the board of education. 51) You can confirm this by calling the Childcare Aware hotline at 800-424-2246. This hotline can refer you to preschools in your area that are fully accredited. Though accreditation doesn't guarantee that a given preschool is perfect for your child, you can be assured that reliable people are managing the school.

52) The last thing you should do before enrolling your kid is to bring him to the school and have a trial day or half day in the environment. Be sure to observe if he's comfortable with the teachers and the students. Always remember that in choosing a preschool, our prime consideration as parents should be our children's comfort and security. Now do you have any questions?

Words

preschool 유치원
elementary school 초등학교
curriculum 교과과정
hotline 직통전화, 상담 (서비스) 전화
prime 주된, 가장 중요한
daycare center 어린이집
pupil (어린) 학생
accredited 인가 받은, 공인된
trial 시험의, 시험 삼아 하는
comfort 안락함, 편안함

해석

신사 숙녀 여러분, 좋은 아침입니다. 저는 아동 교육 협회(the Association for the Education of Young Children)에서 왔습니다. 효과적인 양육에 관한 이번 세미나에 참석하게 되어 기쁩니다. 47) 조기교육의 장점을 장려하는 협회 업무 일부로, 저는 여러분의 자녀들을 위해 어떻게 좋은 유치원을 선택하는 지에 대해 몇 가지 생각을 나누고 싶습니다.

많은 부모들이 '유치원과 어린이집의 차이점이 무엇인가요?'고 물어봅니다. 48) 둘 다 아직 초등학교에 입학하지 않은 어린 아이들을 받아주는 학교입니다. 또한 둘 다 특정 단체들에 의해 운영되며 학습 프로그램을 가지고 있습니다. 차이점은 유치원이 어린이집보다 아이들의 학습에 관심을 더욱 기울인다는 것입니다. 유치원은 또한 일반적으로 어린이집에서 제공하는 것보다 체계적인 반일제반(half-day programs)을 운영하고 있습니다. 그것은 여러분이 유치원의 종일반(full-time preschool programs)에 자녀를 등록시키고 싶다면, 더 많은 비용을 지불해야 할 수도 있음을 의미합니다.

하지만, 49) 유치원에는 장점들이 있습니다. 그중 하나는 어린이집과 달리 유치원은 비슷한 연령대의 아이들만 받는 것입니다. 그러면 여러분의 자녀는 비슷한 나이와 능력을 갖고 있는 또래들에게 둘러싸이게 될 것입니다. 이는 유치원이 그들의 학생들에게 더 최적화 된 활동을 제공할 수 있는 이유입니다. 여러분의 자녀들이 곧 경험하게 될 학교 환경에 더 잘 대비할 수 있게 되므로 이러한 특징은 자녀들에게 진정한 이점이 될 수 있습니다.

저는 확실히 여러분께 자녀를 어린이집 보다는 유치원에 보낼 것을 고려해 보실 것을 권해드리지만, 여러분은 자녀에게 맞는 유치원을 선택하는 방법이 궁금할 것입니다. 무엇보다 먼저, 유치원이 어떻게 운영되고 있는지에 대해 많은 조사를 하셔야 합니다. 여러분의 선택을 단지 유치원 평판에만 치우치지 않도록 주의를 기울이십시오. 50)항상 좋은 유치원이 가지고 있는 다음 몇 가지 사항을 살펴보세요.: 깨끗하고 안전한 시설; 배려심 많고 자격을 갖춘 교사들; 그리고 질병이나 응급 상황에 대처하는 확실한 규칙.

그 다음, 여러분은 유치원의 교과 과정과 교육 시스템에 대해 살펴봐야 합니다. 스스로에게 물어보세요.: Waldorf나 Montessori 프로그램 같이 특정한 학습법을 선호하시나요? 스포츠나 현장학습이 포함된 프로그램을 원하시나요? 미술이나 무용, 음악 수업 같은 창의적 활동에 자녀들이 참여하기를 원하시나요? 아마도 자녀들이 외국어에 노출되기를 원하시나요?

일단 이러한 질문에 대답하셨다면, 유치원이 현재 면허가 있고, 교육위원회로부터 완전하게 인가 받았는지를 확인하세요. 51) Childcare Aware의 직통 전화인 800-424-2246으로 전화해서 확인하실 수 있습니다. 이 직통 전화는 여러분 지역에 있는 완전하게 인가받은 유치원을 알려줄 것입니다. 인가받은 것이 여러분의 자녀에게 완벽한 유치원이라는 것을 보장하지는 않음에도 불구하고, 여러분은 신뢰할 수 있는 사람이 유치원을 관리하고 있다고 확신 할 수 있습니다.

52) 자녀를 등록시키기 전에 여러분이 해야 할 마지막 일은 자녀를 유치원에 데려가서 그 환경에서 시험적인 하루나 반나절동안 지내게 하는 것입니다. 자녀가 선생님과 학생들이랑 편한 지 관찰하세요. 유치원을 선택하는데 있어, 부모로서 가장 중요한 고려사항은 자녀의 안락함과 안전이어야 한다는 것을 항상 기억하세요. 자, 질문 있으신가요?

47 ▶ 정답 ⓑ

What is the task of the Association for the Education of Young Children?

(a) establishing new preschools
(b) promoting quality education for children
(c) designing academic programs
(d) teaching preschool children

해석
아동교육협회(the Association for the Education of Young Children)가 하는 일은 무엇인가요?
(a) 새 유치원 설립
(b) 아이들을 위한 양질의 교육 장려
(c) 학업 프로그램 고안
(d) 취학 전 아동교육

해설 "As part of the association's task of promoting excellence in early childhood education, I would like to share some ideas on how to choose a good preschool for your child."의 내용을 통해 아동교육협회의 업무 중 하나가 유아교육을 장려하는 것임을 알 수 있다.

48 ▶정답 ⓓ

What is a similarity of preschools and daycare centers?
(a) Both are focused on childcare.
(b) They both offer well-prepared learning programs.
(c) Both teach elementary school students.
(d) They both cater to preschoolers.

해석
유치원과 어린이집은 무엇이 유사한가요?
(a) 둘 다 보육에 초점이 맞춰져 있다.
(b) 둘 다 잘 준비된 학습 프로그램을 제공한다.
(c) 둘 다 초등학생들을 가르친다.
(d) 둘 다 미취학아동을 대상으로 한다.

해설 "Well, both are schools that accept young children who don't attend elementary school yet. They're also both regulated by certain agencies and have learning programs."에서 미취학아동을 받는 것이 유치원과 어린이집의 유사점으로 언급되었다.

49 ▶정답 ⓐ

Why most likely can preschools offer activities that are appropriate for the children?
(a) because the children have the same age-related skills
(b) because the children are of different ages
(c) because preschools have better facilities
(d) because preschools offer full-day programs

해석
유치원이 어린이들에게 적합한 활동을 제공할 수 있을 것 같은 이유는 무엇일 거 같나요?
(a) 아이들은 나이에 맞춰 동일한 능력을 가지고 있어서
(b) 아이들의 나이가 다르기 때문에
(c) 유치원은 더 좋은 시설을 가지고 있어서
(d) 유치원에서는 종일반 프로그램을 제공하기 때문에

해설 "There are advantages to preschools, however. One of these is, unlike daycare centers, they only accept pupils of similar ages. Your child would then be surrounded by kids his or her own age and abilities. This is why preschools are able to offer activities that are better suited to their students."에서 유치원의 장점으로 비슷한 나이대의 아이들만 받는다는 내용이 나온다.

50 ▶정답 ⓑ

Which is one of the signs that a preschool is right for a child?
(a) It follows all popular educational systems.
(b) It takes care of the child's safety and welfare.
(c) It encourages a child to adopt a foreign language
(d) It prepares children in dealing with emergencies.

해석
유치원이 아이에게 적합한지 알 수 있는 신호 중 하나는 무엇인가요?
(a) 인기 있는 모든 교육시스템을 따른다.
(b) 아이의 안전과 복지를 신경 쓴다.
(c) 아이가 외국어를 선택하도록 장려한다.
(d) 응급상황을 아이들이 대처할 수 있도록 준비시킨다.

해설 "Always look for the following signs of a good preschool: clean and safe facilities; caring and qualified teachers; and clear rules on handling sicknesses or emergencies."에서 깨끗하고 안전한 시설(=안전과 복지)을 갖추었는지에 대한 내용이 나온다. 유치원의 응급상황 대처능력도 좋은 유치원의 조건으로 언급되었는데 보기 (d)는 '유치원'이 아니라 '아이들'이 응급상황에 대처할 준비가 되었는지에 대한 내용이므로 오답이다.

51 ▶정답 ⓒ

How can the Childcare Aware hotline help parents?
(a) by supplying details about the best daycare centers
(b) by accrediting only competent preschools
(c) by giving details on accredited local preschools
(d) by giving parents free childcare services

해석
어떻게 Childcare Aware의 직통 전화가 부모들을 도울 수 있나요?
(a) 최고의 어린이집에 관한 세부내용을 제공함으로써
(b) 오직 유능한 유치원만 인가를 해줌으로써
(c) 공인된 지역의 유치원에 대한 세부내용을 제공함으로써
(d) 부모에게 무료보육 서비스를 제공함으로써

해설 "You can confirm this by calling the Childcare Aware hotline at 800-424-2246. This hotline can refer you to preschools in your area that are fully accredited."에서 직통전화로 해당지역 공인된 유치원 정보를 얻을 수 있다는 내용이 나온다.

52

▶ 정답 ⓐ

What final step should parents take before enrolling their children in a preschool?

(a) visiting the preschool with the children
(b) considering daycare center services first
(c) asking their children if they're ready for preschool
(d) inquiring about the other children's age

해석

유치원에 자녀들을 등록시키기 전에 부모들은 마지막 단계로 무엇을 해야 하나요?

(a) 아이들과 함께 유치원을 방문할 것
(b) 먼저 어린이집 서비스를 고려할 것
(c) 그들의 아이들에게 유치원에 갈 준비가 되었는지 물어볼 것
(d) 다른 아이들의 나이를 물어볼 것

해설 "The last thing you should do before enrolling your kid is to bring him to the school and have a trial day or half day in the environment."에서 등록 전에 아이를 데리고 유치원에 방문할 것을 권고하고 있다.

Reading and Vocabulary 01회

Question 53-80

ANSWER KEY p.29

53	ⓒ	54	ⓐ	55	ⓓ	56	ⓑ
57	ⓐ	58	ⓒ	59	ⓓ	60	ⓒ
61	ⓑ	62	ⓒ	63	ⓐ	64	ⓑ
65	ⓓ	66	ⓐ	67	ⓓ	68	ⓐ
69	ⓑ	70	ⓒ	71	ⓑ	72	ⓐ
73	ⓒ	74	ⓒ	75	ⓑ	76	ⓒ
77	ⓑ	78	ⓒ	79	ⓓ	80	ⓑ

Question 53-59

ANDRES SEGOVIA

53) Andres Segovia was an influential Spanish guitarist of the 20th century. 57) He was the most important figure in making the guitar a concert instrument. Considered one of the greatest guitarists of all time, he is regarded as the "father of modern classical guitar."

Andres Segovia Torres was born on February 21, 1893 in Linares, Spain, and was raised in Granada. He took piano and violin lessons at an early age, but became more interested in the guitar. Despite the objections of his family and music teachers, young Andres taught himself to play what was considered a lowly instrument and developed his own technique. At the age of 16, he made his musical debut in Granada. Minor performances followed in Madrid and Barcelona.

Segovia gradually became known outside Spain as his artistry matured. He was ready for a major tour by 1919, and performed in South America and Europe, winning over even those who 58) doubted the significance of classical guitar. 54) His most important early performance was his Paris debut in 1924. Arranged at the insistence of the famed Spanish cellist, Pablo Casals, the concert was attended by international celebrities. This and his successful Berlin debut greatly enhanced Segovia's global reputation. In 1928, after his show in New York City, Segovia gained a devoted following in the United States.

Through constant performances, 57) Segovia 59) elevated

the guitar from being a minor musical instrument to one with a distinguished place on the concert stage. He also widened the guitar's musical range by adopting the works of famous classical composers, such as Sylvius Leopold Weiss and Johann Sebastian Bach. 55) Segovia's efforts inspired many modern composers to write music especially for the guitar. They usually did so under Segovia's guidance. Despite his busy schedule, 56) the maestro managed to share his talent with a younger generation of guitarists by establishing and teaching at music schools in different parts of Europe. Classical guitar became an important part of these schools' academic programs due to his influence.

Segovia continued to play his music well into his 90s. He also established competitions and scholarships for young guitarists, and even performed at the 75th anniversary of his debut concert. Later in life, he was conferred the title Marques de Salobreña by the king of Spain. He died in Madrid on June 2, 1987.

Words

influential 영향력 있는, 유력한
instrument 악기
debut 데뷔, 첫 출연, 첫 무대
artistry 예술적 기교
celebrity 유명인사
following 추종자, 팬
composer 작곡가
academic 학업의, 학교의
confer 수여하다, 부여하다
figure 인물
lowly 하찮은, 낮은
mature 성숙되다, 원숙되다
insistence 고집, 주장
devoted 헌신적인, 충실한, 열렬히 사랑하는
elevate 승격시키다, 향상시키다
maestro 거장
anniversary 기념제

해석

안드레스 세고비아

53) 안드레스 세고비아는 20세기 스페인의 영향력 있는 기타 연주자였다. 57) 그는 기타를 콘서트 악기가 되도록 만든 가장 중요한 인물이었다. 전 시대를 통 털어 가장 위대한 기타 연주자 중 한 명으로 여겨지는 그는 현대 클래식 기타의 아버지로 여겨진다.

안드레스 세고비아 토레스는 스페인 Linares에서 1893년 2월 21일 태어났으며, 그라나다에서 자랐다. 그는 어린 나이에 피아노와 바이올린 수업을 받았지만, 기타에 더 관심을 갖게 된다. 가족과 음악교사들의 반대에도 불구하고, 어린 안드레스는 하찮은 악기로 여겨졌던 기타를 독학으로 배웠고 그 자신만의 기술을 개발했다. 16세에 그는 그라나다에서 데뷔공연을 했다. 마드리드와 바르셀로나에서도 작은 공연들이 이어졌다.

세고비아의 예술성이 성숙해짐에 따라, 서서히 스페인 외부로 알려지게 되었다. 그는 1919년 주요 순회공연을 준비했고, 남미와 유럽에서 공연해 클래식 기타의 중요성에 의문을 제기한 사람들조차 끌어들였다. 54) 그의 가장 중요한 초기 공연은 1924년 파리에서의 데뷔였다. 스페인의 유명한 첼리스트인 Pablo Casals의 고집에 의해 주관된 이 공연에 수많은 세계적인 유명인사들이 참석했다. 이 공연과 성공적인 베를린 데뷔는 세고비아의 세계적인 명성을 드높였다. 1928년 뉴욕 공연 후, 세고비아는 미국에 열성적인 팬들이 생겼다.

57) 세고비아는 지속적인 공연을 통해 기타를 비주류악기에서 콘서트 무대에서 독보적인 위치를 갖는 악기로 올렸다. 또한 그는 Sylvius Leopold Weiss 및 Johann Sebastian Bach 와 같은 유명한 클래식 작곡가들의 작품을 채택함으로써 기타의 음악적 범위를 넓혔다. 55) 세고비아의 노력들은 많은 현대작곡가들이 특별히 기타를 위한 곡을 쓰게끔 영감을 주었다. 그들은 보통 세고비아의 지도하에 그렇게 했다. 바쁜 일정에도 불구하고, 56) 이 거장은 유럽 여러 지역 음악학교를 설립하고 가르침으로써 자신의 재능을 젊은 기타학도들과 나누었다. 클래식 기타는 그의 영향으로 인해 이들 학교의 학업 프로그램에 중요한 부분이 되었다.세고비아는 90대에도 계속해서 자신의 음악을 연주했다. 그는 또한 젊은 기타연주자들을 위한 경연대회와 장학금을 설립했고, 자신의 데뷔 75주년 기념공연을 했다. 말년에 그는 스페인 왕으로부터 Marques de Salobreña라는 칭호를 수여 받았다. 그는 1987년 6월 2일 마드리드에서 생을 마감했다.

53 ▶ 정답 ⓒ

What is Andres Segovia famous for?

(a) being the father of a guitarist
(b) designing classical guitars
(c) being a classical guitarist
(d) composing guitar music

해설

무엇으로 안드레스 세고비아는 유명한가요?

(a) 기타리스트의 아버지가 된 것으로
(b) 클래식 기타를 디자인한 것으로
(c) 클래식 기타리스트가 된 것으로
(d) 기타 음악을 작곡한 것으로

해설 글의 첫 문단, 첫 문장에 '영향력 있는 기타리스트'였다는 내용이 나온다.

54 ▶ 정답 ⓐ

What would establish Segovia's worldwide reputation early in his career?

(a) his performances in Paris and Berlin
(b) his friendships with international celebrities
(c) his concerts in Madrid and Barcelona
(d) his musical debut in Granada

해설

그의 경력에서 일찍이 세고비아가 세계적인 명성을 쌓을 수 있도록 한 것은 무엇인가요?

(a) 파리와 베를린에서의 공연
(b) 세계적인 유명인사들과의 우정

(c) 마드리드와 바르셀로나에서의 콘서트
(d) 그라나다에서의 데뷔

해설 "His most important early performance was his Paris debut in 1924. Arranged at the insistence of the famed Spanish cellist, Pablo Casals, the concert was attended by international celebrities. This and his successful Berlin debut greatly enhanced Segovia's global reputation."을 통해 세고비아가 세계적인 명성을 얻는데 파리와 베를린 공연이 큰 역할을 했다는 것을 알 수 있다.

55 ▶ 정답 ⓓ

How did Segovia's music influence the composers of his time?

(a) It made them go back to classical traditions.
(b) It challenged them to perform the guitar in concerts.
(c) It inspired them to copy the classical composers.
(d) It encouraged them to compose guitar music.

해설 어떻게 세고비아의 음악은 당시 작곡가들에게 영향을 미쳤나요?

(a) 그들로 하여금 클래식 전통으로 돌아가게 했다.
(b) 그들에게 콘서트에서 기타를 연주하도록 북돋아 주었다.
(c) 그들에게 클래식 작곡가들을 따라하도록 영감을 주었다.
(d) 그들에게 기타음악을 작곡하도록 장려했다.

해설 "Segovia's efforts inspired many modern composers to write music especially for the guitar. They usually did so under Segovia's guidance."의 진술을 통해 (d)가 가장 적절한 것임을 알 수 있다.

56 ▶ 정답 ⓑ

How was Segovia able to share his skills with young guitarists?

(a) through musical performances
(b) through music school tutorials
(c) by training classical teachers
(d) by designing school programs

해설 어떻게 세고비아는 젊은 기타리스트들에게 자신의 기술을 공유했나요?

(a) 뮤지컬공연을 통해
(b) 음악학교 수업을 통해
(c) 클래식 선생님들을 훈련시킴으로써
(d) 학교프로그램을 만듦으로써

해설 "Despite his busy schedule, the maestro managed to share his talent with a younger generation of guitarists by establishing and teaching at music schools in different parts of Europe."을 통해 음악학교 교육을 통해 후배 양성을 했다는 것을 알 수 있다.

57 ▶ 정답 ⓐ

Based on the article, what could be Segovia's greatest contribution to music?

(a) He improved the guitar's status.
(b) He revived classical music.
(c) He performed great concerts.
(d) He supported many scholars.

해설 이 글을 바탕으로, 세고비아가 음악에 가장 기여한 것은 무엇인가요?

(a) 그는 기타의 지위를 향상시켰다.
(b) 그는 클래식음악을 부활시켰다.
(c) 그는 대형콘서트에서 공연했다.
(d) 그는 많은 학자들을 후원했다.

해설 글의 첫 문단에 세고비아의 영향력에 대해 잘 정리한 문장이 언급되어 있다. "He was the most important figure in making the guitar a concert instrument. Considered one of the greatest guitarists of all time, he is regarded as the "father of modern classical guitar.""을 통해 세고비아의 기여도에 대한 평가로 가장 적절한 것은 (a)이다.

58 ▶ 정답 ⓒ

In the context of the passage, doubted means _____.

(a) trusted
(b) hesitated
(c) questioned
(d) ignored

해설 문맥상 doubted는 _____을 의미한다.

(a) 신뢰하다
(b) 망설이다
(c) 의심하다, 질문하다
(d) 무시하다

해설 doubt 의심하다, 미심쩍어 하다

59 ▶ 정답 ⓓ

In the context of the passage, elevated means _____.

(a) performed
(b) redesigned
(c) devalued
(d) promoted

해설 문맥상 elevated는 _____을 의미한다.

(a) 실행하다, 공연하다
(b) 재설계하다
(c) 평가절하하다
(d) 승격시키다 (승진시키다), 홍보하다, 촉진시키다

해설 elevate 승격시키다, 향상시키다

Question 60-66

TRACKING MARINE ANIMALS CAN HELP IN PROTECTING THEM

60) There has been a continuing decline in the population of fish and other marine species. In the past 20 years, for example, 90% of leatherback turtles and large predatory fish, such as sharks, have disappeared. The reason has been hard to identify because the oceans are difficult to monitor. However, the situation is improving according to research presented to the American Association for Marine Science.

61) Marine biologists can now keep track of their research subjects, thanks to advances in underwater electronic tagging. This system employs electronic tags that are implanted in the bodies of marine animals. The tags then either send location data to satellites or store it on memory chips that can be 65) retrieved when the fish are caught. Either way, 61) the devices can now tell scientists exactly where the animals travel.

Barbara Block of Hopkins Marine Station in California and her team have already tagged around 700 bluefin tuna, a commercially valuable fish. With the help of fishermen, they were able to chart the migration of over 200 bluefin across the Atlantic. 62) All of these fish are born in the Caribbean, and then travel as far as the coast of Southern Spain before returning to breed in their birthplace.

Meanwhile, Andrew Read, a marine biologist at Duke University in North Carolina, is monitoring 45 tagged loggerhead turtles. 63) When these animals come to the surface to breathe, the electronic tags glued to their shells send messages to the nearest satellite. Together, all this work is beginning to fill in the map of marine "highways" used by particular species. It is showing where particular animals prefer to stay close to the water surface and where they prefer deeper waters.

64) The tracking will be helpful in "ocean zoning," a concept being promoted by conservationists. Through zoning, parts of the sea, such as "turtle highways," would be declared sensitive and subject to restrictions against industries that exploit natural resources. Ultimately, scientists like Dr. Read will be able to devise better ways of protecting 66) rare species without interfering too much with the trading of common ones.

Words

leatherback turtle 장수거북이
shark 상어
predatory 포식성의
identify 확인하다, 알아보다
monitor 관찰하다
underwater 수중의
implant 이식하다, 심다
retrieve 되찾다, 회수하다
migration 이주
breed 번식하다, 새끼를 낳다
loggerhead turtle 붉은 바다거북
conservationist 자연보호주의자
subject (to) 권한 아래 있는, (지배)를 받는
rare 드문, 희귀한
keep track of 추적하다
electronic tagging 전자꼬리표
satellite (인공)위성
either way 어느 쪽이든
bluefin 다랑어
birthplace 출생지
fill in 채우다
declare 공표하다, 선언하다
exploit 이용하다
interfere 간섭하다, 개입하다

해석

해양동물 추적이 그들을 보호하는데 도움이 될 수 있다

60) 물고기 및 다른 해양 종들의 개체수가 지속적으로 감소하고 있다. 예를 들어, 지난 20년 동안 90%의 장수 거북이와 상어 같은 거대 포식어류가 사라져 오고 있다. 바다는 관찰하는 것이 어렵기 때문에 이유를 확인하는 것도 어렵다. 그러나 American Association for Marine Science (미국해양과학협회)에 제출된 연구에 따르면, 상황은 나아지고 있다. 61) 수중 전자 꼬리표의 진보덕분에, 해양생물학자들은 이제 그들의 연구대상을 추적할 수 있다. 이 시스템은 해양동물의 몸에 이식해 놓은 전자 꼬리표를 이용한다. 그리고 나면, 이 꼬리표들은 위치정보를 위성에 보내거나, 물고기가 잡힐 때에 되찾을 수 있는 메모리 칩에 저장해 놓는다. 어느 쪽이든, 61) 이 장치는 이제 과학자들에게 동물들이 어디로 이동하는지 정확히 알려줄 수 있다.

California 주 Hopkins Marine Station의 Barbara Block과 그녀의 연구팀은 이미 상업적으로 가치 있는 어류인 대략 700마리의 다랑어에 꼬리표를 달았다. 어부들의 도움으로 그들은 Atlantic (대서양) 전역에 200마리 이상의 다랑어의 이주를 도표화 할 수 있었다. 62) 이 물고기들은 모두 Caribbean (캐리비안)에서 태어나 스페인 남부해안까지 멀리 이동한 후 번식하기 위해 출생지로 되돌아온다.

한편, North Carolina주 Duke University의 해양 생물학자인 Andrew Read는 45마리의 꼬리표가 달린 붉은 바다 거북이들을 관찰하고 있다. 63) 이들이 숨 쉬기 위해 표면으로 올라올 때, 그들의 껍질에 부착된 전자 꼬리표는 가장 가까이에 있는 위성에 신호를 보낸다. 함께, 이 모든 작업은 특정 종에 의해 사용되는 해양 'highway (고속도로)'지도를 채우기 시작하고 있다. 그것은 특정한 동물들이 어디에서 수면 가까이에 머무는 것을 선호하고, 또 어디에서 깊은 바다 속에 머무는 것을 선호하는 지를 보여준다.

64) 추적은 자연보호주의자들에 의해 추진되는 개념인 'ocean zoning (해양 구역화)'에 도움이 될 것이다. 구역화를 통해 'turtle highways (거북이 고속도로)' 같은 바다의 일부지역은 천연자원을 이용하는 산업에 관해 제한을 받게되고, 민감한 지역으로 공표된다. 궁극적으로, Dr. Read와 같은 과학자들은 일반 종 거래에 심한 간섭 없이 희귀종을 보호하기 위한 더 나은 방법을 고안해낼 수 있을 것이다.

60 ▶정답 ⓒ

What is true about the current condition of marine species?

(a) Their populations are increasing.
(b) They are showing previously unobserved behavior.
(c) They are becoming fewer and fewer in number.
(d) They are following new migratory routes.

해석 무엇이 해양생물의 현재 상태에 대해 사실인가요?

(a) 그들의 개체수가 증가하고 있다.
(b) 그들은 이전에 관찰되지 않은 행동을 보여주고 있다.
(c) 그들의 개체수가 점점 더 감소하고 있다.
(d) 그들은 새로운 이동경로를 따르고 있다.

해설 첫 번째 문장에서 "There has been a continuing decline in the population of fish and other marine species."라고 언급되어 있다. 해양생물들의 개체수가 계속해서 감소해왔다는 것을 알 수 있다.

61 ▶정답 ⓑ

What do the electronic tags do?

(a) prevent the fish from being caught
(b) monitor the animals' location
(c) track the fish's activities
(d) record the animals' diet

해석 전자 태그가 하는 일은 무엇인가요?

(a) 물고기가 잡히는 것을 방지한다.
(b) 동물의 위치를 관찰한다.
(c) 물고기의 활동을 추적한다.
(d) 동물의 먹이를 기록한다.

해설 두 번째 문단 첫 번째 문장에서 전자 꼬리표에 대한 진술이 언급되어 있다. "Marine biologists can now keep track of their research subjects, thanks to advances in underwater electronic tagging."을 통해 해양생물들의 이동 경로를 관찰할 수 있다는 것을 알 수 있다.

62 ▶정답 ⓒ

What isn't known about bluefin tuna?

(a) where they breed
(b) how they live
(c) what they eat
(d) where they head to

해석 참 다랑어에 대해 알려져 있지 않은 것은 무엇인가요?

(a) 어디에서 그들이 번식하는지
(b) 어떻게 그들이 사는지
(c) 무엇을 그들이 먹는지
(d) 어디로 그들이 향하는지

해설 "All of these fish are born in the Caribbean, and then travel as far as the coast of Southern Spain before returning to breed in their birthplace."의 언급을 통해 출생지와 번식, 이동경로 등을 확인하면서 사는 법에 대해 알 수 있다. 다만, 무엇을 먹는 지에 대한 언급은 없다.

63 ▶정답 ⓐ

Why do loggerhead turtles come to the surface of the water?

(a) because they need to breathe air
(b) because they are showing their location
(c) because the electronic tags force them to do so
(d) because they have to locate the highway

해석 왜 대머리 거북이가 바다 표면으로 오나요?

(a) 그들은 숨을 쉬어야 하기 때문에
(b) 그들은 자신들의 위치를 보여주고 있기 때문에
(c) 전자 꼬리표가 그들에게 그렇게 하도록 하기 때문에
(d) 그들은 고속도로를 찾아야 하기 때문에

해설 "When these animals come to the surface to breathe"을 통해 대머리 거북이가 표면에 올라오는 이유는 숨을 쉬기 위한 것임을 알 수 있다.

64 ▶정답 ⓑ

How will electronic tagging likely help protect endangered marine animals?

(a) by making them difficult to catch
(b) by helping agencies control the areas that they frequent
(c) by marking them as protected species
(d) by allowing scientists to follow and control them

해석 어떻게 전자 꼬리표가 멸종위기에 처한 해양동물들을 보호하는 데 도움이 될 것 같나요?

(a) 붙잡기 어렵게 함으로써
(b) 기관이 그들이 자주 나타나는 지역을 통제하는 것을 도움으로써
(c) 그들을 보호 종으로 표시함으로써
(d) 과학자들이 그들을 추적해서 통제할 수 있게 함으로써

해설 전자 꼬리표가 해양동물을 보호하는데 도움이 될 것이라는 내용은 마지막 문단에 나온다. 구역화를 통해서 제한을 받고 민감한 지역으로 공표되기 때문이다. (b)의 진술이 같은 내용임을 알 수 있다.

65 ▶정답 ⓓ

In the context of the passage, retrieved means _____.

(a) improved
(b) replaced
(c) emitted
(d) recovered

해석

문맥상 retrieved는 _____을 의미한다.

(a) 향상되다
(b) 대체하다, 대신하다
(c) 방출하다, 내뿜다
(d) 되찾다, 회복하다

해설 retrieve 회수하다

66 ▶ 정답 ⓐ

In the context of the passage, rare means _____.

(a) uncommon
(b) standard
(c) unique
(d) attractive

해석 문맥상 rare는 _____을 의미한다.

(a) 흔하지 않는, 드문
(b) 표준의
(c) 독특한, 유일한
(d) 매력적인

해설 rare 드문, 진기한

Question 67-73

WINDMILL

67) A windmill is a machine that converts wind into useful energy. This energy is derived from the force of wind acting on slanted blades or sails which are attached to a device called a "windshaft." When used with a water pump, grain mill, or any machine that performs simple tasks, the whole 72) mechanism is called a "windmill." When used to generate electricity, it is called a "wind turbine generator."

68-b) d) As early as the 7th century AD, simple windmills were probably already being used in Persia (now Iran) for irrigating farmlands and milling grain. 68-c) Although these windmills were somewhat inefficient, their use spread throughout the Middle East and China. In Europe, the first windmills appeared in England and France during the 12th century and eventually became popular in other parts of the continent. By the 19th century, the Dutch were using around 9,000 windmills.

The use of wind turbines for generating electricity was pioneered in Denmark late in the 1890s. In the US, small wind turbine generators supplied electricity to many rural communities until the 1930s. During that decade, power lines were extended across the nation and the first large wind turbines were built. Modern wind turbines are propelled in either of two ways: 69) the "drag," wherein wind pushes the blades; and the "lift," where the blades move in the same way an airplane's wing rises on an air current.

Used in large-scale power generation, the most successful wind turbine generators can produce 100 to 400 kilowatts of electricity. These generators are sometimes installed in groups called "wind farms." The world's largest wind farms are in California, where the wind turbines can collectively generate up to 1,120 megawatts, a little more than the capacity of a typical nuclear plant.

Wind turbine generators could provide as much as 10% of the world's electricity by the middle of the 21st century. 70) Wind energy creates very little pollution and few greenhouse gases, and is an environment-friendly 73) alternative to non-renewable fuels such as oil. However, 71) countries that have low wind speed and space limitations must come up with specially-designed wind turbines.

Words

windmill 풍차	convert 전환시키다
slanted 비스듬한, 경사가 있는	blade 날
sail (풍차의) 날개	mechanism 기제, 체계
wind turbine generator 풍력터빈 발전기	irrigate 개간하다
farmland 농지	somewhat 다소
continent 대륙	rural 시골의, 지방의
power line 송전선	propel 나아가게 하다
large-scale 대규모의, 광범한	power generation 발전
collectively 총괄하여, 전체적으로	capacity 생산력
typical 전형적인	alternative 대안
renewable 재생 가능한	

해석

풍차

67) 풍차는 바람을 유용한 에너지로 전환시키는 기계이다. 'wind-shaft'로 불리는 장치에 부착된 경사가 있는 날 또는 날개에 작용하는 바람의 힘으로부터 에너지를 얻는다. 수중펌프, 그레인 밀(곡식 찧는 방아) 또는 단순한 작업을 처리하는 기계들이 함께 사용되는 경우, 그 전체 메커니즘을 풍차라고 한다. 전기를 발생시키기 위해 사용될 때는, 그것은 '풍력 터빈 발전기'로 불린다.

68-b) d) 일찍이 7세기 초에 단순한 풍차는 이미 페르시아 (현재의 이란)에서 곡식을 빻고, 농지를 개간하기 위해 사용되었다. 68-c) 이 풍차들은 다소 비효율적이었지만, 중동과 중국 전역에서 사용되었다. 유럽에서는 최초의 풍차가 12세기경 영국과 프랑스에 출현했고, 결국에는 유럽의 다른 지역에서도 인기를 얻었다. 19세기경까지 네덜란드 인들은 대략 9000

대의 풍차를 사용했다.

　　전기를 발생시키기 위해 풍력터빈을 사용한 것은 1890년대 후반 덴마크가 선구적이었다. 미국에서는 소형 풍력발전용 터빈이 1930년대까지 많은 농촌지역에 전기를 공급했다. 그 십년 동안, 송전선은 미국 전역으로 확장되었고 최초의 대형 풍력터빈이 건설되었다. 현대의 풍력터빈은 두 가지 방식중 하나로 움직인다. 69) 바람이 날을 밀어내는 '항력'과 비행기의 날개가 기류에서 상승하는 것과 같은 방식으로 날이 움직이는 '양력'이 있다.

　　대규모 전력생산에 사용되는 가장 성공적인 풍력 터빈 발전기는 100~400 kilowatts의 전기를 생산해 낼 수 있다. 이러한 발전기는 종종 '풍력발전소'라 불리는 단지에 설치되기도 한다. 전 세계에서 가장 큰 풍력발전단지는 캘리포니아에 있으며, 풍력터빈이 모두 합쳐지면 전형적인 원자력 발전소의 생산력보다 약간 더 많은 1,120 megawatts까지 생성할 수 있다.

　　풍력 터빈 발전기는 21세기 중반까지 전 세계 전력의 10%를 공급할 수 있다. 70) 풍력 에너지는 오염이 적고 온실 가스를 거의 만들지 않으며, 석유와 같은 재생 불가능한 연료의 환경친화적인 대안이다. 그러나 71) 풍속이 낮고, 공간적인 제약이 있는 국가에서는 특별히 설계된 풍력 터빈이 필요하다.

67　▶ 정답 ⓓ

What is a windmill used for?
(a) generating wind
(b) controlling the flow of wind
(c) converting into wind
(d) turning wind into power

[해석] 무엇을 위해 풍차가 사용되나요?
(a) 바람을 생산하기 위해
(b) 바람의 흐름을 제어하기 위해
(c) 바람으로 전환시키기 위해
(d) 바람을 에너지로 바꾸기 위해

[해설] 첫 문장에 "A windmill is a machine that converts wind into useful energy."라고 정의되어 있다. 풍차는 바람을 에너지로 전환시키기 위해 사용되는 것임을 알 수 있다.

68　▶ 정답 ⓐ

What is not true about the early windmills?
(a) They were used to generate electricity.
(b) They were mainly used in farms.
(c) They had flaws.
(d) Persians were among the very first to use them.

[해석] 초기 풍차에 관해 사실이 아닌 것은 무엇인가요?
(a) 그들은 전기를 생산하는 데 사용되었다.
(b) 그들은 주로 농장에서 사용되었다.
(c) 그들은 결함이 있었다.
(d) 페르시아인들이 처음으로 그들을 사용했다.

[해설] 두 번째 단락 "As early as the 7th century AD, simple windmills were probably already being used in Persia (now Iran) for irrigating farmlands and milling grain. 68-c) Although these windmills were somewhat inefficient, their use spread throughout the Middle East and China."에서 (b), (c), (d)는 언급되었지만 전기를 생산하는데 사용되었다는 내용은 없다. 전기를 생산하게 된 때는 1890년대로 초기 풍차의 설명이 아니다.

69　▶ 정답 ⓑ

How does the wind propel a wind turbine by means of the "drag"?
(a) by pushing the blades backward
(b) by pressing on the blades
(c) by raising the blades into the air
(d) by moving the blades upward

[해석] 어떻게 바람은 항력(drag)을 이용해서 풍력 터빈을 움직이게 하나요?
(a) 날을 뒤로 밀어냄으로써
(b) 날을 밀어냄으로써
(c) 날을 공기 중으로 들어 올림으로써
(d) 날을 위로 움직임으로써

[해설] 3번째 문단에서 "the "drag," wherein wind pushes the blades"를 통해 (b)가 적절한 것임을 알 수 있다. 방향에 대해서는 언급이 되어 있지 않으므로 (a)는 올바르지 않다.

70　▶ 정답 ⓒ

Based on the article, what could be an advantage of electricity produced by wind turbines?
(a) It is produced more cheaply.
(b) It is much simpler to use.
(c) Its source will never run out.
(d) It can be produced anywhere in the world.

[해석] 글을 토대로, 풍력 터빈에 의해 생산되는 전기의 장점은 무엇이 될 수 있나요?
(a) 더 싸게 생산된다.
(b) 사용하기가 훨씬 쉽다.
(c) 원료가 고갈되지 않을 것이다.
(d) 세계 어디에서나 생산될 수 있다.

[해설] 마지막 문단에 풍력에 의해 생산되는 전기의 장점이 언급되어 있다. 재생 불가능한 연료의 환경 친화적인 대안이라고 했으므로 원료가 고갈되지 않을 것이라는 (c)가 가장 적절하다.

71 ▶ 정답 ⓑ

Why couldn't wind turbines be used to provide all the world's energy requirements?

(a) because lawmakers haven't learned of its benefits
(b) because they need certain climatic conditions
(c) because people prefer non-renewable sources energy
(d) because most countries have space limitations

해석
풍력터빈이 전 세계 에너지 요구량을 충족시키기 위해 사용될 수 없는 이유는 무엇인가요?

(a) 의원들이 그 이점을 알지 못했기 때문에
(b) 풍력터빈은 특정한 기후조건을 필요로 하기 때문에
(c) 사람들이 재생 불가능한 에너지원을 선호하기 때문에
(d) 대부분의 국가들이 공간 제약이 있기 때문에

해설 마지막 문장에서 풍속이 낮고 공간적 제약이 있는 국가에서는 특별 설계된 풍력 터빈이 필요하다고 했으므로 기후조건과 공간적 제약때문에 모든 국가에서 사용될 수 없다는 것을 알 수 있다.

72 ▶ 정답 ⓐ

In the context of the passage, mechanism means _____.

(a) system
(b) idea
(c) device
(d) force

해석
문맥상 mechanism는 _____을 의미한다.

(a) 체계, 시스템
(b) 아이디어
(c) 장치, 도구
(d) 물리력, 힘

해설 mechanism 체계, 작동원리

73 ▶ 정답 ⓒ

In the context of the passage, alternative means _____.

(a) difference
(b) alteration
(c) option
(d) interest

해석
문맥상 alternative는 _____을 의미한다.

(a) 차이
(b) 변경, 변화
(c) 선택
(d) 관심, 흥미

해설
alternative 대안, 선택

Question 74-80

January 15, 2016

Mr. David Gagnon
Director of Operations
Organic Trade Association
Greenfield, MA 01302

Dear Mr. Gagnon:

The United States Department of Agriculture (USDA) is 79) soliciting nominations for membership in the Advisory Committee on Meat and Poultry Inspection. 74) Under the authority of the USDA Food Safety and Inspection Service, the Committee serves as an advice-giving body on product quality and labeling standards for the meat and poultry industries. It also serves as a forum for the sharing of ideas on how our regulatory system can best serve consumers and the industries.

76) In recent years, membership in the Committee was opened up to represent the interests of various sectors. Nominees for membership are generally persons who have shown ability to represent the producers and processors, academe, government, and consumers. 75) Due to the sudden resignation of Mr. Donald Smith, my office is now in need of are presentative from the producers' group. The individual who will fill this vacancy is expected to work with the Committee until March 31, 2018.

78) If your association would like to nominate someone, 77) 78) please send his or her application form, a detailed résumé, and three letters of reference to me at the address indicated below. All nomination materials should be postmarked not later than April 1, 2016. Application forms may be downloaded from www.fsis.usda.gov. Please note that incomplete documents will not be 80) entertained.

For further details, please contact my assistant, Ms. Sonya West, by telephone at (202) 720-2561 or e-mail at sonya.west@fsis.usda.gov. Thank you very much.

Sincerely,

Garry McKee

Garry L. McKee, M.D.
Administrator
Food Safety and Inspection Service, USDA
300 12th Street SW
Washington, DC

Words

- solicit 청하다, 구하다
- advice-giving body 자문기관
- poultry 가금
- nominee 지명(추천)된 후보
- resignation 사임, 사직
- association 협회
- letter of reference 추천서
- postmark (우편물에) 소인을 찍다, (우편의) 소인
- nomination 지명, 추천
- labeling 표시
- regulatory system 규제체제
- represent 대변하다, 대표하다
- vacancy 공석
- application form 신청서
- entertain 받아들이다

[해석]

가농 씨에게:

미국농무부 (USDA)는 육류 및 가금류 검역위원회 (Meat and Poultry Inspection)의 자문위원 후보지명을 요청하고 있습니다. 74) USDA 식품안전검사국의 권한 하에, 위원회는 육류 및 가금류 산업에 대한 제품품질 및 표시기준에 대한 자문 역할을 합니다. 또한, 우리 규제체제가 소비자와 산업에 가장 잘 기여할 수 있는 방법에 대한 아이디어 공유를 위한 포럼으로써의 역할을 합니다.

76) 최근, 위원회 회원자격이 다양한 분야의 이익을 대변하기 위해 개방되었습니다. 회원 후보자는 일반적으로 생산자와 가공업자, 학자, 정부 및 소비자를 대변하는 능력을 보여주는 사람입니다. 75) 도널드 스미스의 갑작스러운 사임으로 인해, 제 사무실은 현재 생산자 그룹의 대표가 필요합니다. 이 공석을 채울 사람은 2018년 3월 31일까지 위원회와 함께 일하게 될 것입니다.

78) 귀하의 협회가 누군가를 후보로 지명하고 싶다면, 77) 78) 신청서, 상세한 이력서, 그리고 세 통의 추천서를 아래의 주소로 저에게 보내주십시오. 모든 추천 자료는 늦어도 2016년 4월 1일까지 소인이 찍혀 있어야 합니다. 신청서는 www.fsis.usda.gov에서 다운로드할 수 있습니다. 완벽히 구비되지 않은 서류는 받지 않습니다.

추가 세부사항은 제 비서인 Ms. 소냐 웨스트에게 전화 (202) 720-2561 또는 이메일 sonya.west@fsis.usda.gov로 연락주세요. 고맙습니다.

74 ▶ 정답 ⓒ

What is the main task of the Committee?

(a) doing safety inspections of meat products
(b) providing capital to meat-processing businesses
(c) developing trade regulations on meat products
(d) promoting the US meat industry in foreign markets

[해석]

위원회의 주된 업무는 무엇인가요?

(a) 육류제품의 안전점검 실시
(b) 육류가공 사업체에 자본을 제공하는 것
(c) 육류제품에 대한 무역규제 개발
(d) 외국 시장에서 미국육류산업 육성

[해설] 첫 번째 문단에 위원회가 하는 일에 대한 소개가 나온다. "Under the authority of the USDA Food Safety and Inspection Service, the Committee serves as an advice-giving body on product quality and labeling standards for the meat and poultry industries. It also serves as a forum for the sharing of ideas on how our regulatory system can best serve consumers and the industries."을 통해 자문기관과 규제정책과 관련된 활동을 하는 곳임을 알 수 있다. 제품의 품질에 대한 자문을 하는 기관이지 실제적으로 점검을 하는 기관이라는 언급은 없으므로 (a)는 올바르지 않다.

75 ▶ 정답 ⓑ

Why does the Committee have a vacancy?

(a) It has just been established.
(b) A representative has left.
(c) It was recently opened to producers.
(d) Gary McKee is resigning.

[해석]

위원회에 공석이 있는 이유는 무엇인가요?

(a) 막 설립되었기 때문
(b) 대표자가 떠났기 때문
(c) 최근에 생산자들에게 개방되었기 때문
(d) 개리 맥키가 사임했기 때문

[해설] "Due to the sudden resignation of Mr. Donald Smith, my office is now in need of are presentative from the producers' group." 에서 기존의 대표자인 도널드 스미스가 사임해서 공석이라는 것을 알 수 있다.

76 ▶ 정답 ⓒ

Who is the Committee most likely to accept as a nominee for the vacancy?

(a) one who can represent all the concerned sectors
(b) one who is commercially successful
(c) one who can speak on behalf of a represented sector
(d) one who can work full-time

[해석]

위원회가 공석의 후보자로 가장 받아들일 것 같은 사람은 누구인가요?

(a) 모든 관심분야를 대표할 수 있는 사람
(b) 상업적으로 성공한 사람
(c) 대표하는 분야를 대신하여 말할 수 있는 사람
(d) 풀타임으로 일할 수 있는 사람

[해설] "In recent years, membership in the Committee was opened up to represent the interests of various sectors. Nominees for membership are generally persons who have shown ability to represent the producers and processors, academe, government, and consumers."를 통해 자신의 분야를 대변할 수 있는 사람을 선호한다는 것을 알 수 있다.

77 ▶ 정답 ⓑ

What was not mentioned as a nomination requirement?

(a) work history
(b) a letter of nomination
(c) recommendation letters
(d) an application form

해석
추천 요건으로 언급되지 않은 것은 무엇인가요?

(a) 이력서
(b) 지명서
(c) 추천서
(d) 신청서

해설 "If your association would like to nominate someone, please send his or her application form, a detailed résumé, and three letters of reference to me at the address indicated below."에서 언급되지 않은 것은 지명서이다.

78 ▶ 정답 ⓒ

If they want to nominate someone, what will the association likely do after reading McKee's letter?

(a) They will apply through the Committee's website.
(b) They will send Sonya West an email.
(c) They will mail the required documents to McKee.
(d) They will visit the USDA office.

해석
만약 그들이 누군가를 지명하기를 원한다면, 맥키의 편지를 읽은 후 협회는 무엇을 할 것 같나요?

(a) 위원회 웹 사이트를 통해 신청할 것이다.
(b) 소냐 웨스트에게 이메일을 보낼 것이다.
(c) 필요한 서류를 맥키에게 우편으로 보낼 것이다.
(d) 그들은 USDA 사무실을 방문 할 것이다.

해설 신청서와 간단한 이력서, 세 통의 추천서를 우편으로 보내달라고 했으므로 가장 적절한 것은 (c)이다. 문의사항이 있는 경우 비서인 소냐 웨스트에게 메일을 보내라고 했으므로 (b)는 오답이다.

79 ▶ 정답 ⓓ

In the context of the passage, soliciting means _____.

(a) granting
(b) rejecting
(c) opening
(d) seeking

해석
문맥상 soliciting는 _____을 의미한다.

(a) 수여하다, 승낙하다
(b) 거절하다
(c) 개방하다, 열다
(d) 청하다, 구하다, 찾다

해설 solicit 청하다, 구하다

80 ▶ 정답 ⓑ

In the context of the passage, entertained means _____.

(a) supported
(b) accepted
(c) amused
(d) used

해석
문맥상 entertained는 _____을 의미한다.

(a) 지지하다, 지원하다
(b) 받아들이다, 허용하다
(c) 즐겁게 하다
(d) 사용하다

해설 entertain 받아들이다.

지텔프코리아 공식지정

G-TELP
LEVEL 2

이현아 취향저격 지텔프 실전모의고사

해설편

2

Answers and Explanations

한 권에 끝내는 G-TELP 실전모의고사 5회

SECTION 01 GRAMMAR
SECTION 02 LISTENING
SECTION 03 READING & VOCABULARY

Grammar Test 02회
Question 1-26

ANSWER KEY   p.41

01	ⓐ	02	ⓓ	03	ⓒ	04	ⓑ
05	ⓐ	06	ⓑ	07	ⓒ	08	ⓑ
09	ⓓ	10	ⓒ	11	ⓑ	12	ⓓ
13	ⓑ	14	ⓓ	15	ⓒ	16	ⓓ
17	ⓐ	18	ⓑ	19	ⓐ	20	ⓑ
21	ⓓ	22	ⓒ	23	ⓐ	24	ⓒ
25	ⓑ	26	ⓓ				

01 ▶ 정답 ⓐ

해석 Mr. Barlow는 최근에 농장이 개각충의 공격을 받았음에도 불구하고, 충분한 양의 레몬과 오렌지를 수확해왔다. 그러나 그를 가장 놀라게 한 것은 병든 나무가 실제로 맛있고 육즙이 많은 과일을 생산했다는 것이다.

해설 해석을 통해 풀어야 하는 접속부사이다. 빈칸 뒤의 내용이 예상하지 못한 사건으로 그를 놀라게 했다는 내용이므로 반전을 표현하는 However가 가장 적절하다.

02 ▶ 정답 ⓓ

해석 어제 열기구가 Texas에서 화재를 일으켜 추락했다. 열기구에는 사고 당시 승객들이 있었다. 현재 조사관들이 희생자의 수와 신원을 파악하고 있다.

해설 시간을 표현하는 부사 at this time (현재)이 있으므로 현재진행시제가 가장 적절하다.

03 ▶ 정답 ⓒ

해석 1965년 Fred DeLuca는 대단히 성공적인 Subway 샌드위치가게를 짓기 위해 Peter Buck으로부터 1,000달러의 대출을 받았다. DeLuca와 Buck은 나중에 프랜차이즈 업계에 있는 사업가를 돕는 Franchise Brands를 설립하기 위해 파트너 관계를 맺었다.

해설 완벽한 문장 뒤에 빈칸이 나왔으므로 들어갈 수 있는 것은 부사밖에 없다. 목적을 표현하는 to 부정사가 가장 적절하다.

04 ▶ 정답 ⓑ

해석 Bert와 Sara는 비치 하우스 개조공사에 많은 비용이 필요할 것이라는 것을 예상하지 못했다. 그러한 이유로 그들은 지난달부터 개조공사 비용을 대기 위해 은행대출을 알아보고 있다.

해설 시간부사 since last month(지난 달 이래로)가 있으므로 주절에는 현재완료진행시제가 가장 적절하다.

05 ▶ 정답 ⓐ

해석 UCLA Downtown Centre는 사회활동 용도로 대여할 수 있지만 장소를 준비하기에 충분한 시간이 필요하다. 그러므로 경영진은 고객이 적어도 4일 전에 미리 센터에 예약을 알려야 한다고 조언한다.

해설 명령, 동의, 제안, 주장, 요구, 충고 동사의 목적어 자리에 that절이 오면 that절의 동사는 「(should) 동사원형」이 되어야 한다.

06 ▶ 정답 ⓑ

해석 잘 만들어진 영화임에도 불구하고 The Spy Who Came in from the Actively Cold는 흥행에 성공하지 못했다. 만약 영화가 흥미로운 시각 효과를 줬더라면, 더 많은 사람들이 영화를 관람했을 텐데.

해설 If절의 동사 시제가 had p.p.이므로 주절에는 「조동사 과거형 + have p.p.」가 와야 한다.

07 ▶ 정답 ⓒ

해석 'Mystery shoppers'란 회사가 비밀리에 자사의 서비스직원을 관찰하기 위해 고용한 아마추어 탐정이다. 영업직원의 효율성 및 전반적인 서비스 질을 조사하기 위해 고급 상점들을 방문하는 것이 그들 업무의 한 부분이다.

해설 빈칸은 upscale stores를 목적어로 취하는 문장 전체의 주어자리이다. 주어 자리에 들어갈 수 있는 것은 동명사이므로 (c)가 적절하다.

08 ▶ 정답 ⓑ

해석 영국의 록스타인 Robert Chalmers는 54세의 나이에 심장 마비로 생을 마감했다. 보고서에 따르면, 심장 마비가 왔을 때에 Chalmers는 일주일 간 프랑스를 여행하고 있었다.

해설 기간을 표현하는 부사 for a just week (딱 주일 동안)이 있으므로 완료시제가 적절하다. 시간부사절 접속사 when이 이끈 절에서 동사가 과거이므로 과거완료진행시제가 들어가야 올바르다.

09 ▶ 정답 ⓓ

해석 부장은 내일 회의에 참석할 것이다. 그녀는 비서에게 누군가가 그녀를 만나고자 한다면, 그녀는 하루 종일 Lakeview Hotel의 Grand Hall에서 보낼 것이라고 말했다.

해설 시간부사 tomorrow가 있으므로 미래를 표현하는 시제가 들어가야 한다. 조동사 will이 들어간 표현들이 우선순위에 들어가며 미리 계획되어 있는 일정을 나타내고 있으므로 미래진행시제가 더 적절하다. 미래완료시제는 앞선 시제부터 미래시제까지 지속적으로 해오는 상황일 때 쓸 수 있다.

10 ▶ 정답 ⓒ

해석 상원은 미국장애아동교육에 자금을 지원하자는 Dayton 상원의 제안을 거부했다. 만약 상원의원들이 이 제안을 승인했다면, 상원은 이 나라의 특수교육프로그램에 약 220억 달러를 지원했을 텐데.

해설 If절의 시제가 had p.p.이므로 주절에는 「조동사 과거형 + have p.p.」시제가 들어가야 한다.

11 ▶ 정답 ⓑ

해석 점점 증가하는 인터넷 사용자들로 인해 전자상거래에 대한 전망은 계속해서 좋아지고 있다. 실제로 전자상거래를 적극적으로 채택하는 대부분의 소매업자들은 비즈니스 성장에 만족하고 있다.

해설 관계사문제이다. 선행사가 retailers(소매업자들)이므로 사람 선행사를 수식할 수 있는 who와 whom이 후보로 남을 수 있다. whom은 목적격이므로 목적어가 없는 불완전한 문장이 와야 하는데, 주어가 없으므로 문법적으로 올바르지 않다. 주격 관계대명사 who의 쓰임이 올바르다.

12 ▶ 정답 ⓓ

해석 시각보조 수단이 없기 때문에, 라디오광고는 청취자의 관심을 끌고 붙잡아야 한다. 이 때문에, 최고의 라디오 광고는 판매수단으로 코미디를 사용한다. 대부분의 소비자들은 만약 그것이 재미있다면, 라디오광고를 기억할 것이다.

해설 해석을 통해서 풀어야 하는 접속사 문제이다. 문맥상 조건을 표현하는 if가 들어가야 자연스럽다. 주절의 시제가 미래(will remember), 부사절의 시제가 현재(is)인 것을 체크한다면 시간/조건 부사절 접속사를 더 쉽게 찾을 수 있다.

13 ▶ 정답 ⓑ

해석 내가 혼자 살기 시작했을 때 나는 요리를 하지 않고, 값비싼 식당에서 식사를 하곤 했다. 그러나 나는 만약 내가 식사를 준비하려고 노력했었다면, 많은 돈을 아낄 수 있었을 것이라는 것을 나중에 깨달았다.

해설 If절의 시제가 had p.p. 이므로 주절의 시제는 「조동사 과거형 + have p.p.」가 들어가야 한다.

14 ▶ 정답 ⓓ

해석 Hong Kong Design Center는 올해 유명한 디자인콘테스트를 개최할 예정이다. 심사위원단은 박람회에서 수상자를 결정하기 위해, 다양한 디자인 학교들로부터 수백 명의 후보자들을 심사할 것이다.

해설 빈칸은 완벽한 문장 뒤에 나왔으므로 들어갈 수 있는 품사는 부사밖에 없다. 목적을 표현하는 to 부정사가 들어가야 한다.

15 ▶ 정답 ⓒ

해석 Leila는 55킬로그램의 체중을 목표로 삼았다. 그녀의 현재 체중에서는 쉽지 않은 일이다. 이상적인 체중에 도달하기까지 그녀는 2년 동안 과일과 채소만 먹을 것이다.

해설 기간을 표현하는 부사 for two years(2년 동안)이 있으므로 완료시제가 적절하다. 시간부사절 before의 동사가 현재시제(reaches)이므로 문맥상 미래완료진행시제가 적절하다.

16 ▶ 정답 ⓓ

해석 기술 회사인 Dell의 경우, 수익성은 적합한 고객선택에 달려 있다. 이 고객들은 정기적으로 컴퓨터를 교체하고 회사에 예측 가능한 매출흐름을 제공 할 수 있는 대기업과 부유한 사람들이다.

해설 해석을 통해서 풀어야 하는 조동사 문제이다. 문맥상 회사의 수익에 영향을 미칠 수 있는 '능력'에 대해서 이야기하고 있으므로 can이 가장 적절하다.

17 ▶ 정답 ⓐ

해석 내 친구는 나에게 교육부에서 상담업무를 수락할 것을 권하고 있다. 그러나 나는 그녀에게 만약 정부에서 일한다면, 국방부에서 좀 더 많은 도전적인 일을 맡을 수 있을 것이라고 말했다.

해설 실현가능성이 희박한 미래의 상황을 가정하는 were to 가정법이다. If절의 동사는 「were to + 동사원형」으로 쓰이고, 주절에는 「조동사 과거형 + 동사원형」이 쓰인다.

18 ▶ 정답 ⓑ

해석 호화 유람선인 Crystal Cruises는 Traveler 잡지의 2015년 Readers' Choice 설문조사에서 가장 높은 점수를 받았다. 관광객들과 여행 작가들은 뛰어난 서비스와 잘 정비된 시설을 이유로 그 유람선을 예약할 것을 권고한다.

해설 recommend는 목적어 자리에 동명사를 목적어로 취하는 3형식 타동사이다.

19 ▶ 정답 ⓐ

해석 Federal Aviation Administration(미국연방항공청)은 비행 중에 항공기의 전자시스템을 방해 할 수 있는 장치를 사용하는 것에 대해 사람들에게 경고했다. FAA는 승객들이 항공기를 위험에 빠뜨릴 수 있는 장치를 사용하지 말 것을 당부했다.

해설 명령, 동의, 제안, 주장, 요구, 충고 동사의 목적어 자리에 that절이 오는 경우 that절의 동사는 「(should) + 동사원형」이 쓰인다.

20 ▶ 정답 ⓒ

해석 최근 설문조사는 벤처자금이 많은 유럽기업에게 매우 중요하다는 것을 보여준다. 조사대상 기업의 대부분은 신생 중소기업이었다. 그들 대부분은 회사가 외부 자금지원 없이는 성장하지 못했을 것이라고 믿었다.

해설 관계사 문제이다. 선행사가 majority of the companies이므로 사람 선행사를 꾸며주는 who와 whom을 쓸 수 없고 장소나 공간을 수식하는 when도 쓰일 수 없다. 주격 관계대명사 that의 쓰임이 문법적, 문맥상 가장 적절하다.

21 ▶ 정답 ⓓ

해석 음악 평론가인 Ernest Hooper는 Florida Orchestra의 재정적 문제는 공연에 관객을 유치함으로써 쉽게 해결될 수 있다고 생각한다. 그는 만약 오케스트라가 대중적인 곡을 공연한다면, 더 많은 사람들이 공연에 갈 것이라고 말한다.

해설 if절의 동사 시제가 과거(played)이므로 가정법 과거임을 알 수 있다. 주절에는 「조동사 과거형 + 동사원형」이 들어가야 한다.

22 ▶ 정답 ⓒ

해석 2개월 전, 시카고는 전자제품 판매가 강세였다고 보고했다. 그러나 그 수치는 지난 달 발표된 수치보다 훨씬 더 낮았다. 보스턴, 뉴욕, 및 아틀란타에서도 수익이 저조했지만, 클리블랜드에서는 수익이 향상되고 있었다.

해설 등위접속사 but에 연결되는 내용이 클리블랜드의 수익성인데, 이는 다른 도시들이 수익이 낮았던 과거의 상황을 묘사하고 있으므로 똑같이 과거(진행)으로 시제 일치를 해줘야 가장 적절하다. 수익이 향상되고 있는 상황이었으므로 단순과거보다 진행시제를 써서 표현하는 것이 자연스럽다.

23 ▶ 정답 ⓐ

해석 Anne은 신용카드를 분실했지만 아직 신용카드회사에 알리지 않았다. 만약 내가 그녀라면, 다른 사람들이 신용 카드를 사용하지 못하도록 가능한 한 빨리 분실 신고를 할 텐데.

해설 if절의 시제가 과거(were)이므로 주절에는 「조동사 과거형 + 동사원형」이 쓰여야 한다.

24 ▶ 정답 ⓒ

해석 Eastern University는 향후 몇 년 이내에 세계대학순위를 올리기를 갈망한다. 이를 위해, 부서를 재편성하고 있다. 총장은 대학순위를 올리기 위해 연구 위주의 교수진을 채용할 것을 제안했다.

해설 명령, 동의, 제안, 주장, 요구, 충고 동사의 목적어 자리에 that절이 오는 경우 that절의 동사는 「(should) 동사원형」이 되어야 한다.

25 ▶ 정답 ⓑ

해석 15살 된 내 사촌 Donny는 우리지역에서 적십자사의 헌혈운동에 참여할 수 없게 되자 실망했다. 자원봉사자들은 적어도 17세 이상의 기증자들로부터 피를 받는 것을 허락한다.

해설 allow는 목적어 자리에 동명사를 목적어로 취하는 3형식 타동사이다.

26 ▶ 정답 ⓓ

해석 Gordon Fisheries, Inc는 공장의 폐수 배출을 줄이는 방법을 실시할 것이다. 그 방법은 또한 물과 전력 소비를 줄일 것이다. 경영진은 회사가 매년 5만 달러를 절약할 것으로 확신하고 있다.

해설 해석을 통해 풀어야 하는 조동사 문제이다. that절의 내용에 대해서 확신하는(confident)하는 상황이 현재시제임(is)을 알 수 있다. 앞 문장에서 공장 폐수 배출을 줄이는 방법을 실시할 것이라고 했으므로 이것이 5만 달러 절약을 할 것으로(미래의 상황) 확신하는 것이 문맥상 자연스러우므로 조동사 will이 들어가야 한다.

Listening Test 02회

Question 27-52

ANSWER KEY p.49

27	ⓓ	28	ⓒ	29	ⓑ	30	ⓐ
31	ⓓ	32	ⓑ	33	ⓐ	34	ⓓ
35	ⓐ	36	ⓑ	37	ⓓ	38	ⓐ
39	ⓒ	40	ⓑ	41	ⓓ	42	ⓒ
43	ⓐ	44	ⓓ	45	ⓐ	46	ⓒ
47	ⓑ	48	ⓒ	49	ⓐ	50	ⓓ
51	ⓑ	52	ⓐ				

[Part 1]

Now listen to the questions.

27: Where will Emily go for the weekend?
28: How did Emily and her daughter become interested in skiing?
29: According to the conversation, what should a person develop first before trying to ski?
30: What term was used to refer to a mountain slope for beginners?
31: Why does Sandy want to go to Colorado?
32: What type of skiing was likened to a marathon?
33: What will Ted most likely do next winter?

해석

27: Emlily는 주말에 어디를 갈까요?
28: Emily와 그녀의 딸은 어떻게 스키에 관심을 갖게 되었나요?
29: 대화에 따르면, 스키를 타기에 앞서 가장 먼저 높여야 할 것은 무엇인가요?
30: 어떤 용어가 초보자용 슬로프를 의미하는 데 사용되나요?
31: 왜 Sandy는 Colorado에 가고 싶어 하나요?
32: 어떤 종류의 스키가 마라톤에 비유되었나요?
33: Ted는 내년 겨울에 무엇을 할 가능성이 높나요?

Now you will hear the conversation.

[conversation]

M Hi, Emily! I'm throwing a small party at home on Saturday. Fiona just got a promotion, and we are celebrating it. Would you like to come over with Mark?

F That would be nice, Ted, but I'm sorry that we can't come on Saturday. 27) Mark and I will be in Colorado this weekend with our daughter, Sandy. Please just give our best wishes to Fiona.

M That's too bad, but it's okay. 27) What will you be doing in Colorado?

F 27) Oh, Mark and Sandy have been eager to go skiing there for months.

M Skiing? I didn't know the three of you liked sports, much less winter sports.

F Sandy and I really didn't until our skiing trip last year near Lake Ontario. Before that, Mark was the only ski enthusiast in the family.

M 28) How did you start learning skiing?

F 28) Well, weeks before our trip last year, he'd been lecturing Sandy and me on the basics of the sport.

M 29) I see. Don't you also need some physical preparation before going skiing?

F 29) Oh yes. He taught us some exercises for improving flexibility and strength, which he said were needed before even trying to ski.

M So, how did your first skiing experience go?

F It went great! When we reached the resort, we immediately put on our ski gear. 30) Then Mark took the two of us to what was called a "bunny slope," a gentle slope for those new to the sport. He showed us how to keep our balance and slide down the slope carefully to avoid injury.

M That must have been difficult!

F Not really, Ted. Once Sandy and I learned the basic techniques, sliding down the slope was easy. The difficult part was stopping. I couldn't reduce my speed and stay balanced at the same time, so I fell on the snow several times!

M Ha-ha-ha! It's a good thing it's only snow you fell on! How did your daughter do?

F Sandy turned out to be quite good for a beginner—definitely better than I was. 31) In fact, it's her idea to go to Colorado this time. She wants to practice "downhill skiing" and watch some professionals do complicated stunts.

M You mean there are different varieties of skiing?

F Yes. Downhill skiing is the easiest because the person

simply slides down a gentle slope. However, trained skiers like those who join the Winter Olympics do downhill racing where their speed in going down a steep slope is measured.

M That must be hard!

F Yes, but an even more complex variety is "freestyle skiing," which involves spins, quick turns, and acrobatic jumps. 32) There's also "cross-country racing," which emphasizes endurance rather than speed, much like a marathon.

M Those skiing styles must require a lot of training.

F They really do, and professional skiers can be really amazing to watch!

M 33) That sounds exciting. I think I'll take Fiona and the kids to a ski resort next winter to try the sport.

F You should, Ted. I'm sure you'll all enjoy the sport as much as we do!

Words

throw a party 파티를 열다
be eager to ~을 하고 싶어하다
physical preparation 준비운동, 체력훈련
strength 체력
professional 전문가
stunt 곡예
steep 가파른
spin 회전
promotion 승진
enthusiast 열광자, 열심인 사람
flexibility 유연성
slide down 미끄러져 내려가다
complicated 어려운, 복잡한
trained 숙련된
endurance 지구력

해석

M 안녕 Emily! 나는 토요일에 집에서 작은 파티를 하려고 해. Fiona가 막 승진이 돼서 우리는 그것을 축하하려고 해. Mark랑 같이 올래?

F 그러면 좋지, Ted. 그런데 미안하지만 토요일에 갈 수가 없어. 27) Mark와 나는 이번 주말에 콜로라도에서 우리 딸 Sandy와 같이 시간을 보낼 예정이야. Fiona에게 안부를 꼭 전해줘.

M 아쉽지만 괜찮아. 27) 콜로라도에서 뭐 할 거야?

F 27) 오, Mark와 Sandy는 몇 달 째 그곳에서 스키를 너무 타고 싶어해.

M 스키? 나는 너희 셋이 겨울 스포츠는 말할 것도 없이 스포츠를 좋아하는지 몰랐어.

F Sandy와 나도 작년에 온타리오 호수 근처에 스키 타러 갈 때까지도 몰랐어. 그 전에는 가족 중에 Mark만 스키를 좋아했지.

M 28) 스키는 어떻게 배우기 시작했어?

F 글쎄, 28) 우리가 작년 여행가기 몇 주 전에 Mark는 Sandy와 나에게 스키의 기본적인 것들을 가르쳐줬어.

M 29) 그렇구나. 너는 스키 타러 가기 전에 약간의 신체적인 준비가 필요하진 않니?

F 29) 맞아. 그는 우리에게 체력과 유연성을 향상 시킬 수 있는 몇 가지 운동을 알려줬는데 그가 말하기를 스키를 타기 전에도 필요하다고 했어.

M 처음으로 스키를 타본 경험은 어땠어?

F 좋았어! 우리가 리조트에 도착했을 때, 우리는 바로 스키 장비를 착용했어. 30) 그리고 나서 Mark는 우리 둘을 'bunny slope'라고 불리는 곳으로 데리고 갔는데 스키 초보자를 위한 경사가 완만한 곳이야. 그는 우리에게 균형을 잡는 법과 부상당하지 않게 경사를 조심해서 내려가는 법을 알려주었어.

M 어려웠겠다!

F 꼭 그렇진 않아, Ted. 일단 Sandy와 내가 기본기를 익히고 나니, 경사를 내려가는 것은 쉬웠어. 어려운 부분은 멈추는 것이었어. 나는 속도를 줄이면서 동시에 균형을 잡을 수가 없어서, 눈에서 몇 번을 넘어졌지!

M 하하하. 네가 눈에서만 넘어져서 다행이야. 네 딸은 어땠어?

F 확실히 나보다 낫게 Sandy는 초보치고는 되게 잘했어. 31) 사실, 이번에 콜로라도에 가는 것은 그녀의 아이디어야. 그녀는 'downhill skiing'을 연습해보고 싶어 하고, 전문가들이 어려운 곡예 하는 것을 보고 싶어 해.

M 다양한 종류의 스키가 있다는 말이니?

F 그럼. Downhill skiing은 사람이 단순히 완만한 경사를 타고 내려오기 때문에 가장 쉬워. 그러나 동계 올림픽에 참가하는 숙련된 스키선수들은 가파른 경사를 타고 내려가고 그 속도를 재는 활강 경기를 해.

M 어렵겠다!

F 맞아. 그런데 훨씬 더 어려운 종류는 'freestyle skiing'인데, 회전, 빠르게 돌기, 그리고 곡예점프를 하는 거야. 32) 또한 'cross-country racing'이 있는데, 이는 마라톤처럼 속도보다는 지구력을 강조해.

M 그런 종류의 스키는 훈련을 많이 해야겠다.

F 그들은 정말 그렇게 하고 전문 스키선수들을 보는 것은 정말로 놀라워!

M 33) 되게 재미있겠다. 나도 내년 겨울에 스키타러 Fiona와 애들을 데리고 스키리조트에 가 봐야겠어.

F 꼭 그래봐 Ted. 내가 확신하건데 너도 우리만큼 스키를 즐기게 될 거야!

27

▶ 정답 ⓓ

Where will Emily go for the weekend?

(a) to a skiing competition
(b) to the beach
(c) to a friend's house
(d) to a ski resort

해석

Emily는 주말에 어디를 갈까요?

(a) 스키대회로
(b) 해변으로
(c) 친구 집으로
(d) 스키 리조트로

해설 Emily는 주말에 Colorado에 가는 이유로 스키를 타고 싶다고 했으므로 스키 리조트로 간다는 (d)가 가장 적절하다.

28 ▶ 정답 ⓒ

How did Emily and her daughter become interested in skiing?

(a) by learning it from Ted
(b) by watching an exhibition
(c) by being introduced to it by Mark
(d) by watching Mark join a competition

해석
Emily와 그녀의 딸은 어떻게 스키에 관심을 갖게 되었나요?

(a) 테드로부터 배움으로써
(b) 시범경기를 봄으로써
(c) 마크가 소개를 해줌으로써
(d) 마크가 대회에 참가하는 것을 봄으로써

해설 스키를 어떻게 배우게 되었냐는 질문에 지난 해 여행가기 전에 마크가 Sandy와 Emily에게 스키의 기본적인 것들을 가르쳐줬다는 말을 통해 정답을 (c)로 체크할 수 있다.

29 ▶ 정답 ⓑ

According to the conversation, what should a person develop first before trying to ski?

(a) the ability to turn quickly
(b) flexibility and strength
(c) speed and coordination
(d) the ability to jump high

해석
대화에 따르면, 스키를 타기에 앞서 가장 먼저 높여야 할 것은 무엇인가요?

(a) 빠르게 회전하는 능력
(b) 유연함과 체력
(c) 속도와 조정력
(d) 높게 점프할 수 있는 능력

해설 Emily의 말 "He taught us some exercises for improving flexibility and strength, which he said were needed before even trying to ski."를 통해 유연함과 체력이 필요한 것을 알 수 있다.

30 ▶ 정답 ⓐ

What term was used to refer to a mountain slope for beginners?

(a) bunny slope
(b) steep slope
(c) practice slope
(d) basic slope

해석
어떤 용어가 초보자용 슬로프를 의미하는 데 사용되어지나요?

(a) bunny slope
(b) steep slope
(c) practice slope
(d) basic slope

해설 "Then Mark took the two of us to what was called a "bunny slope," a gentle slope for those new to the sport."를 통해 bunny slope가 초보자용 코스임을 알 수 있다.

31 ▶ 정답 ⓓ

Why does Sandy want to go to Colorado?

(a) to join the Winter Olympics
(b) to learn some ski stunts
(c) to see the snow-covered mountains
(d) to practice downhill skiing

해석
왜 Sandy는 Colorado에 가고 싶어 하나요?

(a) 동계 올림픽에 참가하기 위해서
(b) 스키 곡예를 배우기 위해서
(c) 눈으로 덮인 산을 보기 위해서
(d) downhill 스키를 연습하기 위해서

해설 "In fact, it's her idea to go to Colorado this time. She wants to practice "downhill skiing" and watch some professionals do complicated stunts."을 통해 (d)가 정답임을 알 수 있다.

32 ▶ 정답 ⓑ

What type of skiing was likened to a marathon?

(a) freestyle skiing
(b) cross-country skiing
(c) downhill ski racing
(d) ski jumping

해석
어떤 종류의 스키가 마라톤에 비유되었나요?

(a) 자유형 스키
(b) 크로스 컨트리 스키
(c) 활강 스키 경기
(d) 스키 점프

해설 "There's also "cross-country racing," which emphasizes endurance rather than speed, much like a marathon."에서 마라톤과 cross-country skiing을 비교하고 있다.

33 ▶ 정답 ⓐ

What will Ted most likely do next winter?

(a) learn how to ski with his wife and children
(b) go to Colorado with Emily's family
(c) watch a professional skiing contest
(d) enroll his children at a ski academy

해석
Ted는 내년 겨울에 무엇을 할 가능성이 높나요?

(a) 그의 아내와 아이들과 스키 타는 법을 배울 것이다
(b) Emily의 가족과 Colorado에 갈 것이다
(c) 프로 스키 대회를 보러 갈 것이다
(d) 아이들을 스키 강좌에 등록시킬 것이다

해설 "That sounds exciting. I think I'll take Fiona and the kids to a ski resort next winter to try the sport."에서 내년 겨울에 스키리조트에 가고 싶어 하는 것을 알 수 있다.

[Part 2]

Now listen to the questions.

34: What is the purpose of the talk?
35: Where can customers use the Milton Premium Shopper Card?
36: What benefit will customers get when using the card?
37: What is the expected benefit of the program to the company?
38: How can customers get the loyalty card?
39: How likely will an advanced information system make customer data secure?

해석

34: 발표의 목적은 무엇인가요?
35: 고객은 어디에서 Milton Premium Shopper Card를 사용할 수 있나요?
36: 고객이 카드를 사용할 때 어떤 이점이 있나요?
37: 회사에 대한 프로그램의 기대 이익은 무엇인가요?
38: 고객은 어떻게 로열티 카드를 얻을 수 있나요?
39: 첨단 정보 시스템이 고객 데이터를 얼마나 안전하게 지킬 수 있나요?

Now you will hear the talk.

Good morning! Just in case some of you still don't know me, I'm Linda Usher, the new Sales Director. 34) Today, I'll be giving you an overview of the company's latest marketing program. It's a customer loyalty program that will reward our loyal shoppers and provide valuable marketing information to our department store.

This program is all about the Milton Premium Shopper Card. 35) It's a plastic, bar-coded card that customers can use every time they shop at any branch of Milton. The card is very convenient to use:the customers simply have to present the card to a store clerk before paying for their purchase.

36) For every purchase, the cardholders will earn points corresponding to the amount spent. These points will be converted to rebates or repayments to be credited quarterly. On the first year, these rebates will be 5% of every $50 worth of purchased merchandise. There are two other benefits:a 10% discount on selected items, and free gift-wrapping. Cardholders will also receive free items during special occasions such as Valentine's Day, Thanksgiving Day, and other major holidays.

37) So, you might ask, how can this program help our marketing efforts? Well, through this program, Milton will be able to keep track of our customers' needs and preferences. We will use the information to achieve two major objectives:to match our business plan with market demand better, and to make Milton more competitive in our area.

Management would like to launch the card before the year ends, so 38) our department store will start issuing application forms next week to interested shoppers. These documents will be available in printed format at our customer service counters, and in digital format at our website, www.miltonstore.com. 38) We will deliver the cards to their respective holders as soon as the applications are processed.

At this point, I would like to say that a program like this raises questions about the possible violation of our consumers' privacy. However, our shoppers have nothing to worry about. 39) In line with Milton's "customer first" policy, we'll give our shoppers written assurance that the data we collect about them will not be shared with other companies and will be kept confidential at all times. In fact, to keep our database secure, our IT department is already using more advanced data encryption and systems monitoring devices.

I would like to end my talk by encouraging all of you to promote this new program to as many customers as possible. Please persuade them to read our brochures or visit our website so they will know more about the Premium Shopper Card. Thank you, ladies and gentlemen! I am now ready to entertain your questions.

Words

Sales Director 영업이사
reward 보답하다, 보상하다
present 보여주다, 제시하다
cardholder 카드 소지자
rebate 환불
credit 입금하다
preference 선호도
issue 발행하다, 발부하다
violation 위반, 위배
written assurance 서면 확인서
secure 안전한
overview 개요
loyal shopper 단골
store clerk 점원
corresponding 상응하는
repayment 상환, 반환
special occasion 특별행사
launch 출시하다
respective 각각의, 각자의
in line with ~에 따라, ~와 함께
confidential 기밀의

해석

좋은 아침입니다. 혹시 여러분 중에 아직도 저를 모르는 분이 계실 수도 있으니까요. 저는 Linda Usher이고 새로 온 영업이사입니다. 34) 오늘 여러분에게 회사의 최신 마케팅 프로그램에 관한 개요를 설명하겠습니다. 단골 고객에게 보답을 하고 소중한 마케팅 정보를 백화점에 제공하는 고객 신뢰 프로그램입니다.

이 프로그램은 모두 Milton Premium Shopper Card에 관한 것 입니다. 35) 이것은 고객들이 Milton의 어떤 지점에서도 매번 사용할 할 수 있는 플라스틱 바코드 카드입니다. 이 카드는 사용하기 매우 편리 합니다: 고객들은 단지 계산하기 전에 가게 점원에게 카드를 보여주기만 하면 됩니다.

36) 구매 할 때마다, 카드 소지자들은 지출한 금액에 상응하는 포인트를 받을 것입니다. 이 포인트는 환급금이나 반환금으로 전환되어 분기별로 입금될 것입니다. 첫 해 환급금은 50달러 상당의 구매마다 5%가 될 것입니다. 추가 혜택 두 가지가 더 있습니다:선별된 품목에서 10% 할인 및 무료 선물포장을 받을 수 있습니다. 카드 소지자들은 또한 발렌타인데이, 추수감사절, 및 기타 주요 공휴일 같은 특별한 행사기간에 무료 사은품을 받을 것입니다.

37) 그렇다면, 여러분은 이 프로그램이 어떻게 우리 마케팅 활동을 도울 수 있는지 궁금할 수 있습니다. 자, 이 프로그램을 통해서, Milton은 우리 고객들의 필요와 선호를 파악할 수 있습니다. 우리는 두 가지 주요 목표를 달성하기 위해 이 정보를 사용할 것입니다. 즉, 우리 비즈니스 플랜과 시장의 수요를 더 잘 조화시키고, Milton이 우리 지역에서 더욱 경쟁력 있게 되는 것입니다.

경영진은 연말 전에 카드를 출시하고 싶어 하므로, 38) 우리 백화점은 다음 주에 관심 있는 고객들에게 신청서를 발행할 것입니다. 이 서류는 우리 고객서비스 카운터에서 출력된 양식 및 웹 싸이트인 www.miltonstore.com에서 디지털 양식으로 이용할 수 있습니다. 38) 신청서가 처리되는 대로 카드를 각 소유자에게 전달할 것입니다.

이때, 저는 이와 같은 프로그램이 고객들의 사생활을 침해할 가능성에 대해 의문을 제기한다는 점에 관해 말하고 싶습니다. 그러나 우리 쇼핑객들은 전혀 걱정할 필요가 없습니다. 39) Milton의 '고객 우선주의' 정책에 따라 우리가 수집한 고객 관련 데이터는 다른 회사와 공유하지 않으며, 항상 기밀로 유지될 것이라는 서면 확인서를 고객들에게 보내드릴 것입니다. 사실 데이터베이스를 안전하게 유지하기 위해, 우리의 IT 부서는 이미 첨단 데이터 암호화 및 시스템 모니터링 장치를 사용하고 있습니다.

여러분 모두가 가능한 많은 고객에게 이 새로운 프로그램을 홍보할 것을 촉구하며 발표를 마치도록 하겠습니다. 고객들에게 안내책자를 읽거나 홈페이지를 방문하도록 권해서, 고객이 Premium Shopper Card에 대해 더 잘 알 수 있도록 해주세요. 고맙습니다, 신사 숙녀 여러분! 지금부터 여러분의 질문을 받겠습니다.

34 ▶ 정답 ⓓ

What is the purpose of the talk?

(a) to promote a department store
(b) to launch a new product
(c) to train new employees
(d) to inform employees about a new marketing strategy

발표의 목적은 무엇인가요?
(a) 백화점 홍보를 하기 위해
(b) 신제품 출시를 하기 위해
(c) 신입 사원을 교육시키기 위해
(d) 직원들에게 새로운 마케팅 전략을 알리기 위해

해설 "Today, I'll be giving you an overview of the company's latest marketing program."를 통해 회사의 최신 마케팅 전략을 설명하려고 한다는 것을 알 수 있다.

35 ▶ 정답 ⓐ

Where can customers use the Milton Premium Shopper Card?

(a) at all Milton department stores
(b) at only one branch of Milton
(c) anywhere customer loyalty cards are honored
(d) at all department stores nationwide

고객은 어디에서 Milton Premium Shopper Card를 사용할 수 있나요?
(a) Milton 백화점 모든 지점에서
(b) Milton의 한 지점에서만
(c) 고객 로열티 카드 (포인트 카드) 가 취급되는 곳은 어디라도
(d) 전국의 모든 백화점

해설 "It's a plastic, bar-coded card that customers can use every time they shop at any branch of Milton."을 통해 Milton 백화점의 모든 지점에서 사용 가능하다는 것을 알 수 있다.

36 ▶ 정답 ⓑ

What benefit will customers get when using the card?

(a) priority checkout lines
(b) rebates on their purchases
(c) discounts during holidays
(d) after-hours shopping privileges

고객은 카드를 사용할 때 어떤 이점이 있나요?
(a) 계산 우선권
(b) 구매에 대한 환급
(c) 휴일 기간 할인
(d) 영업 외 시간의 쇼핑 특권

해설 "For every purchase, the cardholders will earn points corresponding to the amount spent. These points will be converted to rebates or repayments to be credited quarterly."에서 고객들은 구매당 쌓은 포인트를 현금으로 전환하여 환급 받게 될 것이라고 이야기하고 있다.

37 ▶정답 ⓓ

What is the expected benefit of the program to the company?

(a) getting income tax breaks
(b) promotion of merchandise
(c) immediate increase in the number of customers
(d) valuable data on customers' spending habits

해석 회사에 대한 프로그램의 기대 이익은 무엇인가요?

(a) 소득세 감면 혜택을 받는 것
(b) 상품 홍보
(c) 고객 수의 즉각적인 증가
(d) 고객의 소비 습관에 관한 중요한 데이터

해설 "So, you might ask, how can this program help our marketing efforts? Well, through this program, Milton will be able to keep track of our customers' needs and preferences."를 통해 고객들의 필요와 선호도를 얻을 수 있음을 알 수 있다. 고객들의 필요와 선호도가 '소비 습관'이라는 단어로 패러프레이징 되어 보기에 나왔다.

38 ▶정답 ⓐ

How can customers get the loyalty card?

(a) by filling-out an application form
(b) by being a Milton shopper long enough
(c) by paying a membership fee
(d) by being interviewed at a Milton store

해석 고객은 어떻게 로열티 카드를 얻을 수 있나요?

(a) 신청서를 작성하는 것으로
(b) 장기간 Milton의 고객이 되는 것으로
(c) 회비를 지불하는 것으로
(d) Milton 점에서 인터뷰 하는 것으로

해설 "our department store will start issuing application forms next week to interested shoppers.", "We will deliver the cards to their respective holders as soon as the applications are processed."을 통해 백화점에서 발행한 신청서를 작성해서 제출하면 카드를 받을 수 있음을 알 수 있다.

39 ▶정답 ⓒ

How likely will an advanced information system make customer data secure?

(a) It will erase all customer data from the system.
(b) It will keep back-up files of important information.
(c) It will protect the information from being stolen by others.
(d) Only customers will have access to the data.

해석 첨단 정보 시스템이 고객 데이터를 얼마나 안전하게 지킬 수 있나요?

(a) 시스템에서 모든 고객 데이터를 삭제할 것이다.
(b) 중요한 정보의 백업 파일을 보관할 것이다.
(c) 다른 회사가 정보를 빼내가지 못하도록 보호할 것이다.
(d) 고객만이 데이터에 접근할 수 있을 것이다.

해설 "In line with Milton's 'customer first' policy, we'll give our shoppers written assurance that the data we collect about them will not be shared with other companies and will be kept confidential at all times. In fact, to keep our database secure, our IT department is already using more advanced data encryption and systems monitoring devices." 첨단 고객 정보시스템은 고객 관련 데이터를 다른 회사와 공유하지 않고, 기밀사항으로 유지하기 위해 사용된다는 것을 알 수 있다.

[Part 3]

Now listen to the questions.

40: About what did the woman ask the man's advice for?
41: Why was the woman asking about printers?
42: Who did the man say is in the best position to give details about the capability of a particular printer?
43: What did the man cite as a publishing task that could be provided by the printing firm itself?
44: How did the woman initially feel about the schedule of her project?
45: What was said about start-up printing firms?
46: Why likely did the woman feel more positive after the conversation?

해석
40: 여자는 무엇에 관해 남자에게 조언을 구했나요?
41: 여자는 왜 인쇄소에 대해 물어 보았나요?
42: 남자는 특정한 인쇄소의 역량에 관한 세부 정보를 제공하는 데 누가 가장 좋은 위치에 있다고 말했나요?
43: 인쇄소 자체가 제공 할 수 있는 출판 작업으로 남자가 언급한 것은 무엇인가요?
44: 여자는 처음에 그녀의 프로젝트 일정에 대해 어떻게 생각했나요?
45: 신생 인쇄소에 관해 언급된 것은 무엇인가요?
46: 대화 후 여자가 더 긍정적인 기분을 느낀 이유는 무엇인가요?

Now you will hear the conversation.
[conversation]

F Hi, Oliver! I heard you used to do marketing work for a lifestyle magazine, so I suppose you know a lot about printing services. 40) Could you give me some advice on how to choose a good printing company?

M Sure, Cynthia! 41) But what do you need the printing services for?

F Well, 41) I'll be editing a souvenir book for our company's 25th year in business. I was assigned to find a reliable printer that operates right here in Boston.

M Doesn't the company already have an existing printer? Isn't it the one making our corporate brochures and stationery?

F Yes, but unfortunately, it will stop its operations in Boston next week. It is moving its operations to Philadelphia.

M I see. Well, I think your first task is to compare the other printing firms here in Boston. Try to get information directly from their account executives. One fundamental thing to find out is whether the firm is technically equipped to handle your project or not.

F 42) Does that mean I should visit the printing offices and look at their facilities?

M 42) It would be helpful to do that, but you can save time by simply asking the printing account executive all the important questions. Account executives are in an excellent position to answer those.

F I see. What kind of questions do I need to ask the account executives?

M You should ask them the following: Can the printing firm deliver high quality but affordable output? Can it give you a price quote immediately? If the firm can't work within your budget, can it suggest other options? Finally, can the printing staff meet the production schedule you've set?

F I can see that the answers to those questions are important, but to be really honest about it, 44) Oliver, it's my production deadline that worries me. This project requires a full-time book designer for at least two months, but I haven't found one yet. All the designers I know have prior commitments.

M 43) In that case, find out if the printing firm itself can do the design job for you. This is why it's better to get a printer that employs full-time in-house graphic designers and layout artists. That way, pre-press production work, offset printing, and binding can be done in only one place. Coordination would be a lot easier for you.

F Yes, that's right. But are you saying that I should entrust the project only to a well-established printer?

M Not necessarily, Cynthia. 45) Even start-up printing firms can do a good job for you. In fact, since they're just beginning to build a name, they are usually more eager to impress their new clients. Just be sure to look at enough samples of their work and a list of their major clients.

F 46) Thanks, Oliver! Your advice definitely took out some of my worries. Now I'm more confident that the book project will proceed smoothly.

Words

suppose 생각하다, 추정하다
assign 맡기다, 배정하다
printer 인쇄소, 인쇄업자
task 일, 업무
affordable (가격이) 저렴한, 알맞은
in-house 사내의, 조직 내의
well-established 안정적인
impress 깊은 인상을 주다, 감명을 주다
account executive 회계 담당자, 회계부 이사
souvenir book 기념도서
reliable 믿을 만한
operation 기업, 사업체
handle 취급하다, 처리하다
budget 예산
binding 제본
start-up 신흥의, 새로 시작하는
proceed 진행되다

해석

F 안녕, Oliver! 나는 네가 라이프스타일 잡지사에서 마케팅 업무를 하고 있다고 들어서, 나는 네가 인쇄 서비스에 대해 많이 알고 있을 거라고 생각해. 40) 어떻게 하면 좋은 인쇄소를 선택할 수 있는 지에 대해 조언해 줄 수 있어?

M 41) 당연하지, Cynthia! 그런데 너는 인쇄서비스가 왜 필요해?

F 글쎄, 41) 나는 우리 회사 25주년을 축하는 도서를 편집하려고 해. 나는 여기 보스턴에서 운영되는 신뢰할 만한 인쇄소를 찾는 일을 맡았어.

M 회사에서 이미 거래하고 있는 인쇄소가 있지 않아? 그곳에서 회사 안내 책자와 문구류를 제작하지 않아?

F 맞아, 그런데 유감스럽게도 다음 주에 보스턴에서 운영을 중단한대. 필라델피아로 회사를 옮긴다네.

M 그렇구나. 글쎄, 내 생각에 네가 가장 먼저 할 일은 이곳 보스턴에 있는 다른 인쇄소들을 비교하는 거야. 그 회사들의 회계 담당자에게서 직접 정보를 얻으려고 노력해봐. 알아봐야 할 중요한 것은 그 회사가 너희 회사 프로젝트를 처리할 수 있는 장비를 갖추고 있는 지야.

F 42) 네 말은 내가 인쇄소를 방문해서 그들의 시설을 살펴봐야 한다는 거지?

M 42) 그렇게 하면 도움이 되겠지만, 모든 중요한 질문들을 인쇄소 회계 담당자에게 하면 시간을 절약할 수 있어. 회계를 맡고 있는 직원들은 그런 질문에 답변하기에 적합한 직책이야.

F 그렇구나. 나는 회계 담당자에게 어떤 질문을 해야 할까?

M 다음과 같은 질문을 하는 것이 좋아. 인쇄소가 좋은 품질을 저렴한 가격대로 출력 해줄 수 있는지? 즉시 가격 견적서를 보내줄 수 있는지? 만약 인쇄소가 예산 범위 내에서 작업을 할 수 없다면, 다른 선택사항들을 제안할 수 있는지? 마지막으로 인쇄소 직원이 네가 정한 제작 일정을 맞출 수 있는지?

F 나도 그러한 질문들에 대한 답변이 중요하다는 것은 알겠는데, 솔직히, 44) Oliver, 제작 마감일이 걱정돼. 이 프로젝트는 북 디자이너가 전임으로 적어도 두 달은 작업을 해야 하는데, 아직 디자이너를 구하지 못했거든. 내가 아는 모든 디자이너들이 이미 다른 일을 하기로 되어있어서.

M 43) 그런 경우라면, 인쇄소가 자체적으로 디자인 작업을 해줄 수 있는지도 알아봐. 전업 사내 그래픽 디자이너와 레이아웃 아티스트를 고용하는 인쇄소를 이용하는 것이 더 좋은 이유이기도 하지. 그런 방식으로 사전 출력 작업, 오프셋 인쇄, 및 제본도 한 곳에서 할 수 있어. 조직화 작업이 훨씬 더 편해질 거야.

F 맞아. 그런데 네가 말하는 것은 내가 그 프로젝트를 안정적인 인쇄소에만 맡겨야 된다는 거지?

M 꼭 그럴 필요는 없어 Cynthia. 45) 심지어 새로 시작하는 업체라도 일을 잘 해줄 수 있어. 사실 그들은 이제 막 이름을 알리는 시작단계라서, 보통 새로운 고객들에게 더 깊은 인상을 주려고 노력해. 그들이 했던 충분한 작업 샘플과 주요고객 목록은 꼭 확인해.

F 46) 고마워 Oliver! 네 조언이 확실히 몇 가지 우려했던 점들을 해결해 줬어. 이제 도서 프로젝트가 원활하게 진행될 수 있을 거라는 자신감이 생겼어.

40 ▶ 정답 ⓑ

About what did the woman ask the man's advice for?
(a) buying a good printer
(b) choosing a printing company
(c) starting a printing business
(d) working for a magazine

해설
여자는 무엇에 관해 남자에게 조언을 구했나요?
(a) 좋은 프린터 구매
(b) 인쇄소 선택
(c) 인쇄소 사업 시작
(d) 잡지사 작업

해설 "Could you give me some advice on how to choose a good thing company?"를 통해 인쇄소를 선택하는데 있어 조언을 구하는 것임을 알 수 있다.

41 ▶ 정답 ⓓ

Why was the woman asking about printers?
(a) She needed the most affordable printing service.
(b) She wanted a printer with modern facilities.
(c) She needed a printer with highly-skilled technicians.
(d) She needed a good printer in the city where she works.

해설
여자는 왜 인쇄소에 대해 물어 보았나요?

(a) 그녀는 가장 저렴한 인쇄 서비스가 필요했다.
(b) 그녀는 현대적인 시설을 갖춘 인쇄소를 원했다.
(c) 그녀는 고도로 숙련 된 기술자가 있는 인쇄소를 필요로 했다.
(d) 그녀는 그녀가 근무하는 도시에 있는 좋은 인쇄소를 필요로 했다.

해설 "I'll be editing a souvenir book for our company's 25th year in business. I was assigned to find a reliable printer that operates right here in Boston."를 통해 그녀가 근무하는 도시인 보스턴에서 좋은 인쇄소를 찾아야 하기 때문에 남자에게 인쇄소에 대해 물었음을 알 수 있다.

42 ▶ 정답 ⓒ

Who did the man say is in the best position to give details about the capability of a particular printer?
(a) a marketing specialist
(b) a publication designer
(c) an account executive
(d) an editorial assistant

해설
남자는 특정한 인쇄소의 역량에 관한 세부 정보를 제공하는 데 누가 가장 좋은 위치에 있다고 말했나요?
(a) 마케팅 전문가
(b) 출판 설계자
(c) 회계 담당자
(d) 편집 보조원

해설 "you can save time by simply asking the printing account executive all the important questions. Account executives are in an excellent position to answer those."를 통해 회계 담당자가 정보를 주는데 가장 적합한 사람임을 알 수 있다.

43 ▶ 정답 ⓐ

What did the man cite as a publishing task that could be provided by the printing firm itself?
(a) design and layout
(b) distribution
(c) large-format printing
(d) direct mail

해설
인쇄소 자체가 제공 할 수 있는 출판 작업으로 남자가 언급한 것은 무엇인가요?
(a) 디자인 및 레이아웃
(b) 유통
(c) 대형 인쇄
(d) 광고용 우편물

해설 "In that case, find out if the printing firm itself can do the design job for you. This is why it's better to get a printer that employs full-time in-house graphic designers and layout artists."를

인쇄소가 직접 고용한 전문가를 통해 디자인 및 레이아웃 작업이 가능함을 언급하고 있다.

44 ▶ 정답 ⓓ

How did the woman initially feel about the schedule of her project?

(a) excited
(b) annoyed
(c) confident
(d) anxious

해석

여자는 처음에 그녀의 프로젝트 일정에 대해 어떻게 생각했나요?

(a) 신난
(b) 짜증난
(c) 자신감 있는
(d) 염려스러운

해설 "Oliver, it's my production deadline that worries me."를 통해 대화 초반에 업무 마감일을 맞추지 못할 것에 대해 걱정했음을 알 수 있다.

45 ▶ 정답 ⓐ

What was said about start-up printing firms?

(a) They are eager to please their new clients.
(b) They can offer a wider range of services.
(c) They are considered a practical choice by reputable clients.
(d) They offer lower prices than famous printing firms.

해석

신생 인쇄소에 관해 언급된 것은 무엇인가요?

(a) 새로운 고객을 만족시키고자 열성적이다.
(b) 더 넓은 범위의 서비스를 제공 할 수 있다.
(c) 믿을 만한 고객들의 실질적인 선택으로 여겨진다.
(d) 유명한 인쇄소보다 저렴한 가격을 제공한다.

해설 "Not necessarily, Cynthia. Even start-up printing firms can do a good job for you. In fact, since they're just beginning to build a name, they are usually more eager to impress their new clients."를 통해 신생 인쇄소들은 고객을 만족시키려고 더 노력한다는 것을 알 수 있다.

46 ▶ 정답 ⓒ

Why likely did the woman feel more positive after the conversation?

(a) because the man will be doing her job for her
(b) because she already found a printing company
(c) because she became more informed about her task
(d) because she has accepted that the project would fail

해석

대화 이후, 여자가 더 긍정적인 기분을 느낀 이유는 무엇이었나요?

(a) 남자는 그녀를 위해 일할 것이기 때문에
(b) 그녀가 이미 벌써 인쇄소를 발견했기 때문에
(c) 그녀가 그녀의 일에 대해 더 많이 알기 때문에
(d) 그 프로젝트가 실패할 것이라는 것을 그녀가 받아들였기 때문에

해설 "Thanks, Oliver! Your advice definitely took out some of my worries. Now I'm more confident that the book project will proceed smoothly."의 언급을 통해 걱정하던 부분이 해소될 정도로 정보를 얻고 자신감을 얻었음을 알 수 있다.

[Part 4]

Now listen to the questions.

47: To whom is the talk most likely being given?
48: What material is needed to complete the papermaking frame?
49: How was the paper pulp described in the talk?
50: According to the speaker, what should be done when the papermaking frame has dried?
51: Why should the recycled paper be ironed?
52: What was mentioned as an optional material in making recycled paper?

해석

47: 설명은 누구를 대상으로 하고 있나요?
48: 제지 틀을 완성하는 데 필요한 재료는 무엇인가요?
49: 설명에서 종이 펄프가 어떻게 묘사 되었나요?
50: 화자에 따르면, 제지 틀이 말랐을 때 무엇을 해야 하나요?
51: 재활용 종이를 다림질해야 하는 이유는 무엇인가요?
52: 재활용 종이를 만들 때 선택 사항으로 언급 된 것은 무엇인가요?

Now you will hear the talk.

47) I know you are all interested in making money out of recycled materials, so I will be showing you how to make recycled paper in your own home. It's an exciting way to earn extra cash--and it's environment-friendly, too! The process is simple.

First, cut some old newspapers and other used sheets of paper into two-inch squares. Second, fill a big basin with water up to four inches high. Third, get an old food processor or blender, an old wire hanger, used nylon stockings or pantyhose, white glue, extra water, and an electric iron.

48) Fourth, make a papermaking frame out of the old

wire hanger by shaping it into a rectangle or square. After that, take the nylon stocking and stretch it flat to cover the wire frame.

Fifth, put the frame aside while you put a handful of paper and some water into the food processor. Set the processor to "high" and blend the mixture until it turns mushy. 49) Keep adding paper and water until the mixture becomes a big, gray blob, which is called the "pulp." To make the pulp smooth, just add more water to it. Keep the food processor on until all the paper is crushed, and then leave it on for another two minutes.

Sixth, put two tablespoons of white glue in the basin of water and add all of the paper pulp you have just made. Mix it well with your hands. Seventh, take the wire-and-nylon frame, dip it all the way to the bottom of the basin, and lift it slowly. Hold the frame for a minute to drain the water.

50) Eighth, hang the frame on a clothesline, preferably under the sun. Let the frame dry before gently peeling off the paper. 51) Finally, use a flat-iron on low heat to smoothen the paper.

Remember that you can keep making paper until you've used up all the pulp. Just be sure to mix the remaining pulp in the basin every time you decide to make a new piece. You can make as many pieces as you like by using several frames and drying them simultaneously.

52) If you want your recycled paper to have different colors and textures, simply add food coloring, onionskin, small leaves, or flower petals to the paper pulp.

Follow those steps, and soon with a little hard work, you'll be earning money from paper!

Words

extra 가외의, 추가의
blender 믹서기
glue 접착제, 풀
frame 틀
a handful of 소량의
blob 걸쭉한 작은 덩이
dip 담그다
preferably 가급적
smoothen 매끄럽게 하다
texture 질감

basin 물그릇, 대야
wire hanger 옷걸이
electric iron 전기 다리미
flat 평평한
mushy 무른, 흐물흐물한
crush 분쇄하다, 으깨다
drain 물기를 없애다, 배수하다
peel off 벗기다
simultaneously 동시에
flower petal 꽃잎

47

▶ 정답 ⓑ

To whom is the talk most likely being given?

(a) to students who want to practice their skills in the arts
(b) to people who want to earn from a home-based craft
(c) to workers who are learning new jobs in a factory
(d) to volunteers who wish to preserve the environment

48 ▶ 정답 ⓒ

What material is needed to complete the papermaking frame?

(a) white glue
(b) an old cotton shirt
(c) an old wire hanger
(d) an electric iron

해석 제지 틀을 완성하는 데 필요한 재료는 무엇인가요?

(a) 흰색 접착제
(b) 오래된 면 셔츠
(c) 낡은 철사 옷걸이
(d) 전기다리미

해설 "Fourth, make a papermaking frame out of the old wire hanger by shaping it into a rectangle or square."에서 낡은 철사 옷걸이가 제지용 틀을 만드는 데 사용된다는 것을 확인할 수 있다.

49 ▶ 정답 ⓐ

How was the paper pulp described in the talk?

(a) thick and grayish
(b) unevenly textured
(c) completely white
(d) extremely sticky

해석 강연에서 종이 펄프가 어떻게 묘사 되었나요?

(a) 걸쭉하고 회색인
(b) 고르지 않은 질감인
(c) 완전히 흰색인
(d) 매우 끈적끈적한

해설 "Keep adding paper and water until the mixture becomes a big, gray blob, which is called the "pulp"."를 통해 펄프는 회색 빛깔이 나는 걸쭉한 덩어리임을 알 수 있다.

50 ▶ 정답 ⓓ

According to the speaker, what should be done when the papermaking frame has dried?

(a) The frame should be laid on a flat surface.
(b) The paper should be cut into smaller pieces.
(c) The frame should be exposed to direct heat.
(d) The paper should be peeled off carefully.

해석 화자에 따르면, 제지 틀이 말랐을 때 무엇을 해야 하나요?

(a) 틀은 평평한 표면 위에 두어야 한다.
(b) 더 작은 조각들로 종이를 잘라야 한다.
(c) 틀을 직접 열에 노출시켜야 한다.
(d) 종이를 조심스럽게 벗겨야 한다.

해설 "Eighth, hang the frame on a clothesline, preferably under the sun. Let the frame dry before gently peeling off the paper."를 통해 제지 틀이 마르면 종이를 벗겨내는 작업을 해야 한다는 것을 확인할 수 있다.

51 ▶ 정답 ⓑ

Why should the recycled paper be ironed?

(a) to put patterns onto it
(b) to smoothen its surface
(c) to dry it more quickly
(d) to increase its durability

해석 왜 재활용 종이를 다림질해야 하나요?

(a) 그 위에 패턴을 두기 위해서
(b) 그것의 표면을 매끄럽게 하기 위해서
(c) 그것을 더 빨리 말리기 위해서
(d) 그것의 내구성을 더 증가시키기 위해서

해설 "Finally, use a flat-iron on low heat to smoothen the paper."를 통해 종이 표면을 매끄럽게 하기 위해 다림질을 한다고 언급되었다.

52 ▶ 정답 ⓐ

What was mentioned as an optional material in making recycled paper?

(a) colors
(b) glue
(c) blending agents
(d) water

해석 재활용 종이를 만들 때 선택 사항으로 언급된 것은 무엇인가요?

(a) 색상
(b) 접착제
(c) 혼합제
(d) 물

해설 "If you want your recycled paper to have different colors and textures, simply add food coloring, onionskin, small leaves, or flower petals to the paper pulp."에서 다양한 색감이나 질감은 원하면 추가할 수 있다는 것을 알 수 있다.

Reading and Vocabulary 02회

Question 53-80

ANSWER KEY p.55

53	ⓓ	54	ⓐ	55	ⓑ	56	ⓓ
57	ⓒ	58	ⓐ	59	ⓑ	60	ⓒ
61	ⓑ	62	ⓓ	63	ⓒ	64	ⓐ
65	ⓑ	66	ⓐ	67	ⓒ	68	ⓓ
69	ⓒ	70	ⓐ	71	ⓑ	72	ⓐ
73	ⓒ	74	ⓓ	75	ⓒ	76	ⓑ
77	ⓓ	78	ⓐ	79	ⓒ	80	ⓓ

Question 53-59

ISADORA DUNCAN

Isadora Duncan was an American dancer who developed less traditional, freer forms of movement that influenced modern dance techniques. She is widely known as the "Mother of Modern Dance."

Isadora Duncan was born Dora Angela Duncan on May 27, 1878 in San Francisco, California. She was the youngest of the four children of Joseph Charles Duncan, a bank employee and art lover, and Mary Gray, a pianist and music teacher. Dora and her siblings lived with their mother after her parents divorced. 53) At the age of six, Dora helped support her family by teaching local children how to dance. As a teenager, Duncan joined Augustin Daly's theater company and performed in stage productions in Chicago and New York. Although she studied ballet, the young dancer experimented with freer, more natural ballet movements that were less traditional.

In 1899, Duncan moved to London with her family. 54) There, she observed the ancient Greek sculptures at the British Museum and started 58) associating her own dance movements with the free-flowing classical movements found in the artworks. Later on, she would dance barefoot and wear flowing costumes patterned after classical Greek designs. 55) As ballet became a less popular art form in the early 20th century, Duncan's choreography was increasingly admired for its "natural movement," which included skipping, jumping, and running. Her performances in Europe were eagerly received.

Duncan's bohemian attitude applied not only to her profession but also to her personal life. 56) She would have a number of rich male partners and illegitimate children, and was strongly criticized in conservative circles. As an artist, however, she sought to promote among audiences a new awareness of human emotions and social realities. Ultimately, her liberating approach to movement made her known as the pioneer of modern dance.

Duncan established dance schools in Europe to share her art. The first opened in 1904 in Grunewald, Germany, where she welcomed students from poor families. 57) Duncan's career would be 59) disrupted when her two children died in an accident in 1913. She was able to recover only when she returned to teaching and holding dance tours. She was eventually forced to close her school in Germany, and later, another school in Moscow, due to lack of funds. She then spent her time performing mostly in Europe.

In 1922, Isadora Duncan married the Russian poet Sergei Yesenin, but their marriage failed after three years. She spent the rest of her sad life in Nice, France. She died in a car accident on September 14, 1927. Her autobiography, My Life, was published in 1928.

Words

traditional 전통의, 전통적인
local 지역의, 현지의
experiment 시도하다, 실험하다
associate 결부시키다
barefoot 맨발의
attitude 태도, 자세
profession 직업
conservative 보수적인
social reality 사회적인 현실
liberate 자유롭게 해주다
establish 설립하다, 세우다
fund 자금
sibling 형제자매
perform 공연하다
sculpture 조각상, 조각품
free-flowing 자유로운 흐름
choreography 안무
apply 적용하다
illegitimate 사생아로 태어난, 불법인
awareness 의식
ultimately 궁극적으로
pioneer 선구자, 개척자
recover 회복하다
autobiography 자서전

해석

이사도라 던컨

이사도라 던컨은 전통에 얽매이지 않은 좀 더 자유로운 형태의 동작을 개발하여 현대 무용기술에 영향을 끼친 미국의 무용수였다. 그녀는 '현대무용의 어머니'로 널리 알려져 있다.

이사도라 던컨은 캘리포니아의 샌프란시스코에서 1878년 5월 27일 도라 안젤라 던컨으로 태어났다. 그녀는 은행직원이며 예술 애호가인 Joseph Charles Duncan과 피아니스트이며 음악교사인 Mary Gray의 네 자녀 중 막내였다. 도라와 형제들은 그녀의 부모님이 이혼한 후 어머니와 함께 생활했다. 53) 여섯 살 때, 도라는 지역의 아이들에게 춤추는 법을 가르쳐 가족 부양하는 것을 도왔다. 십대 때 던컨은 Augustin Daly's theater company에 입단하여 시카고와 뉴욕에서 연극공연을 했다. 발레를 전공했음에도 불구하고, 그 젊은 무용가는 전통을 따르지 않은 더 자유롭고 자연스러운 발레동작을 시도했다.

1899년, 던컨은 가족과 함께 런던으로 이사했다. 54) 그 곳에서, 그녀는 고대 그리스 조각상들을 대영박물관에서 관찰하고, 예술작품에서 찾아낸 자유로운 흐름의 고전적인 동작들을 그녀의 무용동작에 결부시키기 시작했다. 후에, 그녀는 맨발로 춤을 추었고, 고대 그리스 디자인을 본떠 만든 늘어뜨린 의상을 입었다. 55) 20세기 초반, 발레의 인기가 떨어지자, skipping (줄넘기), jumping (뛰어넘기), 및 running (달리기)을 포함한 던컨의 안무는 '자연스러운 움직임'으로 더욱 찬사를 받았다. 그녀의 유럽 공연은 열렬한 호응을 받았다. 던컨의 보헤미안적인 태도는 그녀의 직업뿐 아니라 그녀의 사생활에도 적용되었다. 56) 그녀는 수많은 부유한 연인들과 사생아가 있었으며, 보수파들로부터 많은 비난을 받았다. 하지만, 예술가로서 그녀는 관객들에게 인간의 감정과 사회적인 현실에 관한 새로운 의식을 고취시키고자 했다. 궁극적으로, 그녀의 자유로운 동작 접근법은 그녀를 현대무용의 선구자로 알려지게 만들었다.

던컨은 그녀의 예술을 공유하기 위해 유럽에 무용학교를 세웠다. 첫 번째 학교가 1904년 독일 Grunewald에서 문을 열었고, 그녀는 가난한 가정의 학생들을 따뜻하게 맞이했다. 57) 던컨의 경력은 1913년 사고로 그녀의 두 자녀가 사망했을 때 중단되었다. 그녀는 무용 순회공연을 할 때와 춤을 가르치러 돌아다닐 때만 (자녀들의 사망으로 인한 슬픔에서) 회복될 수 있었다. 그녀는 결국 독일에 있는 학교를 닫을 수밖에 없었고, 후에 자금부족으로 모스크바에 있는 학교도 문을 닫았다. 그 후에 그녀는 주로 유럽에서 공연을 하며 시간을 보냈다.

1922년 이사도라 던컨은 러시아 시인 Sergei Yesenin (세르게이 예세닌)과 결혼했으나, 그들의 결혼생활은 3년 후 끝났다. 그녀는 남은 생을 프랑스의 니스에서 보냈다. 그녀는 1927년 9월 14일 자동차 사고로 사망했다. 그녀의 자서전인 My Life는 1928년 출간되었다.

53 ▶ 정답 ⓓ

What did the young Isadora Duncan do to help support her family?

(a) perform in ballet productions
(b) teach other children music
(c) develop new dance moves
(d) teach other children dancing

해설

어린 이사도라 던컨이 가족의 부양을 돕기 위해 한 것은 무엇인가요?

(a) 발레 공연을 했다
(b) 다른 아이들에게 음악을 가르쳤다
(c) 새로운 무용동작을 개발했다
(d) 다른 아이들에게 무용을 가르쳤다

해설 "At the age of six, Dora helped support her family by teaching local children how to dance."를 통해 도라는 가족 부양을 돕기 위해 아이들에게 댄스를 가르친 것을 알 수 있다.

54 ▶ 정답 ⓐ

What did Isadora Duncan use as a basis for her dance movements and costumes?

(a) classical Greek art
(b) modern British dance
(c) popular American music
(d) traditional German ballet

해설

이사도라 던컨이 자신의 무용동작과 의상에 관한 기본원리로 사용했던 것은 무엇인가요?

(a) 고전 그리스 예술
(b) 현대 영국 무용
(c) 미국 대중음악
(d) 전통적인 독일의 발레

해설 "There, she observed the ancient Greek sculptures at the British Museum and started 58) associating her own dance movements with the free-flowing classical movements found in the artworks. Later on, she would dance barefoot and wear flowing costumes patterned after classical Greek designs."를 통해 고대 그리스 예술의 영향을 받았다는 것을 알 수 있다.

55 ▶ 정답 ⓑ

Based on the passage, what can be said about modern dance?

(a) It never replaced traditional ballet in the 20th century.
(b) It was a welcome change from an outdated dance style.
(c) It made the audience more emotional.
(d) It is a financially stable art form.

해설

지문을 토대로, 현대무용에 관해 알 수 있는 것은 무엇인가요?

(a) 20세기에 전통발레를 대체하지 못했다.
(b) 시대에 뒤쳐진 무용방식에서 환영받은 변화였다.
(c) 청중들을 좀 더 감성적으로 만들었다.
(d) 경제적으로 안정된 예술형태이다.

해설 "As ballet became a less popular art form in the early 20th century, Duncan's choreography was increasingly admired for its "natural movement," which included skipping, jumping, and running."에서 자연스러운 움직임으로 찬사 받았다는 내용이 언급되어 있다.

56 ▶ 정답 ⓓ

Why did Duncan receive criticisms in traditional circles?

(a) because of her unusual costumes
(b) because of her fast dance moves
(c) because of her wealthy dance partners
(d) because of her unchecked lifestyle

해석
던컨이 보수파로부터 비난 받은 이유는 무엇인가요?
(a) 그녀의 특이한 의상 때문에
(b) 그녀의 빠른 춤 동작 때문에
(c) 그녀의 부유한 무용 파트너들 때문에
(d) 그녀의 문란한 생활방식 때문에

해설 "She would have a number of rich male partners and illegitimate children, and was strongly criticized in conservative circles."를 통해 그녀가 비난 받은 이유가 문란한 생활방식 때문이라는 것을 알 수 있다.

57 ▶ 정답 ⓒ

How did Duncan get over the untimely death of her children?

(a) by building her first school
(b) by marrying a literary artist
(c) by pursuing her career
(d) by closing her schools

해석
던컨은 어떻게 자녀들의 갑작스러운 사망을 극복했나요?
(a) 그녀의 첫 번째 학교를 세움으로써
(b) 문학가와 결혼하는 것으로써
(c) 그녀의 일을 계속 하는 것으로써
(d) 그녀의 학교를 닫는 것으로써

해설 "Duncan's career would be 59) disrupted when her two children died in an accident in 1913. She was able to recover only when she returned to teaching and holding dance tours."를 통해 춤을 추고 가르치는 일을 통해 자녀들의 사망을 극복한 것을 알 수 있다.

58 ▶ 정답 ⓐ

In the context of the passage, associating means _____.

(a) connecting
(b) developing
(c) separating
(d) combining

해석
문맥상, associating는 _____을 의미한다.
(a) 연결하다, 결부시키다
(b) 개발하다
(c) 분리시키다
(d) 결합하다, 연합하다

해설 associate 결부시키다, 연관시키다

59 ▶ 정답 ⓑ

In the context of the passage, disrupted means _____.

(a) offended
(b) stopped
(c) disjointed
(d) promoted

해석
문맥상 disrupted는 _____을 의미한다.
(a) 불쾌하게 했다
(b) 중단했다
(c) 관절을 삐게 했다
(d) 촉진시키다

해설 disrupt 중단하다, 방해하다

Question 60-64

60) 64) RESEARCH SHOWS THAT FIRSTBORNS GAIN HIGHER I.Q.

A study found that the eldest children in families are more likely to have a higher "intelligence quotient" (I.Q., or a person's intelligence as compared to those of other people their age) than their younger siblings. The results, which were published in two journals, Science and Intelligence, are solely due to family dynamics, and are independent of biological factors such as a person's genes and development before birth.

61) In the study, Norweigan scientists analyzed the birth order, health status, and I.Q. scores of 241,000 men, using their military records. The men were aged 18 to 19 and born from 1967 to 1976. The study excluded other factors including the mother's age, parents' education, and family size. The results showed that the average I.Q. score of firstborns was 103.2: almost 3% higher than that of second children (100.3), and over 4% higher than that of thirdborns (99.0).

Although a discrepancy of three IQ points seems small, it is significant: The difference between "gifted" and "above average" intelligence may mean the distinction between admission to an elite school and a common public school, which could open up more opportunities for the firstborn.

62) The study eliminated the biological factor by analyzing the scores of "accidental firstborns," or those who became the eldest after an older sibling died. Their scores

were generally the same as those of biological firstborns.

Different theories explain why the eldest children have higher I.Q. One theory is that firstborns had their parents' undivided attention for a longer time than their younger siblings, giving them an early edge in developing their language and reasoning abilities. Another cites the tendency of elder children to teach their younger siblings, giving them more practice at organizing information, which builds their I.Q.

63) Another theory involves the siblings' inclination to find their place in the family. Firstborns are usually regarded as more responsible and achievement-oriented, so younger siblings distinguish themselves by developing other skills such as high sociability and musical talent. However, these skills are not measured by I.Q. tests.

The results would lead to more in-depth research about family dynamics. Since gender has little effect on I.Q., the results could also apply to females.

Words

intelligence 지능
family dynamics 가족 역학
gene 유전자
firstborn 맏이, 첫째
distinction 차이, 구별
edge 우위, 유리함
cite 언급하다
inclination 경향, 성향, 기질
distinguish oneself 두각을 나타내다, 뛰어나다
solely 오로지, 단지
independent of 관계없이, 별도로
exclude 제외하다, 배제하다
discrepancy 차이, 불일치
eliminate 제거하다
reasoning ability 추리력
tendency 성향, 경향
sociability 사교성

해석

60) 64) 연구는 맏이들이 더 높은 I.Q.를 가지고 있다는 것을 보여 준다

연구에 따르면 가족 중 첫째 아이들은 다른 형제, 자매보다 높은 "지능지수"(I.Q. 또는 다른 또래의 지능과 비교되는 한 사람의 지능)를 가지고 있을 가능성이 더 높다. 두 개의 전문잡지, Science 와 Intelligence에 발표된 결과는 전적으로 가족 역학에 기인하는 것이며 출생 전 유전자 및 발달과 같은 생물학적 요인과는 관련이 없다.

61) 이 연구에서 노르웨이 과학자들은 241,000명의 남성들의 징병 기록을 사용하여 출생 순서, 건강 상태 및 I.Q. 지수를 분석했다. 남성들은 18세~19세였으며, 1967~1976년 사이에 태어났다. 이 연구는 어머니의 나이, 부모의 교육 정도, 가족 수 등 다른 요인들은 배제했다. 결과는 맏이들의 평균 I.Q. 지수는 103.2 : 두 번째 자녀의 지수(100.3)보다 거의 3% 높았으며, 세 번째 자녀의 지수(99.0)보다 4% 이상 높았다.

세 가지 I.Q. 지수 차이는 작지만 중요하다. '영재'와 '평균 이상' 지능 사이의 차이는 엘리트 학교와 일반 공립학교의 입학 여부 차이를 의미할 수 있으며, 이는 첫째들에게 더 많은 기회들을 열어줄 수 있다. 62) 이 연구는 '우연히 맏이가 된 사람들', 즉 손위 형제가 사망한 후 맏이가 된 사람들의 지수를 분석함으로써 생물학적 요인을 제거했다. 그들의 지수는 생물학적인 맏이들 지수와 대체로 같았다.

여러 이론들은 맏이들이 I.Q.가 더 높은 이유를 설명한다. 한 가지 이론은 맏이들이 그들의 어린 형제들보다 더 오랜 시간 동안 그들의 부모로부터 관심을 온전히 받았기 때문에 그들의 언어와 추리력을 발전시키는 데 있어 일찌감치 우위를 가졌다는 것이다. 다른 이론은 맏이들이 어린 동생들을 가르치는 경향이 있고, 그들은 정보를 구성하는 연습을 하게 되고, 그것이 지능을 발달시키게 된다고 말한다.

63) 또 다른 이론은 형제들이 가족 내에서 자신의 위치를 찾으려는 경향을 내포한다. 맏이들은 일반적으로 더 책임 있고 성취지향적인 것으로 간주되어, 어린 형제들은 높은 사교성 및 음악적 재능과 같은 다른 기술을 개발함으로써 두각을 드러낸다. 하지만 이러한 기술들은 I.Q. 테스트로 측정되지 않는다. 이 결과들은 가족 역학에 관한 심층 연구로 이어질 것이다. 성별은 I.Q.에 거의 영향을 미치지 않으므로, 결과는 여성에게도 적용될 수 있다.

60 ▶ 정답 ⓒ

Which was a finding of the study?

(a) Firstborns had an average I.Q.
(b) Secondborns had the lowest intelligence scores.
(c) Firstborns outscored their younger siblings in I.Q.
(d) Most firstborns go to prestigious schools.

해석
어떤 것이 연구 결과인가요?
(a) 맏이들은 평균적인 I.Q.를 가졌다.
(b) 둘째들은 가장 낮은 지능지수를 가졌다.
(c) I.Q에서 맏이들은 어린 동생들보다 높았다.
(d) 대부분의 맏이들은 명문학교에 간다.

해설 연구결과를 묻는 문제인데, 제목에서부터 '맏이들이 IQ 지수가 더 높다'로 했으므로 쉽게 정답을 찾을 수 있다.

61 ▶ 정답 ⓑ

How did the researchers gather information for the study?

(a) by administering I.Q. tests to siblings
(b) by looking at past records of intelligence
(c) by following babies from birth until adulthood
(d) by analyzing the personal records of siblings

해석
어떻게 연구자들은 연구 정보를 수집했나요?
(a) 형제자매들에게 I.Q. 테스트를 함으로써
(b) 과거의 지능 기록들을 봄으로써
(c) 출생부터 성인기까지 아기들을 관찰함으로써
(d) 형제자매들의 개인적인 기록들을 분석함으로써

해설 연구를 위해 남성들의 징병기록을 이용했고, 징병기록은 1967~1976년 사이에 출생한 18~19세였던 남성들이었다고 밝혔다. (b)가 가장 적절한 정답이다.

62 ▶ 정답 ⓓ

What did the results among non-biological firstborns show?

(a) that biological firstborns are more intelligent
(b) that the results only apply to natural firstborns
(c) that I.Q. is a purely biological trait
(d) that the difference in I.Q. isn't inborn

해석
비 생물적 맏이들 간에 결과는 무엇을 보여주나요?
(a) 생물학적 맏이들이 더 지능적이다.
(b) 결과는 자연적인 맏이들에게만 적용이 된다.
(c) I.Q.는 순전히 생물학적인 특성이다.
(d) I.Q.의 차이는 선천적이지 않다.

해설 "The study eliminated the biological factor by analyzing the scores of "accidental firstborns," or those who became the eldest after an older sibling died. Their scores were generally the same as those of biological firstborns."을 통해 형제자매들 간의 IQ차이는 선천적인 것이 아니라는 것을 알 수 있다.

63 ▶ 정답 ⓒ

According to a theory, why most likely do younger siblings have lower I.Q.s?

(a) They only rely on firstborns to gain knowledge.
(b) They are born lacking in intelligence.
(c) They don't pursue what the firstborns are already good at.
(d) Parents give unequal attention to their children.

해석
이론에 따르면, 왜 대부분의 어린 형제자매들이 더 낮은 I.Q.를 가지나요?
(a) 지식을 얻기 위해서 그들은 오직 맏이들에게만 의지한다.
(b) 그들은 지능이 부족한 상태로 태어난다.
(c) 그들은 맏이들이 이미 잘하는 것을 추구하지 않는다.
(d) 부모는 그들의 아이들에게 불공평한 관심을 가진다.

해설 "so younger siblings distinguish themselves by developing other skills such as high sociability and musical talent. However, these skills are not measured by I.Q. tests."를 통해 동생들은 맏이들이 두각을 드러내지 않는 예술적 재주와 같은 것을 추구한다는 것을 알 수 있다.

64 ▶ 정답 ⓐ

What significant conclusion could be inferred from the study?

(a) that intelligence and birth order are related
(b) that firstborns are more successful
(c) that birth order determines school performance
(d) that female firstborns have higher I.Q.s than male ones

해석
연구에서 어떤 중요한 결론을 추론할 수 있나요?
(a) 지능과 출생순서가 연관이 있다.
(b) 맏이들이 더 성공한다.
(c) 출생 순서가 학교 성적을 결정한다.
(d) 여성 맏이들이 남성 맏이들보다 더 I.Q.가 높다.

해설 firstborns들의 지능이 생물학적이건 비생물학적이건 IQ 지수가 동생들보다 높다는 것은 출생순서와 관련있다고 추론할 수 있다.

65 ▶ 정답 ⓑ

In the context of the passage, solely means _____.

(a) clearly
(b) only
(c) simply
(d) also

해석
문맥상 solely는 ____을 의미한다.
(a) 확실히, 명백하게
(b) 오직, 단지
(c) 단지, 간단하게
(d) 또한

해설 solely 오로지, 전적으로

66 ▶ 정답 ⓐ

In the context of the passage, edge means _____.

(a) advantage
(b) boundary
(c) start
(d) border

해석
문맥상 edge는 ____을 의미한다.
(a) 장점, 혜택
(b) 경계(선)
(c) 시작, 출발
(d) 경계, 가장자리

해설 edge 우위, 유리함

Question 67-73

DOMINOES

Dominoes are small, flat, rectangular tiles used to play a variety of games. 67-c) They were probably introduced in Europe from China in the 1300s. 67-b) Most sets of dominoes are made of bone, ivory, plastic, or wood. 67-a) A regular set consists of 28 domino tiles, or "bones," each of which is two inches long. Tiles are one-inch wide and 3/8-inch thick. A line 72) divides each domino into two square "sections." 67-d) Twenty-one of the dominoes have one to six dots, or "pips," on each section. One domino's two sections are both blank, and the six remaining dominoes have one blank section and one section with pips. No two dominoes are alike.

The game was invented in China in the 14th century. Its first recorded reference in Europe is from Italy, where the royalty of Venice and Naples played the game. 68) The tiles were made by gluing two sheets of ebony on either side of the tile. This prevented cheating by allowing a player to see the pip from the back of the tile in certain lights. In the 18th century, the domino game arrived in Britain from France and quickly became popular in inns and taverns. The word "domino" is French for a black and white hood worn by Christian priests in winter.

69) The most commonly played domino games are "blocking games." In these games, one domino is connected to either end of the first domino if the number of its dots 73) matches the number of dots of one (or both) section of the first tile. If, for example, the first tile has a section with four dots, a player can connect to it a tile with one end also marked with a four. 70) A player's goal is to play all his seven tiles (his "hand") while blocking the other player's attempt to do the same. A score may be determined by counting the total pips of the losers' remaining tiles.

71) Dominoes or variants of it are played in almost all countries of the world, but it is most popular in Latin America. The National English Domino and Cribbage Championships have been organized by Keith Masters annually in Stoke on Trent since 1985.

Words

flat 평평한
square 사각형의, 정사각형의
dot 점
alike 같은, 아주 비슷한
royalty 왕족
ebony 흑단
priest 사제, 신부
mark 표시하다
variant 변형, 변종
rectangular 직사각형의
section 부분, 구획
blank 빈
reference 참고(문), 참조(문), 언급
glue 붙이다
hood 두건, 모자
match 일치하다
block 막다

도미노

도미노는 다양한 게임을 하는데 사용되는 작고, 평평한 직사각형 타일이다. 67-c) 그들은 아마도 1300년대 중국에서 유럽으로 소개되었다. 67-b) 대부분 도미노 세트는 뼈, 상아, 플라스틱이나 나무로 만들어진다. 67-a) 일반적인 세트는 28개의 도미노 타일 또는 'bones'로 구성되어 있고, 각각의 길이는 2인치이다. 타일의 폭은 일 인치이고 두께는 3/8인치이다. 각각의 도미노는 하나의 선으로 두 개의 사각형 '섹션'으로 나뉜다. 67-d) 도미노 중에서 21개는 각 섹션에 한 개에서 여섯 개의 점 또는 '핍'을 갖고 있다. 한 도미노의 두 섹션은 모두 비어있고, 나머지 여섯 개의 도미노는 하나의 빈 섹션과 핍으로 되어있는 섹션을 갖고 있다. 두 개의 도미노가 같지 않다.

도미노 게임은 14세기 중국에서 발명되었다. 유럽에서의 최초 기록은 이태리의 베니스와 나폴리 왕족들이 도미노 게임을 했다는 것이다. 68) 이 타일들은 두 장의 흑단을 타일 양면에 붙여서 만들어진 것이었다. 이것은 플레이어가 특정한 불빛에서 타일의 뒤에서 핍을 볼 수 있게 함으로써 부정 행위를 막았다. 18세기, 도미노 게임은 프랑스에서 영국으로 넘어와 여관과 주점에서 빠르게 인기를 얻었다. '도미노'라는 단어는 기독교 사제들이 겨울에 착용하는 흑백 두건을 가리키는 불어이다.

69) 가장 일반적으로 하는 도미노게임은 'blocking games'이다. 이 게임에서, 한 도미노 점들의 수가 첫 번째 타일의 한 섹션(혹은 양 섹션)에 있는 점들의 수와 일치하는 경우, 그것을 첫 번째 도미노의 양쪽 면과 연결할 수 있다. 예를 들어, 첫 번째 타일의 한 섹션에 점이 네 개 있는 경우, 플레이어는 마찬가지로 네 개의 점이 표시된 다른 타일을 그것에 연결할 수 있다. 70) 플레이어의 목표는 자신의 일곱 개 타일들(그의 'hands')을 모두 내면서, 다른 플레이어가 그렇게 하려는 것을 저지하는 것이다. 점수는 패자들에게 남아있는 타일에 있는 핍들을 모두 세어서 결정한다.

71) 도미노나 그 변형된 게임은 전 세계 거의 모든 나라에서 이뤄지지만, 남미에서 가장 인기가 있다. The National English Domino와 Cribbage Championships은 1985년 이후 Keith Masters에 의해 Trent, Stoke에서 해마다 개최되어 오고 있다.

67 ▶ 정답 ⓒ

Which is not a characteristic of dominoes?

(a) They are composed of 28 tiles.
(b) They can be made from different materials.
(c) They first came from Europe.
(d) Most tile sections have dots.

해석

도미노의 특징이 아닌 것은 무엇인가요?

(a) 그들은 28개의 타일로 구성되어 있다.
(b) 그들은 다양한 재료로 만들어질 수 있다.
(c) 그들은 유럽에서 처음 유래했다.
(d) 대부분의 타일 섹션들은 점을 가지고 있다.

해설 도미노는 중국에서 유럽으로 소개되었다고 첫 번째 문단에 나오므로, 유럽에서 처음 유래되었다는 (c)의 진술은 올바르지 않다.

68 ▶ 정답 ⓓ

Why were ebony sheets glued on each side of a domino tile?

(a) to make the tile last longer
(b) to indicate what country the set was made
(c) to make the tile more attractive
(d) to prevent dishonest play during a game

해설 도미노 타일의 각 면에 흑단이 붙어있는 이유는 무엇인가요?

(a) 타일을 더 오래 사용하기 위해
(b) 그 세트를 만든 나라를 표현하기 위해
(c) 타일을 좀 더 보기 좋도록 위해
(d) 게임 중에 부정행위를 예방하기 위해

해설 "The tiles were made by gluing two sheets of ebony on either side of the tile. This prevented cheating by allowing a player to see the pip from the back of the tile in certain lights."을 통해 부정행위를 막기 위해 도미노 타일 각 면에 흑단을 붙인 것을 알 수 있다.

69 ▶ 정답 ⓒ

How is a "blocking game" played?

(a) by linking a tile to one with a smaller number of dots
(b) by being the first to play all tiles with a blank end
(c) by linking tile sections with the same number of dots
(d) by trying to draw the highest total of pips

해설 어떻게 'blocking game'이 이뤄지나요?

(a) 더 적은 점 개수의 타일에 연결함으로써
(b) 빈 면이 있는 타일 모두 먼저 냄으로써
(c) 같은 점 개수의 타일 섹션을 연결함으로써
(d) 가장 높은 핍의 합계를 도출함으로써

해설 The most commonly played domino games are "blocking games." In these games, one domino is connected to either end of the first domino if the number of its dots matches the number of dots of one (or both) section of the first tile.에서 'blocking game'은 점 개수가 같은 타일을 연결하는 게임이라는 것을 확인할 수 있다.

70 ▶ 정답 ⓐ

Who wins in a "blocking game"?

(a) the first player to play all his dominoes
(b) the player with more remaining tiles after the game
(c) the player with the highest total of dots after the game
(d) the last player to play a tile

해설 'blocking game'에서 승자는 누구인가요?

(a) 모든 도미노를 다 낸 첫 번째 플레이어
(b) 게임 종료 후 남은 타일이 많은 플레이어
(c) 게임 종료 후 점의 총합이 가장 높은 플레이어
(d) 타일을 마지막에 낸 플레이어

해설 A player's goal is to play all his seven tiles (his "hand") while blocking the other player's attempt to do the same.의 언급을 통해 도미노를 모두 낸 플레이어가 게임의 승자가 되는 것을 알 수 있다.

71 ▶ 정답 ⓑ

Based on the article, what can be said about the domino game?

(a) One type of dominoes is used worldwide.
(b) It retains its popularity worldwide.
(c) It is exclusively played by Latin Americans today.
(d) It remains an unorganized game.

해설 글을 바탕으로, 도미노 게임에 대해 말할 수 있는 것은 무엇인가요?

(a) 한 종류 도미노가 전 세계에서 사용된다.
(b) 전 세계적으로 인기 있다.
(c) 오늘날 남미 사람들만 하는 게임이다.
(d) 체계적이지 않은 게임이다.

해설 Dominoes or variants of it are played in almost all countries of the world의 언급을 통해 전 세계 모든 국가들에서 행해지고 있다는 것(=인기가 있다)을 알 수 있다.

72 ▶ 정답 ⓐ

In the context of the passage, divides means _____.

(a) separates
(b) decorates
(c) indicates
(d) combines

해설 문맥상 divides는 _____을 의미한다.

(a) 나누다
(b) 장식하다
(c) 나타나다
(d) 결합하다

해설 divide 나누다

73

▶ 정답 ⓒ

In the context of the passage, matches means _____.

(a) exceeds
(b) increases
(c) equals
(d) reduces

해석

문맥상 matches는 _____을 의미한다.
(a) 초과하다
(b) 증가하다
(c) (수나 양 또는 가치가) 같다
(d) 줄이다

해설 match 일치하다

Question 74-80

January 26, 2016

Mr. Christopher D. Gibson
ManagerHamlin Garden Park
2000 Hamlin Boulevard
Tampa, Florida 33612

Dear Mr. Gibson:

I would like to relate to you my family's terrible experience at Hamlin Garden Park. 74) We went to visit your park last Saturday, January 24, to celebrate my birthday. My 1 years old son, Jeff, loved going to Hamlin Garden Park, but that time had not been pleasant for us.

Jeff was enjoying the kiddie rides in your Dinosaur Land until we made the mistake of putting him on one of your little cars that run separately on tracks. 75) He was the last kid to get off a car, and there was an empty toy car behind him. The ride attendant pushed that toy car which hit the back of my son. He sustained a whiplash and started to cry. He was 79) traumatized after that and didn't want to take any more rides.

You must be fully aware of what those rides can do without proper supervision. A fellow park visitor told me a similar accident had happened before. If the cars can possibly hurt kids, why haven't you taken safety measures against it? 76) Obviously, the cars should be operated all together—not independently—to prevent accidents like this from happening.

My husband and I thought that our son's injury wasn't serious until we came home to watch our home video of the incident. We saw how our boy had also been struck on the back of the head by the toy car. 77) If a medical examination shows that something serious happened to our son, I will definitely hold your company responsible and pursue legal actions.

78) I demand that you thoroughly review the safety of all your rides in Dinosaur Land, 80) particularly those for the smaller kids. You have to do this immediately before similar accidents happen. I expect to hear from you soonest about this matter.

Katrina Pitman

Katrina S. Pitman
Ft. Lauderdale, Florida

Words

relate 이야기하다, 들려주다
attendant 안내원
whiplash 외상, 손상
fellow 동료의, 친구 사이인
traumatize 정신적 충격을 주다, 타격을 주다
pursue legal action 소송을 걸다, 법적 조치를 취하다
kiddie ride 어린이용 놀이기구
sustain (피해를) 입다, 당하다
supervision 관리, 감독
safety measure 안전 조치

해석

깁슨 씨께:

저는 Hamlin Garden Park에서 우리 가족이 겪었던 끔찍한 경험을 알려 드리길 원합니다. 74) 지난 1월 24일 토요일에 우리는 제 생일을 축하하기 위해 귀하의 공원에 갔습니다. 제 1살짜리 아들 제프는 Hamlin Garden Park에 가는 것을 좋아했지만, 그 시간은 우리에게 유쾌하지 않았습니다.

우리가 제프를 트랙에서 개별적으로 달리는 작은 차들 중 한 대에 태우는 실수를 하기 전까지, 그는 Dinosaur Land에서 어린이용 놀이기구를 즐기고 있었습니다. 75) 그는 차에서 마지막에 내렸고, 그의 뒤에는 비어있는 장난감 차가 있었습니다. 놀이기구 안내원이 그 장난감 차를 밀어서 아들을 뒤에서 쳤습니다. 그는 다쳐서 울기 시작했습니다. 그 후 그는 충격을 받아 놀이기구를 더 이상 타고 싶어 하지 않았습니다.

당신은 적절한 관리가 되지 않는 그러한 놀이기구들이 무엇을 할 수 있는지 충분히 인지해야 합니다. 공원을 방문했던 제 친구도 전에 비슷한 사고가 있었다고 말했습니다. 자동차가 아이들을 해칠 수 있는데, 왜 당신은 안전 조치를 취하지 않았나요? 76) 명백히, 자동차들은 이와 같은 사고를 예방하기 위해 따로 움직이지 않고 함께 움직여야 합니다.

남편과 나는 우리가 집에 와서 이 사고에 대한 비디오를 볼 때까지 아들의 부상이 심각하지 않다고 생각했습니다. 우리는 장난감 차가 어떻게 우리 아들 뒤통수를 쳤는지 봤습니다. 77) 건강검진에서 우리 아들에게 심각한 일이 생겼다는 것이 드러나면, 나는 당신의 회사에 책임을 묻고 법적 조치를 취할 것입니다.

78) 저는 Dinosaur Land의 모든 놀이기구의 안전성, 특히 어린이를 위한 안전성을 철저히 검토할 것을 요구합니다. 유사한 사고가 발생하기 전에 당신은 즉시 검토하여야 합니다. 나는 이 문제에 대해 곧 소식을 듣게 되기를 기대합니다.

74 ▶ 정답 ⓓ

Why did Katrina Pitman and her family visit the park?

(a) to report about an accident
(b) to try the new rides
(c) to teach her son how to drive
(d) to celebrate a special event

해석 카트리나 피트만과 그녀의 가족이 공원을 방문한 이유는 무엇인가요?

(a) 사고를 보고하기 위해
(b) 새로운 놀이기구를 타기위해
(c) 그녀의 아들에게 운전하는 법을 알려주기 위해
(d) 특별 행사를 기념하기 위해

해설 글의 첫 문단에서 카트리나 피트만의 생일을 축하하기 위해 공원을 방문했다는 내용이 언급되어 있다.

75 ▶ 정답 ⓒ

What happened to Katrina Pitman's son?

(a) His toy car hit another boy.
(b) He wasn't allowed to ride a toy car.
(c) He got hit by an empty toy car.
(d) A ride attendant scolded him.

해석 아들이 놀이기구에서 마지막에 내리는데, 놀이기구 안내원이 비어있는 장난감 차를 뒤에서 밀어 아들 뒤통수를 쳤다는 내용이 언급되어 있다.

76 ▶ 정답 ⓑ

According to Pitman, how can the toy cars be made safer to ride?

(a) by having the kids accompanied
(b) by making the cars run in a series
(c) by having the kids wear safety gear
(d) by making the cars run individually

해석 피트만에 따르면, 어떻게 장난감 자동차를 안전하게 탈 수 있나요?

(a) 아이들과 동행함으로써
(b) 차를 연속해서 달리게 함으로써
(c) 아이들에게 안전장비를 착용시킴으로써
(d) 차를 개별적으로 달리게 함으로써

해설 3문단 마지막 줄에 사고를 예방하기 위해 자동차들이 따로 움직이지 않고 함께 움직여야 한다고 피트만은 말하고 있다.

77 ▶ 정답 ⓓ

Based on the letter, what will Pitman most likely do if her son sustained worse injury?

(a) She won't take him to the park anymore.
(b) She will take him to the hospital.
(c) She will scold the ride attendant.
(d) She will sue Hamlin Garden Park.

해석 편지를 바탕으로, 피트만은 아들의 부상이 심하다면 무엇을 할 것 같나요?

(a) 그녀는 더 이상 그를 공원에 데려가지 않을 것이다.
(b) 그녀는 그를 병원에 데려갈 것이다.
(c) 그녀는 놀이기구 안내원을 꾸짖을 것이다.
(d) 그녀는 Hamlin Garden Park을 고소할 것이다.

해설 건강 검진에서 우리 아들에게 심각한 일이 생겼다는 것이 드러나면 회사에 책임을 묻고 법적 조치를 취하겠다고 했으므로 고소할 것이라 (d)가 가장 적절하다.

78 ▶ 정답 ⓐ

What did Ms. Pitman want Mr. Gibson to do?

(a) to check the safety of the park rides
(b) to retrain the park employees
(c) to stop operating the toy cars
(d) to refund their park entrance fees

해석 피트만은 깁슨이 무엇을 하기를 원했나요?

(a) 공원 놀이기구의 안전을 점검하는 것
(b) 공원 직원을 유지하는 것
(c) 장난감차 운영을 중단하는 것
(d) 공원 입장료를 환불해 주는 것

해설 마지막 문단 첫 번째 문장에서 I demanded that you thoroughly review the safety of all your rides in Dinosaur Land.를 통해 안전 점검을 철저히 할 것을 요구한다는 것을 알 수 있다.

79 ▶ 정답 ⓒ

In the context of the passage, traumatized means _____.

(a) pleased
(b) warned
(c) distressed
(d) injured

해석 문맥상, traumatized는 _____을 의미한다.

(a) 기뻐하는, 만족한
(b) 경고하다, 알리다
(c) 괴롭히다, 고통스럽게 하다
(d) (신체에) 부상을 입히다, (감정, 평판을) 상하게 하다

해설 traumatize 정신적 충격을 주다, 마음에 충격을 주다

80 ▶ 정답 ⓓ

In the context of the passage, particularly means _____.
(a) remarkably
(b) exceptionally
(c) unusually
(d) specifically

해석

문맥상, particularly는 _____을 의미한다.
(a) 두드러지게, 현저하게
(b) 유별나게, 뛰어나게
(c) 유난히, 이상하게, 유별나게
(d) 특별히, 특히

해설 particularly 특히, 특별히

지텔프코리아 공식지정

G-TELP
LEVEL 2

이현아 취향저격 지텔프 실전모의고사

Answers and Explanations

한 권에 끝내는 G-TELP 실전모의고사 5회

해설편 3

SECTION 01 GRAMMAR
SECTION 02 LISTENING
SECTION 03 READING & VOCABULARY

Grammar Test 03회
Question 1-26

ANSWER KEY p.67

01	ⓐ	02	ⓓ	03	ⓒ	04	ⓑ
05	ⓐ	06	ⓒ	07	ⓑ	08	ⓓ
09	ⓒ	10	ⓑ	11	ⓓ	12	ⓐ
13	ⓑ	14	ⓓ	15	ⓒ	16	ⓑ
17	ⓒ	18	ⓓ	19	ⓐ	20	ⓒ
21	ⓑ	22	ⓒ	23	ⓐ	24	ⓒ
25	ⓑ	26	ⓓ				

01 ▶ 정답 ⓐ
해석 중세 필사본은 수도원과 왕실 서가내부에 은밀하게 보관되어 있곤 했다. 오늘날, 그들의 사본은 인터넷상에서 이용 가능하다. 사실, 만약 내가 그들에 관한 연구를 할 기회를 가진다면, 나는 이용 가능한 데이터의 양에 압도당할 것이다.

해설 빈칸이 있는 문장에 If가 있는 것으로 보아 가정법 문제임을 알 수 있다. If절의 시제가 과거이므로 주절에는 [would/should/could/might + 동사원형]이 들어가야 하므로 정답은 (a)가 가장 적절하다.

02 ▶ 정답 ⓓ
해석 Ethiopia에서 가뭄이 많은 죽음을 초래하고 있다. 이 비상사태에 대응하여, 국제기관들이 희생자들을 위한 구조 활동을 시작했다. 지금 현재, 적십자 직원들은 피해를 입은 사회에 식량배급을 하고 있다.

해설 시간부사 right now는 '지금 당장/ 지금 현재'란 뜻으로 이 부분을 체크했다면 '현재진행'시제가 가장 적절하다. 보기에 현재진행시제가 없는 경우에 한해서 현재시제가 정답이 될 수 있다.

03 ▶ 정답 ⓒ
해석 Greenwood's Grocery는 2년 전에 새로운 식료품점 세 곳이 시장에서 경쟁을 시작할 때까지 굉장히 수익성이 좋았다. 그것이 도입한 새로운 가격책정 정책이 이전 고객들을 되찾아 오는 것을 목표로 했다.

해설 빈칸 앞 명사 new pricing scheme을 수식하는 절을 찾는 문제이다. 주어가 빠진 주격 관계대명사절을 이끄는 (C)가 정답이다.

오답분석 관계부사 how가 이끈 절은 완벽해야 하는데 불완전한 문장이 왔고, when은 선행사가 '시간'의 개념이 되어야 하는데 선행사와의 관계가 어울리지 않는다. (d)의 reduced its significant prices는 '그것의 상당한 가격을 줄였던'이 되므로 문맥상 어울리지 않는다.

04 ▶ 정답 ⓑ
해석 Arnold는 어제 새 스마트 폰을 구매했다. 그는 통신기술의 발전을 의심하는 테크노포브(주석: 신기술을 무서워하는 사람)이었다. 그는 스마트 폰이 얼마나 유용한지를 깨닫기 전까지 휴대폰을 소지하는 것을 거부해왔었다.

해설 시간부사절 until이 이끈 절의 시제가 과거이므로 문맥상 과거완료나 과거시제만 올 수 있다. 보기에 해당 시제는 (b)뿐이다.

05 ▶ 정답 ⓐ
해석 Tony 와 Alice는 그들의 18살짜리 딸이 캄보디아 교육 학습투어에 참여할 것이라는 소식을 듣고 기뻤다. 그러나, 그들은 그 여행이 야생 장소들로 도보 투어를 포함하고 있다는 것을 알고서 걱정했다.

해설 보기를 통해 준동사 문제임을 알 수 있다. involve는 동명사만을 목적어로 취하는 3형식 동사이다.

06 ▶ 정답 ⓒ
해석 자격을 갖춘 검안사가 되기 위해서, 면허가 있는 검안사 밑에서 6개월간의 인턴과정을 해야 한다. 인턴십이 끝났을 때, 감독관은 그 인턴의 수행평가서를 Board of Examiners in Optometry에 제출할 것이다.

해설 조동사 문제는 해석을 통해 문맥상 가장 적절한 것을 찾아야 한다. 해석상 '~할 것이다'를 표현하는 will이 가장 적절하다.

오답분석 when 부사절이 현재시제인데 과거의 상황을 나타내는 could는 적절하지 않다. 불확실한 추측을 나타내는 may나 능력/허가를 표현하는 can도 적절하지 않다.

07 ▶ 정답 ⓑ
해석 내 사촌 Dorothy는 고급 이탈리아 레스토랑의 요리사이다. 그녀는 다음 달 우리 가족모임을 위해 저녁 만찬을 준비해달라는 요청을 받았다. 그녀는 우리를 위해 호화로운 식사인 풀코스 요리를 준비할 것이라고 말했다.

해설 ask동사는 5형식에 쓰이면 목적보어자리에 to 부정사를 가진다. 목적어가 주어로 빠지면서 수동태로 형태가 바뀌었을 뿐 목적보어 자리가 빈 칸이므로 to 부정사가 들어가야 한다.

08 ▶ 정답 ⓓ
해석 Dr. Abigail Morton는 좋은 자세와 근골격근 질병간의 관계를 연구하는 물리치료사이다. 그녀의 현재 연구에서, 그녀는 150명의 회사직원들이 다양한 사무실 업무를 하는 동안 그들의 자세를 관찰하고 있다.

해설 문장구조와 문맥을 모두 고려해서 풀어야 하는 접속사 문제이다. 구조상 모든 보기가 들어갈 수 있지만 해석상 '~하는 동안에'를 뜻하는 while이 가장 적절하다.

09 ▶ 정답 ⓒ

해석 지난 수요일 Joseph 삼촌은 가슴 통증을 느꼈다. 그가 건강 검진을 받기 위해 병원에 이송되었을 때, 의사는 그에게 즉시 심장우회수술을 받아야 한다고 말했다.

해설 빈칸 앞에 당위성·이성적 판단의 형용사 necessary가 오고 문맥상 당위적 내용을 표현하고 있다면 that절의 동사는 「(should) 동사원형」이 되어야 한다.

10 ▶ 정답 ⓑ

해석 Peter Darwin은 항상 몇 번의 연승을 거두고 있는 재능 있는 테니스 선수처럼 보여 왔다. 그러나 몇몇 비평가들은 그가 그의 경기력을 향상시키기 위해 금지된 약물을 사용할지도 모른다고 의심하고 있다.

해설 해석을 통해 문맥상 가장 적절한 조동사를 찾는 문제이다. 문맥상 가능성을 표현할 수 있는 could가 가장 적절하다.

11 ▶ 정답 ⓓ

해석 8년 동안 무명의 모델로 일한 후에 Bettina Humphrey는 직업을 바꾸기로 결심했다. 올해 8월쯤이 되면 그녀는 수상경력이 있는 다큐멘터리 영화를 만든 지 3년이 된다.

해설 시간부사 by August this year(이번 해 8월쯤)를 통해서 미래완료시제가 가장 적절함을 알 수 있다.

오답분석 (b)의 will be making은 미래진행시제로 미래의 특정한 시점에 '~하고 있는' 동작을 강조할 때 쓴다.

12 ▶ 정답 ⓐ

해석 Heritage Alliance는 동남아시아의 문화적 소수자들의 권리를 높이는 성공적인 비정부 기구이다. 그것은 민간인들로부터 큰 기부를 받는다. 그러한 지원이 없다면, 그 단체는 그 지역의 원주민 공동체를 보호하지 못할 것이다.

해설 If 가정법절의 시제가 were(과거)인 것을 통해 가정법 과거임을 알 수 있다.

13 ▶ 정답 ⓑ

해석 Edgar는 파티 후에 운전을 해야 했기 때문에, 그는 파티에서 술을 마시지 않겠다고 아빠와 약속했다. 그러나 그는 그렇게 하는 것이 위험하다는 것을 알았음에도 불구하고 데킬라 다섯 잔의 유혹을 뿌리칠 수 없었다.

해설 문장 형식상 빈칸은 부사절 접속사 자리이며 해석상 '~에도 불구하고'를 의미하는 양보부사절 접속사 although가 가장 적절하다.

오답분석 명사절 접속사 that은 문장구조상 들어갈 수 없다.

14 ▶ 정답 ⓓ

해석 Wilmington의 몇몇 주민들은 마을 공원 근처에 고가도로를 짓는 것에 반대했다. 그들이 이미 파업을 계획하고 있었을 때 그 마을 의회에서 고가도로를 지을 대안의 부지를 찾고 있다는 것을 공무원들이 갑작스럽게 발표했다.

해설 시간부사 when절의 시제가 과거인 것을 통해 주절은 과거나 과거완료시제가 와야 한다. 보기에 과거 진행시제인 (d)가 가장 적절하다.

15 ▶ 정답 ⓒ

해석 Travis 와 Georgia는 텔레비전 토크쇼의 진행자이다. 최근에 그들은 쇼가 재미없어지고 있다는 시청자들의 평가를 받아 오고 있다. 프로듀서가 그것의 구성을 바꾼다면, 프로그램은 훨씬 더 재미있을 것이다.

해설 If 가정법 절의 동사 revised가 과거시제인 것을 보아 가정법 과거임을 알 수 있다.

16 ▶ 정답 ⓑ

해석 Schiller Pharmaceuticals의 새 CEO는 파산으로부터 회사를 막으려고 열성적이다. 그녀는 제품 품목을 넓히기로 결정했다. 그녀와 그녀 팀의 화학자들은 이미 새로운 고수익 화장품 개발을 시작했다.

해설 begin은 의미차이 없이 목적어 자리에 to 부정사와 동명사를 모두 취할 수 있다. 보기에 동명사밖에 제시되지 않았으므로 정답은 (b)이다.

17 ▶ 정답 ⓒ

해석 Daniel은 전시회에 출품할 일련의 그림들을 마무리하기 위해 서둘렀다. 그러나 스트레스로 인해 심각한 요통이 생겼고 그로 인해 그는 몸져 누웠다. 만약 그가 지나치게 많은 압력을 그 자신에게 가하지 않았더라면, 그는 그런 불상사를 피할 수 있었을 텐데.

해설 If절의 시제가 had p.p.이므로 가정법 과거완료임을 알 수 있다. 가정법 과거완료 주절에는 [would/ should/ could/ might + have p.p.]가 쓰인다.

18 ▶ 정답 ⓓ

해석 자신의 책인 The Disappearance of Childhood에서 Neil Postman은 인쇄매체가 어른과 아이를 구분하도록 조장했다고 제시한다. 그는 이러한 중요한 구분은 텔레비전이 도입된 이후부터 무너지고 있다고 주장한다.

해설 보기를 통해 시제문제임을 알 수 있다. 전치사 since 뒤에 온 the arrival of the television (텔레비전의 도입 이후)는 문맥상 과거 시점에 해당하므로 주절에는 현재완료 시제가 가장 적절하다.

오답분석 보기 (c)도 현재완료시제인 것은 맞지만 that절의 주어가 this important distinction이므로 3인칭 단수인데 수일치가 맞지 않다.

19 ▶ 정답 ⓐ

해석 내 친구인 Bart는 세간의 주목을 받는 대상을 찍을 때 특별한 방법을 사용한다. 인기 있는 작가인 Georgina Brown의 사진을 찍을 때, 그는 그녀를 커다란 사전 위에 앉게 했다.

해설 관계사 문제이다. 수식을 받는 선행사가 Gergina Brown이며 보기에 주어진 관계사절 중에서 주격관계대명사 who가 이끈 것이 가장 적절하다.

오답분석 (b)은 해석상 글 쓰는 것이 Gerogina Brown에게 인기가 있다는 내용이 되므로 문맥상 어울리지 않는다. (c)에 나온 whose는 소유격 관계대명사이므로 완벽한 문장이 와야하는데, 주어가 없는 불완전한 문장이 나왔으므로 문법상 올바르지 않다. 관계대명사 that은 콤마(,)뒤에 쓰일 수 없으므로 적절하지 않다.

20 ▶ 정답 ⓒ

해석 Anne이 오늘 아침 출근길에 그녀가 평소 다니는 길로 들어섰을 때, 그녀의 차는 교통체증에 꼼짝달싹 못했다. 만약 그녀가 교통방송을 들었더라면, 그녀는 다른 길로 출근을 했을 텐데.

해설 If절의 시제가 had p.p.이므로 가정법 과거완료이다. 가정법 과거완료의 주절에는 [would /should / could / might + have p.p.]가 들어가야 한다.

21 ▶ 정답 ⓑ

해석 JKNY의 대표는 회사의 지출을 줄이겠다는 계획을 발표했다. 그는 모든 매니저들이 전국에 있는 모든 가게에 비용절감정책을 실시할 것을 지시했다. 이 조치는 12% 만큼 간접비용을 줄 일 수 있다.

해설 명령/동의/제안/주장/요구/충고 동사 다음에 오는 that절이 당위적 내용인 경우 동사는 「(should) 동사원형」이 되어야 한다.

22 ▶ 정답 ⓒ

해석 많은 임원들이 세계적으로 유명한 경영전문가인 Benjamin Spade가 다음달 워크샵을 개최하는 것을 기다려오고 있다. 자리를 예약하기 위해서는 행사 주최 측에 즉시 연락해야 한다.

해설 보기를 통해 준동사 문제임을 알 수 있다. [주어 + 동사 + 목적어]가 완벽하게 왔으므로 더 이상 필요한 문장 성분은 없다. 부사만이 들어갈 수 있으며 to 부정사의 부사적 용법이 가장 적절하다.

23 ▶ 정답 ⓐ

해석 Sonia의 소장 도서는 빠르게 늘어나고 있다. 그녀의 책은 실제로 작은 아파트의 책장 두 칸에서 쏟아져 나오고 있다. 그녀는 좀 더 넓은 공간을 찾을 때 까지 책 구매를 자제하는 것이 최선이다.

해설 당위적 · 이성적 판단을 표현하는 형용사 best가 오고 that절이 왔으므로 동사는 「(should) 동사원형」이 되어야 한다.

24 ▶ 정답 ⓒ

해석 일부 정신과 의사들은 'narcissism'이 심각한 성격 장애라고 확신한다. 이 장애는 심리치료를 받는다고 하더라도, 환자가 자신의 결함을 인정하도록 하는 것이 이 치료의 가장 어려운 부분이라고 한다.

해설 동사 is의 주어자리이다. 보기 중에서 주어자리에 들어갈 수 있는 것은 동명사뿐이다.

25 ▶ 정답 ⓑ

해석 나는 5년 전 독일어 수업에 등록했다. 그러나 나는 진짜로 독어를 배우지 않았다. 만약 내가 독일어를 친구들과 해외에서 정기적으로 사용했더라면, 나는 독일어를 익혔을 텐데.

해설 If절의 시제가 had p.p.인 것으로 보아 가정법 과거완료임을 알 수 있다.

26 ▶ 정답 ⓓ

해석 세익스피어의 '리어왕'을 각색한 영화인 Fatherhood는 감독의 높은 기준 때문에 제작하는데 3년이 걸렸다. 세익스피어의 팬들이 기쁘게도, 마침내 극장에서 다음 달에 많이 기다려 온 영화를 상영할 것이다.

해설 시간부사 next month가 있으므로 미래시제가 들어가야 가장 적절하다.

Listening Test 03회

Question 27-52

ANSWER KEY p.75

27	ⓑ	28	ⓒ	29	ⓓ	30	ⓑ
31	ⓒ	32	ⓓ	33	ⓐ	34	ⓑ
35	ⓓ	36	ⓐ	37	ⓓ	38	ⓒ
39	ⓐ	40	ⓓ	41	ⓐ	42	ⓒ
43	ⓐ	44	ⓓ	45	ⓑ	46	ⓒ
47	ⓓ	48	ⓐ	49	ⓓ	50	ⓑ
51	ⓒ	52	ⓑ				

[Part 1]

Now listen to the questions.

> 27: What activity is Alex inviting Carla to?
> 28: What did Alex first think of archery?
> 29: According to Carla, why is flight archery the most difficult type of archery?
> 30: In the type practiced by Carla, how far is the archer from the target?
> 31: What is Carla's instructor coaching her on now?
> 32: Based on the conversation, what is true about archery?
> 33: What will Alex most likely do soon?

해석

27: 알렉스는 무슨 활동에 칼라를 초대하고 있나요?
28: 알렉스는 처음에 양궁에 대해 어떻게 생각했나요?
29: 칼라에 따르면, 원사 양궁(flight archery)이 왜 가장 어려운 종류의 양궁인가요?
30: 칼라가 연습하는 종류에서, 표적에서 궁사까지 거리가 얼마나 되나요?
31: 칼라의 강사는 현재 그녀에게 무엇에 관해 가르치고 있나요?
32: 대화를 바탕으로, 양궁에 대해 사실인 것은 무엇인가요?
33: 곧 알렉스는 무엇을 할 것 같나요?

Now you will hear the conversation.
[conversation]

M Hi, Carla. Some of our officemates want to hold an in-house sports event every Saturday. 27) This weekend, they are thinking of having a badminton game. Would you like to join?

F I'd love to, Alex, but I already have practice sessions for another sport every Saturday afternoon.

M Really? Which sport?

F It's archery. My best friend is on the archery team at Stanford. She convinced me to try it myself two months ago.

M 28) Hmmm... archery. Somehow I think it's a very difficult sport. Is it hard to learn?

F Well, the level of difficulty depends on the type of archery you do. For example, the "field shooting" type is somewhat difficult. It's almost like hunting. It's played in a park or forest, and the targets are placed at varying distances.

M Are there more difficult types of archery?

F Yes. There's "clout archery," which is a bit more difficult because the archers have to shoot a target that's outlined on the ground. 29) But the most difficult of all is "flight archery," because the goal is to shoot an arrow the longest distance.

M So, what type of archery do you do?

F I'm still at the simple "target shooting" stage right now. It's the best place to start archery because you learn the basic skills.

M I see. I'm curious, 30) when you're practicing archery, how far should you be from the target?

F 30) For me, it's only 30 meters. In the more competitive types of archery, of course, the distance may go as far as 70 meters for women and 90 meters for men.

M That is a long distance! I wonder if my arrows could hit anything at that distance! Isn't it a bit dangerous to shoot an arrow that far? I'd worry about accidentally hitting somebody.

F Well, it's actually very safe if you follow the proper safety procedures and only shoot on a target range.

M I see... Anyway, how are your lessons going?

F I'm enjoying them a lot! Of course, I haven't hit the bull's eye yet, but I've improved a lot since I started. I used to make a lot of mistakes, you know. For example, when aiming for the target, I tended to pull the bow toward my right shoulder.

M Well, isn't that the correct way to pull the bow?

F I thought so, too, but the correct way, my instructor

said, was to pull it toward my face because that gives the arrow more accuracy. 31) He also pointed out my major weakness, which was my inability to concentrate on the target. This is what I've been focusing on these past few weeks.

M Now you've made me really curious about archery. Do you think your instructor can accommodate another student?

F Of course, Alex! You can even enroll your wife and kids. 32) The great thing about archery is that anyone can do it. In fact, my instructor conducts two more classes: one for kids and another for retirees.

M 33) That's wonderful, Carla! I think my whole family will love that. Expect us to be trooping to your archery school pretty soon!

Words

officemate 회사동료
archery 양궁
shoot 쏘다
safety procedure 안전수칙
accommodate 수용하다
troop 몰려다, 무리 지어 가다
in-house 사내의
target 과녁
arrow 화살
weakness 단점, 약점
retiree 은퇴자

해석

M 칼라야, 안녕. 우리 회사 동료 몇 명이 매주 토요일에 사내 스포츠모임을 하기를 원해. 27) 이번 주말에 배드민턴 경기를 할 생각인 거 같아. 너도 같이 할래?

F 알렉스, 나도 그러고 싶지만 이미 나는 매주 토요일 오후에 다른 운동 연습이 잡혀 있어.

M 그래? 무슨 운동이야?

F 양궁이야. 내 가장 친한 친구가 Stanford의 양궁 팀에 있거든. 두 달 전에 그녀가 나에게 한번 해 볼 것을 설득했어.

M 28) 음… 양궁. 왠지 아주 어려운 운동 같은데. 배우기 어렵지 않아?

F 글쎄, 난이도는 네가 하는 양궁의 종류에 따라 따르지. 예를 들면, 'field shooting(야외 양궁)'은 다소 어려워. 거의 사냥과 같아. 공원이나 숲에서 하는데, 과녁들도 다양한 거리에 배치되어 있어.

M 더 어려운 종류의 양궁도 있어?

F 그럼. 'clout archery(집중사 양궁)'이 있는데, 땅 위에 그려놓은 과녁을 맞춰야 해서 조금 더 어려워. 29) 하지만 목적이 화살을 가장 멀리 쏘는 것이기 때문에, 가장 어려운 것은 'flight archery(원사 양궁)'이야.

M 그래서 너는 무슨 양궁을 해?

F 지금은 여전히 단순한 'target shooting(과녁 쏘기)' 단계에 있어. 기본적인 기술을 배울 수 있기 때문에 양궁을 시작하기에 최적의 단계지.

M 그렇구나. 30) 궁금한 게 있는데 양궁 연습할 때 과녁에서 얼마나 멀리 떨어져 있어야 해?

F 30) 내 경우에는, 겨우 30미터 정도야. 물론 좀 더 경쟁적인 양궁경기에서는 그 거리가 여자는 70미터, 남자는 90미터까지 될 수 있어.

M 먼 거리구나! 그 정도 거리에서 화살로 무엇인가를 맞출 수 있을지 모르겠어. 그렇게 멀리 화살을 쏘는 것은 좀 위험하지 않아? 의도하지 않게 누군가를 맞출까 봐 걱정이 돼.

F 글쎄, 적절한 안전수칙을 지키고 과녁 범위에서만 쏘면 사실 정말로 안전해.

M 그렇구나.. 어쨌든, 레슨은 어때?

F 정말 재밌어! 물론 아직 과녁의 중앙은 맞추지 못하지만, 처음 시작할 때보다 훨씬 많이 좋아졌어. 내가 실수를 많이 했거든. 예를 들면, 과녁을 조준할 때, 나는 활을 내 오른쪽 어깨 쪽으로 당기는 경향이 있었지.

M 그게 활을 당기는 옳은 방법 아니야?

F 나도 그렇게 생각했는데, 강사가 말하길, 올바른 방법은 그걸 내 얼굴 쪽으로 당기는 거래. 그래야 화살이 더 정확하게 날아가기 때문이야. 31) 그는 또한 내가 과녁에 집중 못 하는 나의 주된 단점을 지적해 줬어. 이게 내가 지난 몇 주 동안 집중해오고 있는 거야.

M 너는 내가 정말 양궁에 대해 호기심을 갖게 만들어. 네 생각에 너의 선생님이 다른 학생을 받을 수 있을 거 같아?

F 물론이지, 알렉스! 아내랑 아이들과 함께 등록할 수도 있어. 32) 양궁의 가장 좋은 점은 누구나 할 수 있다는 거야. 사실, 우리 선생님은 어린이 반과 은퇴하신 분들을 위한 두 반을 더 운영하고 있어.

M 33) 멋지다, 칼라! 우리가족 전부 좋아할 거 같아. 곧 우리가 너의 양궁 학교에 몰려 갈테니 기대하구 있어!

27 ▶ 정답 ⓑ

What activity is Alex inviting Carla to?

(a) an archery class
(b) a badminton game
(c) a company outing
(d) a game of archery

해석

무슨 활동에 알렉스는 칼라를 초대하고 있나요?

(a) 양궁수업
(b) 배드민턴경기
(c) 회사 야유회
(d) 양궁경기

해설 알렉스는 카라에게 "This weekend, they are thinking of having a badminton game. Would you like to join?"라고 물었다. 동료들과의 배드민턴 경기에 칼라를 초대한다는 것을 알 수 있다.

28 ▶정답 ⓒ

What did Alex first think of archery?

(a) that it was exciting
(b) that it was dangerous
(c) that it was difficult
(d) that it was entertaining

해석 알렉스는 처음에 양궁에 대해 어떻게 생각했나요?

(a) 흥미로웠다고
(b) 위험했다고
(c) 어려웠다고
(d) 재미있다고

해설 알렉스가 "Hmmm… archery. Somehow I think it's a very difficult sport."라고 말한 것을 토대로 양궁을 어려운 스포츠로 생각했다는 것을 알 수 있다.

29 ▶정답 ⓓ

According to Carla, why is flight archery the most difficult type of archery?

(a) because the target is outlined on the ground
(b) because it is almost similar to hunting
(c) because it requires target shooting
(d) because it requires long distance shooting

해석 칼라에 따르면, 원사 양궁(flight archery)이 왜 가장 어려운 종류의 양궁인가요?

(a) 과녁이 땅에 그려져 있기 때문
(b) 사냥과 거의 유사하기 때문
(c) target shooting을 해야 하기 때문
(d) 먼 거리를 쏘아야하기 때문

해설 "But the most difficult of all is "flight archery," because the goal is to shoot an arrow the longest distance."에서 화살을 멀리 쏘아야 하기 때문에 어렵다고 칼라가 말한다.

30 ▶정답 ⓑ

In the type practiced by Carla, how far is the archer from the target?

(a) 10 meters
(b) 30 meters
(c) 70 meters
(d) 90 meters

해석 칼라가 연습하는 종류에서, 표적에서 궁사까지 거리가 얼마나 되나요?

(a) 10미터
(b) 30미터
(c) 70미터
(d) 90미터

해설 알렉스가 "when you're practicing archery, how far should you be from the target?"라고 물은 질문에, "For me, it's only 30 meters."라고 답했으므로 (b)가 적절하다.

31 ▶정답 ⓒ

What is Carla's instructor coaching her on now?

(a) her physical energy
(b) her aiming position
(c) her mental focus
(d) her handling of archery gear

해석 칼라의 강사는 현재 그녀에게 무엇에 관해 가르치고 있나요?

(a) 그녀의 체력
(b) 그녀의 조준자세
(c) 그녀의 정신집중
(d) 그녀의 양궁장비 조작

해설 "He also pointed out my major weakness, which was my inability to concentrate on the target. This is what I've been focusing on these past few weeks."에서 칼라가 과녁에 집중하지 못하는 것을 지적한다는 것을 알 수 있다. 조준자세는 과거에 배운 내용이므로 문제의 정답이 될 수 없다.

32 ▶정답 ⓓ

Based on the conversation, what is true about archery?

(a) One must be interested in hunting to learn archery.
(b) It can be played only by people who have strong arms.
(c) One must expect to accidentally hit people to learn archery.
(d) It can be enjoyed by people of almost all ages.

해석 대화를 바탕으로, 양궁에 대해 사실인 것은 무엇인가요?

(a) 양궁을 배우려면 사냥에 관심이 있어야 한다.
(b) 그것은 강한 팔을 가진 사람들만이 할 수 있다.
(c) 양궁을 배우기 위해서 의도치 않게 사람을 맞출 수 있다는 것을 예상해야 한다.
(d) 거의 모든 연령대 사람들이 즐길 수 있다.

해설 "The great thing about archery is that anyone can do it In fact, my instructor conducts two more classes: one for kids and another for retirees."에서 양궁은 모든 연령대의 사람들이 즐길 수 있다는 것을 알 수 있다.

33

▶ 정답 ⓐ

What will Alex most likely do soon?
(a) enroll his whole family in archery classes
(b) purchase the basic archery gear
(c) watch an actual archery competition
(d) contact Carla's archery instructor

해석

곧 알렉스는 무엇을 할 것 같나요?
(a) 그의 가족 모두를 양궁수업에 등록한다.
(b) 기본적인 양궁장비를 구입한다.
(c) 실제 양궁경기를 관람한다.
(d) 칼라의 양궁강사와 연락한다.

해설 대화 마지막에 알렉스는 "That's wonderful, Carla! I think my whole family will love that. Expect us to be trooping to your archery school pretty soon!"이라고 말하고 있다.

[Part 2]

Now listen to the questions.

34: What is one of the provisions of the Americans with Disabilities Act?

35: What improvement was not cited as having been implemented by the city library?

36: Based on the talk, how can "assistive software" most likely help a blind client use online databases?

37: What kind of organization gave a substantial donation to the city library?

38: How is the Webster County Library using the remainder of the donation?

39: Based on the script, what could a librarian do to avoid being overly caring to disabled library clients?

해석

34: 미국 장애인법 조항들 중 하나는 무엇인가요?

35: 시립도서관에 의해 시행된 개선사항으로 언급되지 않은 것은 무엇인가요?

36: 강연에 따르면, 어떻게 '지원 소프트웨어 (assistive software)'가 맹인 고객들이 온라인 데이터베이스를 사용하는 것을 도울 것 같나요?

37: 어떤 종류의 단체가 시립도서관에 상당한 기부를 했나요?

38: Webster County 도서관은 어떻게 남은 기부금을 사용하나요?

39: 내용을 바탕으로, 사서는 장애가 있는 도서관 고객들에게 지나친 관심을 기울이지 않도록 하기 위해 할 수 있는 것은 무엇인가요?

Now you will hear the talk.

Good morning, everyone! I'm the chief librarian of the Webster County Library, and I'd like to welcome all of our newly-hired library workers to this orientation session. We are glad that you've decided to work with us. Before we proceed with our training session, let me give you a brief update on the latest projects and accomplishments of our main library.

As you may know, 34) the Americans with Disabilities Act of 1990 requires that, among other things, all public buildings in the country be accessible to the disabled. In compliance with that, all of our recent buildings have been designed to meet the special needs of people who are in wheelchairs, hearing-impaired, blind, and learning-disabled.

We have also undertaken redesign projects on our buildings that were built before 1990. Our main library on Grant Street in Cedarburg, for example, will re-open in August with some major structural improvements. Our task was to preserve the original style of this beautiful building from 1886 while making it accessible to our citizens with special needs. We've taken great care to ensure that the new additions to the building complement the existing structure.

35) Among these new additions are the installation of access ramps and electrically powered doors at the south and north sides of our building. These ramps and doors make it easier for disabled library clients to enter or leave the building even if they don't have able-bodied companions to help them. And the ramps and doors are as beautiful as the original walls they were added to. 35) We've also added a new wheelchair elevator to the two existing units in the center of the building. The new elevator will be reserved for disabled clients who need to travel from one floor of the library to another.

In addition to this structural work, 36) we're also installing "assistive software" in our computers. With this software, clients who are blind or have hearing disabilities will find it easier to use our computer databases including the now completely digital card catalog and materials check-out system.

Obviously, our library needed huge financial resources to implement these changes. We're very fortunate to have the support of generous benefactors like the Blackwell Foundation. 37) It is a private institution that provided the library system with a grant of $650,000 to fund the renovation.

38) We've already spent part of this substantial donation on the physical improvements to the building and the computer system, and we're using the remainder to expand our book, journal, and audio-visual collections. Since we publicized these past and ongoing development

projects in our latest newsletter, we've been receiving a lot of compliments from our community.

Our work doesn't end there, however. As librarians, we still have many duties and obligations to fulfill and do better, particularly in dealing with disabled clients. I've always emphasized that our job requires an adaptable attitude. This means we should always be ready to help our clients in such basic tasks as retrieving books, photocopying materials, and doing Internet research.

39) But even as we give assistance to our clients, we should avoid being overly caring. We should be mindful of our clients' need for personal space while studying or working inside the library. Let's remember that all of them, regardless of their physical condition or mental capacity, deserve excellent service.

Words

accomplishment 업적, 성과
in compliance with 준수하여, ~에 따라
hearing-impaired 청각 장애가 있는
blind 시각 장애인의
learning-disabled 학습 장애를 가진
preserve 보전하다
complement 보완하다
access ramp 진입 경사로
able-bodied companion 신체 건강한
check-out system 대출 시스템
benefactor 후원자
renovation 보수, 수리
substantial 상당한
remainder 나머지
publicize 홍보하다, 선전하다
ongoing 진행중의
photocopy 복사하다
overly 과도하게, 지나치게
caring 돌봄, 보살핌
mindful 염두에 둔, 유의하는
deserve 자격이 있다

해석

여러분, 안녕하세요! 저는 Webster County 도서관의 수석사서입니다. 이 오리엔테이션에 오신 신입 도서관 직원 여러분들을 모두 환영합니다. 여러분이 우리와 함께 일하기로 결정을 한 것에 대해 기쁘게 생각합니다. 교육을 진행하기 전에, 우리 중앙도서관의 최근 프로젝트와 성과에 관해 간략하게 알려드리겠습니다.

아시다시피, 34) 1990년의 장애인 법은, 다른 모든 것들 중에서도, 장애인들이 미국의 모든 공공건물에 접근할 수 있어야 한다는 것을 요구합니다. 이를 준수해, 우리의 최근 모든 건물들은 휠체어를 타거나 청각장애, 시각장애 및 학습장애가 있는 사람들의 특별 필요를 충족시키도록 설계되었습니다.

또한 우리는 1990년 이전에 지어진 건물의 재설계 프로젝트에 착수하였습니다. 예를 들면, Cedarburg의 Grant Street에 있는 우리 중앙도서관은 몇 가지 주된 구조적인 개선을 거쳐 8월에 재개장될 예정입니다. 우리의 임무는 특별한 도움이 필요한 시민들이 이용할 수 있으면서도, 1886년부터 존재하던 이 아름다운 건물의 본 양식을 보존하는 것이었습니다. 우리는 건물에 새로 추가된 부분들이 기존 구조를 보완하도록 최대한 신경을 썼습니다.

35) 건물의 남쪽과 북쪽에 진입 경사로 및 전동식 문을 설치하는 것이 새로운 추가사항입니다. 이 경사로와 문은 장애가 있는 도서관 고객들이 그들을 도울 신체 건강한 동행이 없더라도 쉽게 건물을 드나들 수 있도록 해줍니다. 아울러, 이 경사로와 문은 그들이 추가되었던 곳의 원래 벽만큼이나 아름답습니다. 35) 또 건물 중앙에 있는 두 개의 기존기기에 새로운 휠체어 엘리베이터를 추가했습니다. 이 새로운 엘리베이터는 도서관 1층에서 다른 층으로 이동해야 하는 장애인 고객들 전용이 될 것입니다.

이러한 구조적 작업 외에도, 36) 우리는 컴퓨터에 '보조 소프트웨어'를 설치하고 있습니다. 이 소프트웨어로, 시각 또는 청각 장애가 있는 고객들은 이제 완벽한 디지털카드 카탈로그와 자료대출 시스템을 포함하는 우리 컴퓨터 데이터베이스를 더욱 쉽게 이용하게 될 것입니다.

분명하게도, 우리 도서관은 이러한 변화를 실행하기 위해 막대한 재정 지원이 필요했습니다. 우리는 굉장히 운 좋게도 Blackwell 재단과 같은 관대한 후원자들의 지원을 받게 되었습니다. 37) 이 재단은 도서관 시스템의 보수자금으로 65만 달러의 보조금을 지원한 사립기관입니다.

38) 우리는 이미 컴퓨터 시스템 및 건물의 물리적 개선에 상당한 금액을 사용했으며, 나머지 기부금을 책이나 잡지, 시청각자료를 늘리는데 사용할 계획입니다. 우리는 최근 소식지에 과거와 현재진행 중인 개발 프로젝트를 홍보했기 때문에, 지역사회로부터 많은 찬사를 받고 있습니다. 그러나 우리 일은 끝나지 않습니다. 사서로서, 우리는, 특히 장애인 고객들을 대하는 면에 있어서, 이행해야 하고 더 잘 해내야 할 많은 의무와 책임이 여전히 있습니다. 저는 항상 우리의 업무는 유연한 태도를 요구한다고 강조합니다. 즉, 우리는 항상 도서검색, 자료복사 및 인터넷검색과 같은 기본적인 업무에서 고객을 도울 준비가 되어 있어야 합니다.

39) 그러나 우리가 고객을 도울 때에도, 지나친 관심을 기울이는 것은 피해야 합니다. 도서관에서 공부를 하거나 일하는 동안 고객이 사적인 공간을 필요로 한다는 것을 염두에 두어야 합니다. 신체 상태나 정신능력에 관계없이 모두가 훌륭한 서비스를 받을 자격이 있다는 것을 기억하세요.

34 ▶ 정답 ⓑ

What is one of the provisions of the Americans with Disabilities Act?

(a) providing free library services to the disabled
(b) making public buildings easier to reach for the disabled
(c) hiring disabled persons to work in public agencies
(d) publishing a regular newsletter for the disabled

해석
미국신체 장애인법의 조항들 중 하나는 무엇인가요?
(a) 장애인들에게 무료 도서관 서비스를 제공하는 것
(b) 장애인들을 위한 공공건물의 접근성을 더 쉽게 만드는 것
(c) 장애인들이 공공기관에서 일할 수 있도록 고용하는 것
(d) 장애인들을 위한 정기적인 소식지를 출간하는 것

해설 "the Americans with Disabilities Act of 1990 requires that, among other things, all public buildings in the country be accessible to the disabled."에서 장애인들의 공공기간 접근성이 가장 우선시 되는 조항임을 알 수 있다.

35 ▶ 정답 ⓓ

What improvement was not cited as having been implemented by the city library?

(a) wheelchair-accessible elevators
(b) electrically powered doors
(c) access ramps for wheelchairs
(d) special furniture for the disabled

해석 시립도서관에 의해 시행된 개선사항으로 언급되지 않은 것은 무엇인가요?

(a) 휠체어로 접근 가능한 엘리베이터
(b) 전동식 문
(c) 휠체어를 위한 진입 경사로
(d) 장애인용 특수 가구

해설 건물의 남쪽과 북쪽에 진입 경사로와 전동식 문을 설치한다고 언급되어 있을 뿐 아니라 건물 중앙에 새로운 휠체어 엘리베이터를 추가했다고 언급했다. 장애인용 특수 가구에 대한 언급은 없다.

36 ▶ 정답 ⓐ

Based on the talk, how can "assistive software" most likely help a blind client use online databases?

(a) by providing voice and sound oriented services
(b) by making the software available on a wheelchair
(c) by helping the client hear better
(d) by making the databases easier to read

해석 강연에 따르면, 어떻게 '지원 소프트웨어 (assistive software)'가 맹인 고객들이 온라인 데이터베이스를 사용하는 것을 도울 것 같나요?

(a) 음성 및 음향 지향적인 서비스를 제공함으로써
(b) 소프트웨어를 휠체어에서 이용할 있도록 함으로써
(c) 고객이 더 잘 듣게 도움으로써
(d) 데이터베이스를 읽기 쉽게 만듦으로써

해설 "we're also installing "assistive software" in our computers. With this software, clients who are blind or have hearing disabilities will find it easier to use our computer databases including the now completely digital card catalog and materials check-out system."를 통해 시각이나 청각에 장애가 있는 분들을 위한 음성 서비스를 지원한다는 것을 추론할 수 있다. 데이트 베이스를 이용하기 쉽게 만든다는 내용이 나왔지, 데이터베이스를 읽기 쉽게 만든다는 내용은 없으므로 정답이 될 수 없다.

37 ▶ 정답 ⓓ

What kind of organization gave a substantial donation to the city library?

(a) a government agency
(b) a civic association
(c) a multinational firm
(d) a private foundation

해석 어떤 종류의 단체가 시립도서관에 상당한 기부를 했나요?

(a) 정부기관
(b) 시민단체
(c) 다국적기업
(d) 사설재단

해설 "It is a private institution that provided the library system with a grant of $650,000 to fund the renovation."을 통해 사설기관이 기부단체임을 알 수 있다.

38 ▶ 정답 ⓒ

How is the Webster County Library using the remainder of the donation?

(a) by hiring more library workers
(b) by holding workshops on library services
(c) by buying more library materials
(d) by publicizing the project

해석 Webster County 도서관은 어떻게 남은 기부금을 사용하나요?

(a) 더 많은 도서관 직원을 고용함으로써
(b) 도서관 서비스에 관한 워크샵을 개최함으로써
(c) 더 많은 도서관자료를 구입함으로써
(d) 프로젝트를 홍보함으로써

해설 "We've already spent part of this substantial donation on the physical improvements to the building and the computer system, and we're using the remainder to expand our book, journal, and audio-visual collections."에서 남은 기부금으로 도서관 자료 및 시청각 자료를 구입하는데 남은 기부금이 사용될 것임이 언급되었다.

39 ▶ 정답 ⓐ

Based on the script, what could a librarian do to avoid being overly caring to disabled library clients?

(a) give them time alone
(b) approach them all the time
(c) require another person to accompany them
(d) expect them to be more demanding

해석 내용을 바탕으로, 사서는 장애가 있는 도서관 고객들에게 지나친 관심을 기울이지 않도록 하기 위해 할 수 있는 것은 무엇인가요?
(a) 그들에게 혼자 있는 시간을 준다.
(b) 그들에게 항상 다가간다.
(c) 다른 사람에게 그들과 동행할 것을 요구한다.
(d) 그들이 더 많은 것을 요구할 것을 예상한다.

해설 "But even as we give assistance to our clients, we should avoid being overly caring. We should be mindful of our clients' need for personal space while studying or working inside the library."에서 혼자 있는 시간을 줌으로써 사적인 공간을 배려할 수 있다고 말하고 있다.

[Part 3]

Now listen to the questions.

> 40: Why does Jonathan find Enterprise magazine useful for gaining knowledge about business?
> 41: Why is Jonathan unable to read the magazine regularly?
> 42: To what did Miriam compare the financial benefit of subscribing to a magazine?
> 43: How do distributors respond to complaints about late deliveries?
> 44: What do subscribers to the print edition get that online subscribers don't?
> 45: According to Miriam, why does she prefer a magazine's print edition to its online edition?
> 46: Based on the conversation, what will Jonathan most likely do?

해설
40: 조나단은 경제에 관한 지식을 얻는데 Enterprise지가 왜 유용하다고 생각하나요?
41: 왜 조나단은 잡지를 정기적으로 읽을 수 없나요?
42: 잡지구독의 경제적 이익을 미리엄은 무엇에 비유하고 있나요?
43: 배급업자들은 늦은 배송에 관한 불만사항을 어떻게 대응하나요?
44: 온라인 구독자들은 안 되고, 인쇄판 구독자들만 얻는 것은 무엇인가요?
45: 미리엄에 따르면, 왜 그녀는 온라인 판보다 인쇄판을 선호하나요?
46: 대화를 바탕으로, 조나단이 무엇을 할 것 같나요?

Now you will hear the conversation.
[conversation]

> F I've noticed you enjoy reading Enterprise magazine, Jonathan. That publication is quite popular, isn't it?
>
> M Yes, Miriam, it's my favorite business magazine. I really learn a lot about the stock market and management practices reading it.
>
> F I can see how that would be valuable. Are the articles really readable?
>
> M Oh, yes. 40) They explain things in simple language in all the articles. Because of this, I find the stories very useful for expanding my knowledge about areas of business I'm not familiar with.
>
> F Really? They must have a good writing style.
>
> M Yes, I like their writing style. They don't take themselves too seriously and are surprisingly funny from time-to-time.
>
> F That's good to hear. Business writing can be so dry sometimes. So you read it every month then?
>
> M 41) Unfortunately, I don't get to read all of the monthly issues. Sometimes, when I try to buy it from a newsstand, the copies are already sold out.
>
> F Why don't you just get a subscription? That will be convenient. It will also assure you of getting a copy each month.
>
> M I wish I could, but I'm afraid I can't afford that right now. Judging from the cover price of Enterprise, I think subscribing to it would cost a small fortune.
>
> F Actually, the exact opposite is true. 42) You can save a lot by having a subscription. It's like buying groceries in bulk. It's so much cheaper!
>
> M How do you know that? Do you have a subscription to Enterprise?
>
> F No, but I have a one-year subscription to Art Review. If I bought a year's worth of monthly issues from a newsstand, I would have to pay a total of $59 the total of the cover prices for all 12 issues. But with the discounted subscription fee of $20, I actually save $39. That's more than 60% off the cover price!
>
> M Mmm… That sounds like a very good deal! But is the magazine delivered to you on time?
>
> F So far, they have been. But if you do encounter a problem with the delivery, all you have to do is inform the distributor about it. 43) Most distributors act on subscribers' complaints right away.
>
> M I see. But just one more question: Is there a big difference between the print and online formats of a magazine? I'm just thinking that if I could access the Internet edition, why should I still subscribe to the print

edition?

F That's a good point. 44) I think the print and electronic contents are basically the same. The main difference is that most leading magazines also have what they call "premium materials," which can be accessed only by subscribers to the print edition.

M That sounds like a good deal.

F It is. Moreover, if you're a subscriber to the print edition, you can read all the contents of the magazine -- even the online archives -- without any hassle. 45) Personally, I prefer reading the print edition. It's a relaxing break from staring at my computer monitor for long hours.

M That's true for me, too. Also, I print out a lot of electronic articles when I fail to get a copy of the print edition of Enterprise. If I compute the amount I spend on paper and printer ink, it would almost equal a year's subscription fee.

F 46) If that's the case, you might as well get a subscription!

Words

publication 간행물, 출판물
monthly issue 월간 발행물
afford 여유가 되다, 형편이 되다
in bulk 대량으로
distributor 배급업자, 유통업자
content 내용
hassle 번거로움, 귀찮은 일
might as well ~하는 편이 낫다
article 기사
subscription 구독
cover price 정가
encounter 맞닥뜨리다, 접하다
subscriber 구독자
online archive 온라인 자료실
compute 계산하다

해석

F 조나단, 난 네가 Enterprise 잡지 읽는 것을 좋아한다는 걸 알게 됐어. 그 간행물은 꽤 유명해, 그렇지?

M 응, 미리엄, 그건 내가 제일 좋아하는 비즈니스 잡지야. 난 그 잡지를 읽으면서 주식 시장과 경영 관행에 대해 정말 많은 것을 배워.

F 그 잡지가 얼마나 유용한지 알겠다. 기사들은 읽기 쉬워?

M 응. 40) 모든 기사들이 쉬운 언어로 설명되어 있어. 덕분에 나는 낯선 경제 분야에 대한 지식을 넓히는데 글들이 매우 유용하다는 것을 깨달았어.

F 정말? 기사들의 문체가 정말 좋음에 틀림없구나.

M 응, 나는 그들의 문체가 좋아. 너무 심각하지도 않고, 의외로 가끔씩 재밌어.

F 그거 참 반가운 소리다. 비즈니스 관련 글은 때때로 너무 지루할 수 있거든. 그러면 너는 매달 그 잡지를 읽어?

M 41) 안타깝게도, 매달 잡지를 사보지는 않아. 가끔, 가판대에서 사려고 하면, 잡지가 이미 다 팔리고 없어.

F 정기구독을 하는 건 어때? 그렇게 하는 게 편리할 거야. 매달 그 잡지를 받는 것이 보장되잖아.

M 나도 그러고 싶은데, 지금 당장은 그럴 여유가 없어. Enterprise의 정가로 판단해보면, 정기구독을 하면 상당한 비용이 들 거 같아.

F 실제로는, 정확하게 그 반대야. 42) 정기구독으로 훨씬 절약할 수 있어. 그건 식료품을 대량으로 사는 것과 같은 것이야. 그게 훨씬 싸!

M 너는 그걸 어떻게 알아? 너 Enterprise 정기 구독하고 있어?

F 아니, 근데 나는 Art Review를 1년 정기구독하고 있어. 만약 내가 가판대에서 1년 치를 구매한다면, 나는 12권 전부의 정가 총액인 59달러를 지불해야만 해. 하지만, 할인된 구독료 20달러로, 사실상 39달러를 절약하고 있어. 그건 정가의 60%이상 할인된 가격이야.

M 흠... 그거 괜찮은 거래 같아! 그런데 잡지는 제때에 배달돼?

F 지금까지는 그래. 그런데 만약 배달과 관련된 문제가 발생하면, 배급업자에게 그것에 관해 알려주기만 하면 돼. 43) 대부분의 배급업자들은 정기구독자들의 불만사항에 즉각적으로 처리해줘.

M 이해했어. 그런데, 한 가지 더 질문이 있는데: 인쇄판과 온라인 판에 큰 차이가 있어? 내 생각에 인터넷 판으로 이용할 수 있다면 왜 활자판으로 구독해야 해?

F 좋은 지적이야. 44) 인쇄물이나 온라인 상의 내용은 기본적으로 동일한 것 같아. 주된 차이는 대부분의 주요 잡지에는 인쇄판 구독자만 이용할 수 있는 소위 '고급 자료'가 있다는 거야.

M 그거 좋은 거래네.

F 그렇지. 게다가, 인쇄판의 정기 구독자인 경우, 잡지의 모든 내용을-심지어 온라인 자료실에 있는 내용까지- 번거로움 없이 모두 읽을 수 있어. 45) 개인적으로, 나는 인쇄판을 더 선호해. 장시간 컴퓨터 화면을 응시하는 것에서 벗어나 편안한 휴식을 취할 수 있거든.

M 그건 나도 그래. 게다가 난 Enterprise의 인쇄판을 구하지 못했을 때는 많은 양의 인터넷 기사를 출력하거든. 내가 종이와 프린터 잉크에 소비한 금액을 계산해보면, 1년 치 구독료와 거의 같을 거야.

F 46) 그런 경우라면, 너는 정기구독하는 편이 낫겠다.

40 ▶ 정답 ⓓ

Why does Jonathan find Enterprise magazine useful for gaining knowledge about business?

(a) It is a popular magazine.
(b) It is very accessible.
(c) It is his favorite magazine.
(d) It is easy to understand.

해석

조나단은 경제에 관한 지식을 얻는데 Enterprise지가 왜 유용하다고 생각하나요?

(a) 인기 있는 잡지이기 때문에
(b) 쉽게 구할 수 있기 때문에
(c) 그가 가장 좋아하는 잡지이기 때문에
(d) 이해하기 쉽기 때문에

해설 "They explain things in simple language in all the articles. Because of this, I find the stories very useful for expanding my knowledge about areas of business I'm not familiar with."에서 경제 분야의 지식이 쉽게 쓰여져서 유용하다고 언급하고 있다.

41 ▶정답 ⓐ

Why is Jonathan unable to read the magazine regularly?

(a) He is sometimes unable to buy a copy of the latest issue.
(b) He frequently misplaces his copy of it.
(c) He often can't access its online edition.
(d) He is usually too busy to read it.

해석
왜 조나단은 잡지를 정기적으로 읽을 수 없나요?
(a) 그는 가끔 최신판을 살 수 없기 때문에
(b) 그는 자주 잡지를 제자리에 두지 않기 때문에
(c) 그는 종종 온라인 판에 접속할 수 없기 때문에
(d) 그는 평상시에 너무 바빠서 읽을 수 없기 때문에

해설 "Unfortunately, I don't get to read all of the monthly issues. Sometimes, when I try to buy it from a newsstand, the copies are already sold out."에 잡지가 이미 다 팔려서 최신판을 구매할 수 없다고 언급되어 있다.

42 ▶정답 ⓒ

To what did Miriam compare the financial benefit of subscribing to a magazine?

(a) to borrowing magazines from a library
(b) to ordering artwork over the Internet
(c) to buying grocery items wholesale
(d) to buying old magazine issues

해석
잡지구독의 경제적 이익을 미리엄은 무엇에 비유하고 있나요?
(a) 도서관에서 잡지를 빌리는 것
(b) 인터넷을 통한 작품 주문하는 것
(c) 대량으로 식료품을 구입하는 것
(d) 오래된 잡지를 구입하는 것

해설 미리엄은 "You can save a lot by having a subscription. It's like buying groceries in bulk. It's so much cheaper!"라고 말하며 정기구독으로 할인 받는 것을 식료품 대량 구입에 비유했다.

43 ▶정답 ⓐ

How do distributors respond to complaints about late deliveries?

(a) by resolving the complaints immediately
(b) by ignoring the complaints indefinitely
(c) by blaming the publishers
(d) by giving away free copies

해석
어떻게 배급업자들은 늦은 배송에 관해 불만사항을 응대하나요?
(a) 불만들을 즉시 해결함으로써
(b) 불만을 기한 없이 무시함으로써
(c) 출판사들을 비난함으로써
(d) 무료 잡지를 제공함으로써

해설 "Most distributors act on subscribers' complaints right away."에서 배급없자들이 불만사항을 즉각적으로 해결해 준다는 것을 알 수 있다.

44 ▶정답 ⓓ

What do subscribers to the print edition get that online subscribers don't?

(a) more updated information
(b) articles that are better written
(c) more humorous writers
(d) special printed contents

해석
온라인 구독자들은 안 되고, 인쇄판 구독자들만 얻는 것은 무엇인가요?
(a) 더 업데이트된 정보
(b) 더 잘 작성된 기사들
(c) 더 유머러스한 작가들
(d) 특별히 기재된 내용들

해설 "I think the print and electronic contents are basically the same. The main difference is that most leading magazines also have what they call "premium materials," which can be accessed only by subscribers to the print edition."를 통해 고급정보가 인쇄판 구독자들에게만 제공된다는 것을 알 수 있다.

45 ▶정답 ⓑ

According to Miriam, why does she prefer a magazine's print edition to its online edition?

(a) because it can be hand-carried
(b) because it is more relaxing to read
(c) because it is released much earlier
(d) because it has a more attractive design

해석
미리엄에 따르면, 왜 그녀는 온라인 판보다 인쇄판을 선호하나요?
(a) 휴대할 수 있기 때문에
(b) 읽기에 더 편안하기 때문에
(c) 더 빨리 발행되기 때문에
(d) 더욱 매력적인 디자인을 갖고 있기 때문에

해설 "Personally, I prefer reading the print edition. It's a relaxing break from staring at my computer monitor for long hours."에서 인쇄판 기사는 컴퓨터 화면을 계속 응시하지 않고 편하게 읽을 수 있다고 말하고 있다.

46 ▶ 정답 ⓒ

Based on the conversation, what will Jonathan most likely do?
(a) He will buy cheaper ink and paper.
(b) He will just read the magazine's online version.
(c) He will subscribe to Enterprise magazine.
(d) He will get a subscription to Art Review.

해석
대화를 바탕으로, 조나단이 무엇을 할 것 같나요?
(a) 그는 값싼 잉크와 종이를 살 것이다.
(b) 그는 잡지의 온라인 버전을 읽을 것이다.
(c) 그는 Enterprise 잡지를 정기 구독할 것이다.
(d) 그는 Art Review을 정기 구독할 것이다.

해설 대화의 마지막에 미리엄의 말 "If that's the case, you might as well get a subscription!"을 통해 조나단은 Enterprise 잡지를 정기구독을 할 것이라는 추론할 수 있다.

[Part 4]

Now listen to the questions.

47: How does the speaker describe the atmosphere in the emergency room?
48: Based on the talk, which patients are most likely to be seen first by a doctor?
49: Why do ER patients rarely have medical records to base a diagnosis on?
50: Which term refers to the record of the possible causes of the patient's illness?
51: What is true about the general surgeon?
52: What should ER personnel do about patients who are unable to pay their medical bills?

해석
47: 응급실의 분위기를 강연자는 어떻게 묘사하고 있나요?
48: 강의에 따르면, 어떤 환자가 가장 먼저 의사의 진료를 받을 것 같나요?
49: 왜 응급 환자들은 진단의 근거인 의료기록을 거의 갖고 있지 않나요?
50: 어떤 용어가 환자의 가능한 질병의 원인에 관한 기록을 표현하나요?
51: 일반 외과의에 관해 사실인 것은 무엇인가요?
52: 병원비를 지불할 능력이 없는 환자들에 대해 응급실 직원들은 무엇을 해야 하나요?

Now you will hear the talk.

Good morning, everybody. I'm your instructor for this course, Introduction to Emergency Medicine. I'm the head of the Emergency Medicine Department here at the university hospital. I'm also a doctor and an Assistant Professor at the university's medical school.

Welcome to another challenging part of your medical training. 47) The emergency room is one of the busiest parts of the university hospital. And even on the rare days when it is slow at the ER, time is very important in emergency medicine. This is because an ER doctor is always making quick decisions. Unless you know how to work systematically, it's very easy to get confused in this environment, and that can lead to making a wrong decision. For this reason, I'd like to review certain guidelines, which I'm sure you've already learned, but are important nonetheless.

First of all, as soon as a patient arrives in the ER, he should be given immediate attention, and a nurse should record his medical complaints and vital signs right away. The patient's temperature, blood pressure, and pulse rate should be taken regardless of the reason for admission or reported symptoms. This is important for two reasons. One is that they will help us determine how urgent a specific case is. 48) Not all patients need to see a doctor right away, so it is helpful to have an objective way to decide how critical or minor a given case is. Vital signs like blood pressure and temperature can help you determine these.

Another reason is that these readings are usually the only information we have to begin recording the patient's complete medical chart. 49) Doctors who have dealt with certain patients will have detailed records of their medical history. However, this is rarely the case in the ER because most emergency patients are new to the hospital. Should the patient's condition suddenly change during their ER visit, this information could be vital to making a good diagnosis.

The next step is registration. At this stage, another nurse obtains more details, usually about the patient's medical history and health insurance coverage. However, if the patient's condition is life threatening, registration may be done much later. What's important is that after registration, the patient is immediately taken to the examination room. The ER physician comes in to examine the patient and his medical records thoroughly.

50) Based on the findings, the physician creates a list of the possible causes of the illness. What do we call this list? It's the "differential diagnosis," of course. Let's say that based on the differential diagnosis, the physician suspects that the patient has appendicitis. In that case, blood, urine, and other laboratory tests will be required. 51) The physician may also consult the general surgeon

who will further examine the patient and review the test results. If the surgeon confirms that the patient is suffering from appendicitis, then she will get the patient's consent to perform an operation.

Now, one last reminder: 52) Because we serve in a state medical institution, we must attend to all ER patients properly regardless of their capacity to pay. Do you have any questions? Well, since there's none, let's now get down to work.

Words

- emergency room 응급실
- pulse rate 맥박
- urgent 긴급한
- medical history 병력 기록
- threaten 위협하다
- diagnosis 진단
- appendicitis 맹장염
- consent 동의, 동의서
- vital sign 활력징후
- admission 입원
- critical 위태로운, 중요한
- vital 매우 중요한, 필수적인
- physician 의사
- urine 소변
- surgeon 외과의

해석

여러분, 안녕하세요. 저는 여러분들의 응급의학 입문 과정의 강사입니다. 저는 이 대학병원의 응급의학과 장입니다. 또한 의사이며, 의과대학의 조교수입니다.

의학교육의 또 다른 어려운 분야에 온 것을 환영합니다. 47) 응급실은 대학병원에서 가장 바쁜 곳 중 한 곳입니다. 드물게 응급실이 한가한 날에도, 시간은 응급의학에서 정말 중요합니다. 응급실 의사들이 항상 신속한 결정을 내리기 때문입니다. 만약 여러분이 체계적으로 일하는 방법을 알지 못한다면, 이런 환경에서 쉽게 혼란스러워질 것이고, 그것은 잘못된 결정을 내리는 결과를 초래할 수 있습니다. 이런 이유로, 저는 여러분이 이미 배웠지만, 그럼에도 굉장히 중요한 지침들을 검토하고자 합니다. 무엇보다, 환자가 응급실에 도착하자마자, 응급치료를 받아야 하며, 간호사는 즉시 환자의 의학적인 문제와 활력 징후(vital sign)를 기록해야 합니다. 입원 이유나 기재된 증상과 상관없이 환자의 체온, 혈압, 및 맥박을 확인해야 합니다. 이것은 두 가지 이유에서 중요합니다. 한 가지 이유는, 그들이 특정 경우가 얼마나 긴급한지를 결정하는 데 도움을 줄 것이기 때문입니다. 48) 모든 환자가 의사의 즉각적인 진료를 받을 필요는 없으므로, 특정 경우가 얼마나 위태로운지, 사소한지를 판단하는 객관적인 방법을 갖는 것이 도움이 됩니다. 혈압과 체온 같은 활력징후들은 여러분이 이들을 결정하는 데 도움을 줄 수 있습니다.

또 다른 이유는 이러한 기록들이 환자의 완전한 의료차트를 기록하기 시작하는 데에 있어 우리가 가지고 있는 유일한 정보이기 때문입니다. 49) 특정 환자들을 진료해 온 의사들은 그들의 자세한 병력기록을 갖게 됩니다. 그러나 대부분의 응급환자들은 그 병원이 처음이기 때문에, 이런 경우는 드뭅니다. 응급실에 있는 동안 환자의 상태가 갑자기 변한다면, 이 정보는 적절한 진단을 내리는 데 중요할 수 있습니다.

다음 단계는 접수입니다. 이 단계에서 다른 간호사는 환자의 병력 및 건강보험 보장범위에 관해 더욱 자세한 정보를 얻습니다. 그러나 환자의 상태가 생명을 위협하는 경우 접수는 좀 더 후에 할 수 있습니다. 중요한 것은 접수 후에, 환자를 즉시 검사실로 보내는 것입니다. 응급실 의사가 환자와 그의 의료기록을 철저하게 검토하기 위해 들어옵니다. 50) 결과를 바탕으로, 의사는 가능한 질병의 원인목록을 작성합니다. 우리는 이 목록을 무엇이라고 부르나요? 물론, 이것은 '감별 진단'입니다. 감별 진단을 근거로, 의사가 환자를 맹장염으로 의심했다고 가정해봅시다. 이 경우, 혈액, 소변 및 기타 검사실검사가 필요합니다. 51) 또한 의사는 환자를 꼼꼼하게 검사하고 결과를 검토할 일반 외과의사와 상의할 수 있습니다. 만약 외과의사가 환자가 맹장염으로 고통 받고 있다는 것을 확인하면, 그러면 그녀는 수술을 시행하기 위해 환자의 동의서를 받을 것입니다. 이제, 마지막 주의사항입니다: 52) 우리는 국립의료기관에서 근무하기 때문에 환자들의 지불능력에 관계없이 모든 응급환자들을 적절하게 보살펴야 합니다. 질문 있으신가요? 그럼, 질문 없으니 이제 일하러 갑시다.

47 ▶ 정답 ⓓ

How does the speaker describe the atmosphere in the emergency room?

(a) It is very relaxed.
(b) It is very disturbing.
(c) It is very boring.
(d) It is very hectic.

해석 응급실의 분위기를 강연자는 어떻게 묘사하고 있나요?

(a) 매우 편안하다.
(b) 매우 혼란스럽다.
(c) 매우 지루하다.
(d) 매우 바쁘다.

해설 강연자는 "The emergency room is one of the busiest parts of the university hospital."라고 말했다.

48 ▶ 정답 ⓐ

Based on the talk, which patients are most likely to be seen first by a doctor?

(a) those whose vital sign readings are more critical
(b) those whose vital sign readings are most stable
(c) those who have records of their medical history
(d) those who arrived at the ER first

해설 강의에 따르면, 어떤 환자가 가장 먼저 의사의 진료를 받을 것 같나요?

(a) 활력징후 수치가 위태로운 환자들
(b) 활력징후 표시가 가장 안정적인 환자들
(c) 병력기록이 있는 환자들
(d) 응급실에 처음 도착한 환자들

해설 "Not all patients need to see a doctor right away, so it is helpful to have an objective way to decide how critical or minor a given case is. Vital signs like blood pressure and temperature can help you determine these."에서 특정한 환자가 얼마나 심각하고 미미한지를 활력징후를 통해서 판단한다고 했다. 활력징후가 위태롭거나 좋지 않은 환자들은 의사들의 진료를 곧 받을 것이다.

49 ▶ 정답 ⓓ

Why do ER patients rarely have medical records to base a diagnosis on?

(a) because they refused to give information the first time
(b) because they have never been to any hospital before
(c) because they are usually minor cases
(d) because it is usually their first ER admission

해석
왜 응급환자들은 진단의 근거인 의료기록을 거의 갖고 있지 않나요?
(a) 처음에 정보 제공하는 것을 거부했기 때문에
(b) 어떤 병원에도 이전에 가본 적이 없으므로
(c) 대개 경미한 경우이기 때문에
(d) 보통 응급실 첫 입원이므로

해설 "Doctors who have dealt with certain patients will have detailed records of their medical history. However, this is rarely the case in the ER because most emergency patients are new to the hospital."를 통해 응급실에는 환자들이 위급상황에 처음 오는 경우가 대부분이므로 진료기록이 없는 경우가 많다는 것을 알 수 있다.

50 ▶ 정답 ⓑ

Which term refers to the record of the possible causes of the patient's illness?

(a) emergency response
(b) differential diagnosis
(c) laboratory examination
(d) surgical procedure

해석
어떤 용어가 환자의 가능한 질병의 원인에 관한 기록을 표현하나요?
(a) 비상대처
(b) 감별진단
(c) 실험실검사
(d) 외과적 시술

해설 "Based on the findings, the physician creates a list of the possible causes of the illness. What do we call this list? It's the "differential diagnosis," of course."에서 언급했다.

51 ▶ 정답 ⓒ

What is true about the general surgeon?

(a) She performs the required laboratory tests.
(b) Only she can determine the patients' condition.
(c) She confirms the findings of the emergency doctor.
(d) Only she can explain to the patients their condition.

해석
일반 외과의에 관해 사실인 것은 무엇인가요?
(a) 그녀는 필요한 실험실검사를 수행한다.
(b) 그녀만이 환자의 상태를 결정할 수 있다.
(c) 그녀는 응급실 의사가 내린 결과를 확인한다.
(d) 그녀만이 환자들에게 그들의 상태를 설명할 수 있다.

해설 "The physician may also consult the general surgeon who will further examine the patient and review the test results."의 언급을 통해 외과의사는 응급실에서 실시한 검사결과를 검토한다는 것을 알 수 있다.

52 ▶ 정답 ⓑ

What should ER personnel do about patients who are unable to pay their medical bills?

(a) refer them to a specialist at once
(b) give them proper medical attention nonetheless
(c) send them away as soon as possible
(d) give them priority over other patients

해석
병원비를 지불할 능력이 없는 환자들에 대해 응급실 직원들은 무엇을 해야 하나요?
(a) 그들을 즉시 전문가에게 보낸다.
(b) 그럼에도 불구하고 그들에게 적절한 치료를 해준다.
(c) 가능한 빨리 그들을 보낸다.
(d) 그들에게 다른 환자보다 우선권을 준다.

해설 "Because we serve in a state medical institution, we must attend to all ER patients properly regardless of their capacity to pay."를 통해 응급환자의 목숨이 위태로운 경우, 접수보다 치료가 우선시 된다는 것을 알 수 있다.

Reading and Vocabulary 03회

Question 53-80

ANSWER KEY p.81

53	ⓓ	54	ⓓ	55	ⓒ	56	ⓑ
57	ⓐ	58	ⓒ	59	ⓓ	60	ⓐ
61	ⓓ	62	ⓐ	63	ⓑ	64	ⓒ
65	ⓓ	66	ⓑ	67	ⓐ	68	ⓒ
69	ⓑ	70	ⓓ	71	ⓐ	72	ⓑ
73	ⓒ	74	ⓓ	75	ⓒ	76	ⓑ
77	ⓐ	78	ⓑ	79	ⓒ	80	ⓓ

Question 53-59

MARGARET MEAD

Margaret Mead was an American anthropologist who was famous for her research on cultural anthropology and her insights on how the world functioned. Through her writings and interviews in mass media, she has made anthropology 58) accessible to many people.

Margaret Mead was born in 1901 in Philadelphia, Pennsylvania. She was the eldest of the four children of Edward Sherwood Mead, a professor of economics at the University of Pennsylvania, and Emily Fogg, a sociologist. 53) She was studying a sociology at Barnard College in New York when she became keenly interested in anthropology. There, she met the anthropologist Franz Boas who would later become her mentor at Columbia University graduate school.

At age 23, Mead traveled to the South Pacific to do research for her doctoral dissertation. The resulting book, Coming of Age in Samoa, became a bestseller. She continued studying the cultures of North America and Southeast Asia after earning her PhD. 54) In Bali, Indonesia, she pioneered the use of photography in anthropological research, taking more than 30,000 pictures of the Balinese.

In the course of her career, Mead had important insights about childrearing, women's roles, and gender relations in many cultures. She was one of the first to introduce the idea that society expected individuals to behave in certain "acceptable" ways, and that these ways varied greatly between cultures. 55) She further proposed that masculine and feminine behavior were not all caused by biological differences but by cultural conditioning or socialization.

Mead taught at the New School for Social Research, Yale University, and Emory University. She was also the first woman anthropologist to become president of the American Association for the Advancement of Science. During her lifetime, she produced more than 40 books and 1,000 scholarly articles. Although Mead was controversial, 56) it is widely acknowledged that her research and numerous documentary films promoted a greater understanding of cultures that had been ignored by mainstream American society.

From 1926 until her retirement, Mead worked at the American Museum of Natural History. A committed activist, she often commented on social and environmental issues. 57) In recognition of her achievements, Time magazine named her "Mother of the World" in 1969. Her memoirs, Blackberry Winter, were published in 1972. She died in New York in 1978. A year later, she was posthumously 59) awarded the Presidential Medal of Freedom.

Words

anthropologist 인류학자
insight 통찰(력), 식견
accessible 접근 가능한, 이용 가능한
keenly 강렬하게, 깊게
pioneer 개척하다
behave 행동하다, 처신하다
masculine 남성적인
behavior 행동, 행실
retirement 은퇴
comment 논평하다
anthropology 인류학
mass media 대중매체
sociology 사회학
doctoral dissertation 박사학위논문
childrearing 육아, 자녀양육
propose 제안하다, 제시하다
feminine 여성적인
mainstream 주류
committed 헌신적인
posthumously 사후에

해석

마가렛 미드

마가렛 미드는 문화 인류학에 관한 연구와 어떻게 세계가 역할을 했는지에 대한 통찰로 유명했던 미국 인류학자였다. 그녀는 저서와 대중매체와의 인터뷰를 통해, 많은 사람들이 인류학에 접근할 수 있도록 했다.

마가렛 미드는 1901년에 펜실베니아주 필라델피아에서 태어났다. 그녀는 펜실베니아 대학의 경제학 교수인 Edward Sherwood Mead와 사회학자인 Emily Fogg의 네 자녀 중 첫째였다. 53) 그녀가 뉴욕 주 Barnard College에서 사회학을 공부할 때, 인류학에 깊은 흥미가 생겼다. 그곳에서 그녀는 후에 콜롬비아 대학원에서 그녀의 멘토가 될 인류학자인 프란츠 보아스를 만났다.

23세의 나이에, 미드는 박사학위 논문 연구를 위해 남태평양에 갔다.

그 결과물인 Coming of Age in Samoa는 베스트셀러가 되었다. 그녀는 박사학위를 받은 후, 북미와 동남아시아 문화를 계속해서 연구했다. 54) 인도네시아의 발리에서 그녀는 인류학 연구에 사진촬영을 처음으로 사용하여 30,000장 이상의 발리 족 사진을 찍었다.

미드는 경력을 쌓는 중에, 많은 문화권에서 육아, 여성의 역할과 성별 관계에 관해 중요한 통찰을 하게 되었다. 그녀는 사회가 개인이 '허용된' 특정한 방식으로 행동할 것을 기대하고, 이 방식은 문화마다 크게 달라진다는 생각을 처음으로 도입한 학자 중 한 명이었다. 55) 더 나아가, 그녀는 남성적인 행동과 여성적인 행동이 생물학적인 차이에서만 비롯되는 것이 아니라 문화 조건화 또는 사회화에 의해서도 기인한다는 것을 제시했다.

미드는 Emory University과 Yale University 그리고 New School for Social Research에서 강의 했다. 그녀는 또한 American Association for the Advancement of Science (미국과학진흥협회)의 회장이 된 최초의 여성 인류학자였다. 그녀는 일생 동안 40권 이상의 책과 1000권 이상의 학술논문을 발표했다. 미드는 논란이 많았음에도 불구하고, 56) 그녀의 연구 및 수많은 다큐멘터리 영화가 미국 주류 사회에 의해 간과되었던 문화에 대한 이해를 증진시켰다는 것은 널리 인정받았다.

1926년부터 은퇴할 때까지 미드는 American Museum of Natural History (미국 자연사 박물관)에서 근무했다. 헌신적인 행동주의자로서, 그녀는 사회문제 및 환경문제와 관련된 논평을 자주 했다. 57) 그녀의 업적을 인정하여, Time지는 1969년 그녀를 'Mother of the World'로 선정했다. 그녀의 회고록인 Blackberry Winter는 1972년 출간됐다. 그녀는 1978년 New York에서 사망했다. 일 년 후, 그녀는 사후에 Presidential Medal of Freedom를 수여 받았다.

53 ▶ 정답 ⓓ

What field of study did Margaret Mead pursue before becoming an anthropologist?

(a) journalism
(b) economics
(c) filmmaking
(d) sociology

해설
마가렛 미드는 인류학자가 되기 전에 어떤 분야의 연구를 했나요?

(a) 언론
(b) 경제학
(c) 영화제작
(d) 사회학

해설 "She was studying a sociology at Barnard College in New York when she became keenly interested in anthropology."에서 사회학을 공부하던 중에 인류학에 관심이 생겼다고 했으므로 사회학을 연구했다는 것을 알 수 있다.

54 ▶ 정답 ⓓ

What was probably Mead's major contribution while studying Balinese society?

(a) building a large collection of Balinese artifacts
(b) writing a bestselling book about Bali
(c) founding a center for women's studies in Indonesia
(d) making photography a part of field research

해설
발리 사회를 연구하는 동안 미드의 주된 공헌은 아마도 무엇이었나요?

(a) 많은 발리 공예품을 수집하는 것
(b) 발리에 관한 베스트셀러 책을 쓴 것
(c) 인도네시아에서 여성학 센터를 설립한 것
(d) 사진촬영을 현장 연구 일부가 되게 한 것

해설 "In Bali, Indonesia, she pioneered the use of photography in anthropological research, taking more than 30,000 pictures of the Balinese."에서 사진 30,000장을 사용하여 발리 사회를 연구했다고 언급되어 있다.

55 ▶ 정답 ⓒ

How did Mead explain gender behavior?

(a) It is determined at birth.
(b) It is similar across all cultures.
(c) It is shaped by one's society.
(d) It can only be explained by biology.

해설
성별 행동양식을 미드는 어떻게 설명했나요?

(a) 태어날 때 결정된다.
(b) 모든 문화권에서 비슷하다.
(c) 자신의 사회에 의해 형성된다.
(d) 오직 생물학에 의해서만 설명될 수 있다.

해설 "She further proposed that masculine and feminine behavior were not all caused by biological differences but by cultural conditioning or socialization."에서 성별에 따른 행동이 생물학적 차이뿐 아니라 조건화나 사회화에 따라서 달라질 수 있다고 언급되어 있다.

56 ▶ 정답 ⓑ

Which was a result of Mead's work in the US?

(a) an interest in modern societies
(b) an increased awareness of other cultures
(c) a sudden growth in research
(d) a preference for more primitive research subjects

해설
미국에서 미드가 했던 활동의 결과는 무엇이었나요?

(a) 현대사회에 관한 관심
(b) 다른 문화에 대한 인식증가

(c) 연구에서의 급격한 성장
(d) 더 원시적인 연구 주제에 관한 선호도

해설 "it is widely acknowledged that her research and numerous documentary films promoted a greater understanding of cultures that had been ignored by mainstream American society."을 통해서 미국 주류 사회에서 간과되었던 비주류 문화에 대한 관심과 이해가 높아졌 다고 했으므로 (b)가 가장 적절하다.

57 ▶ 정답 ⓐ

Based on the passage, why most probably was Mead named "Mother of the World"?
(a) for her efforts in promoting the understanding of cultures
(b) for her work in modernizing ancient cultures
(c) because she has raised the status of women
(d) because she acted like a mother to her research subjects

해석 지문에 따르면, 미드는 왜 'Mother of the World'로 선정되었나요?
(a) 문화에 관한 이해를 증진시키려는 그녀의 노력 때문에
(b) 고대 문화의 현대화에 관한 그녀의 연구 때문에
(c) 여성의 지위를 높였기 때문에
(d) 그녀가 연구 피실험자들에게 어머니처럼 행동했기 때문에

해설 그녀의 업적에 관해 세 번째 단락에서 북미와 동남아시아 문화연 구, 네 번째 단락에서 개인의 사회화에 관한 연구, 다섯 번째 단락에서 다른 문화를 이해하는 데 끼친 공헌이 나와 있다. 이러한 업적들로 인해 미드가 Mother of the World로 선정되었다고 마지막 단락에 나온다. 따라서 가 장 적절한 것은 (a)이다.

58 ▶ 정답 ⓒ

In the context of the passage, accessible means _____.
(a) handy
(b) restricted
(c) available
(d) nearby

해석 지문의 문맥상, accessible은 _____을 의미한다.
(a) 편리한
(b) 제한된
(c) 이용 가능한
(d) 근처의

해설 accessible 이용 가능한, 접근 가능한

59 ▶ 정답 ⓓ

In the context of the passage, awarded means _____.
(a) donated
(b) allowed
(c) paid
(d) given

해석 문맥상, awarded는 _____을 의미한다.
(a) 기부하다
(b) 허용하다, 받아들이다
(c) 지급하다
(d) 주다

해설 award 주다, 수여하다

Question 60-66

ITALIAN SUPERVOLCANO IS GETTING ACTIVE

Located near a densely populated area and inactive for more than 400 years, the "supervolcano" Campi Flegrei is starting to show signs of becoming active. 60-c) Named "burning fields" in Italian, and also known as the Phlegraean Fields, 60-b) the volcano is near the Bay of Naples in Italy. Recent monitoring has shown that it is heating up and getting active, and 60-d) scientists are saying that it may erupt in the near future.

61) Like all supervolcanoes, Campi Flegrei is characterized by a large depression, called "caldera," that spans more than six miles. The volcano is not a single volcanic cone, but a large 65) complex of 24 craters and geysers that release hot gases. A large portion of the volcano is submerged in the Mediterranean Sea.

The volcano is believed to have formed hundreds of thousands of years ago. 62) Its first eruption, which occurred 200,000 years ago, 66) spewed so much ash that it blocked sunlight from reaching the earth's surface, triggering a volcanic winter or global cooling. The volcano erupted again 40,000 years ago, and scientific evidence suggests it might be one of the reasons why Neanderthals have become extinct. 63) The volcano's most recent eruption in 1538 lasted for eight straight days, spreading ash all over Europe and forming a new mountain. Since its last eruption, Campi Flegrei has been inactive.

Recently, there have been signs that Campi Flegrei is approaching a critical pressure point that can trigger another eruption. 64) The location of the volcano is quite problematic. It is near the metropolitan area of Naples, Italy: one of the densely populated areas of the world. Most of the increasing rock deformation and heating have been observed in the area.

Despite these findings, it is very hard to determine the volcano's "tipping point" or the time it will erupt. The eruption may not even happen for the next 100 years. However, as a precautionary measure, the government has already raised the threat level from green ("quiet") to yellow ("requires scientific monitoring"). The Italian National Institute of Geophysics is monitoring the situation and analyzing real-time findings.

Words

densely populated 인구가 밀집한	active 활동중인, 활성의
erupt 분화하다, 분출하다	depression 함몰지, 움푹한 곳
span 걸쳐있다	volcanic cone complex 화산 원뿔
crater 분화구	geyser 간헐 온천
release 방출하다	submerge 가라앉다, 잠기다
spew 뿜어내다, 분출하다	ash 재
block 막다, 차단하다	extinct 멸종된
critical pressure point 임계 압력점	trigger 촉발시키다
eruption 폭발, 분화	problematic 문제가 있는
metropolitan area 수도권	deformation 변형
precautionary measure 예방조치	

이탈리아 초화산이 활성화되고 있다

인구밀도가 높은 지역 근처에 위치하며, 400년 이상 활동하지 않은 '초화산'인 Campi Flegrei(캄피 플레그레이)가 활성화될 조짐을 보이기 시작한다. 60-c) 이탈리아어로 '불타는 들판'이라고 이름이 붙여진, Phlegraean Fields으로도 알려진 60-b) 이 화산은 이탈리아의 나폴리 만 근처에 있다. 최근 모니터링은 그것이 뜨거워지고 있으며, 활발해지고 있음을 보여주었고 60-d) 가까운 미래에 분화할 가능성이 있다고 과학자들은 말하고 있다.

61) 모든 초화산들과 마찬가지로 Campi Flegrei는 6마일 이상에 걸쳐있는 '칼데라(caldera)'라고 불리는 거대한 함몰지가 특징이다. 화산은 하나의 화산 원뿔이 아닌 뜨거운 가스를 방출하는 24개의 분화구와 간헐 온천의 거대한 복합체이다. 화산 대부분은 지중해에 가라 앉아 있다.

이 화산은 수십만 년 전에 형성된 것으로 간주된다. 62) 20만 년 전에 발생했던 첫 번째 폭발은 엄청난 화산재를 분출해 햇빛이 지구 표면에 닿지 못하게 막아뒀고, 이는 '화산 겨울' 또는 지구 냉각현상을 야기시켰다. 이 화산은 4만 년 전에 다시 분화했으며, 과학적인 증거에 따르면, 그것은 네안데르탈인이 멸종된 이유 중 하나가 될 지도 모른다. 63) 1538년에 있었던 가장 최근 화산 폭발은 8일 연속으로 지속되었으며, 유럽전역에 화산재를 퍼뜨리고 새로운 산을 형성했다. 마지막 분화 이후, Campi Flegrei는 비활

성 상태이다. 최근, Campi Flegrei가 또 다른 분출을 유발시킬 수 있는 임계 압력 지점에 접근하고 있다는 징후가 있다. 64) 화산 위치는 상당한 문제가 있다. 그것은 이탈리아 나폴리의 수도권 근처에 있다; 세계의 인구밀집지역 중 하나이다. 증가하는 암석의 변형과 가열의 대부분이 이 지역에서 관측되고 있다.

이러한 발견에도 불구하고, 화산의 '전환점' 또는 분출할 시점을 결정하는 것은 매우 어렵다. 다음 100년 동안 분출이 일어나지 않을 수도 있다. 그러나 예방 조치로서 정부는 이미 위협수준을 이미 녹색('조용한')에서 황색('과학적 모니터링 필요')으로 올렸다. 이탈리아 국립 지구물리학연구소 (State Institute of Geophysics)는 상황을 모니터링하고 실시간 결과를 분석하고 있다.

60 ▶ 정답 ⓐ

What does not describe Campi Flegrei?

(a) It is the largest volcano in the world.
(b) It is in close proximity to a bay.
(c) Its name suggests its deadly effects.
(d) It might erupt in the coming years.

해설
Campi Flegrei (캄피 플레그레이)를 묘사하지 않는 것은 무엇인가요?
(a) 그것은 세계에서 가장 큰 화산이다.
(b) 그것은 만에 굉장히 가깝다.
(c) 그 이름은 그것의 치명적인 결과를 암시한다.
(d) 향후 몇 년 내에 분출 할 수 있다.

해설 (b), (c), (d)의 내용이 모두 첫 번째 단락에서 나오지만 (a)의 진술은 언급되지 않았다.

61 ▶ 정답 ⓓ

What makes Campi Flegrei a supervolcano?

(a) It has erupted many times in the past.
(b) It was formed hundreds of thousands of years ago.
(c) It was an inactive volcano that is now becoming active.
(d) Its depression is very big.

해설
Campi Flegrei가 초화산이 되게 하는 것은 무엇인가요?
(a) 그것은 과거에 여러 번 분출했다.
(b) 그것은 수십만 년 전에 형성되었다.
(c) 그것은 현재는 활동 중인 비활성 화산이었다.
(d) 그 함몰지는 매우 거대하다.

해설 Campi Flegrei는 6마일 이상에 걸쳐 있는 '칼데라'라는 함몰지가 특징이며 칼데라는 모든 초화산의 특징이라는 내용이 언급되어 있다. Campi Flegrei에 칼데리가 있다는 것은 초화산으로 분류될 수 있다고 추론할 수 있다.

62 ▶ 정답 ⓐ

How most likely did Campi Flegrei cause the "volcanic winter"?

(a) by covering the atmosphere with ash
(b) by forming another volcano nearby
(c) by spreading ash across European lands
(d) by forming a snow-like terrain around the world

해설

어떻게 Campi Flegrei가 '화산겨울'을 발생시켰을 것 같은가?
(a) 화산재로 대기를 덮음으로써
(b) 또 다른 화산을 근처에 형성함으로써
(c) 유럽전역 토지에 화산재를 퍼트림으로써
(d) 전 세계에 눈과 같은 지형을 조성함으로써

해설 "Its first eruption, which occurred 200,000 years ago, 66) spewed so much ash that it blocked sunlight from reaching the earth's surface, triggering a volcanic winter or global cooling."을 통해 화산겨울로 인해 지구 냉각현상이 일어난다는 것을 알 수 있다.

63 ▶ 정답 ⓑ

According to the article, when did the volcano last erupt?

(a) 200,000 years ago
(b) during the 16th century
(c) when the Neanderthals were wiped out
(d) 500 years ago

해설

이 글에 따르면, 언제 화산이 마지막으로 폭발했나요?
(a) 200,000년 전
(b) 16세기 동안
(c) 네안데르탈인이 멸망했을 때
(d) 500년 전

해설 "The volcano's most recent eruption in 1538 lasted for eight straight days, spreading ash all over Europe and forming a new mountain."에서 최근 마지막으로 폭발한 화산이 1538년이라고 했으므로 (b)의 16세기가 가장 적절하다.

64 ▶ 정답 ⓒ

What is the likely reason why the location of the volcano is problematic?

(a) It makes the volcano difficult to access.
(b) It makes its eruption hard to predict.
(c) Many people could die if it erupts.
(d) It generates rock deformation and heat.

해설

화산의 위치가 문제가 되는 이유는 무엇일 것 같은가?
(a) 그것은 화산에 접근하기 어렵게 만든다.
(b) 그것은 분출을 예측하기 어렵게 만든다.
(c) 그것이 분출하면, 많은 사람들이 죽을 수 있다.
(d) 그것은 암석변형과 열을 발생시킨다.

해설 "The location of the volcano is quite problematic. It is near the metropolitan area of Naples, Italy: one of the densely populated areas of the world."에서 인구 밀집 지역 사람들이 피해를 볼 수 있다고 했으므로 (c)가 가장 적절하다.

65 ▶ 정답 ⓓ

In the context of the passage, <u>complex</u> means _____.

(a) cone
(b) union
(c) building
(d) group

해설

문맥상, <u>complex</u>는 _____을 의미한다.
(a) 원뿔
(b) 단결, 결합
(c) 건물
(d) 무리, 집단

해설 complex 복합체, 집합체

66 ▶ 정답 ⓑ

In the context of the passage, <u>spewed</u> means _____.

(a) dripped
(b) ejected
(c) absorbed
(d) increased

해설

문맥상, <u>spewed</u>는 _____을 의미한다.
(a) (액체가) 떨어지다
(b) 내뿜다, 분출하다
(c) 흡수하다
(d) 증가하다

해설 spew 뿜어내다, 분출하다

Question 67-73

MEDITERRANEAN SEA

The Mediterranean Sea is a body of water bordered by three continents: Europe, Asia, and Africa. 67) <u>The sea served as a 72) major route for merchants and travelers during ancient times.</u> This was due to the many opportunities for trade and cultural exchange the Mediterranean provided the peoples of the region. Often called the "cradle of civilization," the region around the Mediterranean Sea was home to many early cultures and civilizations.

The sea covers an area of 2,509,000 square kilometers and has an average depth of 1,500 meters. Due to its limited tidal range and high rate of evaporation, the Mediterranean is much saltier than the Atlantic Ocean to which it is connected through a narrow channel called The Strait of Gibraltar.

The Mediterranean Sea is believed to be a remnant of Tethys, the vast ancient sea that has been shrinking since the African and Eurasian tectonic plates began to collide 30 million years ago. 68) <u>Slight movements of these plates cause the eruption of volcanoes such as Etna, Vesuvius, and Stromboli in Italy, and trigger earthquakes in parts of Europe and Africa.</u>

Some of the world's first civilizations flourished around the Mediterranean. The sea was used as a thoroughfare by merchants trading from Phoenicia. Carthage, Greece, Sicily, and Rome all 73) <u>rivaled</u> for commercial and political control of the Mediterranean region. 69) <u>Under the Roman Empire, the citizens referred to the Mediterranean as Mare Nostrum, meaning "our sea."</u> Later, the Byzantine Empire and the Arabs gained supremacy in the area. Between the 11th and 14th centuries, trading states such as Genoa, Venice, and Barcelona dominated the region. These states struggled with the Turkish territories for naval dominance. 70) <u>Commodities from Asia passed to Europe over Mediterranean routes until the late 15th century when a new passage was established around the Cape of Good Hope.</u>

At present, the Mediterranean Sea facilitates European and American access to the petroleum of Libya, Algeria, and the Persian Gulf region via the Suez Canal. The Mediterranean region has also become a popular tourist destination because of its beautiful beaches and warm climate. 71) <u>To protect the sea, countries bordering the Mediterranean agreed in 1995 to eliminate toxic waste disposal.</u>

Words

Mediterranean 지중해의
tidal 조수의
channel 해협
collide 충돌하다
flourish 번창하다, 번성하다
rival 경쟁하다
dominate 지배하다
dominance 지배
facilitate 용이하게 하다
bordered (국경, 경계를) 접하다
evaporation 증발
shrink 줄어들다
civilization 문명
thoroughfare 통행로, 직통로
supremacy 패권
struggle 갈등을 겪다
commodity 상품, 물품
via 경유하여, 통해

해석

지중해

지중해는 유럽, 아시아, 아프리카의 세 대륙에 둘러 싸여 있는 바다이다. 67)고대에 지중해는 상인들과 여행객들에게 중요한 항로였다. 이는 지중해가 그 지역 사람들에게 무역과 문화교류를 위한 수많은 기회를 제공했기 때문이었다. 종종 '문명의 요람'으로 불리던 지중해 주변지역은 초기 많은 문화와 문명의 본고장이었다.

지중해는 250만 9,000㎢의 면적을 포함하고, 평균수심은 1,500m 이다. 제한된 조수 간만 차와 높은 증발비율 때문에, 지중해는 'Strait of Gibraltar'라는 좁은 해협을 통해서 연결되는 Atlantic Ocean (대서양) 보다 훨씬 더 염분이 많다.

지중해는 테티스해의 잔재로 여겨지는데, 테티스해는 아프리카와 유라시아의 지질구조 판이 3천만 년 전에 충돌하기 시작한 이래로 가라앉고 있는 고대의 광활한 바다다. 68) <u>이 판들이 약간만 움직여도 이탈리아의 Etna, Vesuvius, 그리고 Stromboli 등의 화산들이 분출하고, 유럽 및 아프리카 일부지역에서 지진이 발생한다.</u>

세계 최초의 문명들 중 일부는 지중해 주변에서 번성했다. 이 바다는 페니키아 무역상인들의 통행로로 사용되었다. 카르타고, 그리스, 시칠리 그리고 로마는 모두 지중해 지역의 상권 및 정치권을 장악하기 위해 경쟁을 벌였다. 69) 로마제국 아래에, 시민들은 지중해를 '우리의 바다'를 의미하는 <u>Mare Nostrum으로 불렀다.</u> 후에, 비잔틴 제국과 아랍인들은 이 지역에서 패권을 얻었다. 11세기와 14세기 사이에는 제노아, 베니스, 바르셀로나 등의 무역 국가가 이 지역을 지배했다. 이 국가들은 해군지배권을 놓고 터키의 영토들과 갈등을 빚었다. 70) <u>Cape of Good Hope 주변에 새로운 통로가 생겼던 15세기 후반까지, 아시아 상품은 지중해를 통해 유럽으로 전달되었다.</u>

현재, 지중해는 수에즈운하를 통해 유럽인과 미국인이 리비아, 알제리와 페르시아 만 지역의 석유로 접근하는 것을 용이하게 한다. 지중해지역은 또한 아름다운 해변과 온난한 기후로 인해 인기 있는 관광지가 되었다. 71) <u>바다를 보호하기 위해, 지중해 연안국들은 1995년 독성의 쓰레기폐기물을 제거하는 것에 동의했다.</u>

67 ▶ 정답 ⓐ

What is true about the Mediterranean Sea?

(a) It has been used for economic trade for centuries.
(b) It lies between four continents.
(c) It has fewer salt deposits than the Atlantic Ocean.
(d) Its surrounding areas had been unlivable.

해석
지중해에 관해 사실은 무엇인가요?
(a) 수세기 동안 경제무역을 목적으로 사용되었다.
(b) 네 대륙 사이에 놓여있다.
(c) 대서양보다 소금 매장량이 적다.
(d) 주변 지역은 살아남을 수 없다.

해설 "The sea served as a major route for merchants and travelers during ancient times."의 언급을 통해 경제무역 목적으로 사용되었음을 알 수 있다.

68 ▶ 정답 ⓒ

Which disaster remains a threat to the Mediterranean region?

(a) droughts
(b) wars
(c) earthquakes
(d) tsunamis

해석
어떤 재앙이 지중해 지역에 여전히 위협적인가요?
(a) 가뭄
(b) 전쟁
(c) 지진
(d) 쓰나미

해설 "Slight movements of these plates cause the eruption of volcanoes such as Etna, Vesuvius, and Stromboli in Italy, and trigger earthquakes in parts of Europe and Africa."에서 지진이 언급되었다.

69 ▶ 정답 ⓑ

How did the early Romans consider the Mediterranean Sea?

(a) as the remains of an older sea
(b) as a property of the empire
(c) as the cradle of civilization
(d) as the source of Roman culture

해석
어떻게 초기 로마인들은 지중해를 여겼나요?
(a) 오래된 바다 유물로
(b) 제국의 소유물로
(c) 문명의 요람으로
(d) 로마 문화의 원천으로

해설 로마제국에서 로마인들은 지중해를 Mare Nostrum으로 불렀는데 이는 '우리의 바다'를 의미한다고 언급되어 있다. 지중해를 로마제국의 소유물로 여긴 것이라고 할 수 있다.

70 ▶ 정답 ⓓ

What probably happened to the Mediterranean Sea after the 15th century?

(a) It was acquired by the Turks.
(b) It became useless to European traders.
(c) It became even more crowded.
(d) It became a less important trade route to Asia.

해석
15세기 이후 지중해에 무슨 일이 일어났던 거 같나요?
(a) 터키에 의해 인수되었다.
(b) 유럽 상인들에게 쓸모없게 되었다.
(c) 더 많은 사람들이 몰려들었다.
(d) 아시아 무역항로로써의 중요성이 떨어졌다.

해설 "Commodities from Asia passed to Europe over Mediterranean routes until the late 15th century when a new passage was established around the Cape of Good Hope."에서의 언급을 통해 15세기 후반 이후에는 새로운 통로로 아시아와의 무역이 이뤄졌음을 알 수 있다.

71 ▶ 정답 ⓐ

In the 1990s, what did the countries in the region decide to do?

(a) stop dumping poisonous waste into the sea
(b) promote the region as a tourist destination
(c) increase their trade of petroleum
(d) open the Suez Canal

해석
1990년대, 이 지역의 국가들은 무엇을 하기로 결정했나요?
(a) 유독성 폐기물을 바다에 버리는 것을 중단하기
(b) 관광지로써 그 지역을 홍보하기
(c) 그들의 석유 교역을 확대하기
(d) 수에즈 운하를 개방하기

해설 "To protect the sea, countries bordering the Mediterranean agreed in 1995 to eliminate toxic waste disposal."에 지중해 연안 국들이 1995년에 독성 쓰레기 폐기물을 제거하는 것에 동의했다는 내용이 나온다.

72

▶ 정답 ⓑ

In the context of the passage, major means _____.

(a) serious
(b) important
(c) heavy
(d) old

해석

문맥상, major는 _____을 의미한다.

(a) 심각한
(b) 중요한
(c) 무거운
(d) 오래된

해설 major 중요한, 주된

73

▶ 정답 ⓒ

In the context of the passage, rivaled means _____.

(a) cooperated
(b) played
(c) competed
(d) shared

해석

문맥상 rivaled는 _____을 의미한다.

(a) 협력하다
(b) 경기하다
(c) 경쟁하다
(d) 공유하다, 나누다

해설 rival 경쟁하다, 겨루다

Question 74-80

April 22, 2016

Dr. Michael Smith
Dean, College of Engineering
California Polytechnic State University
San Luis Obispo, CA 93407

Dear Dr. Smith:

74) Colby Systems, Inc., a global leader in the production of consumer technology devices, 79) announces its "Create the Future" Design Contest for 2016. 75) The contest is open to all full-time designers, college professors, and students currently living in the United States.

Design ideas may be submitted in any of the following categories:

(1) *Everyday product*: an original design of a functional product that 76) enhances consumers' quality of life.
(2) *Safety device*: an original design of a mechanical or electronic device that 76) ensures people's safety at home, in the office, or outdoors.
(3) *Transportation equipment*: an original design of a mechanical or electro mechanical tool that improves the quality of cars, trains, and other 80) modes of transport.

78) We emphasize that all design entries should be original and have never been patented before. 77) Contestants are required to submit an essay that focuses on how the product works; how it would be manufactured; where it could be used; and how it would benefit both its intended market and the world as a whole. They must also include an illustration of the product in one of the formats listed on the entry form.

Entry forms are available at www.colbycontest.com. For guidelines, prizes, and other details about the contest, please refer to the attached brochure. Kindly share this information with the California Polytechnic community. Thank you.

Sincerely,

Geraldine Klein
Head, Industrial Division
Colby Systems, Inc.

87 Shelton Technology Center
P.O. Box 598

Words

consumer technology device 소비자 기술 장치
announce 발표하다, 알리다
contest 대회
enhance 향상시키다
ensure 보장하다, 확실하게 하다
tool 도구
transport 운송수단
entry 출품작, 출품물
original 독창적인, 창의적인
patent 특허를 받다, 특허권
contestant (대회) 참가자
manufacture 제조하다
the entry form 참가신청서
available 얻을 수 있는, 이용할 수 있는
guideline 지침

해석

스미스 씨께:

74) 소비자 기술 장치 생산의 글로벌 리더인 Colby Systems, Inc.는 2016년 'Create the Future' 디자인 공모전을 발표했습니다. 75) 이 대회는 현재 미국에 거주하는 전임 디자이너, 대학교수 및 학생이면 누구나 참여할 수 있습니다.

디자인 아이디어는 다음 범주 중 하나로 제출 될 수 있습니다.

(1) 일상용품: 76) 소비자의 삶의 질을 향상시켜주는 기능성 제품의 독창적인 디자인.
(2) 안전장치: 가정, 사무실 또는 실외에서 76) 사람들의 안전을 보장하는 기계 또는 전자장치의 독창적인 디자인.
(3) 운송장비: 자동차, 기차 및 기타 운송 수단의 질을 향상시키는 기계 또는 전자기계 도구의 독창적 디자인.

78) 우리는 모든 디자인 출품작이 독창적이어야 하며, 전에 특허를 받은 적이 없어야 한다는 것을 강조합니다. 77) 참가자들은 제품이 어떻게 작동하는지, 그것이 어떻게 제조될 것인지, 어디에 사용될 수 있는지, 그리고 그것이 겨냥된 시장과 전 세계에 어떻게 이익을 줄 수 있을 것인지에 관한 에세이를 제출해야 합니다. 또한 참가신청서에 열거된 형식 중 하나에 제품삽화를 포함해야 합니다.

참가 신청서는 www.colbycontest.com에서 볼 수 있습니다. 대회에 관한 가이드라인, 상품 및 기타 세부사항은 첨부된 팜플렛을 참조하세요. California Polytechnic 지역사회와 이 정보를 공유해주세요. 고맙습니다.

74 ▶ 정답 ⓓ

What kind of organization is sponsoring the contest?

(a) a state university
(b) a transportation agency
(c) a research institute
(d) a manufacturing firm

해석 대회를 어떤 종류의 기관이 후원하고 있나요?

(a) 주립대학
(b) 운송기관
(c) 연구소
(d) 제조회사

해설 "Colby Systems, Inc., a global leader in the production of consumer technology devices, 79) announces its "Create the Future" Design Contest for 2016."를 통해 대회를 후원하는 회사 Colby systems, Inc.는 소비자 기술 장치를 만드는 제조회사인 것을 알 수 있다.

75 ▶ 정답 ⓒ

Who may join the contest?

(a) only those who are employees of an academic institution
(b) only those who are working as professional designers
(c) only those who are US residents at the time of the contest
(d) only those who have advanced degrees in engineering

해석 대회에 누가 참가할 수 있나요?

(a) 교육기관의 직원에 한해서
(b) 전문 디자이너로 일하는 사람들에 한해서
(c) 대회 당시 미국 거주자에 한해서
(d) 공학석사 및 박사학위 소지자에 한해서

해설 "The contest is open to all full-time designers, college professors, and students currently living in the United States."의 언급을 통해 이 대회는 미국에 거주하는 사람들 모두가 참가 가능하다는 것을 알 수 있다.

76 ▶ 정답 ⓑ

How can the design ideas required for the contest be described?

(a) as solely for household use
(b) as beneficial to the consumers
(c) as adaptations of earlier designs
(d) as hi-tech digital products

해석 공모전에 필요한 디자인 아이디어는 어떻게 묘사될 수 있나요?

(a) 가계 전용으로
(b) 소비자에게 유익한 것으로
(c) 초기 설계의 응용으로
(d) 하이테크 디지털 제품으로

해설 디자인 아이디어에 관해서 설명하는 단락에서 '소비자 삶의 질을 향상시키고', '사람들의 안전을 보장하는'이라는 내용이 나온다. 소비자에게 도움이 되는 디자인 아이디어를 대회가 원한다는 것을 알 수 있다.

77 ▶ 정답 ⓐ

Which doesn't need to be described in the essay about the proposed product?

(a) how it would be profitable
(b) how it would be produced
(c) how it would be used
(d) how it would be helpful

해석 에세이에서 제안된 제품에 관해 설명할 필요가 없는 것은 어떤 것 인가요?

(a) 어떻게 수익을 낼 것인지
(b) 어떻게 생산이 될 것인지
(c) 어떻게 사용이 될 것인지
(d) 어떻게 도움이 될 것인지

해설 "Contestants are required to submit an essay that focuses on how the product works; how it would be manufactured; where it could be used; and how it would benefit both its intended market and the world as a whole."에서 제조, 사용, 유익함에 관한 내용은 나오지만 수익성에 대한 언급이 없다.

78 ▶ 정답 ⓑ

Why most likely is Colby Systems, Inc. sponsoring the contest?

(a) They want more publicity.
(b) They are looking for new products to make.
(c) They would like to support the designers.
(d) They are seeking to promote their products.

해설
Colby Systems, Inc.는 왜 대회를 후원하는 것 같나요?

(a) 그들은 더 많은 홍보를 원한다.
(b) 그들은 생산할 새로운 제품을 찾고 있다.
(c) 그들은 디자이너를 지원하려고 한다.
(d) 그들은 자사제품을 홍보하고자 한다.

해설 "We emphasize that all design entries should be original and have never been patented before."를 통해 Colby Systems, Inc.는 공모전을 통해 얻은 새로운 디자인을 토대로 새로운 제품을 생산하려는 것임을 추론할 수 있다.

79 ▶ 정답 ⓒ

In the context of the passage, announces means _____.

(a) hides
(b) reveals
(c) declares
(d) shows

해설
문맥상, announces는 _____을 의미한다.

(a) 감추다
(b) 밝히다, 드러내다
(c) 공표하다, 선언하다
(d) 보여주다

해설 announce 공표하다, 알리다

80 ▶ 정답 ⓓ

In the context of the passage, modes means _____.

(a) objects
(b) trends
(c) processes
(d) ways

해설
문맥상, modes는 _____을 의미한다.

(a) 목적, 대상
(b) 경향, 추세
(c) 과정, 절차
(d) 방식, 방법

해설 mode 방식, 방법

Answers and Explanations

한 권에 끝내는 G-TELP 실전모의고사 5회

해설편 4

SECTION 01 GRAMMAR
SECTION 02 LISTENING
SECTION 03 READING & VOCABULARY

Grammar Test 04회

Question 1-26

ANSWER KEY   p.93

01	ⓒ	02	ⓐ	03	ⓑ	04	ⓒ
05	ⓑ	06	ⓐ	07	ⓒ	08	ⓐ
09	ⓓ	10	ⓑ	11	ⓓ	12	ⓐ
13	ⓑ	14	ⓒ	15	ⓓ	16	ⓑ
17	ⓐ	18	ⓓ	19	ⓐ	20	ⓓ
21	ⓐ	22	ⓑ	23	ⓐ	24	ⓓ
25	ⓒ	26	ⓑ				

01 ▶정답 ⓒ

해석 Neal Livingston은 존경 받는 독립 영화 제작자이다. 그는 다양한 주제에 관한 텔레비전 다큐멘터리 영화를 제작한다. 많은 사람들이 천재로 여기는 그는 열두 살 때부터 35년 넘게 수상작들을 제작해오고 있다.

해설 '35년 넘는 동안'이라는 기간을 나타내는 시간 부사 for more than 35 years이 있으므로 완료시제가 적절하다. 부사절 접속사 since절에서 동사가 과거시제이므로 현재완료시제가 쓰여야 하는데, 현재도 제작하고 있는 상황을 강조하는 현재완료진행시제가 있으므로 문맥상 가장 자연스럽다.

02 ▶정답 ⓐ

해석 인터넷으로 인해, 요즘 학생들은 개인 학습 수요 및 일정에 따라 개인별 맞춤 학습을 할 수 있다. 만약 오늘날 인터넷 교육이 가능하지 않다면, 직장인들은 대학원 학위를 취득하는 데 어려움이 있을 것이다.

해설 가정법 과거의 문제이다. if절의 동사가 were이므로 주절에는 「조동사 과거형 + 동사원형」이 와야 한다.

오답분석 시간부사 today만 보고 혼합가정법과 헷갈려서는 안 된다. 혼합가정법이 성립하려면, today는 주절에 쓰여야 한다.

03 ▶정답 ⓑ

해석 Bruce는 Nexar Films 회사가 자사의 광고 서비스를 이용하면, 그의 수수료가 상당할 것이라는 것을 알고 있었다. 그는 결국 회사대표가 한 달 전에 승인하기 전까지, Nexar의 광고 수요를 3년 동안 관리해줄 것을 제안했었다.

해설 기간을 표현하는 for three years가 왔으므로 완료시제가 쓰여야 한다. 보기 중에 완료시제는 (B)밖에 없다.

04 ▶정답 ⓒ

해석 새로운 컴퓨터 게임은 심하게 학생들이 그들의 학업을 방해하여 수업에서 낮은 출석률과 부진한 수행평가를 야기한다. 학교 관계자들은 자녀들의 방과 후 활동에 학부모들이 더 신경을 써야 한다고 촉구했다.

해설 명령/동의/제안/주장/요구/충고 동사의 목적어 자리에 '당위성'을 표현하는 that절이 오는 경우, that절의 동사는 「(should)+동사원형」이 되어야 한다.

05 ▶정답 ⓑ

해석 나의 사촌인 Jeff는 처음으로 전국 사진 촬영 대회에 참가하여 일등상을 수상했다. 우리는 그가 18세에 첫 전문가용 카메라를 갖게 된 이후부터 사진 기술을 익혀왔다는 것을 알지 못했다.

해설 빈칸 앞 뒤로 절이 나왔으므로 접속사가 들어가야 한다. 보기중에 접속사는 (b),(C),(d)이므로 해석상 가장 적절한 접속사를 찾아야 한다. 명사절 that절 안에서 주절 시제가 현재완료진행(has been perfecting)이고 부사절의 시제가 과거(got)이므로 가장 적절한 것은 '~이래로'를 뜻하는 since이다. ever는 부사로 쓰였다.

오답분석 at last는 '마침내'라는 뜻의 부사이다.

06 ▶정답 ⓐ

해석 제2형 당뇨병은 미국 성인의 8%를 괴롭게 하는 심각한 질병이다. 이 질병의 위협에도 불구하고, 많은 의사들은 이 질병을 예방하는 것이 규칙적인 신체 운동을 통해 가능할 수 있다고 말한다.

해설 빈칸은 명사절 접속사 that절 안에서의 주어자리이다. 주어 자리에는 동명사와 to 부정사를 쓸 수 있는데, 지텔프 시험에서는 보기에 함께 나온 경우 동명사를 정답 우선순위로 한다.

07 ▶정답 ⓒ

해석 Joanne은 사람들에게 농담하는 것을 좋아한다. 어제, 그녀는 Greg에게 잔인한 농담을 했다. 그녀는 Greg이 보복하지 않을 것이라고 생각했었음에 틀림없는데, 그는 그녀의 못된 장난질로 그녀를 상대로 소송을 제기 할 것이다.

해설 보기를 통해 조동사 문제임을 알 수 있다. 문맥상 '~했었음에 틀림없다'를 뜻하는 must have p.p.가 가장 적절하다.

오답분석 조동사 may have p.p. '~했었을 지도 모른다' / should have p.p. '~했었어야 했는데'를 뜻한다.

08 ▶정답 ⓐ

해석 라이프 스타일 매거진의 인테리어 디자이너이자 작가인 Agnes는 편집자가 정한 월 마감일을 항상 놓친다. 만약 그녀가 주택 수리에 바쁘지 않다면 이런 일은 일어나지 않을 텐데.

해설 가정법 과거 문제이다. if 절의 시제가 과거시제 (weren't)이므로 주절에는 「조동사 과거형 +동사원형」이 들어가야 한다.

09 ▶ 정답 ⓓ

해석 Mark는 20년 이상 전문 파일럿으로 일한 후에, 비행을 그만 두고 개인 사업을 시작하기로 결정했다. 다음 달에 그는 국제공항의 골동품 체인점을 통해 여행 기념품을 판매하고 있을 것이다.

해설 본동사 자리에 들어갈 동사의 시제 문제이다. 시간부사 next month가 있으므로 가장 적절한 시제는 미래이다. 미래의 특정한 시점에 하고 있는 동작을 강조하고 있는 미래진행 시제가 쓰일 수 있다.

10 ▶ 정답 ⓑ

해석 친구들과 나는 Tater's에서 점심식사를 하기로 동의했다. 하지만, 나는 가는 도중에 타이어에 펑크가 나 늦었다. 친구들이 나를 기다리는 것을 원하지 않아 디저트를 먹을 때 합류하겠다고 말했다.

해설 빈칸은 목적보어자리이며, want가 5형식에 쓰이면 목적보어자리에 to 부정사를 쓸 수 있다.

11 ▶ 정답 ⓓ

해석 2개월 전부터 Martin은 이유를 알 수 없는 심한 편두통으로 고통 받아 오고 있다. 그의 상태가 심각할 수 있다는 두려움으로, 그는 진료 예약하는 것을 늦춰오고 있다.

해설 빈칸은 동사 delay의 목적어 자리이다. delay는 동명사만을 목적어로 취하는 3형식 타동사이므로 정답은 (d)이다.

오답분석 having p.p.는 기준 시점보다 앞선 완료의 상태를 표현할 때 쓸 수 있는데 문맥상 올바르지 않다.

12 ▶ 정답 ⓐ

해석 Junior Jaycees International은 그들의 회원들이 훌륭한 리더가 되기 위해 훈련을 하는 청년 단체이다. 이전의 회원 중 많은 사람들이 현재 고위 직책을 맡고 있다. 만약 그것이 조직을 위한 것이 아니었다면, 현재 만큼 성공하지 못했을 것이다.

해설 가정법 과거완료 문제이다. if절의 시제가 had p.p.이므로 주절에는 「조동사 과거형 + have p.p.」가 들어가야 한다.

13 ▶ 정답 ⓑ

해석 많은 시민들이 진짜로 훌륭하고 능력 있는 대통령이 있길 기대해오고 있다. 그래서 훌륭한 국정운영 옹호자인 Robert Powell이 그의 출마를 발표했을 때, 국민들은 환호했다.

해설 문장 주어 Robert Powell과 동사 announced 사이가 빈칸으로 나왔으므로 주어에 해당하는 명사를 수식하는 형용사절 문제임을 알 수 있다. 선행사가 사람이고 동사를 바로 데리고 온 주격 관계대명사 who의 쓰임이 올바르다.

오답분석 whose는 완벽한 문장을 데리고 와야 하는데 명사만이 왔으므로 불가능하며, why는 관계부사로 쓰일 때 선행사가 장소명사이다. 관계대명사 that은 콤마 뒤에 쓸 수 없다.

14 ▶ 정답 ⓒ

해석 Arkansas 노인 교육 센터는 노인들을 돌보는 전문가에게 무료 교육을 제공한다. 일 년에 몇 번씩, 그 센터는 노인을 돌보는 것과 관련해 교육을 하기 위해 무료 세미나를 후원한다.

해설 빈칸이 있는 문장이 완벽하므로 부사만이 들어갈 수 있다. 문맥상 to 부정사의 부사적 용법 중 목적을 나타내는 '~하기 위해서'로 쓰였다.

15 ▶ 정답 ⓓ

해석 Mr. Greeley는 새로운 그리스 레스토랑인 Ethos-Gallery로 차로 가기 위해서, 적어도 한 시간 전에 떠났어야 했다. 교통체증이 너무 심해서 그가 10시에 도착했을 때에 그 식당은 이미 문을 닫았다.

해설 when 부사절의 시제가 과거이므로 주절의 시제는 과거진행시제가 가장 적절하다.

16 ▶ 정답 ⓑ

해석 내가 처음에 Discover Magazine을 읽기 전에는 과학과 기술에 관심이 없었다. 그 잡지는 이해하기 쉬운 기사들과 인상적인 사진들이 있다. 만약 내가 과학을 주로 다루는 출판물을 구독한다면, 나의 첫 번째 선택은 Discover일 것이다.

해설 가정법 과거의 문제이다. 주절의 동사가 「would +동사원형」이므로 if절의 시제는 과거가 되어야 하는데, 가정법에서 be동사는 were만 쓴다.

17 ▶ 정답 ⓐ

해석 학부 4년과 의대 4년을 보낸 후, Greta는 3년간의 레지던트 생활을 했다. 그녀가 소아과 전문의 자격을 받을 때 쯤, 그녀는 11년 연속으로 공부하고 있는 것이 된다!

해설 기간 부사 for eleven straight years가 있고 시간 부사절 접속사 by the time의 시제가 현재이므로 주절에는 미래완료시제가 적절하다. 보기에 미래완료를 포함하고 있는 시제는 (a)의 미래완료진행시제뿐이다.

18 ▶ 정답 ⓓ

해석 경찰청장은 지난 금요일 Garfield 백화점에서 2천 달러 상당의 현금과 상품이 도난당했다고 보고했다. 그는 백화점 소유주들이 건물의 보안을 향상시키는 것이 중요하다고 말했다.

해설 당위성·이성적 판단의 형용사 important가 오고 that절이 오는 경우 that절의 동사는 「(should) + 동사원형」이 되어야 한다.

19 ▶ 정답 ⓐ

해석 Istanbul에 있는 한 극장은 20세기 터키 여배우 인 Afife Jale의 이름을 따서 이름 지어졌다. 그 당시 터키 정부는 여성들이 연기하는 것을 금지했음에도 불구하고, 그녀는 무대에서 공연하는 것을 고집했던 것으로 기억된다.

해설 빈칸은 절과 절을 연결하는 접속사가 필요한 자리이다. 문맥상 가장 자연스러운 것은 '~에도 불구하고'를 의미하는 양보 부사절 although가 가장 적절하다.

오답분석 therefore는 '그러므로'라는 뜻의 접속 부사이다.

20 ▶ 정답 ⓓ

해설 Oregon으로 가는 Louie의 출장은 겨우 이틀밖에 되지 않았다. 회의와 발표로 가득 찬 그의 스케줄은 그에게 자유 시간을 주지 않았다. 만약 그의 출장이 조금만 더 길었더라면, 그는 Hillsboro에 계신 이모를 방문했을 것이다.

해설 If only절의 시제가 had p.p.이므로 주절에는 「조동사 과거형 + have p.p.」가 들어가야 한다.

21 ▶ 정답 ⓐ

해설 캐나다에 있는 몇몇 대학 및 연방 기관들은 기후 변화와 그것(기후 변화)이 동물의 삶에 미치는 해로운 영향에 관한 연구를 하고 있다. 현재, 환경 과학자들은 숲의 변화와 그 변화가 곤충 및 조류 개체 수에 끼치는 영향을 조사하고 있다.

해설 시간 부사 at present는 '현재'라는 뜻이므로 가장 잘 어울리는 시제는 현재진행이다.

22 ▶ 정답 ⓑ

해설 1차 세계 대전 동안, 많은 미국 사업가들은 전투기 엔진에 대한 엄청난 수요 때문에 항공 산업에 뛰어들었다. 전쟁 후, 비행기 엔진을 제작했었던 대부분의 회사들이 즉시 그들의 원래 사업으로 돌아갔다.

해설 빈칸은 앞서 나온 most of the companies를 수식하는 형용사절이 들어가야 한다. 주격 관계대명사로 쓰인 that이 문법적으로, 문맥상 가장 적절하다.

오답분석 who는 선행사가 사람일 때만 쓰는데 선행사가 companies이므로 올바르지 않다. where는 관계부사이므로 완벽한 문장을 데리고 와야 하는데, 목적어가 없는 불완전한 문장이 왔으므로 문법적으로 오류이다. (d)는 which가 목적격 관계대명사로 쓰여서 문법적으로는 오류가 없으나 해석상 올바르지 않다.

23 ▶ 정답 ⓐ

해설 독감 바이러스가 굉장히 빠르게 진화하고 있어서 작년의 독감 백신이 더 이상 효과적이지 않을 지도 모른다. 이러한 이유로 매년 새로운 독감 백신이 출시된다. 건강 전문가들은 또한 모든 사람들이 매년 독감 백신 접종을 받아야 한다고 조언한다.

해설 명령/동의/제안/주장/요구/충고 동사의 목적어 자리에 당위적 내용을 담은 that절이 목적어로 오는 경우 that절의 동사는 「(should) + 동사원형」이 되어야 한다.

24 ▶ 정답 ⓓ

해설 상원이 에너지 법안 승인을 연기한 것에 대해 많은 관찰자들이 실망했다. 많은 사람들은 만약 그 법안이 통과되었더라면, 그것은 농업과 기술을 포함한 모든 분야에서 새로운 일자리 기회를 창출했을 것이라고 말한다.

해설 가정법 과거완료의 문제이다. if절의 시제가 had p.p.이므로 주절에는 「조동사 과거형 + p.p.」가 들어가야 한다.

25 ▶ 정답 ⓒ

해설 Marina는 체중 감량을 위해 다이어트 약을 복용 한 후부터 두통과 설사를 겪기 시작했다. 그녀는 그 약이 그녀에게 긍정적인 것보다 더 많은 해를 입히기 때문에 약 사용하는 것을 중단해야 한다고 즉시 깨달았다.

해설 stop은 1형식과 3형식에 쓰는 동사로 해석을 통해 문맥상 자연스러운 것을 찾아야 한다. '약 복용하는 것을 중단하다'가 문맥상 적절하므로 정답은 (c)이다.

오답분석 she must stop to use the pill이 되면 '그녀는 그 약을 사용하기 위해 (하던 것을) 멈춰야 한다'는 의미가 된다.

26 ▶ 정답 ⓑ

해설 Damian은 강의실에서 강의하던 것이 그리워, Brown University에서 연구 담당 부 대표직을 사임했다. 이에 따라 그는 내년 봄, 응용 물리학 교수로서 Brown 대학으로 돌아갈 것이다.

해설 보기를 통해 조동사 문제임을 확인할 수 있다. 시간 부사 next spring이 있으므로 미래의 상황을 묘사하는 조동사 will이 가장 적절하다.

Listening Test 04회

Question 27-52

ANSWER KEY p.101

27	ⓐ	28	ⓓ	29	ⓑ	30	ⓒ
31	ⓐ	32	ⓒ	33	ⓒ	34	ⓑ
35	ⓒ	36	ⓐ	37	ⓓ	38	ⓒ
39	ⓐ	40	ⓒ	41	ⓐ	42	ⓓ
43	ⓐ	44	ⓓ	45	ⓒ	46	ⓑ
47	ⓑ	48	ⓓ	49	ⓐ	50	ⓓ
51	ⓑ	52	ⓐ				

[Part 1]

Now listen to the questions.

27: What are James and Carol talking about?

28: What was said about the crafts center in Phnom Penh?

29: Aside from the royal residence and its function halls, what else did Carol mention seeing in the Royal Palace compound?

30: Based on the dialogue, what description is most appropriate for the Angkor Wat?

31: What does James always look for when visiting another country?

32: How did Carol feel about meeting some handicapped Cambodians?

33: What was Carol's suggestion to James?

해석

27: 제임스와 캐롤은 무엇에 관해 이야기하고 있나요?

28: 프놈펜 공예 센터에 대해 언급된 것은 무엇인가요?

29: 왕실 거주지와 function hall 이외에, 캐롤은 Royal Palace compound에서 그 밖에 본 것이 무엇이라고 언급 했나요?

30: 대화를 바탕으로, 앙코르 와트에 가장 적절한 묘사는 무엇인가요?

31: 다른 나라를 방문 할 때 제임스가 항상 찾는 것은 무엇인가요?

32: 장애가 있는 몇몇 캄보디아 인들을 만나는 것에 대해 캐롤은 어떻게 느꼈나요?

33: 캐롤이 제임스에게 한 제안은 무엇이었나요?

Now you will hear the conversation.
[conversation]

M 27) Hi, Carol! Is it true that you just came back from Cambodia? That's an interesting place for a vacation!

F Hi James, That wasn't really a planned vacation. My sister and two of her co-workers were going there on business, and they convinced me to go with them.

M Oh, I see. How long did you stay in Cambodia?

F Only seven days. We just made a quick tour of Phnom Penh and nearby places. A very efficient travel guide named Arun showed us around. He brought us to a crafts center named Bassac, where Susan's team had a meeting with some community development groups.

M What do these groups do?

F 28) These groups make and sell traditional Cambodian crafts and donate all the proceeds to poor and disabled people. Susan's company, by the way, is doing a documentary on the crafts center to be shown on national TV next month.

M That's interesting! So, what other places in Cambodia did you visit?

F 29) Well, we went to the most popular landmarks, of course. The National Museum and the Royal Palace in Phnom Penh were on the top of our list. The royal residence and its function halls were magnificent, and so was the Buddhist pagoda in the palace grounds. Then we shopped for books and souvenirs at the city's Central Market.

M You didn't miss visiting Angkor Wat by any chance?

F Of course not! Angkor Wat was simply amazing! I had seen it in so many pictures before, but the pictures of the ancient city's ruins just pale in comparison to the real thing. 30) But, what's so beautiful about Angkor Wat is not only the structure but the atmosphere as well. It was how do I say it?--very soulful!

M I've heard some people say that Angkor Wat is magical. 31) Anyway, you know me, I love going to nice beaches when traveling abroad. Are there any in Cambodia?

F Oh, yes! Arun took us to a very nice beach in Sihanoukville. We all had a great time swimming and, of course, eating fresh seafood.

M Oh, Carol, now you're making me envious with all that talk about swimming and seafood!

F Don't think that all we did was to have fun in Cambodia! We experienced something much more than that. Most of the people I met in Phnom Penh were actually wartime survivors, particularly the native vendors in the markets.

M Wow! It must be great to hear about their experiences.

F Actually, hearing their stories was heartbreaking. They have gone through a very difficult time in their country. 32) Some of them are even landmine victims and physically handicapped. It was amazing how they could remain hopeful despite their disfigured bodies and difficult situation.

M I understand how you feel, Carol, but that's enough about the bad things! After all, you have already sold Cambodia to me as a vacation destination.

F I did? Well, James, now that you mentioned it, 33) why don't you go to Cambodia with my family and me next year? Susan and I are taking our parents there for two weeks.

M I'll seriously think about it, Carol. Thanks for the invitation!

Words

craft 공예
disabled 장애를 가진
royal residence 왕실 거주지
magnificent 웅장한
ruin 유적, 유물
soulful 감동적인 넋이 담긴
vendor 상인
handicapped 장애가 있는
proceeds 수익금
landmark 명소, 주요 지형물
function hall 펑션 홀 (행사 등을 여는 곳)
souvenir 기념품
atmosphere 분위기
envious 부러워하는
landmine 지뢰
amazing 놀라운

해석

M 27) 안녕, 캐롤! 방금 캄보디아에서 돌아온 거 맞지? 캄보디아는 휴가를 보내기에 흥미로운 곳이지!

F 안녕, 제임스, 그건 사실 계획된 휴가는 아니었어. 언니와 동료 두 명이 그곳에 출장을 가게 되었고, 그들이 나보고 같이 가자고 설득했어.

M 그랬구나. 캄보디아에서 얼마나 머물렀어?

F 일주일밖에 안 있었어. 우리는 단지 프놈펜과 근처에 있는 지역들을 빠르게 둘러봤을 뿐이야. 애런이라고 하는 굉장히 유능한 여행 가이드가 우리를 안내했어. 그는 Bassac이라는 공예 센터에 우리를 데리고 갔는데, 그곳에서 수잔 팀은 몇몇 지역 개발 그룹들과 미팅을 가졌어.

M 그러한 그룹들은 무엇을 하는데?

F 28) 그 그룹들은 전통적인 캄보디아 공예품을 만들고 판매해서 모든 수익금을 가난한 사람과 장애인에게 기부해. 그런데 수잔 회사는 다음 달에 전국 TV에 방영될, 그 공예센터에 대한 다큐멘터리를 제작중이야.

M 재미있네! 그래서, 캄보디아에서 그밖에 어떤 곳들을 방문했어?

F 음, 29) 우리는 물론 가장 인기 있는 명소들에도 갔어. 프놈펜의 국립 박물관과 왕궁은 방문목록 1 순위였지. 왕실 거주지와 function hall은 웅장했고, 궁전 부지 불탑도 훌륭했어. 그 다음에 우리는 책과 기념품을 사기 위해 도시의 중앙 시장에서 쇼핑했지.

M 혹시 앙코르와트 방문을 놓친 건 아니지?

F 당연히 아니지! 앙코르와트는 정말 환상적이었어! 나는 전에 많은 사진에서 앙코르와트를 봤는데, 고대 도시의 유적 사진들은 실제와 비교하면 단지 무색할 뿐이야. 30) 그런데, 앙코르와트는 매우 아름다운 것은 구조물뿐 만이 아니라, 분위기이기도 해. 그것은 – 어떻게 말해야 할까 – 진짜 감동적이야!

M 나는 몇몇 사람들이 앙코르와트는 마법이라고 말하는 것을 들어봤어. 31) 어쨌든, 너도 알다시피, 나는 해외여행할 때 멋진 해변으로 가는 것을 너무 좋아하잖아. 캄보디아에도 멋진 해변이 있어?

F 당연하지. 애런은 우리를 Sihanoukville에 있는 매우 멋진 해변으로 데리고 갔어. 우리 모두 수영을 했고, 신선한 해산물을 먹으면서 좋은 시간을 보냈지.

M 오, 캐롤, 지금 네가 이야기하는 수영과 해산물에 관한 모든 것이 나를 부럽게 하고 있어.

F 우리가 캄보디아에서 그저 즐기기만 했다고 생각하지는 마!. 우리는 그 이상을 경험했어. 우리가 프놈펜에서 만난 사람들 대부분, 특히 시장의 현지인 상인들의 대부분은 실제로 전쟁의 생존자들이었어.

M 와우! 그들의 경험을 듣는 것은 분명 굉장할 거야.

F 실제로, 그들의 이야기를 듣는 것은 가슴 아팠어. 그들은 자신들의 나라에서 매우 힘든 시기를 겪었어. 32) 그들 중 일부는 심지어 지뢰 희생자이며 신체적으로 장애인이야. 망가진 몸과 어려운 상황에도 불구하고 그들이 어떻게 계속해서 희망을 품을 수 있었는지 놀라웠어.

M 네가 어떻게 느꼈을지 이해가, 캐롤. 그렇지만 나쁜 일은 이것으로 충분해! 결국, 너는 이미 내게 캄보디아를 휴가지로 매료시켰어.

F 내가 그랬어? 음, 제임스, 네가 말한 김에, 33) 내년에 우리가족이랑 나와 함께 캄보디아에 가는 건 어때? 수잔과 나는 2주 동안 부모님을 모시고 갈 거야.

M 진지하게 생각해 볼게, 캐롤. 초대해줘서 고마워.

27 ▶ 정답 ⓐ

What are James and Carol talking about?

(a) Carol's out-of-country trip
(b) the history of Cambodia
(c) where to spend a vacation
(d) James' business trip

해석

제임스와 캐롤은 무엇에 관해 이야기하고 있나요?

(a) 캐롤의 해외여행
(b) 캄보디아 역사
(c) 어디서 휴가를 보낼 지
(d) 제임스의 출장

해설 대화의 시작이 캐롤의 캄보디아 방문에 관한 이야기로 시작하고 있다.

28 ▶ 정답 ⓓ

What was said about the crafts center in Phnom Penh?

(a) It employs people from different parts of Cambodia.
(b) It receives donations from charitable groups.
(c) It exports expensive crafts.
(d) It provides assistance to poor Cambodians.

해석
프놈펜 공예 센터에 대해 언급된 것은 무엇인가요?
(a) 그곳은 캄보디아 각지의 사람들을 고용한다.
(b) 그곳은 자선 단체로부터 기부금을 받는다.
(c) 그곳은 값비싼 공예품을 수출한다.
(d) 그곳은 가난한 캄보디아인들에게 도움을 준다.

해설 프놈펜 공예 센터는 전통적인 캄보디아 공예품을 만들어서 판매한 수익금을 가난한 사람들과 장애인에게 기부한다고 캐롤이 언급했다.

29 ▶ 정답 ⓑ

Aside from the royal residence and its function halls, what else did Carol mention seeing in the Royal Palace compound?

(a) antique works of art
(b) a Buddhist temple
(c) historical documents
(d) a souvenir shop

해석
왕실 거주지와 function hall 이외에, 캐롤은 Royal Palace compound에서 그 밖에 본 것이 무엇이라고 언급 했나요?
(a) 골동 예술품
(b) 불교 사원
(c) 역사적 문서
(d) 기념품 가게

해설 "Well, we went to the most popular landmarks, of course. The National Museum and the Royal Palace in Phnom Penh were on the top of our list. The royal residence and its function halls were magnificent, and so was the Buddhist pagoda in the palace grounds."에서 궁전부지 불탑이 훌륭했다는 언급을 통해 불교사원을 방문했다는 것을 알 수 있다.

30 ▶ 정답 ⓒ

Based on the dialogue, what description is most appropriate for the Angkor Wat?

(a) gloomy
(b) complicated
(c) touching
(d) intimidating

해석
대화를 바탕으로, 앙코르와트에 가장 적절한 묘사는 무엇인가요?

(a) 우울한
(b) 복잡한
(c) 감동적인
(d) 위협적인

해설 캐롤은 앙코르와트가 멋진 건축물 구조뿐 아니라 분위기까지 멋져서 감동적이라고 말했다.

31 ▶ 정답 ⓐ

What does James always look for when visiting another country?

(a) beautiful beaches
(b) historical sites
(c) magic shows
(d) seafood markets

해석
다른 나라를 방문 할 때 제임스가 항상 찾는 것은 무엇인가요?
(a) 아름다운 해변들
(b) 사적지
(c) 마술 쇼
(d) 해산물 시장

해설 제임스는 해외여행갈 때 멋진 해변 가는 것을 좋아한다고 직접 말했다.

32 ▶ 정답 ⓒ

How did Carol feel about meeting some handicapped Cambodians?

(a) She was shocked.
(b) She was scared.
(c) She was amazed.
(d) She was amused.

해석
장애가 있는 몇몇 캄보디아 인들을 만나는 것에 대해 캐롤은 어떻게 느꼈나요?
(a) 그녀는 충격을 받았다.
(b) 그녀는 무서웠다.
(c) 그녀는 놀랐다.
(d) 그녀는 즐거웠다.

해설 "Some of them are even landmine victims and physically handicapped. It was amazing how they could remain hopeful despite their disfigured bodies and difficult situation."을 통해 캄보이아의 장애인을 만난 것은 놀라웠다는 것을 알 수 있다.

33

▶ 정답 ⓒ

What was Carol's suggestion to James?

(a) he should consult a travel agency about trips to Cambodia
(b) he should assist in making a documentary about Cambodia
(c) he should go with her family the next time they visit Cambodia
(d) he should read materials about Cambodian history and culture

해석

캐롤이 제임스에게 한 제안은 무엇이었나요?

(a) 그가 캄보디아여행에 관해 여행사와 상의하는 것
(b) 그가 캄보디아에 관한 다큐멘터리제작을 지원하는 것
(c) 다음에 그녀의 가족들이 캄보디아를 방문할 때 그가 그들과 함께 가는 것
(d) 그가 캄보디아 역사와 문화에 관한 자료를 읽는 것

해설 대화 마지막 부분에서 캐롤은 내년에 우리가족이랑 같이 캄보디아로 휴가가는 건 어떻냐고 제안을 하고 제임스는 이에 대해 진지하게 생각해보겠다고 대답했다.

[Part 2]

Now listen to the questions.

34: What is this talk about?
35: According to the speaker, when is the company least efficient in its use of electricity?
36: What is the advantage of installing a localized heating system in the company's buildings?
37: How can the workers make sure that the heat is circulating properly?
38: Why did the speaker ask the listeners to discuss the plan among themselves?
39: What will the listeners likely be doing after the talk?

해석

34: 주제는 무엇인가요?
35: 화자에 따르면, 회사의 전기 사용 효율이 가장 낮은 시기는 언제인가요?
36: 회사의 건물에 지역난방 시스템을 설치하면 어떤 장점이 있나요?
37: 직원들은 열이 적절하게 순환하고 있는지 어떻게 확신할 수 있나요?
38: 화자는 왜 청중들에게 그들끼리 계획을 의논할 것을 요청했나요?
39: 청중들은 연설 후 무엇을 할 것 같나요?

Now you will hear the talk.

Good afternoon, ladies and gentlemen! I'm Jane Connor and I'm the new head of the Facilities Maintenance Department. One of my first assignments with the company is to review its current energy use and develop a conservation plan that reduces our energy needs. 34) Our operations manager asked me to share this conservation plan with you today, so we can all do our part to help the company become more eco-friendly. I would like to lay out the steps we need to take to achieve our company's goals.

Our first step was to inspect our electrical facilities and study our annual energy consumption. Based on those findings, we began our second step by creating a preliminary set of proposals for a new energy-saving measure.

Our third step is what we are doing this morning, sharing those findings with employees. 35) Fortunately, our company is energy-efficient for much of the year. The winter months unfortunately are a problem. Obviously, the increase in power consumed during winter is due to heating our buildings. Now, to achieve better energy efficiency, I recommend that the centralized heating systems of our buildings be replaced with localized heating systems for each department.

36) This will allow us to turn on the heating system for a work area only when it is needed. We'll consume less electricity since we would be able to switch off the air-handling units in parts of the building when they are not in use. Once the new heating system is in place, we'll require all departments to set their heating thermostats during working hours at a minimum but comfortable temperature level. The temperature I recommend is 68 degrees Fahrenheit.

For each degree the thermostat is lowered, our company can reduce its average wintertime power consumption by about 5%. 37) To ensure proper heat circulation, of course, we also have to make sure that the heating vents in our work areas are not blocked by office furniture or equipment.

Also, to prevent cold air from entering the building, everyone should make it a point to close all doors and windows tightly. Any irregular procedure or practice, such as poor insulation or faulty heating filters, should be reported at once to the Facilities Maintenance Department for immediate remedial measures. I believe this is the best way for us to save energy while ensuring the comfort of all personnel.

39) Now that you have the information, let's begin the fourth and most important step of the process by having lunch. Let us break into small groups and discuss how these changes will affect your work on both a departmental and personal level. I need your inputs to make the proposals and the overall strategy workable.

38) Nobody understands how our company functions

as well as you do. As valued employees, you are the experts in how we get things done and how changes in processes will affect our workflow. I'm sure you'll be eating with friends and long time co-workers today so this is a good time to discuss how this will affect you and your department.

After the small group discussions, we'll meet again as a large group to compare your opinions. Thanks for your attention.

Words

assignment 업무
eco-friendly 친 환경적인
preliminary 예비의
thermostat 온도 조절 장치
vent 통풍구, 환기구
insulation 단열
overall 전체의, 전반적인
valued 소중한, 귀중한
energy-saving measure 에너지 절약 정책
centralized heating system 중앙난방시스템
localized heating system 지역난방시스템
conservation 절약, 보존
consumption 소비
turn on 켜다
Fahrenheit 화씨
block 막다, 가리다
remedial 개선하는
workable 실행 가능한
workflow 작업 흐름

해석

신사 숙녀 여러분, 안녕하세요! 저는 Jane Connor이고 설비유지관리부서의 새로운 책임자입니다. 회사에서 저의 주된 업무 중 하나는 현재의 에너지 사용을 검토하고 에너지 필요성을 줄일 수 있는 절약 계획을 개발하는 것입니다. 34) 우리 운영관리자가 오늘 저에게 여러분과 절약계획을 공유할 것을 요청했기 때문에, 우리는 모두 회사가 좀 더 환경 친화적으로 될 수 있도록 돕는데 본분을 다할 것 입니다. 저는 회사의 목표를 달성하기 위해 취해야 할 조치를 계획하기를 원합니다.

우리의 첫 번째 단계는 전기 시설을 점검하고 연간 에너지 소비량을 조사하는 것이었습니다. 이러한 결과를 바탕으로, 우리는 새로운 에너지절약 정책을 위한 예비 제안서를 만듦으로써 두 번째 단계를 시작했습니다.

세 번째 단계는 오늘 아침에 우리가 하고 있는 일, 즉 직원들과 이러한 결과들을 공유하는 것입니다. 35) 다행히도 당사는 일 년 중 대부분의 기간 동안 에너지 효율이 뛰어납니다. 명백히, 겨울에 소비되는 전력 증가는 건물 난방이 원인입니다. 이제 에너지 효율성을 높이기 위해, 저는 건물의 중앙난방 시스템을 각 부서의 지역난방 시스템으로 교체하는 것을 권고합니다.

36) 이렇게 하면 필요한 경우에만 작업하는 장소만 난방 시스템을 켤 수 있습니다. 우리는 사용하지 않을 때 건물 일부의 공기 조화기를 끌 수 있기 때문에 전기 소비량을 줄일 수 있습니다. 새로운 난방 시스템이 갖추어지면, 우리는 모든 부서에게 근무 시간 동안 최저이지만 쾌적한 온도 수준으로 난방 자동 온도 조절 장치를 맞추도록 요구 할 것입니다. 제가 권장하는 온도는 화씨 68도입니다.

자동 온도조절 장치 온도가 1도 내려갈 때마다, 우리 회사는 평균 겨울 소비 전력을 약 5%까지 줄일 수 있습니다. 37) 물론, 적절한 열 순환을 확실히 하기 위해, 작업 공간의 난방 통풍기가 사무용 가구 또는 장비로 막히

지 않도록 해야 합니다.

또한, 차가운 공기가 건물 내부로 유입되는 것을 방지하기 위해, 전 직원은 모든 문과 창문을 꼭 닫아야만 합니다. 단열이 잘 안되거나 난방 필터에 결함이 있는 경우와 같은 변칙적인 절차나 실행은 즉각적인 개선 조치를 위해 설비 유지 보수 부서에 즉시 보고되어야 합니다. 저는 이것이 전 직원의 편안함을 보장하면서 에너지를 절약하는 최선의 방법이라고 생각합니다.

39) 여러분들은 이러한 정보를 갖게 되었기 때문에, 네 번째이자 이 과정에서 가장 중요한 단계는 점심식사를 하면서 시작하도록 합시다. 소그룹으로 나누어, 이러한 변화가 부서별 및 개인적 차원에서 여러분의 업무에 어떻게 영향을 미치는지 토론합시다. 저는 계획과 전체적인 전략이 실행될 수 있도록 하기 위해 여러분의 의견이 필요합니다.

38) 누구도 여러분만큼 우리 회사가 어떻게 돌아가는지 잘 알지 못 합니다. 소중한 직원으로서, 여러분은 우리가 어떻게 일을 처리하는지, 그리고 절차상 변화가 어떻게 우리 업무진행상황에 영향을 미치는지에 관한 전문가들입니다. 저는 오늘 여러분이 친구이자 오랜 동료들과 함께 식사를 할 것이고, 이것이 여러분과 여러분의 부서에 어떻게 영향을 줄 것인지 토론할 좋은 시간이라 확신합니다.

소그룹 토론 후, 우리는 여러분의 의견을 비교할 수 있도록 큰 그룹으로 다시 모일 것입니다. 주목해 주셔서 고맙습니다.

---

34 ▶ 정답 ⓑ

What is this talk about?

(a) a revised company policy
(b) a new energy-saving strategy
(c) a new information systems design
(d) a detailed expense report

해석

주제는 무엇인가요?

(a) 개정된 회사정책
(b) 새로운 에너지절약 전략
(c) 새로운 정보시스템 디자인
(d) 상세한 지출보고서

해설 "Our operations manager asked me to share this conservation plan with you today, so we can all do our part to help the company become more eco-friendly."에서 직원들에게 말할 주제는 에너지 절약 계획임을 알 수 있다.

---

35 ▶ 정답 ⓒ

According to the speaker, when is the company least efficient in its use of electricity?

(a) in summer
(b) in autumn
(c) in winter
(d) in spring

해석
화자에 따르면, 회사의 전기 사용 효율이 가장 낮은 시기는 언제인가요?
(a) 여름시기
(b) 가을시기
(c) 겨울시기
(d) 봄시기

해설 대부분 에너지 효율이 뛰어나지만 겨울에는 에너지 효율이 떨어진다는 내용이 언급되어 있다.

36 ▶ 정답 ⓐ

What is the advantage of installing a localized heating system in the company's buildings?
(a) The heating system in each work area can be switched on and off as needed.
(b) Each department's power use can be recorded.
(c) The heating system can function at all times.
(d) The maintenance department can repair heating vents easily.

해석
회사의 건물에 지역난방 시스템을 설치하면 어떤 장점이 있나요?
(a) 각 작업 장소의 난방 시스템을 필요에 따라 켜고 끌 수 있다.
(b) 각 부서의 전력 사용을 기록할 수 있다.
(c) 난방 시스템이 항상 작동될 수 있다.
(d) 관리부서가 난방 환기구를 쉽게 수리 할 수 있다.

해설 "This will allow us to turn on the heating system for a work area only when it is needed. We'll consume less electricity since we would be able to switch off the air-handling units in parts of the building when they are not in use."을 통해 지역 난방시스템이 도입되면 필요에 따라 난방시스템을 켜고 끌 수 있다는 것을 알 수 있다.

37 ▶ 정답 ⓓ

How can the workers make sure that the heat is circulating properly?
(a) by blocking the air vents
(b) by using as few furniture as possible
(c) by not lowering the thermostat
(d) by ensuring that the heat outlets are not blocked

해석
직원들은 열이 적절하게 순환하고 있는지 어떻게 확신할 수 있나요?
(a) 통풍구를 막음으로써
(b) 최대한 가구를 적게 사용함으로써
(c) 온도조절 장치를 낮추지 않음으로써
(d) 열배출구가 막히지 않도록 확실히 함으로써

해설 적절한 열 순환을 확실히 하기 위해, 작업 공간의 난방 통풍기가 사무용 가구 또는 장비로 막히지 않도록 확실히 해야 한다는 내용이 언급되어 있다.

38 ▶ 정답 ⓒ

Why did the speaker ask the listeners to discuss the plan among themselves?
(a) so they can plan the company's energy use
(b) so they can eat together and become friends
(c) because they know the company the most
(d) because they have better energy-saving ideas

해석
화자는 왜 청중들에게 그들끼리 계획을 의논할 것을 요청했나요?
(a) 그들이 회사 에너지 사용을 계획할 수 있도록 하기 위해
(b) 그들이 함께 식사하고 친구가 될 수 있도록 하기 위해
(c) 그들이 회사를 가장 잘 알고 있기 때문에
(d) 그들에게 더 나은 에너지 절약 아이디어가 있기 때문에

해설 청중들은 이 회사의 직원들이므로 회사에 관해 가장 잘 아는 전문가들이라고 화자는 말하고 있다. 그러므로 회사의 문제점이나 개선 방안에 대해 자유롭게 의견을 내달라고 요청한다는 것을 알 수 있다.

39 ▶ 정답 ⓐ

What will the listeners likely be doing after the talk?
(a) They will be sharing their opinions.
(b) They will be listening to another speaker.
(c) They will go back to their work.
(d) They will go home.

해석
청중들은 연설 후 무엇을 할 것 같나요?
(a) 그들은 의견을 나눌 것이다.
(b) 그들은 다른 연사의 말을 듣게 될 것이다.
(c) 그들은 다시 일할 것이다.
(d) 그들은 집에 갈 것이다.

해설 "Now that you have the information, let's begin the fourth and most important step of the process by having lunch. Let us break into small groups and discuss how these changes will affect your work on both a departmental and personal level."을 통해 점심을 먹으면서 토론을 할 것임을 알 수 있다.

[Part 3]

Now listen to the questions.

40: Why was Alan asking Clarissa about gardening?
41: What term is used to refer to the conditions that influence the growth of a garden?
42: What was not said about the effect of light on gardens?
43: What did Clarissa say one must do before buying plants?
44: What did Clarissa say about healthy soil?
45: What was said about garden centers?
46: What will Alan most likely do during the weekend?

해석

40: 왜 앨런은 클라리사에게 정원 가꾸기에 대해서 물었나요?
41: 정원을 가꾸는 데 영향을 미치는 조건을 가리키기 위해 어떤 용어가 사용되었나요?
42: 정원에 끼치는 빛의 영향에 대해 언급되지 않은 것은 무엇인가요?
43: 클라리사는 식물을 사기 전에 무엇을 해야 한다고 말했나요?
44: 비옥한 토양에 관해 클라리사가 말한 것은 무엇인가요?
45: 원예 용품점에 관해 언급된 것은 무엇인가요?
46: 앨런은 주말에 무엇을 할 가능성이 높나요?

Now you will hear the conversation.
[conversation]

M Hi, Clarissa! I hear you've got the most beautiful garden in your neighborhood. 40) <u>Can you give me some advice on how to start a flower garden? Jennifer and I want to have one in the backyard of our new house, but we don't know how to begin.</u>

F I'd be happy to help, Alan, and you won't regret your decision to have a flower garden. It's so simple yet so beautiful. The first thing you should do is to get to know the "character" of your yard.

M 41) What do you mean by "character"?

F 41) <u>Oh. It's the various conditions that determine how well different types of plants would grow on the garden.</u>

M I see, but what are those conditions?

F The most important is the amount of natural sunlight available to the plants in the garden. 42-b) <u>You see, different plants grow best in different levels of light</u>, so the amount of light in the garden will strongly influence your choices of what to plants. The direction your garden faces, of course, will have a lot to do with how much light your garden will get.

M You're right.

F 42-c) <u>North-facing gardens get the least light, so they tend to be damp</u> and south-facing gardens get the most light, so they're normally dry. West-facing gardens get lots of afternoon and evening light. But I prefer east-facing gardens because they get lots of morning light. 42-a) <u>It's the kind of light that makes plants very healthy and makes backyard gardens such a joy for early morning walks.</u>

M I'm excited about the whole idea! What kind of plants would you recommend?

F It all depends on how you want the garden to look like. Do you want trees, shrubs, or flowers? Or, do you want a mix of all three? 43) <u>Of course, before even thinking of buying plants, you must make an accurate record of the conditions of your backyard.</u>

M I see. Then based on it, I'll know which plants are suitable?

F Yes. You'll know which plants can survive the weather conditions in your area. For example, you should avoid getting plants that die during winter. You can just imagine how much work it is to take care of them every spring.

M Right. What else should I remember before I plant?

F You must also carefully prepare the soil. You have to completely remove weeds, then mix the correct fertilizer into the soil. 44) <u>If the soil is healthy, of course, you'll need less fertilizer. That could mean a lot of savings for you.</u>

M I can imagine! Anyway, where can we get good seedlings for our garden?

F 45) <u>Just go to any garden center in your neighborhood. Most of them sell a wide variety of "everyday" plants—even gardening equipment and outdoor furniture.</u> If you want some rare plants, however, you need to get them from nurseries. Nurseries and garden centers are usually managed by professional horticulturists who really know a lot about plants. They can give you excellent advice on which plants would be best for your garden.

M Thanks for the information, Clarissa! I can hardly wait to start that backyard garden of ours! 46) <u>I'll survey our yard this weekend and take down notes about its character as you have suggested.</u>

F You're welcome Alan.

Words

yard 마당
damp 습기 있는, 눅눅한
weed 잡초
seedling 묘목
horticulturist 원예가
backyard 뒤뜰
shrub 관목
fertilizer 비료
nursery 묘목장

해석

M 클라리사, 안녕! 네가 너희 동네에서 가장 아름다운 정원을 가지고 있다고 들었어. 40) 꽃밭을 어떻게 시작하는 지에 관해 조언 좀 해줄 수 있어? 제니퍼와 나도 우리 새 집 뒤뜰에 정원을 만들고 싶은데 어떻게 시작해야 할지 모르겠어.

F 기꺼이 도와줄게, 앨런, 꽃밭을 가꾸기로 한 너의 결정을 후회하지 않을 거야. 그것은 아주 간단하지만 정말 아름다워. 가장 먼저 해야 할 일은 네 뜰의 '특색'을 파악하는 것이야.

M 41) '특색'이 뭘 의미해?

F 41) 응. 그건 다양한 종류의 식물들이 정원에서 얼마나 잘 자라게 될 지를 결정해주는 여러 가지 조건들이야.

M 아, 알겠어. 그런데 이 조건들이 뭐야?

F 가장 중요한 것은 정원에 있는 식물들이 이용할 수 있는 자연 광(光)의 양이야. 42-b) 너도 알다시피, 식물마다 최상으로 자라는 빛의 수준이 각각 다르기 때문에, 정원에 드는 빛의 양이 네가 어떤 식물을 선택할지에 크게 영향을 끼칠 거야. 당연히, 너의 정원이 향하고 있는 방향이 정원에서 얻게 될 빛의 양과 상당한 관련이 있을 거야.

M 맞아.

F 42-c) 북쪽을 향하는 정원은 빛을 가장 덜 받기 때문에 습한 경향이 있고, 남향의 정원은 가장 많은 빛을 받기 때문에 대체로 건조해. 서향의 정원은 오후와 저녁에 빛을 많이 받아. 그런데 나는 아침햇살을 많이 받을 수 있어서, 동향 정원을 선호하는 편이야. 42-a) 그런 빛은 식물을 아주 건강하게 만들고 뒤뜰정원을 이른 아침 산책의 즐거움이 되도록 해주거든.

M 생각만으로도 신난다. 추천해 줄만한 식물의 종류로는 뭐가 있어?

F 전적으로 네가 어떤 모습의 정원을 원하는지에 달려있어. 나무를 원해, 덤불이나 꽃을 원해? 아니면 이 세 가지 모두가 섞인 것을 원해? 43) 물론, 식물 사는 것을 고려하기 전에 네 뒤뜰의 상태를 정확히 기록해 봐야 해.

M 알겠어. 그러면 그걸 바탕으로 어떤 종류의 식물이 적당할지 알 수 있을까?

F 응. 너희 지역의 기상조건에서 살아남을 수 있는 식물에 대해 알 수 있을 거야. 예를 들면, 겨울동안 죽어버리는 식물을 사는 것은 피해야 해. 매년 봄마다 그들을 관리하기 위해 할 일이 얼마나 많을지 생각해봐.

M 맞아. 그밖에 또 내가 식물을 기르기 전에 명심해야 할 게 뭐가 있을까?

F 토양도 신중하게 준비해야 돼. 잡초를 완벽하게 제거하고 나서 토양에 잘 맞는 비료를 섞어줘야 해. 44) 물론 토양이 비옥하다면 비료가 덜 필요할거야. 그렇게 되면 절약이 많이 될 거야.

M 알겠어! 그런데 우리 정원에 맞는 좋은 묘목은 어디서 얻을 수 있어?

F 45) 그냥 너희 동네에 있는 화원에 가봐. 대부분 다양한 종류의 일상적인 식물들과, 심지어 원예장비와 야외용 가구까지 팔아. 근데 네가 다소 희귀한 식물을 원하면 묘목장에서 구해야 할 거야. 보통 묘목장이나 화원은 식물에 대해 정말 많이 아는 전문적인 원예가들이 운영하거든. 그들은 네 정원에 어떤 식물이 가장 적합한지에 관해 훌륭한 조언을 해줄 수 있을 거야.

M 알려줘서 고마워, 클라리사! 뒤뜰에 정원 꾸미기를 빨리 시작하고 싶다! 46) 이번 주말에 우리 뒤뜰에 대해 조사한 다음 네가 추천해 준 내용대로 그 특징들이 어떤지 메모를 해야겠어.

F 천만에, 앨런.

40 ▶ 정답 ⓒ

Why was Alan asking Clarissa about gardening?

(a) He wants to take up a short course in gardening.
(b) He plans to join an organization of amateur gardeners.
(c) He wants to have a garden at his new home.
(d) He and his wife want to put up a flower business.

해석

왜 앨런은 클라리사에게 정원 가꾸기에 대해 물었나요?

(a) 그는 원예에 관한 단기과정 수업을 듣기 원한다.
(b) 그는 아마추어 정원사 단체에 가입할 계획이다.
(c) 그는 새 집에 정원을 갖고 싶어 한다.
(d) 그와 그의 아내는 화훼사업을 하고 싶어 한다.

해설 "Can you give me some advice on how to start a flower garden? Jennifer and I want to have one in the backyard of our new house, but we don't know how to begin."을 통해 앨런은 새집에서 정원을 가꾸고 싶어 한다는 것을 알 수 있다.

41 ▶ 정답 ⓐ

What term is used to refer to the conditions that influence the growth of a garden?

(a) character
(b) health
(c) personality
(d) climate

해석

정원을 가꾸는 데 영향을 미치는 조건을 가리키기 위해 어떤 용어가 사용되었나요?

(a) 특색
(b) 건강
(c) 성격
(d) 기후

해설 클라리사는 정원 가꾸기에서 가장 먼저 할 일은 뜰의 특색을 파악하는 것이며, 이 특색은 다양한 종류의 식물들이 정원에서 얼마나 잘 자라게 될 지를 결정해주는 것이라고 말하고 있다.

42 ▶ 정답 ⓓ

What was not said about the effect of light on gardens?

(a) Morning light makes a garden both healthy and attractive.
(b) Different plants need varying amounts of light to survive.
(c) Gardens that face north tend to be damp due to very little light.
(d) Plants need more artificial light than sunlight to survive.

해석
정원에 끼치는 빛의 영향에 대해 언급되지 않은 것은 무엇인가요?
(a) 아침 햇살은 정원을 건강하고 매력적으로 만든다.
(b) 식물마다 생존에 필요한 빛의 양이 다르다.
(c) 북향의 정원은 빛이 거의 없기 때문에 습한 경향이 있다.
(d) 식물은 생존을 위해 햇빛보다 인공 빛을 필요로 한다.

해설 대화의 중반부에 클라리사는 식물마다 자라는데 최상의 빛의 수준이 각각 다르며 북향의 정원은 빛을 가장 덜 받아서 습한 경향이 있다고 말한다. 또한 빛은 식물을 건강하게 만들고 뒤뜰 정원을 아침 산책의 즐거움이 되도록 도움을 준다고 이야기했으나 인공 빛에 관해서는 전혀 언급을 하지 않았다.

43 ▶ 정답 ⓐ

What did Clarissa say one must do before buying plants?
(a) study and record the features of the garden site
(b) consult a horticulturist about the garden's look
(c) prepare the soil for planting by applying fertilizer
(d) buy gardening equipment and outdoor furniture

해석
클라리사는 식물을 사기 전에 무엇을 해야 한다고 말했나요?
(a) 정원 부지의 특징을 조사하고 기록하는 것
(b) 원예사와 정원의 모양을 상의하는 것
(c) 비료를 뿌려 식물을 심기 위해 토양을 준비하는 것
(d) 원예 장비 및 야외용 가구를 구입하는 것

해설 클라리사는 식물을 사기 전에 뒤뜰 상태를 먼저 확인해야 한다고 말했으므로 (a)의 진술이 가장 적절하다.

44 ▶ 정답 ⓓ

What did Clarissa say about healthy soil?
(a) It helps plants survive during winter.
(b) It can nourish more trees.
(c) It is highly resistant to weeds.
(d) It means big savings in gardening costs.

해석
비옥한 토양에 관해 클라리사가 말한 것은 무엇인가요?
(a) 겨울동안 식물이 사는 것을 돕는다.
(b) 더 많은 나무에 영양분을 줄 수 있다.
(c) 잡초에 내성이 매우 강하다.
(d) 원예 비용을 크게 절약한다는 것을 의미한다.

해설 "If the soil is healthy, of course, you'll need less fertilizer. That could mean a lot of savings for you."를 통해 비료가 덜 들게 되면 비용을 절약할 수 있다고 말했다.

45 ▶ 정답 ⓒ

What was said about garden centers?
(a) They sell only expensive and unusual plant varieties.
(b) They charge high for assistance.
(c) They can usually supply the basic gardening materials.
(d) They promote the exclusive use of organic fertilizers.

해석
원예 용품점에 관해 언급된 것은 무엇인가요?
(a) 값 비싸고 특이한 식물 품종만을 판매한다.
(b) 그들은 도움을 주는데 높은 비용을 부과한다.
(c) 일반적으로 그들은 기본적인 원예 재료를 공급할 수 있다.
(d) 그들은 유기질 비료를 전용으로 사용할 것을 장려한다.

해설 원예 용품점은 동네에 있는 화원으로 대부분 다양한 종류의 일상적인 식물들과 원예장비 등을 판다고 언급되어 있다.

46 ▶ 정답 ⓑ

What will Alan most likely do during the weekend?
(a) show Clarissa his plans for the garden
(b) start recording the conditions of his backyard
(c) buy seedlings from a nursery
(d) gather organic matter to be used as fertilizer

해석
앨런은 주말에 무엇을 할 가능성이 높나요?
(a) 클라리사의 정원 계획을 보여 준다
(b) 뒷마당 상태를 기록하는 것을 시작한다.
(c) 묘목장에서 묘목을 산다.
(d) 비료로 사용하기 위해 유기물을 모은다.

해설 앨런은 이번 주말에 클라리사가 제안한대로 자신의 뒤뜰을 조사하고 특징들에 대해서 메모를 하겠다고 말했으므로 (b)의 진술이 가장 적절하다.

[Part 4]

Now listen to the questions.

47: What is the purpose of the talk?
48: What was said about the blood donation process?
49: Where are blood donations usually held?
50: Why is the potential donor's blood likely tested for abnormalities?
51: What does the speaker suggest the potential donor do at least two hours before the bloodletting?
52: What will the next speaker talk about?

해석

47: 이야기의 목적은 무엇인가요?
48: 헌혈 절차에 대해 언급된 것은 무엇인가요?
49: 보통 헌혈은 어디에서 행해지나요?
50: 잠재적 기증자의 혈액이 비정상 검사를 받는 이유는 무엇인가요?
51: 강연자는 잠재적 기증자에게 채혈하기 적어도 두 시간 전에 하도록 권하는 것은 무엇인가요?
52: 다음 강연자는 무엇에 대해 이야기할까요?

Now you will hear the talk.

Good morning, everyone! I'm Luke Williams from the Chippewa Valley Chapter of the American Red Cross. 47) As you might have heard, our chapter will be having a blood donation drive next month. I'd like to tell you more about this activity and the blood donation process because I hope to convince you to contribute to our efforts.

To begin with, contrary to what some of you might think, giving blood is one of the easiest ways to help other people. You don't have to spend anything, and you certainly don't have to travel far in order to help. If you're at least 17 years old, weigh 110 pounds or more, and, are healthy, you can become a blood donor.

48) The process itself is very simple. 49) You need to visit the collection center where blood donations are accepted. These are temporary facilities that are usually set up in malls and high schools. Next month for example, we will be collecting blood at Grandville High School Auditorium and at both Bayview and Central City Malls.

Once there, all you have to do is simply read a pamphlet about the blood donation process and then sign a document stating that you have understood what you read in the pamphlet. The blood collection itself will be handled by a team of health professionals.

Before taking your blood, the medical team will do a basic physical examination to determine if you are a suitable donor. As part of the examination, you'll be asked to answer a few questions about your medical history and lifestyle. Afterwards, a nurse will check your blood pressure, pulse, and temperature, then take a few drops of blood from you. 50) The sample will be immediately tested for anemia and other blood tissue abnormalities.

50) If the sample is found okay, you'll be asked to sit on a reclining chair for the donation. I'd like to reassure you that the collection process is completely safe and not painful at all aside from the moment the nurse puts the needle into your arm. And even that is, as they say, just a pin prick. Also, you can be assured that the nurse will collect no more than one pint of blood from you.

You might feel a little weak afterwards, but don't worry. You'll regain your strength once you've rested for a few minutes and had a snack. After that you'll feel good as new and be able to go about your day with the knowledge that you are helping people in need.

51) For your own convenience, I suggest you have a light meal and drink some water two to three hours before donating blood. In closing, let me say that we in the Red Cross appreciate your willingness to participate in this blood donation drive. Your blood donation will be benefiting around 100 patients in our community hospitals, and I think you'll agree that few things can compare with the good work of donating one's own blood for other people.

Thank you so much! 52) I will now call on Ms. Anne Brooks to talk about the times and places where you can join next month's Blood Drive. Thanks and have a great day!

Words

blood donation drive 헌혈운동
physical examination 신체검사
anemia 빈혈
tissue 조직
pint 파인트 (액량 단위)
blood donor 혈액 기증자
pulse 맥박
abnormality 이상, 기형
reassure 안심시키다
willingness 기꺼이 하기

해석

여러분, 안녕하세요! 저는 미국 적십자사 소속 Chippewa Valley 지부의 루크 윌리엄스입니다. 47) 들으셨겠지만, 우리 지부는 다음 달에 헌혈운동을 할 것입니다. 저는 여러분들이 우리의 노력에 기여하도록 설득하고자, 이 활동과 헌혈 절차에 대해 더 자세히 말씀드리고 싶습니다.

우선, 몇몇 사람들이 생각하는 것과는 반대로, 헌혈은 다른 사람을 돕는 가장 쉬운 방법 중 하나입니다. 도움을 주기 위해 뭔가를 소비하거나 멀리 갈 필요도 없습니다. 17세 이상인 경우, 110파운드 이상 체중에, 건강하다면 헌혈자가 될 수 있습니다.

48) 그 절차는 매우 간단합니다. 49) 여러분은 헌혈을 할 수 있는 채혈센터를 방문해야 합니다. 이러한 곳들은 보통 쇼핑몰이나 고등학교에 설치되어 있는 임시 시설입니다. 예를 들어 다음달에는, Grandvile 고등학교 강당과 Bayview 쇼핑 몰, Center City 쇼핑 몰에서 채혈할 것입니다. 일단 그 곳에 가면, 여러분이 해야 할 일은 헌혈 절차에 관한 책자를 읽고 그 내용을 이해했다는 것을 나타내는 서류에 서명을 하는 것뿐입니다. 채혈은 의료전문가들에 의해 진행될 것입니다.

혈액을 채취하기 전에, 의료팀은 여러분이 적합한 기증자인지를 결정하기 위해 기본적인 신체검사를 실시할 것입니다. 검사의 일부로, 여러분은 병력과 생활방식에 관한 몇 가지 질문을 받을 것입니다. 그리고 나서, 간호사가 여러분의 혈압, 맥박 그리고 체온을 검사할 것이고 혈액을 약간 뽑을 것입니다. 50) 그 샘플은 곧바로 빈혈과 혈액 조직 이상 여부와 관련된 검사를 받을 것입니다. 50) 샘플에 이상이 없다면, 여러분은 헌혈을 위해 등받이가 뒤로 젖혀지는 의자에 앉으라고 요청받을 것입니다. 저는 여러분에게 헌혈과정은 완벽하게 안전하며 간호사가 여러분의 팔에 바늘을 꽂는 순간을 제외하고는 전혀 아프지 않다고 안심시켜 드리고 싶습니다. 그것마저도 간호사들이 말하는 것처럼, 단지 핀으로 살짝 찌르는 것에 불과합니다. 또한, 간호사는 여러분에게서 1파인트 이상의 혈액을 채취하지 않을 것이니 염려하지 않으셔도 됩니다.

헌혈 후 다소 체력이 떨어졌다고 느끼실 수도 있지만 걱정하지 마십시오. 잠깐 휴식을 가지고 간식을 먹고 나면 다시 기력을 회복하게 될 것입니다. 그 후, 새롭게 기분이 좋아질 것이고 도움이 필요한 사람들을 돕고 있다는 생각으로 여러분은 하루를 보낼 수 있을 것입니다.

51) 여러분의 편의를 위해, 헌혈하기 2~3시간 전에 가벼운 식사를 하고 약간의 물을 마실 것을 권해드립니다. 마지막으로 저희 적십자사는 기꺼이 이 헌혈 운동에 참여해 주시려는 여러분께 감사의 말씀을 드리고자 합니다. 여러분의 헌혈이 우리 지역 병원에 있는 약 100명의 환자들에게 도움이 될 것이고, 다른 사람을 위해 헌혈하는 것만큼 좋은 일은 거의 없다는데 동의하시리라 생각합니다. 정말 감사합니다! 52) 이제 다음 달 헌혈 운동에 참여할 수 있는 시간과 장소에 대해 이야기해 드릴 앤 브룩스를 모셔보겠습니다. 다시 한 번 감사드리며 즐거운 시간 보내시길 바랍니다!

47 ▶ 정답 ⓑ

What is the purpose of the talk?

(a) to launch a non-government organization
(b) to encourage people to donate blood
(c) to collect funds for a health center
(d) to educate about the need for blood donors

해석 이야기의 목적은 무엇인가요?

(a) 비정부기구를 발족하는 것
(b) 사람들에게 헌혈을 장려하는 것
(c) 보건소 기금을 모금하는 것
(d) 헌혈자의 필요성에 관해 교육하는 것

해설 화자는 연설의 첫 부분에서 헌혈 운동에 대해 소개하고 함께 동참하자는 이야기를 할 것이라고 밝히고 있다.

48 ▶ 정답 ⓓ

What was said about the blood donation process?

(a) It should be promoted in more American communities.
(b) It can be a profitable activity for health agencies.
(c) It requires the use of complex medical equipment.
(d) It is simpler than many prospective donors think.

해석 헌혈 절차에 대해 언급된 것은 무엇인가요?

(a) 그것은 더 많은 미국 사회에서 추진되어야 한다.
(b) 그것은 보건당국에 유익한 활동이 될 수 있다.
(c) 그것은 복잡한 의료장비 사용을 요구한다.
(d) 그것은 많은 장래 기증자들이 생각하는 것보다 간단하다.

해설 화자는 "The process itself is very simple."이라고 말하고 있다.

49 ▶ 정답 ⓐ

Where are blood donations usually held?

(a) at temporary collection centers
(b) at the local health center
(c) at university clinics
(d) at all hospitals nationwide

해석 보통 헌혈은 어디에서 행해지나요?

(a) 임시 채혈센터에서
(b) 지역 건강센터에서
(c) 대학병원에서
(d) 전국의 모든 병원에서

해설 연설자는 채혈을 하기 위해서, 보통 쇼핑몰이나 고등학교에 설치된 임시 시설을 방문해야 한다고 언급했다.

50 ▶ 정답 ⓓ

Why is the potential donor's blood likely tested for abnormalities?

(a) to diagnose the donor's illness right away
(b) to ensure that the donor can produce enough blood samples
(c) to check if the donor is honest about his medical history
(d) to make sure that the donor's blood is safe for donation

해석 잠재적 기증자의 혈액이 비정상 검사를 받는 이유는 무엇인가요?

(a) 즉시 기증자의 질병을 진단하기 위해서
(b) 기증자가 충분한 혈액 샘플을 만들어 낼 수 있는지 확실히 하기위해서
(c) 기증자가 자신의 병력과 관련해 정직한지를 확인하기 위해
(d) 기증자의 혈액이 기증에 안전한지 확인하기 위해서

해설 샘플은 즉시 빈혈과 혈액 조직 이상 여부에 관한 검사를 받을 것이라고 언급되어 있으며, 샘플에 이상이 없는 경우 채혈하는 의자에 앉게 된다. 혈액 검사에서 이상이 발견되면 채혈을 할 수 없다는 내용이므로 기증자의 혈액이 안전한 지를 확인하기 위함이라는 (d)의 진술이 올바르다.

51 ▶ 정답 ⓑ

What does the speaker suggest the potential donor do at least two hours before the bloodletting?

(a) have a blood test done
(b) eat some food and drink some water
(c) get three hours of sleep
(d) take a multivitamin pill

해석 강연자는 잠재적 기증자에게 채혈하기 적어도 두 시간 전에 하도록 권하는 것은 무엇인가요?

(a) 혈액검사를 마치는 것
(b) 음식을 먹고 약간의 물을 마시는 것
(c) 3시간의 수면을 취하는 것
(d) 종합 비타민제를 먹는 것

해설 "For your own convenience, I suggest you have a light meal and drink some water two to three hours before donating blood."을 통해 간단한 음식과 물을 마시는 것이 권고된다는 것을 알 수 있다.

52
▶ 정답 ⓐ

What will the next speaker talk about?

(a) the schedule of blood drive
(b) the medical personnel involved
(c) the other requirements for donors
(d) the intended recipients of the donation

해석
다음 강연자는 무엇에 대해 이야기할까요?

(a) 헌혈운동 일정
(b) 관련된 의료전문가
(c) 기증자에 관한 기타 요구사항
(d) 기부자가 지정한 수령자

해설 "I will now call on Ms. Anne Brooks to talk about the times and places where you can join next month's Blood Drive."에서 다음 강연자는 다음 달에 있을 헌혈운동 일정과 장소에 관해 이야기할 것임을 알 수 있다.

Reading and Vocabulary 04회

Question 53-80

ANSWER KEY p.107

53	ⓑ	54	ⓒ	55	ⓑ	56	ⓐ
57	ⓓ	58	ⓒ	59	ⓓ	60	ⓑ
61	ⓓ	62	ⓓ	63	ⓒ	64	ⓐ
65	ⓑ	66	ⓒ	67	ⓑ	68	ⓒ
69	ⓐ	70	ⓓ	71	ⓒ	72	ⓑ
73	ⓐ	74	ⓓ	75	ⓐ	76	ⓓ
77	ⓒ	78	ⓐ	79	ⓓ	80	ⓑ

Question 53-59

EDWIN HUBBLE

Edwin Hubble was an American astronomer 53) who was the first to show that there are other galaxies in the universe besides the Milky Way. He created a classification system for galaxies that is still in use today. One of the leading astronomers of the 20th century, he is also the namesake of the Hubble Space Telescope.

Edwin Powell Hubble was born in Marshfield, Missouri on November 20, 1889. As a young man, Hubble was a fine student and athlete, and was fond of reading science fiction novels. He received a degree in mathematics and astronomy from the University of Chicago. His athletic and academic 58) excellence would later earn him a Rhodes scholarship at Oxford University in England, where he studied law.

Upon returning to the US in 1913, 54) he worked halfheartedly as a lawyer. 54) He eventually quit law and pursued advanced studies in astronomy at the Yerkes Observatory in Wisconsin, and received his PhD in 1917. Two years later, he began working at Mount Wilson Observatory in California.

55) Most astronomers of Hubble's time believed that the Milky Way galaxy made up the whole universe and that the spots of light called "nebulae" were simply clouds of glowing gas that were quite near to Earth. In 1924, however, 55) Hubble found proof that 59) negated this claim. He showed that the Andromeda nebula was nearly a

million light-years away, far beyond the bounds of the Milky Way. Thereafter, Hubble established the presence of other galaxies. He also proved that the universe is expanding – a discovery that confirmed Albert Einstein's earlier theory that the universe is able to expand or contract.

56) In 1929, Hubble formulated what is now known as Hubble's Law, which states that the farther a galaxy is from another point in space, the faster it appears to move away. 57) This scientific law helped astronomers estimate the age of the universe. His reputation as an astronomer was strengthened by his publication of such papers as The Velocity-Distance Relation among Extra-Galactic Nebulae (1931), The Realm of Nebulae (1936), and The Problem of the Expanding Universe (1942), among others.

Hubble later transferred to the Palomar Observatory in California, where he continued doing space research until his death in 1953. Besides his many awards, NASA also named the Hubble Space Telescope after him for his groundbreaking discoveries in modern astronomy.

Words
Milky Way 우리 은하 (우리 지구가 속해 있는 은하계), 은하(수)
galaxy 은하계
astronomer 천문학자
astronomy 천문학
namesake 이름을 딴 사람(물건)
athlete 운동선수, 운동을 잘 하는 사람
scholarship 장학금
be fond of ~을 좋아하다
halfheartedly 성의 없이, 건성으로
pursue 추구하다, 추진하다
degree 학위
earn 얻다, 받다
claim 주장하다, 요구하다
classification system 분류법, 분류체계
confirm 확인하다
contract 줄어들다, 수축하다
establish 입증하다, 밝히다
estimate 추정하다
expand 팽창하다, 확장하다
farther 더 멀리
negate 부정하다, 무효화하다
presence 존재(함), 참석
spot 점, 반점, 장소, 위치
thereafter 그 후에
transfer 옮기다, 이동하다
reputation 명성
strengthen 강화시키다
ground breaking 획기적인

해석

에드윈 허블

53) 에드윈 허블은 우주에 은하수 외에도 다른 은하가 존재한다는 것을 최초로 보여준 미국인 천문학자였다. 그는 오늘날에도 여전히 사용되고 있는 은하 분류체계를 만들었다. 20세기 최고의 천문학자 중 한 명인 Hubble의 이름을 따서 만든 것이 허블 우주 망원경이다.

Edwin Powell Hubble은 1889년 11월 20일, Missouri의 Marshfield에서 태어났다. 젊은 시절의 허블은 우수한 학생이자 운동선수였으며, 공상과학소설을 좋아했다. 그는 시카고대학에서 수학과 천문학으로 학위를 받았다. 그의 탁월한 운동 실력과 학업 능력으로 후에 영국 옥스퍼드 대학에서 로즈 장학금을 받았고, 그곳에서 법을 전공했다.

1913년 미국으로 돌아왔을 때, 54) 그는 건성으로 변호사로써 일을 했다. 54) 결국, 그는 법을 그만두고, 위스콘신에 있는 여키스 천문대에서 천문학 고등과정을 수료하고, 1917년에 박사학위를 받았다. 2년 후, 그는 캘리포니아에 있는 윌슨 산 천문대에서 일하기 시작했다.

55) 허블 시대의 대부분 천문학자들은 은하수가 우주전체를 구성한다고 믿었고, '성운'이라 불리는 빛의 반점은 지구 가까이에서 빛나는 가스 구름일 뿐이라고 여겼다. 55) 그러나, 1924년에 허블은 이 주장을 부정하는 근거를 발견했다. 그는 안드로메다 성운은 은하수 경계를 넘어 거의 백만 광년 멀리 떨어진 곳에 존재한다는 것을 보여 주었다. 그 후, 허블은 다른 은하계의 존재를 입증하였다. 그는 또한 우주는 팽창하고 있다는 것을 입증했는데, 이는 알버트 아인슈타인의 앞선 이론으로 우주는 팽창하거나 수축할 수 있다는 것을 확인하는 발견이었다.

56) 1929년, 허블은 오늘날 허블의 법칙이라고 알려진 법칙을 만들었는데, 이는 은하계가 우주의 다른 한 지점으로부터 더 멀리 떨어져 있을수록 더 빨리 멀어지는 것처럼 보인다고 말하는 것이다. 이 과학법칙은 천문학자들이 우주 나이를 추정하는 것을 도왔다. 천문학자로서 그의 명성은 The Velocity-Distance Relation among Extra-Galactic Nebulae (1931), The Realm of Nebulae (1936)과 The Problem of the Expanding Universe (1942) 같은 논문을 발표함으로써 더욱 알려졌다.

허블은 후에 캘리포니아에 있는 팔로마산 천문대로 이직해서, 그 곳에서 그가 1953년에 사망할 때까지 우주에 관한 연구를 계속했다. 그의 많은 수상 외에도, NASA는 그의 이름을 따 Hubble Space Telescope 라고 이름 지었는데 이는 현대 천문학에서 허블의 획기적인 발견을 기리기 위함이었다.

53 ▶ 정답 ⓑ

What was Edwin Hubble most famous for?

(a) his work in science fiction
(b) his discoveries about outer space
(c) his discovery of the Milky Way
(d) his invention of a telescope

해석

에드윈 허블은 무엇으로 가장 유명한가요?
(a) 공상과학 소설에서 그의 작품
(b) 우주공간에 관한 발견들
(c) 은하수의 발견
(d) 망원경의 발명

해설 첫 번째 단락에서 "Edwin Hubble was an American astronomer who was the first to show that there are other galaxies in the universe besides the Milky Way."를 통해 우주에서 다른 은하를 발견한 최초의 천문학자임을 알 수 있다.

54 ▶ 정답 ⓒ

Why most likely did Hubble give up his job as a lawyer?
(a) because he wanted to return to Chicago
(b) because he preferred studying to working
(c) because it wasn't really his interest
(d) because law was too difficult

해석

허블은 왜 변호사 업무를 그만두었나요?
(a) 그는 시카고로 되돌아가기를 원했기 때문에
(b) 그는 일하는 것보다 공부하는 것을 더 좋아했기 때문에
(c) 변호사는 그가 진정으로 원했던 것이 아니기 때문에
(d) 법이 너무 어려웠기 때문에

해설 "Upon returning to the US in 1913, he worked halfheartedly as a lawyer."를 통해 진정으로 원했던 것이 아니라고 추측할 수 있다.

55 ▶ 정답 ⓑ

How was Hubble able to prove that the entire universe wasn't just made up of the Milky Way?
(a) by establishing that Earth was within the Milky Way
(b) by showing that a nebula was far outside the Milky Way
(c) by discovering the universe is expanding
(d) by learning that the universe is getting smaller

해석

허블은 우주전체가 은하수로만 이루어진 것이 아니라는 것을 어떻게 입증할 수 있었나요?
(a) 지구가 은하수 안에 있다는 것을 입증함으로써
(b) 성운이 우리 은하에서 멀리 있음을 보여줌으로써
(c) 우주가 팽창하고 있다는 것을 발견함으로써
(d) 우주가 점점 더 작아지고 있다는 것을 알게 됨으로써

해설 "He showed that the Andromeda nebula was nearly a million light-years away, far beyond the bounds of the Milky Way."를 통해 안드로메다 성운이 은하수에서 아주 멀리 떨어져 있음을 보여줬음을 확인할 수 있다.

56 ▶ 정답 ⓐ

What is the basic principle of Hubble's Law?
(a) The farther a galaxy is, the faster it seems to move away.
(b) There are other galaxies in the universe besides the Milky Way.
(c) The size of the universe is not changing.
(d) Nebulae are clouds of gas that are very close to Earth.

해석

Hubble's Law (허블의 법칙)의 기본원리는 무엇인가요?
(a) 은하계는 멀리 있을수록 더 빨리 움직이는 것처럼 보인다.
(b) 우주에는 은하수 외에도 다른 은하계가 있다.
(c) 우주의 크기는 변하지 않는다.
(d) 성운은 지구와 매우 가까운 가스 구름이다.

해설 "In 1929, Hubble formulated what is now known as Hubble's Law, which states that the farther a galaxy is from another point in space, the faster it appears to move away."를 통해 은하계는 멀리 떨어져 있을수록 더 빨리 움직이는 것처럼 보인다는 (a)가 가장 적절하다.

57 ▶ 정답 ⓓ

Based on the passage, what can be said about Edwin Hubble?
(a) He always supported the accepted theories of his time.
(b) His scientific discoveries are no longer relevant today.
(c) He was the best astronomer who ever lived.
(d) His discoveries led to a better understanding of the universe.

해석

지문에 따르면, 에드윈 허블에 관해 말할 수 있는 것은 무엇인가요?
(a) 그는 항상 그 당시 인정받았던 이론을 지지했다.
(b) 그의 과학적인 발견은 오늘날과 더 이상 관련이 없다.
(c) 그는 지금까지 살았던 최고의 천문학자이다.
(d) 그의 발견은 우주를 더 잘 이해하도록 이끌었다.

해설 "This scientific law helped astronomers estimate the age of the universe."를 통해 우주 나이를 측정하는 것이 가능해지고 우주를 더 잘 이해할 수 있도록 이끌었다고 추측할 수 있다.

58 ▶ 정답 ⓒ

In the context of the passage, excellence means _____.
(a) image
(b) appeal
(c) ability
(d) interest

해설 excellence 뛰어남, 탁월함 = ability

59 ▶ 정답 ⓓ

In the context of the passage, negated means _____.

(a) approved
(b) enriched
(c) fought
(d) contradicted

해석

지문의 문맥상 negated는 _____을 의미한다.

(a) 찬성하다, 인정하다
(b) (질, 가치를) 높이다, 풍요롭게 하다
(c) 싸우다, 겨루다
(d) 부인하다, 반박하다

해설 negate 부정하다, 부인하다 = contradict

Question 60-66

STUDY SHOWS THAT SOME ASTHMA PATIENTS ACTUALLY DON'T HAVE ASTHMA

60) A study shows that adults who have been diagnosed with asthma may not have the disease after all. According to the study, which was held at the Ottawa Hospital Research Institute in Canada, about a third of more than 600 asthma patients did not suffer from asthma, a condition wherein a person's airway swells and breathing becomes difficult when exposed to external causes.

Researchers tested 613 Canadian adults who had been diagnosed with asthma in the past five years, 45 percent of whom were taking asthma medications daily. 61) The participants were first asked to go through a lung-function test to measure how much air they could blow out of their lungs. If the test proved that a patient was negative of asthma, he was made to inhale methacholine, a chemical that commonly 65) triggers an asthma attack.

62) The tests showed that 203 of the participants did not test positive for asthma. They were then asked to lower, and eventually, stop their medication during weeks of observation. When their condition did not worsen after stopping asthma medication, they were observed for another year to see if the disease might return. 62) Over 90 percent remained asthma-free even without any medication. The researchers concluded that the subjects may have been cured of the disease or incorrectly diagnosed.

Many of the asthma-free participants were proven to be completely healthy all the while. Most weren't surprised with the finding, suspecting all along that their medications weren't really working. 63) Others were diagnosed with different diseases that had been improperly identified as asthma, including obesity-related breathing difficulties and allergies, and even more serious conditions such as heart disease and lung infection. The participants went on to receive proper treatment for their illnesses.

According to Dr. Shawn Aaron, the study head and professor at the University of Ottawa in Ontario, the results show that some adult asthma patients may need to have their diagnosis 66) reassessed. 64) They may be undergoing asthma medication when they don't need to, and are putting themselves at risk of harmful side effects from the drugs. Moreover, they continue paying for the costs of treatment without any real benefit.

Words

diagnose 진단하다	asthma 천식
disease 질병	patient 환자
airway 기도	swell 부풀다, 부어오르다
external 외부의	medication 약물, 약물치료
blow 불다	negative (검사 결과가) 음성의
inhale 들이마시다	trigger 촉발시키다, 일으키다
positive (검사 결과가) 양성의	lower 낮추다, 내리다
observation 관찰	observe 관찰하다
subject 피험자, 실험 대상	cure 고치다, 치유하다
suspect 의심하다	obesity 비만
lung infection 폐감염	reassess 재평가하다
side effect 부작용	

해석

연구는 일부 천식 환자들이 사실상은 천식이 아니라는 것을 보여준다.

60) 한 연구는 천식으로 진단받은 성인은 결국 이 병에 걸린 것이 아닐 수도 있다는 것을 보여준다. 캐나다 오타와 병원 연구소 (Ottawa Hospital Research Institute)에서 실시된 이 연구에 따르면 천식 환자 600 명 중 약 1/3이, 외부 원인에 노출되었을 때 기도가 부풀어 올라 호흡이 어려워지는 상태인 천식으로 고통스러워하지 않았다.

연구원들은 지난 5년간 천식으로 진단받은 캐나다 성인 613명을 대상으로 시험했고, 이들 중 45%가 천식 치료제를 매일 복용하고 있었다. 61) 참가자들은 먼저 폐에서 얼마나 많은 양의 공기를 불어낼 수 있는지를 측정하는 폐 기능 검사를 받도록 요청받았다. 검사에서 환자가 천식에 음성으로 판명되면, 그는 천식 발작을 유발하는 화학 물질인 메타 콜린 (methacholine)을 흡입하도록 했다. 검사 결과 참가자 중 203명은 천식에 양성 반응이 아님을 나타냈다. 그런 다음, 그들은 약물치료를 줄이고, 최종적으로는 관찰을 받는 주 동안에 약을 중단할 것을 요청 받았다. 천식 치료를 중단한 후 상태가 악화되지 않은 경우에는, 그 병이 혹시라도 다시 재발하지는 않는지 보기 위해 그들을 1년 더 관찰했다. 62) 90% 이상이 약물 치료

없이도 천식 증상이 나타나지 않았다. 연구원들은 피험자들이 병에서 치료되었거나 오진이었을 수 있다고 결론 내렸다. 천식이 없는 상당수의 참가자들은 그 동안 온전히 건강한 상태였다고 판명되었다. 대부분은 약물 치료가 실제로 효과가 없었다고 의심하며 결과에 놀라지 않았다. 63) 다른 사람들은 천식이라고 부적절하게 확인된 다른 질병으로 진단받았고, 이는 비만과 관련된 호흡 곤란, 알레르기 및 심장 질환이나 폐 감염과 같은 더욱 심각한 질병과 같은 것이다. 참가자들은 질병에 대한 적절한 치료를 받았다.

온타리오에 있는 오타와 대학교 (University of Ottawa)의 연구 책임자이자 교수인 Shawn Aaron 박사에 따르면, 그 결과는 일부 성인 천식 환자들이 진단을 다시 재검토할 필요가 있음을 나타낸다. 64) 그들은 약물 치료를 받을 필요가 없음에도 불구하고 치료를 받고 있을 수도 있으며, 그들 자신을 약물의 해로운 부작용 위험에 놓이고 있다. 또한, 그들은 실제적인 이익 없이 치료비용을 지불하는 것을 계속한다.

60 ▶정답 ⓑ

What did the study find out about some asthma patients?

(a) that they could be easily cured of asthma
(b) that their disease is non-existent
(c) that they could get rid of asthma themselves
(d) that they didn't know they had the disease

해석

이 연구는 천식 환자들에 관해 발견한 것이 무엇인가요?

(a) 그들은 쉽게 천식을 치료할 수 있다는 것
(b) 그들의 질병이 존재하지 않는다는 것
(c) 그들이 천식을 그들 스스로 없앨 수 있다는 것
(d) 그들이 병에 걸렸다는 것을 인지하지 못했다는 것

해설 "A study shows that adults who have been diagnosed with asthma may not have the disease after all."를 통해 천식으로 진단받은 환자들이 사실상은 천식 환자가 아님을 연구를 통해 나타났다.

61 ▶정답 ⓓ

How most likely did a participant pass the lung-function test?

(a) by being immune to a chemical
(b) by blowing air as loudly as they could
(c) by having an asthma attack
(d) by blowing a sufficient amount of air

해석

실험 참가자는 어떻게 폐 기능 검사를 통과했을 가능성이 높은가?

(a) 화학 물질에 면역이 됨으로써
(b) 가능한 한 큰 소리로 공기를 불어 냄으로써
(c) 천식 발작을 일으킴으로써
(d) 충분한 양의 공기를 불어냄으로써

해설 "The participants were first asked to go through a lung-function test to measure how much air they could blow out of their lungs."을 통해 정답은 (d)임을 알 수 있다.

62 ▶정답 ⓓ

What was the study able to learn about a third of the participants?

(a) that they needed less asthma medication
(b) that their drugs were working
(c) that their asthma would return
(d) that their medication was useless

해석

연구가 실험 참가자의 3분의 1에 대해서 알게 된 것은 무엇인가?

(a) 그들은 천식 치료제가 덜 필요했다는 것
(b) 그들의 약이 효과가 있었다는 것
(c) 그들의 천식이 재발할 것이라는 것
(d) 그들의 약물 치료가 효과가 없다는 것

해설 "The tests showed that 203 of the participants did not test positive for asthma.", "Over 90 percent remained asthma-free even without any medication. The researchers concluded that the subjects may have been cured of the disease or incorrectly diagnosed."를 통해 실험대상 613명의 1/3에 해당하는 203명의 환자들이 사실상 약물 치료가 도움이 되지 않았음을 알 수 있다.

63 ▶정답 ⓒ

Why most likely were the patients misdiagnosed as having asthma?

(a) Their real diseases were cured by asthma drugs.
(b) Their real diseases always lead to asthma.
(c) Their real diseases showed the same symptoms.
(d) They claimed that they had asthma during diagnosis.

해석

환자들을 천식으로 오진하게 된 가장 큰 이유는 무엇일까?

(a) 그들의 실제 질병은 천식 약으로 치료되었다.
(b) 그들의 실제 질병이 항상 천식을 유발했다.
(c) 그들의 실제 질병이 같은 증상을 보였다.
(d) 그들은 진단동안 천식이 있다고 주장했다.

해설 "Others were diagnosed with different diseases that had been improperly identified as asthma, including obesity-related breathing difficulties and allergies, and even more serious conditions such as heart disease and lung infection."를 통해 천식의 증상과 이러한 질병들의 증상이 유사함을 추론할 수 있다.

64 ▶정답 ⓐ

According to the study, what is a cause of harmful side effects?

(a) taking an asthma drug when it isn't necessary
(b) taking the wrong drug for asthma
(c) taking more than the prescribed dosage for asthma
(d) not taking asthma drugs daily

해석

이 연구에 따르면, 유해한 부작용의 원인은 무엇인가?

(a) 필요하지 않을 때 천식 약을 복용하는 것
(b) 천식에 적합하지 않은 약을 복용하는 것
(c) 천식으로 처방된 용량 이상의 약을 복용하는 것
(d) 천식 약을 매일 복용하지 않는 것

해설 마지막 문단에서 언급된 "They may be undergoing asthma medication when they don't need to, and are putting themselves at risk of harmful side effects from the drugs."를 통해 약물 치료가 불필요한 경우 부작용이 발생할 수 있음을 알 수 있다.

65 ▶ 정답 ⓑ

In the context of the passage, triggers means _____.

(a) fires
(b) starts
(c) prevents
(d) cures

해설 지문의 문맥상 triggers는 _____을 의미한다.

(a) 발사하다, 해고하다
(b) 시작하다, 일으키다
(c) 예방하다, 막다
(d) 치료하다

해설 trigger 촉발시키다, 방아쇠를 당기다 = start

66 ▶ 정답 ⓒ

In the context of the passage, reassessed means _____.

(a) renewed
(b) changed
(c) reviewed
(d) maintained

해설 지문의 문맥상 reassessed는 _____을 의미한다.

(a) 재개하다, 갱신하다
(b) 바꾸다, 변경하다
(c) 재검토하다, 복습하다
(d) 유지하다, 관리하다, 주장하다

해설 reassess 재평가하다 = review

Question 67-73

STONEHENGE

67) Stonehenge is a prehistoric monument that consists of large standing stones, or "megaliths," located on the Salisbury Plain in Wiltshire, southern England. Constructed 5,000 years ago, both who built it and 70) why it was built remain a mystery.

The stones are enclosed in a circular ditch about 300 feet in diameter. The ditch has an earth bank on the inner side and is approached through a wide pathway called the Avenue. 68) The monument's outer part is a circle of sandstones about 13.5 feet high and connected by stone beams. Within it is a circle of bluestone megaliths, a horseshoe-shaped group, and in the innermost part, an oval group.

Archaeological research shows that the stones were made somewhere else before they were installed on the site, and that building Stonehenge required careful planning and advanced knowledge of geometry and symmetry.

Most archaeologists think that Stonehenge was constructed between 3000 BC and 2000 BC. The older circular earth bank and ditch have been dated to about 3100 BC. However, the 72) existing stones are only the ruins of what is believed to have been a bigger structure.

The creation of Stonehenge has been credited to many ancient peoples from throughout thousands of years. The most believable theory is that the construction was begun by the people of the late Neolithic period, around 3000 BC, and 69) continued by the so-called Beaker Folk who lived in a more advanced economy and were more closely knit way than their ancestors.

70) The purpose of Stonehenge has also been the 73) subject of much debate. 70) Some have assumed that the structure was a temple used for worshipping the gods. 70) Others have regarded it as an astronomical observatory for marking significant events on the prehistoric calendar. 70) Still others believe it was a sacred burial site for high-ranking citizens of ancient times. 71) Regardless of its purpose, there is agreement that Stonehenge had played a key role in the lives of those who invested considerable effort in its creation.

Today, Stonehenge is regarded as a British national icon that represents mystery, power, and endurance. It was designated as a UNESCO World Heritage Site in 1986.

Words

prehistoric monument 선사시대 기념물
circular 원형의, 둥근
diameter 직경, 지름
pathway 길, 진로, 통로
beam 기둥
geometry 기하학
credit (공을) ~게 돌리다
debate 논쟁
temple 사원, 신전
regard 간주하다, 여기다
significant 중요한
burial 매장
considerable 상당한, 많은
designate 지정하다, 선정하다
enclose 둘러싸다
ditch 도랑, 배수로
bank 둑, 제방
sandstone 사암
oval 타원형의
symmetry 대칭
subject 주제
assume 가정하다, 생각하다
worship 숭배하다
observatory 관측소, 천문대
sacred 신성한, 성스러운
site 위치, 장소
endurance 인내

해석

스톤헨지

67) 스톤헨지는 잉글랜드 남부 윌트셔의 솔즈베리 평야에 위치한 거대한 입석들 또는 'megaliths(거석)'로 구성된 선사 시대의 기념물이다. 5000년 전에 지어졌지만, 누가 만들었고, 70) 왜 만들었는지는 알려져 있지 않다.

거석들은 직경 약 300 피트의 원형도랑에 둘러싸여있다. 이 도랑은 안쪽에 흙으로 된 둑이 있고, Avenue라고 불리는 대로를 통해 접근가능하다. 68) 이 기념비의 바깥 부분은 13.5 피트 정도 높이의 사암이 원형을 이루고, 돌기둥들로 연결되어 있다. 그 안에는 말발굽 형태의 블루스톤 거석이 원형으로 있으며, 가장 안쪽 부분에는 타원형의 무리가 있다. 고고학 연구는 이 거석들은 그 곳에 설치되기 전에 다른 어딘 가에서 만들어졌으며, 스톤헨지를 짓는 것은 신중한 계획과 기하학과 대칭에 관한 고도의 지식을 요구한다는 것을 나타낸다.

대부분의 고고학자들은 스톤헨지가 기원전 3000년에서 2000년 사이에 지어졌다고 생각한다. 더 오래된 원형의 흙으로 된 둑과 도랑은 대략 기원전 3100년으로 거슬러 올라간다. 그러나 현존하는 거석들은 추측되어지는 더 거대한 구조물들의 잔해에 불과하다.

스톤헨지의 건설은 수천 년에 걸친 수많은 고대인들에게 공이 있다. 가장 믿을 만한 이론은 대략 기원전 3000년경 신석기 후반기에 사람들이 만들기 시작했으며, 69) 조상보다 더욱 발전된 경제생활을 했고 더 긴밀한 유대 방식을 갖고 있었던 Beaker Folk라고 불리던 민족이 계속 이어갔다는 것이다.

70) 스톤헨지의 목적은 또한 수많은 논쟁의 주제가 되어 오고 있다 70) 일부 학자들은 그 구조물(=스톤헨지)이 신을 숭배하기 위해 사용된 신전이라고 여긴다. 70) 다른 학자들은 그것을 선사시대 달력 기준에 중요한 사건을 표시하기 위한 천문관측대로 간주한다. 70) 또 다른 학자들은 스톤헨지를 고대의 높은 신분에 있던 사람들을 위한 신성한 매장지였다고 믿는다. 71) 목적과 상관없이, 스톤헨지는 그것을 만드는 데 상당한 노력을 들인 사람들의 삶에 중요한 역할을 했다는 데에는 이견이 없다.

오늘날 스톤헨지는 신비, 권력, 그리고 인내를 드러내는 영국의 국가적인 상징으로 여겨진다. 스톤헨지는 1986년에 UNESCO 세계문화유산으로 지정되었다.

67 ▶ 정답 ⓑ

What is Stonehenge?

(a) a rock formation
(b) a group of stones
(c) a prehistoric house
(d) a religious monument

해석

스톤헨지는 무엇인가?

(a) 암반층
(b) 암석군
(c) 선사시대의 가옥
(d) 종교적인 기념물

해설 "Stonehenge is a prehistoric monument that consists of large standing stones, or "megaliths," located on the Salisbury Plain in Wiltshire, southern England."를 통해 스톤헨지는 거석들로 이루어진 암석군임을 알 수 있다.

68 ▶ 정답 ⓒ

Which is true about Stonehenge's formation?

(a) It is believed to be added to the structure later on.
(b) It was only discovered recently.
(c) It is composed of three layers of stone structures.
(d) It was constructed in 3000 BC.

해석

스톤헨지의 형성에 대해서 사실인 것은 무엇인가?

(a) 나중에 구조물에 추가된 것으로 여겨진다.
(b) 최근에서야 발견되었다.
(c) 3단계의 암석 구조물로 구성되어있다.
(d) 기원전 3000년에 설립되었다.

해설 "The monument's outer part is a circle of sandstones about 13.5 feet high and connected by stone beams. Within it is a circle of bluestone megaliths, a horseshoe-shaped group, and in the innermost part, an oval group."를 통해 가장 바깥 부분, 그 안 부분, 가장 안쪽 부분으로 나누어 설명하고 있음을 확인할 수 있다. 3단계 암석 구조물로 구성되어 있다는 (c)가 가장 적절하다.

69 ▶ 정답 ⓐ

What is said about the Beaker Folk?

(a) Their social system was more advanced than their ancestors.
(b) They most likely started building of Stonehenge.
(c) They rebuilt Stonehenge into a more modern structure.
(d) Stonehenge was damaged during their time.

해석

Beaker Folk에 대해 언급한 것은?

(a) 그들의 사회체제는 그들의 조상들보다 더욱 발전되었다.

(b) 그들은 스톤헨지를 짓기 시작했을 가능성이 있다.
(c) 그들은 더욱 현대적인 구조물로 스톤헨지를 다시 지었다.
(d) 스톤헨지는 그 당시 손상되었다.

해설 "continued by the so-called Beaker Folk who lived in a more advanced economy and were more closely knit way than their ancestors."를 통해 조상들보다 더욱 윤택하고 친밀한 삶을 살았음을 알 수 있다.

70 ▶ 정답 ⓓ

Why has there been much discussion about Stonehenge?
(a) because it is regarded as sacred
(b) because it has high academic significance
(c) because it has great economic value
(d) because its purpose is still unknown

해설 왜 스톤헨지에 관해서 많은 논란이 있나요?
(a) 그것은 신성한 것으로 여겨지기 때문에
(b) 그것은 학문적인 중요성이 높기 때문에
(c) 그것은 경제적인 가치가 크기 때문에
(d) 그것의 목적은 여전히 알려져 있지 않기 때문에

해설 "The purpose of Stonehenge has also been the subject of much debate"가 언급된 단락에서 보면 많은 학자들이 스톤헨지의 목적에 대해서 다른 주장을 하고 있다. 확실한 근거를 토대로 한 목적이 알려져 있지 않다는 것을 드러낸다.

71 ▶ 정답 ⓒ

Why most likely do experts believe that Stonehenge served an important purpose to its builders?
(a) because it was well preserved
(b) because it is now a heritage site
(c) because it was difficult to make
(d) because remains have been found around it

해설 전문가들은 왜 스톤헨지가 건설자들에게 중요한 역할을 했다고 믿는 것 같은가?
(a) 그것이 잘 보존이 되어있었기 때문에
(b) 그것이 현재 유적지이기 때문에
(c) 그것은 만들기 어려웠기 때문에
(d) 유물들이 그 주변에서 발견되었기 때문에

해설 "Regardless of its purpose, there is agreement that Stonehenge had played a key role in the lives of those who invested considerable effort in its creation."을 통해 많은 사람들이 상당한 노력을 한 것을 알 수 있다. 상당한 노력을 했다는 것은 공을 많이 들였다는 것이므로 그만큼 작업이 어렵고 고되었다는 것으로 추론할 수 있다.

72 ▶ 정답 ⓑ

In the context of the passage, existing means _____.
(a) fresh
(b) present
(c) past
(d) missing

해설 지문의 문맥상 existing는 _____을 의미한다.
(a) 신선한, 새로운
(b) 현재의, 참석한, 존재하는
(c) 과거의
(d) 없어진, 누락된

해설 existing 현존하는, 현재 있는 = present

73 ▶ 정답 ⓐ

In the context of the passage, subject means _____.
(a) topic
(b) result
(c) course
(d) belief

해설 지문의 문맥상 subject는 _____을 의미한다.
(a) 주제
(b) 결과
(c) 과정
(d) 신념, 믿음

해설 subject 주제 = topic

Question 74-80

January 10, 2004

Mr. Thomas Dillon
Vice President for Operations
Beckman Associates, Inc.
4102 Pine Ridge Road
Abington, PA 19001

Dear Mr. Dillon:

I know that your organization is very much concerned about efficiency and productivity. We at the 74) 78) People Company can help you achieve those goals by organizing a team-building program to help make your employees more efficient and your entire company more productive.

78) Our industrial psychologists at the People Company have developed the Team Survival Program, a two-day team-building 79) session that will teach participants how to cope with a fast-paced business environment. On the first day, the participants will attend a seminar that focuses on strategic planning, time management, and work process improvement. 75) On the second day, the participants will undergo outdoor search-and-rescue exercises designed to improve communication and teamwork among them.

The Team Survival Program will be an effective learning experience because it is based on the following principles:

76) (1) Alignment – to bridge the gap between corporate goals and current performance;
(2) Engagement – to standardize the different working styles of team members;
(3) Commitment – to open communication lines between management and staff;
(4) Action – to enable team members to work on shared values and goals.

The People Company would 80) welcome the opportunity to assist Beckman Associates in building a unified team. 77) Please feel free to contact me anytime to discuss the Team Survival Program in detail.

Sincerely,

Miranda S. Barnett

Accounts Manager
The People Company
Tel:(215) 884-4887

Words

efficiency 효율(성)
achieve 달성하다, 성취하다
participant 참가자, 참석자
undergo 겪다, 경험하다
alignment 정렬, 연대, 협력
engagement (업무관련) 약속, 일
commitment 전념, 헌신, 개입
enable 할 수 있게 하다, 가능하게 하다
productivity 생산성
session 강습회, 활동, 모임
cope with 대처하다
principle 원칙
performance 성과
standardize 표준화하다

해석

딜런 씨께:

저는 귀하의 조직이 효율성과 생산성에 굉장히 많은 관심을 가지고 있다는 것을 알고 있습니다. 74) 78) People Company는 직원들의 효율성과 회사 전체 생산성을 높일 수 있도록 도움을 주는 팀-빌딩 프로그램을 구성함으로써, 귀하가 목표를 이룰 수 있도록 도와드릴 수 있습니다.

78) People Company의 산업 심리학자들은 참가자들에게 급변하는 비즈니스 환경에 대응하는 방법을 가르치는 이틀간의 팀-빌딩 연수과정인 Team Survival Program을 개발했습니다. 첫날, 참석자들은 전략기획, 시간관리, 그리고 작업처리과정 개선에 초점을 둔 세미나에 참석할 것입니다. 75) 둘째 날, 참석자들은 팀원들 사이의 결속력과 의사소통을 향상시킬 수 있도록 만들어 진 외부 수색 및 구조훈련을 받을 것입니다.

Team Survival Program은 다음 원칙들을 기본으로 하고 있기 때문에 효과적인 학습 기회가 될 것입니다.

76) (1) Alignment – 기업 목표와 현재 성과 사이의 격차를 줄이기
(2) Engagement – 팀 구성원들의 서로 다른 업무방식을 표준화하기
(3) Commitment – 경영진과 직원들 사이의 소통 통로를 개방하기
(4) Action – 팀 구성원들이 공통의 가치와 목표를 달성할 수 있게 하기

People Company는 Beckman Associates이 단결된 팀을 구성 할 수 있도록 지원할 수 있는 기회를 환영합니다. 77) 언제든지 제게 편히 연락하시어 Team Survival Program에 대해 자세히 상의하세요.

안녕히 계세요,

74 ▶ 정답 @

Why did Miranda Barnett write Thomas Dillon the letter?
(a) to inquire about the services of his company
(b) to ask what goals his company wants to achieve
(c) to apply for as a manager at his company
(d) to offer a program suited to his company's need

해석
미란다 바넷이 토마스 딜런에게 편지를 쓴 이유는 무엇인가요?
(a) 그의 회사 서비스에 대해 문의하기 위해
(b) 그의 회사가 달성하고자 하는 목표를 묻고자
(c) 그의 회사에 매니저로 지원하기 위해
(d) 그의 회사 요구에 맞는 프로그램을 제안하려고

해설 Part 4 편지의 목적은 주로 첫 번째 단락에 나오는 경우가 대부분이다. "We at the People Company can help you achieve those goals by organizing a team-building program to help make your employees more efficient and your entire company more productive."에서 수신인의 사업 목표를 이루는데 도움이 될 수 있도록 도와주겠다고 했으므로 홍보가 목적임을 추론할 수 있다.

75 ▶ 정답 @

How does the Team Survival Program aim to improve teamwork among participants?
(a) through pretend search-and-rescue activities
(b) by undergoing psychology tests
(c) through a seminar on time management
(d) by planning strategies together

해석 어떻게 Team Survival Program은 참가자들 간의 팀워크를 향상시키는 것을 목표로 하는가?

(a) 가상의 수색 및 구조 활동들을 통해
(b) 심리 테스트를 실시함으로써
(c) 시간 관리에 관한 세미나를 통해
(d) 함께 전략을 계획함으로써

해설 "On the second day, the participants will undergo outdoor search-and-rescue exercises designed to improve communication and teamwork among them."를 통해 (a)가 정답임을 알 수 있다.

76 ▶ 정답 ⓓ

What does the principle of Alignment most likely say?

(a) Team members should have the same goals.
(b) Managers should communicate with their staff.
(c) Various working styles should be standardized.
(d) Employee performance should meet management goals.

해석 Alignment의 원칙은 무엇이라고 말하는 거 같은가?

(a) 팀 구성원들은 동일한 목표를 가져야 한다.
(b) 관리자는 그들의 직원들과 의사소통해야 한다.
(c) 다양한 업무 방식을 표준화해야 한다.
(d) 직원성과는 경영목표를 충족시켜야 한다.

해설 "Alignment - to bridge the gap between corporate goals and current performance;"를 통해서 경영목표와 직원성과 사이의 간격 줄이기는 경영목표를 충족 시킨다는 (d)의 내용으로 요약할 수 있다.

77 ▶ 정답 ⓒ

What did Barnett request Dillon to do?

(a) to inform his employees about the program
(b) to set a schedule for the team-building session
(c) to contact her if he is interested in the program
(d) to prepare a budget for the team-building session

해석 바넷이 딜런에게 요청한 것은 무엇인가요?

(a) 그의 직원들에게 프로그램에 대해 알리는 것
(b) 팀-빌딩 연수과정에 관한 일정을 정하는 것
(c) 그가 프로그램에 대해서 관심이 있다면 그녀에게 연락을 하는 것
(d) 팀-빌딩 연수과정에 대한 예산을 준비하는 것

해설 "Please feel free to contact me anytime to discuss the Team Survival Program in detail"를 통해 관심이 있다면 연락할 것을 요청하고 있다.

78 ▶ 정답 ⓐ

What business is Miranda Barnett most probably involved in?

(a) an employee-training company
(b) an account management firm
(c) an emergency response team
(d) a recruitment company

해석 미란다 바넷은 어떤 직종에서 일하는 거 같나요?

(a) 직원교육회사
(b) 회계관리회사
(c) 응급구조팀
(d) 채용회사

해설 "People Company can help you achieve those goals by organizing a team-building program to help make your employees more efficient and your entire company more productive."를 통해 직원들을 교육하는 회사인 것을 알 수 있다.

79 ▶ 정답 ⓓ

In the context of the passage, session means _____.

(a) plan
(b) subject
(c) council
(d) activity

해석 지문의 문맥상 session는 _____을 의미한다.

(a) 계획
(b) 주제, 과목, 피실험자
(c) 의회, 자문회
(d) 활동

해설 session 활동, 강습회, 모임 = activity

80 ▶ 정답 ⓑ

In the context of the passage, welcome means _____.

(a) secure
(b) appreciate
(c) admit
(d) disallow

해석 지문의 문맥상 welcome는 _____을 의미한다.

(a) 보호하다, 고정시키다, 획득하다
(b) 감사하다, 환영하다, 진가를 알아보다
(c) 인정하다
(d) 허락하지 않다

해설 welcome 환영하다, 기꺼이 받아들이다 = appreciate

지텔프코리아 공식지정

G-TELP
LEVEL 2

이현아 취향저격 지텔프 실전모의고사

해설편 5

Answers and Explanations

한 권에 끝내는 G-TELP 실전모의고사 5회

SECTION 01 GRAMMAR
SECTION 02 LISTENING
SECTION 03 READING & VOCABULARY

Grammar Test 05회
Question 1-26

ANSWER KEY p.119

01	ⓓ	02	ⓐ	03	ⓒ	04	ⓑ
05	ⓒ	06	ⓐ	07	ⓓ	08	ⓐ
09	ⓓ	10	ⓒ	11	ⓑ	12	ⓓ
13	ⓒ	14	ⓐ	15	ⓒ	16	ⓑ
17	ⓐ	18	ⓑ	19	ⓒ	20	ⓐ
21	ⓓ	22	ⓑ	23	ⓓ	24	ⓐ
25	ⓒ	26	ⓑ				

01 ▶ 정답 ⓓ

해석 연구원들은 하루에 20그램 미만의 지방을 섭취하는 사람들은 편두통의 횟수가 더 적고 정도가 심하지 않다는 것을 발견했다. 이를 바탕으로, 일부 의사들은 편두통이 있는 환자에게 지방섭취를 줄이도록 조언하고 있다.

해설 보기에 시간부사 now가 있으므로 현재진행시제와 가장 잘 어울린다.

02 ▶ 정답 ⓐ

해석 Sarah는 육군 중위인 아버지가 아프리카로 배정되었을 때, 겨우 다섯 살이었다. 이제 20대의 Sarah는 야생 동물들이 돌아다니는 것을 보기 위해 Savanna로 갔던 것을 기억한다.

해설 3형식 타동사 remember는 목적어 자리에 to 부정사와 동명사를 둘 다 취할 수 있다. 지나간 '완료'의 상황을 기억하는 것을 표현할 때는 동명사를 목적어로 취하는데 이 문제는 과거의 회상이므로 (a)가 적절하다.

03 ▶ 정답 ⓒ

해설 어떤 사람들은 카페인이 여드름을 유발한다고 믿는다. 그러나 UCLA의 피부과 교수 Joshua Wieder는 여드름이 신체적 스트레스와 호르몬 문제로 인해 발생한다고 말한다. 그는 커피 마시는 사람들이 커피 섭취를 걱정하지 말 것을 조언한다.

해설 명령, 동의, 제안, 주장, 요구, 충고 동사의 목적어 자리에 that절이 오는 경우 동사는 「(should) 동사원형」이 되어야 한다.

04 ▶ 정답 ⓑ

해설 최근에 친구 한 명이 나에게 아름다운 양장본 시집을 주었다. 책이 무겁기 때문에 집 밖에서 읽으려고 가지고 다닐 수는 없다. 그러나 만약 내가 휴가를 간다면, 나는 꼭 그 책을 가져갈 텐데.

해설 If절의 동사가 were로 과거시제이므로 주절에는 「조동사 과거형 + 동사원형」이 와야 한다. 부사 definitely는 조동사와 본동사 사이에 들어가는 것이 적절하다.

05 ▶ 정답 ⓒ

해설 Jerome은 미술사 졸업생이 아니며 미술기관에서 풀타임으로 일한 적이 없다. 그럼에도 불구하고 그는 한 실험예술박물관의 큐레이터로 고용되어 현재 수개월 동안 공동감독으로 근무하고 있다.

해설 기간을 표현하는 부사 for several months가 나왔으므로 완료시제가 들어가야 하며 시간부사 now가 있으므로 현재완료 진행 시제가 가장 적절하다.

06 ▶ 정답 ⓐ

해설 Jake는 종종 CD-ROM 드라이브에서 디스크를 꺼내는 것을 잊는다. 컴퓨터 엔지니어인 형이 그 사실을 알았을 때 그는 Jake가 디스크와 CD-ROM이 손상되지 않도록 항상 디스크를 빼야 한다고 말했다.

해설 문맥의 흐름상 디스크와 CD-ROM이 손상되지 않도록 주의해서 디스크를 꺼내야 한다는 내용이 들어가는 것이 자연스럽다. '의무'나 '당위성'을 표현하는 조동사 should가 가장 적절하다.

07 ▶ 정답 ⓓ

해설 Susanna Moore는 흥미로운 여성 캐릭터가 등장하는 소설을 몇권 썼다. 이 소설들 중에는 영화로 개작된 In the Cut과 One Last Look이 있다. 그녀의 다음 작품에서, 무어는 이 이야기에 가증스러운 범죄를 저지른 엄마에 관한 이야기를 할 것이다.

해설 관계사 문제로 빈칸 앞에 놓인 소설 In the Cut이 선행사이다. 선행사가 사람이 아니므로 who가 쓰일 수 없고, 콤마(,)뒤에는 관계대명사 that을 쓸 수 없다. 관계부사 where가 완벽한 문장을 이끈 것은 올바르지만 선행사와의 관계에서 문맥상 올바르지 않다. 계속적 용법의 주격 관계대명사 which의 쓰임이 올바르다.

08 ▶ 정답 ⓐ

해설 지난 해 Gibson은 알츠하이머 진단을 받았다. 그의 아내는 그가 질병에 대처하도록 돕는 최선의 방법은 질병에 대해 아는 것이라는 것을 깨달았다. 이것이 그들이 알츠하이머 인식캠페인에 참여한 이유이다.

해설 빈칸 앞에 the best way 명사를 수식할 수 있는 것은 to 부정사이다.

09 ▶ 정답 ⓓ

해설 내 사촌인 Denise는 세계 최대 테마파크의 놀이 공원 중 몇몇을 만든 디자이너이다. 그녀의 디자인에 대한 사랑은 어린 시절부터 분명했다. 우리 모두가 밖에서 노는 동안, 그녀는 항상 방에서 레고로 집을 짓고 있었다.

해설 시간부사절 while의 동사 시제가 과거(played)이므로 주절에는 과거진행 시제가 가장 적절하다.

10 ▶ 정답 ⓒ

해석 테크놀로지 회사인 Constellation Corp는 일반 DVD보다 20배 더 많은 저장 공간을 갖춘 차세대 디스크를 공개하길 갈망한다. 그러나 마케팅 부서는 올해 너무 일찍 제품을 출시하는 것에 반대한다.

해설 빈칸은 전치사 against 뒤이므로 동명사가 들어가는 것이 가장 적절하다.

11 ▶ 정답 ⓑ

해석 1998년 캘리포니아 주지사는 HIV 감염사례를 검토하기 위해 주 전체적인 시스템을 제안했던 입법안을 허용하지 않았다. 보건 당국자는 만약 법안이 통과되었다면, HIV를 예방할 수 있는 효과적인 수단으로 사용되었을 것이라고 말하면서 실망했다.

해설 If절의 시제가 had p.p.이므로 가정법 과거완료임을 알 수 있다. 주절에는 「조동사 과거형 + have p.p.」가 들어가야 한다.

12 ▶ 정답 ⓓ

해석 Andre는 Romanov 왕조 시대의 패션 트렌드에 관한 글을 쓰기 위해 모스크바로 갔다. 병기박물관에서 훌륭한 의상을 보고 난 후, 그는 큰 영감을 받아 모스크바에 있는 동안 기사를 다 작성했다.

해설 접속사 문제로 해석을 요구한다. 문맥상 '~하는 동안'을 의미하는 while이 가장 적절하다.

13 ▶ 정답 ⓒ

해석 Leo Fender의 전자 제품에 대한 관심은 어릴 때 시작되었다. 1928년 고등학교를 졸업한 후, 그는 사교행사 주최측에게 빌려주었던 확성기와 앰프를 이미 만들었다.

해설 관계사 문제이며 선행사가 public address systems and amplifiers이므로 선행사를 포함하는 what과 사람 선행사를 수식하는 who를 쓸 수 없다. 관계부사 when은 완벽한 문장을 이끌어야 하는데 (a)는 목적어가 없는 불완전한 문장이다.

14 ▶ 정답 ⓐ

해석 일부 영화 비평가들은 썩 흥미롭지 않은 장면들 때문에 Woody Allen의 Mighty Aphrodite를 비판했다. 그들은 만약 감독과 편집자가 대본에 더 많은 생각을 넣었더라면, 몇몇 지루한 대화와 장면을 제거했을 것이라고 말했다.

해설 if절의 시제가 had p.p. 이므로 주절에는 「조동사 과거형 + have p.p.」가 들어가야 한다.

15 ▶ 정답 ⓒ

해석 William Magee 박사는 성형외과 의사이고 그의 아내는 간호사이며 사회복지사이다. 1982년에 그들은 얼굴 기형이 있는 가난한 어린이들에게 무료 재건 수술을 제공하기 위해 Operation Smile을 설립했다.

해설 빈칸 앞에 완벽한 문장이 왔으므로 빈칸에는 부사만 들어갈 수 있다. 목적을 나타내는 to 부정사가 가장 적절하다.

16 ▶ 정답 ⓑ

해석 Ospreys는 오직 중간 정도의 성공밖에 이루지 못한 1950년대 밴드였다. 그 이유는 그 밴드가 독특한 사운드를 개발하는 것 대신에, 성공을 거둔 그룹을 단지 흉내냈기 때문이었을 것이다.

해설 해석을 통해 풀어야 하는 접속사 문제이다. 이유를 표현하는 because가 가장 적절하다. 부사절 접속사로만 쓰이는 although는 문법적으로 올바르지 않다.

17 ▶ 정답 ⓐ

해석 Louise는 결혼기념일에 샴페인 한 병을 그녀의 부모님께 드리기를 원한다. 내일, 그녀는 수많은 빈티지 와인 중에서 선택을 하기 위해 Rafael's Winery를 방문할 것이다.

해설 시간부사 tomorrow가 있으므로 미래시제가 가장 적절하다.

18 ▶ 정답 ⓑ

해석 Alabama에 있는 아프리카계 미국인 여성들은 지금 여러 세대 동안 누빔이불을 만들어 오고 있다. 만약 나이 든 세대가 기술을 자녀들에게 전달하지 못했다면, 생계 수단은 오늘날까지 지속되지 않았을 것이다.

해설 If절의 시제가 had p.p. 이므로 가정법 과거완료임을 알 수 있다. 주절에는 「조동사 과거형 + have p.p.」가 들어가야 하는 것을 알 수 있다.

19 ▶ 정답 ⓒ

해석 단 일 년 만에, River Dogs는 Oregon의 아마추어 야구 리그에서 유망한 팀이 되었다. 팀 매니저는 만약 팀이 더 많은 팬 층과 후원을 좀 더 만들어낸다면, 진정으로 성공할 것이라고 말한다.

해설 가정법 문제이며 주절의 동사가 would succeed이므로 가정법 과거임을 알 수 있다. if절에는 동사의 과거시제가 들어가야 한다.

20 ▶ 정답 ⓐ

해석 자동차 정비사는 만약 네 개의 타이어 중 하나가 균형 잡혀 있지 않다면 차가 순조롭게 달리지 않을 것이라고 말한다. 따라서 그들은 차주가 차량의 한 부분이 다른 부분보다 무겁지 않게 해야 한다고 조언한다.

해설 명령, 동의, 주장, 제안, 요구, 충고 동사의 목적어 자리에 that절이 오면 동사는 「(should) 동사원형」이 되어야 한다.

21 ▶정답 ⓓ

해석 Irene은 지구과학을 가르치는 창의적인 방법을 가지고 있다. 그녀는 학생들이 단지 강의가 아니라 실제 적용을 통해 배울 수 있도록 확실히 한다. 다음 주에, 그녀는 학생들에게 과학박람회를 위해 소형 지진 방지 건물을 짓게 할 것이다.

해설 시간 부사 next week이 있으므로 미래의 상황을 묘사하는 것임을 알 수 있다. 미래를 표현하는 조동사 will이 가장 적절하다.

22 ▶정답 ⓑ

해석 Puerto Vallarta는 Mexico Riviera에 있는 아름다운 마을이다. 그곳은 매력적인 해변 휴양지, 정원 및 기념품 가게가 있는 인기 있는 관광명소이다. 또한 관광객들은 도시의 활기 넘치는 밤 문화에 참여하는 것을 즐긴다.

해설 enjoy는 목적어 자리에 동명사만을 취하는 3형식 타동사이다.

23 ▶정답 ⓓ

해석 University of Iowa를 졸업한 신입 교사의 거의 50%는 현재 인접한 주에서 가르치고 있다. 만약 Iowa에 좋은 기회가 있었으면 이 선생님들은 Iowa에 머물러 있었을 텐데.

해설 가정법 문제이며 주절의 동사가 would have p.p.이므로 if절에는 had p.p.가 들어가야 한다.

24 ▶정답 ⓐ

해석 데이비드는 BookFinder.com에서 절판 도서를 검색하여 도서 당 4~16 달러만 지불한다. 돈을 절약하기 위해, 그는 웹 사이트를 발견하기 전에는, 수 년 동안 할인 서점에서 흥미 있는 책을 찾아 왔다.

해설 기간을 표현하는 for years(몇 년 동안)이 있으므로 완료시제가 적절하다. 시간부사 before 절의 시제가 과거이므로 문맥상 과거완료(진행)시제가 적절하다.

25 ▶정답 ⓒ

해석 동 티모르 초대 대통령인 Xanana Gusmão는 신생 공화국이 법률, 경제 및 교육 시스템을 구축하도록 애썼다. 심지어 오늘날에도, 그는 정치가들이 동티모르인들의 기대에 부합하는 훌륭한 통치를 할 것을 촉구한다.

해설 명령, 동의, 제안, 주장, 요구, 충고 동사의 목적어 자리에 that절이 오는 경우 that절의 동사는 「(should) 동사원형」이 되어야 한다.

26 ▶정답 ⓑ

해석 Julia는 회사 웹 사이트의 유용성을 평가하는 업무를 맡은 IT 전문가이다. 다음 달에 사이트가 'live'로 바뀔 때 쯤 이면, 그녀는 3개월 동안 다양한 사용자들과 함께 조율해 오는 것이 될 것이다.

해설 기간을 나타내는 표현 for three months가 있으므로 완료시제가 적절하다. 완료시제는 (b)밖에 없다. 시간 부사절 접속사 by the time절에 미래를 표현하는 부사 next month와 함께 쓰였으므로 주절에 미래완료(진행)시제가 잘 어울린다.

Listening Test 05회

Question 27-52

ANSWER KEY p.127

27	ⓓ	28	ⓐ	29	ⓑ	30	ⓒ
31	ⓑ	32	ⓒ	33	ⓒ	34	ⓑ
35	ⓒ	36	ⓐ	37	ⓒ	38	ⓑ
39	ⓓ	40	ⓑ	41	ⓐ	42	ⓒ
43	ⓓ	44	ⓒ	45	ⓑ	46	ⓓ
47	ⓓ	48	ⓐ	49	ⓓ	50	ⓒ
51	ⓑ	52	ⓒ				

[Part 1]

Now listen to the questions.

27: What did Anne do in the past week?
28: Why is foil fencing best for amateurs and beginners?
29: Which move probably earns a point in foil fencing?
30: How did Anne start being interested in the sport?
31: What event does Matt say made Anne love the sport?
32: What was not mentioned as a characteristic of a highly-skilled fencer?
33: Based on the conversation, what will Matt most likely do on Saturday?

해석

27: 지난주에 앤은 무엇을 했나요?
28: 포일 펜싱이 비전문가와 초보자에게 좋은 최고의 이유는 무엇인가요?
29: 포일 펜싱에서 어떤 움직임이 점수를 얻을 수 있을까?
30: 앤은 어떻게 스포츠(펜싱)에 관심을 가지게 되었나?
31: 매트 말에 따르면, 무엇이 앤을 스포츠(펜싱)를 좋아하게 만들었나?
32: 고도로 숙련된 검객의 특징으로 언급되지 않은 것은?
33: 대화에 따르면, 매트는 토요일에 무엇을 할 것인가?

Now you will hear the conversation.
[conversation]

M Hi, Anne! 27) I heard you won a fencing competition last week. I didn't know you were into such a difficult sport!

F Yes, Matt, I am. But I won only in an amateur competition. It was in the women's foil category.

M Hmmm… I don't really understand what you mean. What is the "foil category"?

F In fencing, the categories are based on the weapons used: "foil," "epee," or "saber." 28) The foil is a flexible sword, and it bends easily. It only weighs less than one pound, that's why it's ideal for amateurs and beginners. On the other hand, the epee is about as long as the foil but it has a wider blade, while the saber is shorter and has a Y-shaped blade.

M I see. You know, I've always wondered how scores in a fencing game are recorded. The scoring must be a complicated process!

F Well, every fencing game or "bout" follows strict rules, which are just too many to mention. 29) In the foil category, a fencer earns a point if his or her weapon hits, or "touches," the opponent's upper body, but definitely not the head and arms.

M How do they know exactly when a touch is made?

F To monitor touches closely, long wires are attached to the players' foils and the protective vests they wear. These wires are, in turn, hooked up to an electrical machine that registers the touches. These allow the judges to award corresponding points.

M That's interesting. I didn't know that fencing matches had gone electronic! 30) How did you get started in fencing, anyway?

F My father was an amateur fencer himself. 30) When I was about 10 years old, Dad encouraged me and my brother Jude to read books about fencing. It was actually Jude whom Dad expected to follow in his footsteps, but he didn't. I was the one who chose to have formal training.

M That's good for you! How did you train for the sport?

F I attended summer fencing classes when I was 15 and a high school student. Later on, I joined my college fencing team. That's where I first got the chance to join amateur bouts.

M 31) You must have enjoyed that first bout so much to pursue fencing as a sport!

F Oh, yes, I really did! But what I enjoyed much more than competing was learning more from my fencing masters. They taught me that fencing is not merely about physical strength.

M I thought that fencing was just all about being fast.
F It does require speed, but more importantly, mental focus and tactic. 32) My masters stressed that the best fencers plan their attacks, are prepared for their opponent's attacks, and even use both hands in fencing if needed.
M That's fascinating! I wish I could watch you in a fencing bout one of these days.
F Of course you can, 33) Matt! Why don't you visit my fencing club on Saturday? I think you'll enjoy watching me practice. You might even decide to get into the sport yourself!
M You know, 33) I've always wanted to learn a new sport... See you on Saturday, Anne.

Words
bend 구부러지다
blade 날
opponent (시합 등의) 상대
protective vest 보호조끼
corresponding point 상응하는 점수
follow in one's footstep 남의 뒤를 따르다
bout 시합
merely 단지
tactic 전술, 전략
master 사범, 스승

해석
M 안녕 앤. 27) 네가 지난주 펜싱 경기에서 우승했다는 소식을 들었어. 나는 네가 그렇게 어려운 스포츠에 빠져있는지 몰랐어.
F 맞아, 매트. 근데 나는 아마추어 경기에서 이겼을 뿐이야. 그것은 여성 포일 카테고리에 들어가.
M 흠, 나는 네가 말하는 걸 정확하게 모르겠어. '포일 카테고리'가 뭐야?
F 펜싱에서, 사용하는 무기를 기준으로 나뉘는데 그 종류에 포일(foil), 에페(epee), 그리고 사브르(saber)가 있어. 28) 포일(foil)은 유연한 검이라 쉽게 구부러져. 그 검은 1 파운드 미만의 무게라서, 아마추어와 초보자에게 가장 알맞아. 반면에, 에페(epee)는 포일(foil)만큼 길지만 더 넓은 날을 가지고 있고, 사브르(saber)는 더 짧고, Y자 모양의 칼날이야.
M 이해가 된다. 너도 알다시피, 나는 펜싱경기에서 점수가 어떻게 기록되는지 항상 궁금했어. 채점방식이 복잡함에 틀림없어.
F 음, 모든 펜싱 경기나 '한판 시합'은 엄격한 규칙들을 따르는데, 언급하기엔 너무 많아. 29) 포일(foil) 카테고리에서는 선수가 자신의 검으로 상대방의 상체를 찌르거나 닿으면 점수를 얻지만, 상대의 머리와 팔은 (찔러서는) 안 돼.
M 언제 닿는지 정확히 어떻게 알아?
F 터치를 엄밀히 보기 위해서, 선수의 foil과 선수들이 착용하는 보호조끼에 긴 전선들이 부착되어 있어. 이 전선들은 터치를 기록하는 전자기기에 연결돼. 이것들은 심사위원들이 상응하는 점수를 줄 수 있는 걸 가능하게 해.
M 흥미롭다. 나는 펜싱 경기가 전자화 되었다는 것을 몰랐어. 30) 무튼, 너는 어떻게 펜싱을 시작하게 된 거야?
F 우리 아빠가 아마추어 펜싱선수셨어. 30) 내가 10살쯤 되었을 때, 아빠는 나와 내 동생 주드에게 펜싱에 관한 책을 읽도록 장려하셨어. 사실 아빠는 주드가 자신의 뒤를 이을 것이라고 기대하셨지만, 그는 그렇게 하지 않았어. 정규 훈련을 받기로 결심한 사람은 나였거든.
M 너한테 잘된 일이네. 훈련은 어떻게 했어?
F 내가 15살 고등학생이었을 때, 여름 펜싱수업에 참가했어. 나중에, 대학 펜싱 팀에 합류했지. 바로 거기서 아마추어 시합에 참가할 기회를 얻었어.
M 31) 너는 스포츠로 펜싱을 계속한 것으로 보아 첫 번째 시합을 엄청나게 즐겼음에 틀림없구나!
F 오, 맞아, 정말 그랬어! 그런데 경기보다 훨씬 더 즐거웠던 건 내 펜싱 사부님들로부터 더 많은 것을 배운 것이야. 그들은 펜싱이 단지 육체적인 것과 관련된 것만은 아니라는 것을 알려주셨어.
M 나는 펜싱은 속도가 빠른 것이 전부일 거라 생각했어.
F 속도도 중요하지만, 집중력과 전술이 더 중요해. 32) 내 사부님들은 최고의 펜싱선수들은 공격을 계획하고, 상대방 공격에 대비하고, 필요한 경우 펜싱에서 양손까지 사용한다고 강조하셨어.
M 매력적인데! 조만간 펜싱 시합에서 너를 볼 수 있었으면 좋겠다.
F 당연히 볼 수 있지, 33) 매트! 토요일에 펜싱 클럽에 올래? 너는 내가 연습하는 걸 보는 걸 즐길 거 같아. 심지어 너는 펜싱을 하겠다고 할지도 모르지!
M 너도 알겠지만, 33) 나는 항상 새로운 스포츠를 배우고 싶어 했지. 토요일에 봐, 앤.

27 ▶ 정답 ⓓ

What did Anne do in the past week?
(a) teach a sports class
(b) organize a sports event
(c) enroll in a sports class
(d) join a sports competition

해석
지난주에 앤은 무엇을 했나요?
(a) 스포츠 수업을 했다
(b) 스포츠 이벤트를 계획했다
(c) 스포츠 수업에 등록했다
(d) 스포츠 대회에 참가했다

해설 대화 " I heard you won a fencing competition last week."을 통해 앤이 지난주에 스포츠 대회에 참가했다는 것을 알 수 있다.

28 ▶ 정답 ⓐ

Why is foil fencing best for amateurs and beginners?

(a) because the foil sword is light
(b) because the foil sword's blade is wide
(c) because the foil sword's blade is Y-shaped
(d) because the foil sword doesn't bend easily

해석 포일 펜싱이 비전문가와 초보자에게 좋은 최고의 이유는 무엇일까?
(a) 포일 검이 가볍기 때문에
(b) 포일 검의 칼날이 넓기 때문에
(c) 포일 검의 칼날이 Y 자 모양이기 때문에
(d) 포일 검은 쉽게 구부러지지 않기 때문에

해설 "The foil is a flexible sword, and it bends easily. It only weighs less than one pound, that's why it's ideal for amateurs and beginners."의 언급을 통해 검의 무게가 가볍기 때문에 비전문가와 초보자에게 이상적이라는 것을 확인할 수 있다.

29 ▶ 정답 ⓑ

Which move probably earns a point in foil fencing?

(a) using both hands at the same time
(b) hitting the opponent's chest
(c) bending the sword the farthest
(d) hitting the opponent's arm

해석 포일 펜싱에서 어떤 움직임이 점수를 얻을 수 있을까?
(a) 양손을 동시에 사용하는 것
(b) 상대방의 가슴을 찌르는 것
(c) 검을 최대한 구부리는 것
(d) 상대방의 팔을 찌르는 것

해설 "In the foil category, a fencer earns a point if his or her weapon hits, or "touches," the opponent's upper body, but definitely not the head and arms."을 통해 상체에 속하는 가슴을 찌르는 것이 점수 획득을 할 수 있다는 것을 알 수 있다.

30 ▶ 정답 ⓒ

How did Anne start being interested in the sport?

(a) Her brother introduced her to the sport.
(b) She had practice bouts with her father.
(c) Her father pushed her to learn about the sport.
(d) She wrote a book about the sport.

해석 앤은 어떻게 스포츠(펜싱)에 관심을 가지게 되었나?
(a) 그녀의 남동생이 그녀에게 펜싱을 소개했다.
(b) 그녀는 아빠와 시합했다.
(c) 그녀의 아빠가 그녀에게 펜싱을 배우도록 권했다.
(d) 그녀는 펜싱에 관한 책을 썼다.

해설 "When I was about 10 years old, Dad encouraged me and my brother Jude to read books about fencing."의 언급을 통해 그녀의 아빠 권유로 펜싱에 관심을 가지게 되었다는 내용이 적절하다.

31 ▶ 정답 ⓑ

What event does Matt say made Anne love the sport?

(a) the advice of her instructors
(b) her participation in her first competition
(c) watching her father win an amateur bout
(d) her training as a high school student

해석 매트 말에 따르면, 무엇이 앤을 스포츠(펜싱)를 좋아하게 만들었나?
(a) 강사들의 조언
(b) 그녀의 첫 번째 대회 참가
(c) 그녀의 아빠가 아마추어 경기에서 승리하는 것을 본 것
(d) 고등학생으로서 받았던 그녀의 훈련

해설 "You must have enjoyed that first bout so much to pursue fencing as a sport!", "Oh, yes, I really did!"를 통해서 앤은 첫 시합으로 펜싱에 흥미를 갖게 된 후 계속해서 펜싱을 하게 되었다는 것을 확인할 수 있다.

32 ▶ 정답 ⓒ

What was not mentioned as a characteristic of a highly-skilled fencer?

(a) being ready to deal with any of the opponent's attacks
(b) being able to use both hands during a bout
(c) being able to beat the opponent simply through strength
(d) being good at planning an attack strategy

해석 고도로 숙련된 검객의 특징으로 언급되지 않은 것은?
(a) 상대방의 어떤 공격에도 대응할 준비가 되어있는 것
(b) 시합하는 동안 양손을 사용할 수 있는 것
(c) 체력만으로 상대를 이길 수 있는 것
(d) 공격 전략을 세우는 것에 능숙한 것

해설 "My masters stressed that the best fencers plan their attacks, are prepared for their opponent's attacks, and even use both hands in fencing if needed."에 a), b), d)의 근거가 언급되어 있지만 체력에 관한 내용은 언급되지 않았다.

33 ▶ 정답 ⓒ

Based on the conversation, what will Matt most likely do on Saturday?

(a) watch some professional fencing sessions
(b) read a book about fencing
(c) join Anne's fencing club
(d) get fencing lessons from Anne

해석

대화에 따르면, 매트는 토요일에 무엇을 할 것인가?
(a) 일부 프로펜싱 세션을 볼 것이다.
(b) 펜싱에 관한 책을 읽을 것이다.
(c) 앤의 펜싱 클럽에 합류할 것이다.
(d) 앤에게서 펜싱수업을 받을 것이다.

해설 "Matt! Why don't you visit my fencing club on Saturday?", "You know, I've always wanted to learn a new sport… See you on Saturday, Anne."의 대화를 통해 매트는 토요일에 앤의 펜싱클럽에 방문하여 함께할 것임을 유추할 수 있다.

[Part 2]

Now listen to the questions.

34: What is the speaker's designation?
35: What is the purpose of the talk?
36: According to the speaker, what will be done to an electronic mail that is infected with a virus?
37: How should employees exchange official messages?
38: What is the company policy on personal electronic mail?
39: What can the records of security violations be used for?

해석

34: 화자의 직책은 무엇인가요?
35: 이야기의 목적은 무엇인가요?
36: 화자에 따르면, 바이러스에 감염된 이메일은 어떻게 될 것인가?
37: 공식적인 메시지들을 직원들은 어떻게 주고받아야 하나요?
38: 개인 이메일과 관하여 회사 정책은 무엇인가요?
39: 보안 위반 기록은 어떤 용도로 사용될 것인가요?

Now you will hear the talk.

Good morning, everyone! 35) I assume all of you have already read the memo circulated yesterday about the company's new Information Security Policy. As you know, the policy was developed by our Information Technology Department and will be implemented by the Human Resources Department beginning tomorrow. 34) 35) As head of HR, I would like to explain some of the points in the memo, and that's why I called this short meeting.

Let me begin by emphasizing some of the policy provisions concerning the use of electronic mail. 36) Our Information Security Policy provides that any e-mail infected with a virus or worm, or found to contain any code that can harm our information system, will not be delivered to the addressee. Please understand that our network administrators have no choice but to remove such e-mail immediately from the delivery system. That's the best way to avert any possible breakdown of our system.

Now, I'm sure you all realize how important it is to keep our business plans, product designs, and financial figures strictly confidential. Because of this, 37) all personnel may exchange official e-mail only through our local area network and never through Internet-based e-mail service providers. 38) But you might ask: what about personal e-mail? Of course, we can still send and receive personal e-mail using our official addresses, but as the memo states, we can do so only on a limited basis beginning tomorrow. It simply means that we should compose and read personal e-mail only during breaks and outside our regular work hours.

If we must save personal messages in our mailboxes, we have to make sure that they don't take up more than 25% of mailbox capacity. In relation to this, I am reminding everyone to refrain from distributing material that may be considered threatening, discriminating, or obscene by anyone within or outside our organization. Management is concerned that such material may reflect the discipline of our personnel, and therefore affect our corporate reputation.

Finally, I would like to repeat this very important aspect of our IT policy: all systems activity and network traffic will be monitored all throughout the day by our IT department. 39) Our network administrators will be recording security violations, and their records may be used as bases for policy review and disciplinary action. I would like everyone to understand that our new Information Security Policy is meant to protect the interest of everyone in our company, and this is why I am calling on all of you to strictly comply with its provisions. Thank you for your attention. Now, I'll entertain your questions.

Words

assume 가정하다, 생각하다
implement 실행하다, 시행하다
call the meeting 회의를 소집하다
network administrator 네트워크 관리자
local area network 기업내 정보 통신망 (=LAN)
refrain from 삼가다, 자제하다
obscene 외설적인, 추잡한
discipline 징계, 제재
network traffic 네트워크 통신량
comply with 따르다, 준수하다
circulate 배포하다, 유포하다
HR 인사과
infect 감염시키다, 전염시키다
personnel 직원
discriminate 차별하다
reflect 반영하다
aspect 측면
security violation 보안 위반
provision 규정, 조항

해석

여러분, 좋은 아침입니다! 35) 저는 여러분 모두가 이미 어제 회사의 새로운 정보 보안 정책에 관해 배포된 메모를 읽었다고 생각해요. 아시다시피, 그 정책은 IT부서에서 개발했고, 인사부에서는 내일부터 정책을 실행할 것입니다. 34) 35) 인사과의 총 책임자로서 메모에 있는 몇 가지 점을 설명하고자 이 짧은 회의를 소집했습니다.

이메일 사용과 관련된 몇 가지 규정을 강조하는 걸로 시작하겠습니다. 우리의 정보 보안 정책은 바이러스나 웜에 감염되었거나, 36) 우리 정보 시스템을 손상시킬 수 있는 코드를 포함하고 있는 어떠한 이메일도 수신인에게 전송되지 않도록 규정하고 있습니다. 우리 네트워크 관리자들이 그런 이메일을 전달 시스템으로부터 즉각 제거해야 한다는 것을 이해해주셔야 합니다. 우리 시스템이 고장 날 가능성을 막을 수 있는 최선책입니다.

이제, 저는 여러분 모두가 우리 사업계획, 제품 디자인, 그리고 재무상 수치에 대해 엄격하게 기밀을 유지하는 것이 얼마나 중요한지 깨달았을 것이라 확신합니다. 이것 때문에, 37) 전 직원들은 사설 인터넷 기반 이메일 서비스업체가 아닌 당사의 통신망을 통해서만 업무상 이메일을 주고받을 수 있습니다. 38) 그러나 여러분은 개인 이메일 사용에 관하여도 문의할 수 있습니다. 물론, 우리는 여전히 개인 이메일을 업무상 주소로도 주고받을 수 있지만, 메모에서 나와 있듯이, 내일부터는 제한적으로만 가능합니다. 이는 우리가 개인 이메일을 작성하고 읽는 것은 근무 외 시간이나 휴식시간에만 가능하다는 것을 의미합니다.

사서함에 개인 메일을 저장해야 하는 경우, 개인메일이 사서함 용량의 25%이상을 차지하지 않도록 해야 합니다. 이와 관련해서, 저는 여러분에게 회사 내외부의 누구에게도 위협적이거나 차별적, 외설적으로 여겨질 수 있는 내용을 보내는 것을 자제할 것을 부탁드립니다. 경영진은 그러한 내용이 직원의 징계에 반영될 수 있고, 그에 따라 회사의 평판에 영향을 끼칠 수 있는 점을 우려하고 있습니다.

마지막으로 IT 정책의 중요한 측면을 다시 반복하고 싶습니다. IT 부서에서 모든 시스템 활동과 네트워크 통신량을 하루 종일 모니터 할 것입니다. 39) 본사의 네트워크 관리자들은 보안위반사항을 기록할 것이고, 이 기록은 징계조치 및 정책검토의 근거가 될 것입니다. 새로운 정보보안정책은 당사의 모든 직원들의 이익을 보호하기 위한 것임을 이해해 주시기 바라며, 여러분 모두가 규정을 엄격하게 준수해줄 것을 요구하는 바입니다. 집중해 주셔서 고맙습니다. 지금부터, 여러분들의 질문을 받겠습니다.

34 ▶ 정답 ⓑ

What is the speaker's designation?

(a) company manager
(b) human resources head
(c) network administrator
(d) information technology chief

해석

화자의 직책은 무엇인가요?

(a) 회사 매니저
(b) 인사부 책임자
(c) 네트워크 관리자
(d) 정보 기술 책임자

해설 "As head of HR, I would like to explain some of the points in the memo, and that's why I called this short meeting."에서 화자의 직책이 인사부 총 책임자임을 알 수 있다.

35 ▶ 정답 ⓒ

What is the purpose of the talk?

(a) to gather ideas needed for a proposed policy
(b) to ask questions about a recent memorandum
(c) to introduce the development of a new policy
(d) to emphasize the success of a new policy

해석

이야기의 목적은 무엇입니까?

(a) 제안된 정책에 필요한 생각들을 모으기 위해
(b) 최근 메모에 관해 질문하기 위해
(c) 새로운 정책 개발을 소개하기 위해
(d) 새로운 정책 성공을 강조하기 위해

해설 "I assume all of you have already read the memo circulated yesterday about the company's new Information Security Policy.", "As head of HR, I would like to explain some of the points in the memo, and that's why I called this short meeting."를 통해 메모로 알린 새로운 정책 개발을 이야기하기 위해 미팅을 소집한 것임을 알 수 있다.

36 ▶ 정답 ⓐ

According to the speaker, what will be done to an electronic mail that is infected with a virus?

(a) It will be erased immediately from the delivery system.
(b) It will be saved in a remote server for further analysis.
(c) It will be delivered after the virus has been removed.
(d) It will be returned to the sender within 24 hours.

해설

화자에 따르면, 바이러스에 감염된 이메일은 어떻게 될 것인가?

(a) 전달 시스템에서 바로 지워질 것이다.
(b) 추가 분석을 위해 원격 서버에 저장될 것이다.
(c) 바이러스가 제거된 후에 전달될 것이다.
(d) 24시간 이내에 발송인에게 반송될 것이다.

해설 "Our Information Security Policy provides that any e-mail infected with a virus or worm, or found to contain any code that can harm our information system, will not be delivered to the addressee. Please understand that our network administrators have no choice but to remove such e-mail immediately from the delivery system."에서 바이러스에 감염된 이메일은 즉각 전달 시스템에서 제거된다는 것을 확인할 수 있다.

37 ▶ 정답 ⓒ

How should employees exchange official messages?

(a) through an Internet-based service provider
(b) using a third-party e-mail address
(c) through the company's local area network
(d) using a secure corporate website

해석
공식적인 메시지들을 직원들은 어떻게 주고받아야 하나요?

(a) 인터넷기반 서비스 업체를 통해
(b) 제3자의 이메일 주소를 사용해서
(c) 회사의 LAN을 통해
(d) 안전한 회사 웹 사이트를 이용해서

해설 "all personnel may exchange official e-mail only through our local area network and never through Internet-based e-mail service providers."을 통해 업무상 이메일은 회사의 통신망을 통해서만 주고받을 수 있는 것을 알 수 있다.

38 ▶ 정답 ⓑ

What is the company policy on personal electronic mail?

(a) Its volume is limited to half of the employee's mailbox space.
(b) It may be sent and received only on a limited basis.
(c) It must be erased as soon as the recipient has read it.
(d) It may be only sent and received using an unofficial address.

해석
개인 이메일과 관련된 회사 정책은 무엇인가요?

(a) 그것의 용량이 직원들의 사서함 절반으로 제한된다.
(b) 제한적으로만 주고받을 수 있게 된다.
(c) 수신자가 이메일을 읽자마자 지워져야 한다.
(d) 비공식적인 주소로만 주고받을 수 있게 된다.

해설 "But you might ask: what about personal e-mail? Of course, we can still send and receive personal e-mail using our official addresses, but as the memo states, we can do so only on a limited basis beginning tomorrow."에서 개인 이메일은 사용이 가능하긴 하지만, 제한적으로만 이용가능하다고 언급되어 있다.

39 ▶ 정답 ⓓ

What can the records of security violations be used for?

(a) for improving the reputation of the company
(b) for evaluating the performance of the IT department
(c) as basis for giving a worker a promotion
(d) as basis for disciplining a worker

해석
보안위반 기록은 어떤 용도로 사용될 것인가요?

(a) 회사의 명성을 높이는데
(b) IT 부서 성과를 평가하는데
(c) 직원 승진의 근거로
(d) 직원 징계의 근거로

해설 "Our network administrators will be recording security violations, and their records may be used as bases for policy review and disciplinary action."에서 보안위반 기록은 징계조치의 근거가 될 지도 모른다고 언급되어 있다.

[Part 3]

Now listen to the questions.

40: Why does the woman want to do online shopping?
41: In online shopping, where should purchased items be placed?
42: What is not included in computing the customer's total purchase?
43: What is the customer advised to do before sending the electronic order form to the merchant?
44: What was mentioned as a possible physical proof of the online transaction?
45: How was data encryption described?
46: How did the woman feel after the conversation?

해석
40: 왜 여자는 온라인 쇼핑을 하고 싶어 하나요?
41: 온라인 쇼핑에서는 구입한 품목들을 어디에 두어야 하나요?
42: 고객의 총 구매 계산에 포함되지 않는 것은 무엇인가요?
43: 전자 주문 양식을 판매자에게 보내기 전, 고객은 무엇을 하도록 권고를 받나요?
44: 온라인 거래의 가능한 물리적 증거로 언급된 것은 무엇인가요?
45: 데이터 암호화는 어떻게 묘사되었나요?
46: 대화 후 여자는 어떻게 느꼈나요?

Now you will hear the conversation.
[conversation]

F Dave, you frequently order books over the Internet, don't you? Can you teach me how to shop online? 40) I'd like to try it since I'm too busy to shop in stores these days.

M Sure, Lara! Online shopping is easy so long as you have a credit card, a computer, and an Internet connection.

F So, how exactly is it done?

M Well, let's say you want to buy a dress. The first thing you should do is visit a web-based store that sells dresses. As you browse through the store's online catalog, you'll see on your computer screen pictures of the products as well as their prices.

F I see. And if I find the dress I like?

M 41) Once you've chosen the dress you want to buy, you can put it in your electronic "shopping cart" by simply clicking a button displayed onscreen. If you want to buy another dress, just add it to the shopping cart.

F Okay, I get it. But online stores charge additional fees, right?

M Yes, Lara. 42) Tax and shipping rates will be added to the price of what you bought, and the total amount will appear onscreen. After that, you should fill out an electronic order form with your name, e-mail address, and the address where you want your order delivered.

F How do I pay for my purchase?

M You will be asked to type in your credit card number and the card's expiration date. However, to make sure you have given accurate information about the card, 43) you must review the online form before sending it to the merchant. Once you've sent the form, you'll see a confirmation of your order on screen. The store usually sends a confirmation form to your e-mail address.

F But I'll want a physical proof that I placed an order. How will I have it?

M 44) The proof you'll need is the confirmation form itself. Just print it out, then write the date and time of your transaction on it.

F So it's actually simpler than I thought! I just have one more question, Dave. How can I be sure my credit card information will be safe?

M Well, most online merchants now have very secure Internet connections. When you visit their site, you'll see a key icon on one corner of the webpage. If the icon appears whole, you can be sure that your transaction details would be encrypted before they are sent to the merchant.

F What does "encrypted" mean?

M It means the data will be translated into codes that nobody will understand. 45) Only the merchant can restore the data to their original form by using a secret password. However, if there's no such assurance from the store, I'd advise you not to give any sensitive information to it.

F I'll keep that in mind, Dave. Thanks for sharing with me all that information. 46) Now I can shop online without worrying about it!

Words

browse (인터넷을) 검색하다, 살펴보다
expiration date 만료일
restore 복원하다, 복구하다
fill out 기입하다, 작성하다
encrypt 암호화하다
sensitive information 민감한 정보

해석

F 데이브, 너 인터넷으로 책 자주 주문하지, 그렇지? 온라인으로 쇼핑하는 방법 좀 가르쳐줄래? 40) 매장에서 쇼핑하기에는 요즘 너무 바빠서 인터넷으로 구매하려고.

M 물론이지, 라라! 온라인 쇼핑은 신용 카드와 컴퓨터 및 인터넷이 연결되어 있기만 하면 쉬워.

F 그래서 정확히 어떻게 하는 거야?

M 음, 드레스를 사고 싶다고 가정하자. 네가 우선해야 할 일은 드레스를 판매하는 온라인 상점을 방문하는 거야. 상점의 온라인 카탈로그를 살펴볼 때, 컴퓨터 화면에서 제품 가격과 사진을 보게 될 거야.

F 알겠어, 그럼 내가 좋아하는 드레스를 발견하면?

M 41) 네가 구매하려는 드레스를 선택하고, 화면에 표시된 버튼을 클릭하기만 하면 전자 '장바구니'에 그 드레스를 넣을 수 있어. 다른 드레스를 구매하고 싶으면, 장바구니에 추가하기만 하면 돼.

F 좋아, 알겠어. 그런데 온라인 상점은 추가 비용을 청구하지, 그렇지?

M 맞아, 라라. 42) 세금 및 배송료가 구입한 가격에 추가되고, 총 금액이 화면에 표시될 거야. 그 후, 전자 주문서에 네 이름, 이메일 주소 및 주문이 배송될 주소를 기입해야 해.

F 구매한 물품 비용은 어떻게 지불해?

M 신용카드 번호와 카드 만료일을 입력하라고 할 거야. 그런데, 확실하게 정확한 카드 정보를 제공하기 위해서, 43) 판매자에게 양식을 보내기 전에 온라인 양식을 검토해야 해. 양식을 보내면, 화면에서 주문을 확인할 수 있어. 상점은 보통 이메일로 주문확인서를 보내줘.

F 내가 주문을 했다는 물리적인 증명을 원하면, 어떻게 받아?

M 44) 네가 필요한 증명은 확인서 그 자체야. 그냥 확인서를 인쇄하고, 거래 날짜와 시간을 기록하면 돼.

F 생각했던 것보다 실제는 더 간단하네! 한 가지 질문이 더 있어, 데이브. 신용 카드 정보가 안전하다는 건 어떻게 확신 할 수 있어?

M 음, 요즘 대부분의 온라인 판매자들은 인터넷 연결 보안을 굉장히 철저히 해. 그들의 사이트에 들어가면, 웹 페이지 한쪽 구석에 키 아이콘이 표시되어 있는 걸 볼 수 있을 거야.. 아이콘이 온전하게 보이면, 네 거래 세부정보가 암호화되어 판매자에게 전송되는지를 확인할 수 있어.

F '암호화되는' 건 무슨 의미야?

M 이는 누구도 이해할 수 없는 코드로 데이터가 변환되는 것을 말해. 45) 판매자만이 비밀 암호를 사용해서 데이터를 원래 양식으로 복원할 수 있어. 그런데, 상점에서 그러한 확신이 들지 않으면, 민감한 어떤 정보도 제공하지 마.

F 명심할게, 데이브. 모든 정보를 나한테 공유해줘서 고마워. 46) 이제는 걱정 없이 온라인 쇼핑을 할 수 있겠어.

40 ▶ 정답 ⓑ

Why does the woman want to do online shopping?

(a) She needs to buy a product that is sold only on the web.
(b) She does not have time to shop at regular stores.
(c) She thinks online stores charge lower than regular stores.
(d) She wants to try out her new credit card.

해석 왜 여자는 온라인 쇼핑을 하고 싶어 하나요?
(a) 그녀는 웹에서만 판매되는 제품을 구입해야 한다.
(b) 그녀는 오프라인 매장에서 쇼핑 할 시간이 없다.
(c) 그녀는 온라인 매장이 오프라인 매장보다 더 저렴하다고 생각한다.
(d) 그녀는 새로운 신용카드를 사용해보고 싶어 한다.

해설 "I'd like to try it since I'm too busy to shop in stores these days."에서 오프라인 매장에서 쇼핑할 시간이 없다고 말하고 있으므로 인터넷 쇼핑을 하려는 이유로 가장 적절한 것은 (b)이다.

41 ▶ 정답 ⓐ

In online shopping, where should purchased items be placed?

(a) on an electronic shopping cart
(b) on a special network server
(c) on a Web-based product catalog
(d) on an electronic message board

해석 온라인 쇼핑에서는 구입한 품목들을 어디에 두어야 하나요?
(a) 전자 장바구니에
(b) 특수 네트워크 서버에
(c) 웹 기반 제품 카탈로그에
(d) 전자 메시지 게시판에

해설 "Once you've chosen the dress you want to buy, you can put it in your electronic "shopping cart" by simply clicking a button displayed on screen."을 통해 구매품은 전자 장바구니에 담으면 된다는 것을 알 수 있다.

42 정답/(c)

What is not included in computing the customer's total purchase?

(a) the price of the item bought
(b) the shipping fee
(c) the Internet service charge
(d) the tax rate

해석 고객의 총 구매 계산에 포함되지 않는 것은 무엇인가요?
(a) 구매한 물품 가격
(b) 배송비
(c) 인터넷 서비스요금
(d) 세금

해설 "Tax and shipping rates will be added to the price of what you bought, and the total amount will appear on screen."에서 세금, 배송료, 구매물품 가격이 총 금액에 포함되는 것을 알 수 있고 인터넷 서비스 비용은 대화에서 언급되지 않았다.

43 ▶ 정답 ⓓ

What is the customer advised to do before sending the electronic order form to the merchant?

(a) pay additional charges in cash
(b) contact the online store by phone
(c) verify her credit card account balance
(d) review the information in the form

해석 전자 주문 양식을 판매자에게 보내기 전, 고객은 무엇을 하도록 권고를 받나요?
(a) 현금으로 추가비용을 지불한다.
(b) 전화로 온라인매장에 문의한다.
(c) 신용카드 계좌잔액을 확인한다.
(d) 양식에 있는 정보를 검토한다.

해설 "you must review the online form before sending it to the merchant."에 온라인 양식을 검토해야 된다는 내용이 언급되어 있다.

44 ▶ 정답 ⓒ

What was mentioned as a possible physical proof of the online transaction?

(a) a receipt sent by mail
(b) the store's printed catalog
(c) a printout of the confirmation form
(d) the customer's credit card bill

해석 온라인 거래의 가능한 물리적 증거로 언급된 것은 무엇인가요?
(a) 우편으로 발송된 영수증
(b) 상점 카탈로그 인쇄물
(c) 확인서 출력물
(d) 고객의 신용카드 청구서

해설 "The proof you'll need is the confirmation form itself."에 물건을 구매했다는 것을 입증해주는 자료가 구매확인서라고 언급되어 있다.

45 ▶ 정답 ⓑ

How was data encryption described?

(a) It is the fastest way of transmitting data.
(b) It ensures that only the store will see the customer's data.
(c) It is used by all online stores at all times.
(d) It checks whether customers gave accurate information.

해석

데이터 암호화는 어떻게 묘사되었나요?

(a) 데이터를 전송하는 가장 빠른 방법이다.
(b) 매장만이 고객 데이터를 볼 수 있도록 한다.
(c) 모든 온라인매장에서 항상 사용된다.
(d) 고객이 정확한 정보를 제공했는지 확인한다.

해설 "Only the merchant can restore the data to their original form by using a secret password."에서 판매자만이 고객의 암호화된 데이터를 볼 수 있다는 것을 알 수 있다.

46 ▶ 정답 ⓓ

How did the woman feel after the conversation?

(a) confused
(b) nervous
(c) hesitant
(d) relieved

해석

대화 후 여자는 어떻게 느꼈나요?

(a) 혼란스러운
(b) 긴장하는
(c) 주저하는
(d) 안도하는

해설 "Now I can shop online without worrying about it!"를 통해 걱정 없이 안도하고 있음을 알 수 있다.

[Part 4]

Now listen to the questions.

47: What is the subject of the talk?
48: Based on the talk, why is a social worker assigned in the adoption process?
49: What did the speaker cite as the cause of major problems in local adoption in the U.S.?
50: When does the child finally move into the new parents' home?
51: How is the adjustment of the child and parents to the new family setup determined?
52: What could adoptive children expect to receive from their parents after the adoption is finalized?

해설

47: 이 이야기의 주제는 무엇인가요?
48: 대화에 따르면, 사회복지사가 입양과정에 배정되는 이유는 무엇인가요?
49: 화자는 미국 현지 입양의 주된 문제점의 원인이 무엇이라고 언급했나요?
50: 아이는 언제 최종적으로 새로운 부모님 집으로 옮겨가나요?
51: 새 가족 구성에 관한 자녀 및 부모의 적응은 어떻게 판단이 되나요?
52: 입양이 확정된 후, 입양아는 부모로부터 무엇을 받을 것이라고 예상할 수 있나요?

Now you will hear the talk.

47) Now that you've decided to adopt a child, I will explain the various stages in the legal adoption process. Regardless of the type of adoption you're considering, you'll have to go through four basic phases.

First is the pre-placement stage where you, the prospective parents, will be required to submit a number of documents. The most important of these are your marriage license, proof of employment, and medical records. You'll also have to attend some routine interviews and meetings at the adoption agency.

48) Then, under the adoption law, a social worker has to be assigned to evaluate your suitability to adopt a child. This evaluation is called the "home study process." It begins once you've completed all the required documents, and takes two to three months. However, in the case of international adoption, the pre-placement stage may be more complicated. This is because it involves visits to the home country of the child you plan to adopt, and in some cases, meetings with his birth parents.

49) Even in local adoption, some major problem often crop up because family laws here in the US may vary from state to state. That's why it's very important that you engage the services of a lawyer to handle the legal aspect of adoption. Once you've passed the home study process, however, the placement stage immediately follows.

50) The placement stage is when the child you want to adopt moves into your home. Shortly after is the post-placement stage, which lasts from six to 12 months. 51) As required by law, a social worker will visit your home several times to determine how well you and the child are adjusting to the new family setup. If necessary, the social worker will help you get professional counseling to make the placement successful.

The last stage is the finalization process. 52) This is when the law courts formally make your child a legal member of your family and he or she will be entitled to all the legal rights the new status entails. During finalization, you'll be required to appear in court with the social worker or lawyer who's assisting you with the adoption process. For international adoption cases, the finalization hearing will take place in the child's home country; for local adoption cases, it will be conducted in your home state.

Words

adopt 입양하다
pre-placement 사전-배정
evaluate 평가하다
crop up 발생하다
entail 수반하다
hearing 심리, 공판
go through 거치다, 겪다
social worker 사회복지사
suitability 적합성
post 뒤에, 후에
court 법정

해석

47) 여러분들은 입양을 결정했기 때문에, 법적인 입양 절차에 있어서 여러 단계를 설명해드리겠습니다. 여러분은 고려중인 입양 유형과 상관없이, 기본 네 단계를 거쳐야 합니다.

첫 단계는 예비부모인 여러분들이 많은 서류를 제출해야 하는 사전배정단계입니다. 가장 중요한 것은 결혼증명서, 고용증명서, 의료기록입니다. 여러분은 또한 입양기관과 진행하는 몇 번의 정기인터뷰와 미팅에 참석해야 합니다.48) 그런 다음, 입양법에 따라, 사회복지사가 여러분이 아이를 입양하는 데 적합한 지를 평가하도록 배정될 것입니다. 이 평가는 '가정조사과정'이라고 합니다. 이 과정은 필요한 모든 서류를 작성하고 나면 시작되며, 두 달에서 세 달 정도 걸립니다. 그렇지만, 해외입양의 경우라면 사전 배정단계가 좀 더 복잡해질 수 있습니다. 이는 여러분이 입양하고자 하는 자녀의 모국방문과, 경우에 따라, 친부모와의 만남을 포함하기 때문입니다.49) 현지 입양에서조차, 미국의 가족법은 주마다 다양하기 때문에 일부 주요문제들이 종종 발생합니다. 그렇기 때문에 입양의 법률적인 측면을 다루는 변호사 서비스를 이용하는 것이 매우 중요합니다. 하지만, 여러분이 가정조사과정을 통과하면, 배정단계가 바로 시작됩니다.

50) 배정단계는 입양하려는 자녀가 여러분 가정으로 들어오는 때입니다. 바로 그 다음 단계가 배정 후 단계인데, 6개월에서 12개월까지 걸립니다. 51) 법에 따라, 여러분과 아이가 새로운 가정환경에 얼마나 잘 적응하고 있는지 판단하기 위해, 사회복지사가 여러분의 가정을 여러 번 방문할 것입니다. 필요하다면, 사회복지사는 성공적인 배정을 위해, 여러분이 전문상담을 받을 수 있게 도움을 줄 것입니다. 마지막 단계는 최종승인과정입니다. 52) 이 단계에서 법정은 공식적으로 자녀를 여러분 가정의 합법적 구성원이 되게 하고, 자녀는 새로운 신분이 수반하는 모든 법적인 권리를 부여받게 됩니다. 최종승인과정이 진행되는 동안, 여러분은 여러분의 입양과정을 도와주는 변호사나 사회복지사와 함께 법정에 출두해야 합니다. 해외입양의 경우, 최종승인과정 심리는 자녀의 출생국가에서 이루어지고, 현지입양의 경우 여러분 고향에서 실시됩니다.

47 ▶ 정답 ⓓ

What is the subject of the talk?
(a) the ideal type of child to adopt
(b) the best countries to apply for an adoption
(c) the best time to adopt a child
(d) the steps in adopting a child

해석

이 이야기의 주제는 무엇인가요?
(a) 입양하기에 이상적인 아이의 유형
(b) 입양을 신청하기에 최상의 국가들
(c) 아이를 입양하기 위한 가장 좋은 시기
(d) 아이를 입양하는 단계

해설 "Now that you've decided to adopt a child, I will explain the various stages in the legal adoption process."에서 아이 입양 단계에 대해 이야기할 것임을 알 수 있다.

48 ▶ 정답 ⓐ

Based on the talk, why is a social worker assigned in the adoption process?
(a) to determine if one is fit to adopt a child
(b) to confirm the validity of one's documents
(c) to help one find a suitable child to adopt
(d) to help one complete the documents

해석

대화에 따르면, 사회복지사가 입양과정에 배정되는 이유는 무엇인가요?
(a) 아이를 입양하기에 적합한가를 결정하기 위해
(b) 서류 유효성을 확인하기 위해
(c) 입양하기에 적합한 자녀를 찾도록 돕기 위해
(d) 문서작성을 돕기 위해

해설 "Then, under the adoption law, a social worker has to be assigned to evaluate your suitability to adopt a child."를 통해 사회복지사 역할이 아이를 입양하고자 하는 가정이 입양에 적합한 지를 평가하는 것을 확인할 수 있다.

49 ▶ 정답 ⓓ

What did the speaker cite as the cause of major problems in local adoption in the U.S.?
(a) the high cost of legal services involved in adoption
(b) the difficulty of obtaining required documents
(c) the lack of social workers to help in the process
(d) the different family laws of the various U.S. states

해석

화자는 미국 현지입양의 주된 문제점의 원인이 무엇이라고 언급했나요?
(a) 입양에 관련된 법률 서비스의 높은 비용
(b) 필요한 서류를 받는 어려움
(c) 입양과정에서 도움을 줄 수 있는 사회복지사의 부족
(d) 미국의 여러 주들의 다양한 가족법

해설 "Even in local adoption, some major problem often crop up because family laws here in the US may vary from state to state."에서 미국현지입양의 문제 발생의 원인은 미국의 주에 따른 다양한 가족법 때문임을 알 수 있다.

50 ▶ 정답 ⓒ

When does the child finally move into the new parents' home?

(a) during the pre-placement stage
(b) once the home study process begins
(c) during the placement stage
(d) once all the papers are completed

해석
아이는 언제 최종적으로 새로운 부모님 집으로 옮겨가나요?
(a) 사전배정단계 동안
(b) 일단 가정 조사과정이 시작되면
(c) 배정단계 동안
(d) 일단 모든 서류가 완성되면

해설 "The placement stage is when the child you want to adopt moves into your home."에서 입양아가 새로운 가정으로 가는 시기는 배정단계임을 알 수 있다.

51 ▶ 정답 ⓑ

How is the adjustment of the child and parents to the new family setup determined?

(a) through court appearances
(b) through visits by the social worker
(c) through legal investigations
(d) through visits by the child's true parents

해석
새 가족 구성에 관한 자녀 및 부모의 적응은 어떻게 판단이 되나요?
(a) 법정 출두를 통해
(b) 사회복지사의 방문을 통해
(c) 법적조사를 통해
(d) 자녀의 친부모 방문을 통해

해설 "As required by law, a social worker will visit your home several times to determine how well you and the child are adjusting to the new family setup."에서 사회복지사가 가정방문을 통해 입양 가정과 입양되는 아이의 적응도를 판단한다는 것이 언급되어 있다.

52 ▶ 정답 ⓒ

What could adoptive children expect to receive from their parents after the adoption is finalized?

(a) everything the child demands the new parents
(b) what the child used to get from his former parents
(c) everything the law entitles them to
(d) only what the new parents decide to give the child

해석
입양이 확정된 후, 입양아는 부모로부터 무엇을 받을 것이라고 예상할 수 있나요?
(a) 아이가 새로운 부모에게 요구하는 모든 것
(b) 아이가 그의 전 부모로부터 받았던 것
(c) 법이 그들에게 허용하는 모든 것
(d) 새 부모가 자녀에게 주기로 결정한 것만

해설 "This is when the law courts formally make your child a legal member of your family and he or she will be entitled to all the legal rights the new status entails."를 통해 입양가정의 합법적 구성원이 된다는 것은 입양단계가 마무리 되었다는 것을 의미하며, 입양아는 모든 법적인 권리를 부여 받는다는 것을 유추할 수 있다.

Reading and Vocabulary
05회

Question 53-80

ANSWER KEY   p.133

53	ⓒ	54	ⓐ	55	ⓑ	56	ⓒ
57	ⓑ	58	ⓑ	59	ⓓ	60	ⓓ
61	ⓑ	62	ⓒ	63	ⓐ	64	ⓒ
65	ⓑ	66	ⓐ	67	ⓐ	68	ⓑ
69	ⓐ	70	ⓒ	71	ⓑ	72	ⓓ
73	ⓑ	74	ⓒ	75	ⓓ	76	ⓑ
77	ⓓ	78	ⓐ	79	ⓓ	80	ⓓ

Question 53-59

BERTRAND RUSSELL

Bertrand Arthur William Russell was a British philosopher, mathematician, and political activist. He was a Nobel Prize recipient for his influential literary work on improving people's lives.

Bertrand Arthur William Russell was born in Trelleck, Wales on May 18, 1872. His parents were John Russell, Viscount Amberley, and Katherine. He was also the grandson of John Russell, a British prime minister. Russell was orphaned at age three, and was raised by his grandparents. 53) Early in life, he learned French and German. He was eleven years old when he was introduced to the work of the Greek mathematician Euclid, an event that changed his life.

After obtaining a first-class degree from Trinity College, Cambridge, Russell worked as an assistant at the British embassy in Paris. 54) In 1903, he published his Principles of Mathematics, which argued that mathematics could be derived from logic. The ideas in this book were further developed in the influential Principia Mathematica, which he co-wrote with Alfred North Whitehead in 1913.

Russell was appointed lecturer at Trinity College in 1910. 55) 56) However, when World War I broke out, his refusal to bear arms brought him in conflict with the British government. He lost his teaching position in 1916 and was sent to jail two years later. His bad experiences due to his anti-war beliefs, and his three marriages and two divorces in less than 20 years, 58) resulted in his highly controversial 1932 book, Marriage and Morals.

In 1938, Russell went to the United States to teach. However, his lectureship at City College, New York was 59) terminated in 1940 due to complaints that he was an enemy of religion and traditional morality. 56) He abandoned his pacifist stand in 1939, and supported the allied cause in World War. After the war, he was granted an Order of Merit. He was then awarded the Nobel Prize for Literature in 1950 and was cited as "the champion of humanity and freedom of thought." Russell had published many important works in his life, including the best-selling History of Western Philosophy and various papers on social, moral, and religious issues.

Russell became a supporter of nuclear disarmament. 57) At the age of 89, he was again imprisoned after an antinuclear demonstration. His last major publication was his three-volume autobiography (1967-1969). Today, Russell is considered as a major philosopher and a leading social reformer of the 20th century. Bertrand died in Wales on February 2, 1970.

Words

recipient 수상자, 수령인
embassy 대사관
derive 도출하다, 끌어내다
appoint 지명하다, 임명하다
controversial 논쟁의, 물의를 일으키는, 논쟁의 여지가 있는
terminate 해고하다, 끝내다
abandon 버리다, 단념하다
stand 입장, 견해, 태도
grant 주다, 수여하다
imprison 감금하다
social reformer 사회 개혁가
orphan 고아가 되다, 고아
mathematics 수학
logic 논리
bear arms 싸우다, 무기를 들다
morality 도덕(성), 윤리성
pacifist 평화주의자, 반전론자
ally 동맹을 맺다, 제휴하다
award 주다, 수여하다
demonstration 시위, 데모

해석

버트란드 러셀

Bertrand Arthur William Russell은 영국의 철학자이자 수학자이며 정치 활동가였다. 그는 사람들의 삶의 질을 높이는데 영향력을 끼친 문학작품으로 노벨상을 수상했다.

Bertrand Arthur William Russell은 1872년 5월18일 Wales의 Trelleck에서 태어났다. 그의 부모님은 엠벌리 자작인 존 러셀과 캐서린 이었다. 그는 또한 영국수상이었던 존 러셀의 손자였다. 러셀은 세 살 때 고아가 되어, 조부모의 손에 자랐다. 53) 그는 일찍부터 불어와 독어를 배웠다. 그는 11세에 그리스 수학자인 Euclid의 연구를 접하였고, 이는 그의 생애를 바꾸어 놓은 사건이었다.

Cambridge의Trinity College를 수석으로 졸업한 후, 러셀은 파리 주재 영국대사관에서 비서로 근무했다. 54) 1903년 그는 Principles of

Mathematics을 출간했고, 수학은 논리에서 도출될 수 있다고 주장했다. 이 책에 있는 개념은 1913년 Alfred North Whitehead와 공동 저술한 영향력 있는 Principia Mathematica에서 더욱 발전되었다. 러셀은 1910년 트리니티 대학에서 교수로 임명되었다. 55) 56) 그러나 1차 세계대전이 발발했을 때, 그는 반전운동으로 인하여 영국정부와 갈등을 겪게 된다. 그는 1916년 교수직을 잃고, 2년 후 감옥에 갔다. 그의 반전 믿음과 20년도 채 안 되는 기간 동안 겪은 세 번의 결혼과 두 번의 이혼과 같은 불행한 경험은 1932년 심각한 물의를 일으켰던 책인 Marriage and Morals를 만들었다.

1938년, 러셀은 강의를 하기 위해 미국에 갔다. 그러나 그는 전통윤리 및 종교의 적이라는 불만으로 인해 New York의 City College교수직에서 해임되었다. 56) 1939년 그는 평화주의자 입장을 버리고 제2차 세계대전에서 연합군을 지지했다. 전쟁 후 그는 훈장을 수여받았다. 1950년에는 노벨 문학상을 받았고, '인류와 자유로운 사상의 수호자'로 선정되었다. 러셀은 베스트셀러인 History of Western Philosophy 와 사회, 윤리, 도덕, 종교적인 쟁점들에 관한 다양한 논문을 포함한 중요한 작품을 출간했다.

러셀은 핵무기 감축의 지지자가 되었다. 57) 그는 89세의 나이에 반핵시위로 다시 투옥되었다. 그의 마지막 주요 출판물은 세 권의 자서전이었다. 오늘날 러셀은 20세기의 주요 철학자이며 중요한 사회개혁가로 여겨진다. 그는 1970년 2월2일 웨일스에서 사망했다.

53 ▶ 정답 ⓒ

What attribute did Bertrand Russell show as a young child?

(a) being politically ambitious
(b) being deeply religious
(c) an inclination for learning
(d) a talent for literary writing

해석
버트란드 러셀은 어렸을 때 어떤 특성을 보였나요?

(a) 정치적인 야망
(b) 깊은 신앙심
(c) 학구적인 성향
(d) 문필과 관련된 재능

해설 어려서부터 불어와 독어를 배우고 11세에 그리스 수학자인 Euclid의 연구를 접했다는 내용을 통해 어린 시절 그의 학구적인 모습을 짐작할 수 있다.

54 ▶ 정답 ⓐ

What statement did Russell make in his book, Principles of Mathematics?

(a) that logic can be translated into mathematics
(b) that Euclid's mathematical principles are timeless
(c) that mathematics doesn't agree with logic
(d) that life could be improved through mathematics

해석
러셀은 그의 책 Principles of Mathematics에서 언급한 것은 무엇인가요?

(a) 논리는 수학으로 바뀔 수 있다.
(b) Euclid의 수학원리는 영원하다.
(c) 수학은 논리와 일치하지 않는다.
(d) 수학을 통해 인생을 향상시킬 수 있다.

해설 1903년 그는 Principles of Mathematics을 출간하고, 수학은 논리에서 도출될 수 있다고 주장했다는 내용이 나와 있다.

55 ▶ 정답 ⓑ

Why most likely was Russell sent to jail in 1918?

(a) He was lecturing at Trinity College illegally.
(b) He opposed his government's war activities.
(c) He couldn't make his marriages last.
(d) His divorces were not approved by the government.

해석
왜 1918년에 러셀이 감옥에 가게 되었을 것 같나요?

(a) Trinity College에서 불법으로 강의했기 때문에
(b) 정부의 전쟁활동에 반대했기 때문에
(c) 결혼생활을 유지할 수 없었기 때문에
(d) 그의 이혼이 정부로부터 승인되지 않았기 때문에

해설 반전운동으로 영국정부와 갈등을 겪고 1916년에 교수직을 잃고 2년 후 감옥에 갔다는 내용을 통해 정부의 전쟁활동에 반대한 이유로 투옥했음을 유추할 수 있다.

56 ▶ 정답 ⓒ

What can be said about Russell's views on the two world wars?

(a) They were consistent.
(b) They didn't affect his teaching career.
(c) They were opposing.
(d) They both earned him awards.

해석
두 번의 세계 대전에 관해 러셀의 견해라고 말할 수 있는 것은?

(a) 견해들이 일관되었다.
(b) 그의 견해들은 그의 교수 경력에 영향을 끼치지 않았다.
(c) 입장이 반대였다.
(d) 둘 다 그에게 상을 안겨주었다.

해설 1939년 그는 평화주의자 입장을 버리고 제2차 세계대전에서 연합군을 지지했다는 내용을 통해 1차 세계대전과 2차 세계대전에서 러셀의 견해가 상반되는 것을 알 수 있다.

57

▶ 정답 ⓑ

How did Bertrand Russell spend his last days?

(a) by supporting the use of nuclear weapons
(b) by writing a book about his life
(c) by writing a book about Western philosophy
(d) by staying away from politics

해석

어떻게 버트란드 러셀은 말년을 보냈나요?

(a) 핵무기 사용을 지원함으로써
(b) 그의 일생에 관한 책을 쓰면서
(c) 서양철학에 관한 책을 쓰면서
(d) 정치를 멀리함으로써

해설 그는 반핵시위로 89세에 투옥되었고, 3권의 자서전이 마지막 출판물이라고 언급되어 있다. 자서전을 썼다는 (b)의 내용이 가장 적절하다.

58

▶ 정답 ⓑ

In the context of the passage, resulted means _____.

(a) stopped
(b) produced
(c) affected
(d) printed

해석

문맥상, resulted는 _____을 의미한다.

(a) 중단하다
(b) 생산하다, (결과를) 낳다, 생기게 하다
(c) 영향을 끼치다
(d) 인쇄하다

해설 result (결과로) 생기다, 발생하다

59

▶ 정답 ⓓ

In the context of the passage, terminated means _____.

(a) promoted
(b) delayed
(c) continued
(d) ended

해석

문맥상, terminated는 _____을 의미한다.

(a) 승격시키다 (승진시키다), 홍보하다, 촉진시키다
(b) 지연시키다, 연기하다
(c) 계속하다
(d) 끝내다

해설 terminate 끝내다, 종료하다

Question 60-66

60) THE GENDER GAP IN SCIENCE SHOULD BE BRIDGED

When Austrian sociologist, Helga Nowotny, began a graduate fellowship at Berlin's Institute for Advanced Study in 1981, only one of her 19 fellow graduates was also female. Today, Nowotny is back at the Institute as a visiting professor, and things have changed. Over half of the current group of students are female.

Researchers across the European Union agree that things are now better for women in science, but say that there is still a lot to be done. Europe has a 65) growing need for scientific talent, but many of its female scientists still don't enjoy equal opportunities. 61) While roughly 40% of recent doctoral degrees awarded in Europe were earned by women, they make up only 15% of researchers in the private sector. Scientific laboratories are still a male-dominated work place despite the fact that women are "as talented as men." She suggests that there must be a mechanism to encourage women to compete.

The E.U. is trying to bridge the gender gap by funding programs to support women scientists and requiring gender-based hiring plans. However, many researchers say that the scientific community tends to suffer when factors such as gender are used to determine funding. They suggest that longer-term solutions that encourage both young men and women to pursue science are a better option. 62) Hannele Kurki, an adviser at the Academy of Finland, says that an early introduction to science may help break down gender stereotypes.

Jürgen Hambrecht, the chief executive of German chemicals giant BASF, agrees. 63) He says that women are important because of the differences in character between men and women. Hambrecht also states that women scientists are exactly the bridge needed in the workplace. BASF runs a laboratory where children of both genders get hands-on exposure to chemistry.

Scientific institutions are also realizing that the best way to inspire young scientists, female or male, is by example. Nowotny recalls how, 20 years ago, the fellows at the Berlin Institute were incredulous that the only other female fellow was pregnant. 64) Today, fellows are encouraged to bring their families to work. By 66) promoting a family-friendly environment, institutions can make science a fulfilling career for more women.

Words
sociologist 사회학자
private sector 민간부문, 사기업
stereotype 고정관념
inspire 영감을 주다, 고무하다
promote 조성하다, 조장하다
doctoral degree 박사학위
mechanism 방법
hands-on 실제로 참가하는, 직접해보는
incredulous 믿지 않는, 의심하는
fulfill 충족시키다, 실현하다

해석

60) 과학에서의 성차별은 해소되어야 한다

호주의 사회학자인 Helga Nowotnys가 1981년 Berlin's Institute for Advanced Study에서 연구원으로 일을 시작했을 때, 19명 연구원 중 한 명만이 여성이었다. 오늘날 Nowotny이 초빙교수로서 연구소로 되돌아 왔을 때는 모든 것이 바뀌었다. 현재 학생들의 절반 이상이 여성이다.

EU 전역의 연구원들은 현재 상황이 과학 분야의 여성들에게 더 나아졌다는 것에 동의하지만, 아직 갈 길이 멀다고 입을 모은다. 유럽은 과학적 재능에 관한 필요성이 더 커지고 있지만, 여성 과학자들 중 상당수는 여전히 동등한 기회를 누리지 못하고 있다. 61) 유럽에서 수여된 대략 40%의 박사학위는 여성들이 받았지만, 그들은 민간부문 연구원의 겨우 15%만을 구성하고 있다. 과학 실험실은 여성들이 '남성만큼 재능이 있다'는 사실에도 불구하고 여전히 남성들이 장악하고 있다. 그녀는 여성들의 경쟁을 장려할 방안이 있어야 한다고 제안한다.

EU는 여성과학자들을 후원하는 프로그램에 자금을 지원하고 성별에 기반을 둔 고용계획을 요청함으로써 성차별을 해소하기 위해 애쓰고 있다. 하지만, 많은 연구원들은 과학계는 성별과 같은 요인으로 지원금을 결정할 때 어려움을 겪는 경향이 있다고 말한다. 그들은 젊은 남녀가 과학을 추구하도록 장려하는 장기적 해결책이 더 나은 선택이라고 제안한다. 62) Academy of Finland의 고문인 Hannele Kurki는 조기 과학 입문이 성차별적 편견을 무너뜨리는데 도움이 될 것이라고 말한다.

독일 굴지의 화학기업인 BASF의 최고 경영자인 Jürgen Hambrecht도 동의한다. 63) 그는 남녀의 성격 차이 때문에 여성들이 중요하다고 말한다. Hambrecht는 또한 여성 과학자들이 직장에서 필요한 가교라고 말한다. BASF는 남녀아이들 모두가 화학에 직접적인 경험을 할 수 있는 실험실을 운영한다.

과학기관은 또한 젊은 남녀 과학자들에게 영감을 줄 수 있는 최선의 방법은 실례에 의한 것임을 깨닫고 있는 중이다. Nowotny는 20년 전 Berlin 연구소에서 연구원들은 유일한 여성 연구원이 임신 중이었다는 것을 믿지 못했던 것을 회고했다. 64) 오늘날, 연구원들에게 가족들을 직장에 데려오도록 장려하고 있다. 가족 친화적인 환경을 조성함으로써, 기관들은 과학을 더 많은 여성에게 충족감을 주는 직업으로 만들 수 있다.

60 ▶정답 ⓓ

What is the article about?
(a) new opportunities for female scientists in Germany
(b) the career of Helga Nowotny
(c) the restructuring of a graduate program in Berlin
(d) the lack of opportunities for female scientists in Europe

해석

이 글은 무엇에 관한 것인가요?
(a) 독일 여성 과학자들을 위한 새로운 기회
(b) Helga Nowotny의 경력
(c) 베를린대학원의 프로그램 개편
(d) 유럽 여성 과학자들의 기회 부족

해설 글의 주제에 관해 묻는 문제로 보통 article은 제목에 주제를 담고 있다. 제목을 통해 과학계에서의 성차별이 있다는 것을 알 수 있으며 두 번째 문단에서 여성 연구원들이 동등한 기회를 누리지 못하고 있다는 내용이 나온다.

61 ▶정답 ⓑ

How can the status of European female scientists with doctoral degrees be described?
(a) Only a few of them earn doctor's degrees.
(b) Only a few of them are hired by the industries.
(c) Europe needs more of them.
(d) Most of them join the private sector.

해석

박사 학위를 가진 유럽 여성 과학자들의 지위가 어떻게 묘사될 수 있나요?
(a) 오직 그들 중 소수만이 박사 학위를 취득한다.
(b) 오직 그들 중 소수만이 산업체에 고용된다.
(c) 유럽은 그들을 더 많이 필요로 한다.
(d) 그들 대부분은 민간 부문에 참여한다.

해설 유럽에서 수여된 박사학위의 40%가 여성들이지만, 민간부문 연구원의 여성비율은 겨우 15%밖에 안 된다고 언급되어 있다. 극소수만이 산업체에 고용된다는 (b)의 진술과 같은 말이다.

62 ▶정답 ⓒ

Why does Hannele Kurki suggest that people be introduced to science early?
(a) to produce female science graduates in the future
(b) to prevent male scientists from advancing
(c) to save female scientists from unfair labeling.
(d) to give female science students better training

해석

Hannele Kurki은 왜 사람들이 과학을 일찍 접하도록 제안하나요?
(a) 미래에 여성 과학 졸업생을 배출하기 위해
(b) 남성 과학자들이 발전하는 것을 막기 위해

(c) 여성 과학자들을 편견으로부터 보호하기 위해
(d) 여성 과학 학생들에게 더 나은 교육을 제공하기 위해

해설 Hannele Kuriki는 조기 과학 입문이 성차별에 관한 편견을 무너뜨리는 데 도움이 될 것이라고 말했다.

63 ▶ 정답 ⓐ

What is Jürgen Hambrecht most likely suggesting?
(a) that women scientist's work can balance those of men
(b) that girls make better scientists
(c) that men should bridge the workplace
(d) that girls are good at chemistry

해설
Jürgen Hambrecht이 제시하는 것은 무엇인가요?
(a) 여성 과학자들의 업무는 남성의 업무와 균형을 이룰 수 있다는 것
(b) 여자 아이들이 더 나은 과학자가 된다는 것
(c) 남성들이 직장에서 교량 역할을 해야 한다는 것
(d) 여자 아이들이 화학을 잘한다는 것

해설 Jürgen Hambrecht는 여성들이 중요한 이유로 남녀의 성격 차이를 들었다. 여성 과학자들은 남성 과학자들과 다른 성격으로 인해 남성 과학자들과 서로 보완적인 일을 할 수 있다고 말했으므로 (a)의 진술을 유추할 수 있다.

64 ▶ 정답 ⓒ

How can institutions make women have a satisfying scientific career?
(a) by encouraging them to have families
(b) by accepting only women
(c) by making favorable work environments for women
(d) by accepting male associates who tolerate women

해설
어떻게 과학기관은 여성들이 과학 분야에서 만족스러운 경력을 갖게 할 수 있나요?
(a) 그들이 가족을 갖도록 장려함으로써
(b) 여성만을 수락함으로써
(c) 여성에게 유리한 근무 환경을 조성함으로써
(d) 여성을 참아내는 남성 동료를 받아들임으로써

해설 글의 후반부에, 가족 친화적인 환경을 만들어서 과학이 더 많은 여성들에게 충족감을 주는 직업이 될 수 있는 환경을 만들어야 한다고 제안하고 있다.

65 ▶ 정답 ⓑ

In the context of the passage, growing means _____.
(a) producing
(b) increasing
(c) raising
(d) shrinking

해석
문맥상, growing은 _____을 의미한다.
(a) 생산하는
(b) 증가하는
(c) 올리는
(d) 줄어드는

해설 growing 증가하는

66 ▶ 정답 ⓐ

In the context of the passage, promoting means _____.
(a) upholding
(b) marketing
(c) upgrading
(d) assisting

해석
문맥상, promoting은 _____을 의미한다.
(a) 지지하다
(b) 마케팅하다
(c) 개선하다
(d) 돕다

해설 promote 조성하다, 조장하다, 장려하다

Question 67-73

PLASTIC

Plastic is a manmade or natural material that is used in a variety of products. Plastics are made of long chains of carbon molecules called "polymers" that give them their many unique and highly useful properties.

67) The word "plastic" is derived from the Greek word plastikos which means "to mold." Plastic can be made as strong as steel, as transparent as glass, as light as wood, and as elastic as rubber. They can also be produced in almost any color. Different types of plastic can be 72) alloyed into more useful varieties. More than 50 families of plastics have already been produced through combinations, and new types are currently being developed.

Although synthetic plastics are relatively new, natural plastics have been in use for thousands of years. The ancient Egyptians wrapped their mummies in burial cloths that were soaked in gum-like and semisolid substances called "resins." Many cultures also used natural resin-bearing animal horns and turtle shells to make spoons, combs, and buttons. 68) During the mid-19th century, "shellac," a substance secreted by an insect called "lac," was used in molding small cases, phonograph records, and mirror frames.

69) In the late 19th century, scientists began to develop many more types of plastics in the laboratory and more efficient ways of producing them. 70) Among the inventors who contributed to the development of plastics was Leo Baekeland, who created what is known today as "phenolic resin," also called Bakelite. It has been used to make telephones, pot handles, and many other products. By the 1930s, water-soluble, flexible, and durable polymers, called "acrylics," were already being produced by German, British, and American companies.

Plastics are very important to modern life. They are widely used in automobile and aircraft manufacturing, food packaging, and health care. Although plastics are extremely useful, they also have some disadvantages. 71) When burned, some plastics produce 73) noxious fumes that cause health risks. Their use has also resulted in a growing garbage problem in many parts of the world. To address the problem, consumers are being encouraged to reduce their use of plastics and recycle used plastic products.

Words

molecule 분자	property 특성
mold 만들다, 주조하다	transparent 투명한
elastic 탄력(성)이 있는	alloy 합금하다
variety 여러 가지, 각양각색	synthetic 합성의
burial 매장	mummy 미라
soak 담그다, 적시다	semisolid 반고체의
horn 뿔	shell 껍데기, 껍질
secrete 분비하다	contribute (to) 기여하다
water-soluble 수용성의	flexible 적응성 있는, 유연한
aircraft 항공기	fume 연기, 가스
garbage 쓰레기	address 다루다, 해결하다

해석

플라스틱

플라스틱은 다양한 제품에 사용되는 인공 또는 천연 재료이다. 플라스틱은 그들에게 그들의 독특하고, 매우 유용한 특징을 주는 'polymers'로 불리는 carbon molecules의 긴 사슬로 만들어진다.

67) 단어 '플라스틱'은 '만드는 것'을 의미하는 그리스어 plastikos에서 유래했다. 플라스틱은 강철처럼 강하고, 유리처럼 투명하며, 나무처럼 가볍고, 고무처럼 탄력적이게 만들어 질 수 있다. 그들은 또한 거의 어떠한 색상으로도 생산이 가능하다. 다른 종류의 플라스틱은 더 유용한 종류로 합금될 수 있다. 50종 이상의 플라스틱 제품군은 이미 조합을 통해 생산이 되어 오고 있으며, 새로운 종류들이 현재 개발되고 있다.

합성 플라스틱은 상대적으로 새로운 것인 반면, 천연 플라스틱은 수천년 동안 사용되어 오고 있다. 고대 이집트인들은 'resins'라고 불리는 고무와 같은 및 반고체물질에 적셨던 매장용 천에 미라를 감쌌다. 많은 문화들도 숟가락과 빗, 단추를 만들기 위해 천연 'resin'을 함유한 동물 뿔과 거북이 껍질을 사용했다. 68) 19세기 중반, 'lac'이라는 곤충의 분비 물질인 'shellac'은 작은 상자 및 축음기 판, 그리고 거울 틀을 주조하는데 사용이 되었다.

69) 19세기 후반, 과학자들은 더 많은 종류의 플라스틱과 훨씬 효율적인 생산방법을 실험실에서 개발하기 시작했다. 70) 플라스틱 개발에 기여한 발명가들 중 한 명인 Leo Baekland는 오늘날 'phenolic resin'이라고 알려진, 또는 Bakelite라고도 불리는 것을 만들어냈다. 그것은 전화기, 냄비 손잡이, 그리고 많은 다른 제품들을 만드는데 사용되었다. 1930년대에는 'acrylics'로 불리는 수용성, 유연성, 내구성을 갖춘 폴리머가 이미 독일, 영국, 그리고 미국회사들에 의해 생산되었다.

플라스틱은 현대의 삶에 굉장히 중요하다. 그들은 자동차 및 비행기 제조, 식품포장과 건강관리에 널리 사용되고 있다. 플라스틱은 굉장히 유용함에도 불구하고, 그들은 또한 몇몇 단점을 갖고 있다. 71) 탈 때, 일부 플라스틱은 건강에 위험한 73) 유독 기체를 만든다. 그들의 사용으로 또한 전세계 많은 지역에서 쓰레기 문제를 이끌고 있다. 이 문제를 해결하기 위해, 소비자들에게 플라스틱 사용을 줄이고 사용한 플라스틱 제품들을 재활용하는 것을 장려하고 있다.

67 ▶ 정답 ⓐ

Which property of plastic does the origin of its name suggest?

(a) its flexibility
(b) its lightness
(c) its durability
(d) its transparency

해석

플라스틱의 어떤 특성이 그 이름의 유래를 표현하나요?

(a) 그것의 유연성
(b) 그것의 가벼움
(c) 그것의 내구성
(d) 그것의 투명성

해설

두 번째 문단에서 '플라스틱'이란 단어가 그리스어 plastikos에서 유래되었는데 강철처럼 강하고, 유리처럼 투명하며, 나무처럼 가볍고 고무처럼 탄력 있게 만들어질 수 있다고 언급되어 있다. 고무와 같이 탄력적인 유연성이 플라스틱이란 단어의 유래를 담고 있다.

68
▶ 정답 ⓑ

How were phonographs made in the 19th century?
(a) by using the horns of animals
(b) by using a material from an insect
(c) by employing the shells of a turtle
(d) by harvesting gum from a tree

해석
어떻게 축음기는 19세기에 만들어졌나요?
(a) 동물들의 뿔을 사용하여
(b) 곤충의 재료를 사용하여
(c) 거북이 껍질을 사용하여
(d) 나무에서 고무를 채취하여

해설 19세기 중반에 'lac'이라는 곤충 분비 물질 shellac이 작은 상자 및 축음기 판을 만드는데 사용되었다는 내용이 언급되어 있다.

69
▶ 정답 ⓐ

What major development in the history of plastics occurred in the late 19th century?
(a) the development of better ways of making plastic
(b) the discovery of natural plastic
(c) the invention of more durable types of plastic
(d) the promotion of plastic waste recycling

해석
19세기 후반에 플라스틱 역사에 있어 어떤 중요한 발전이 있었나요?
(a) 플라스틱 만드는 더 나은 방법들의 발전
(b) 천연 플라스틱의 발견
(c) 내구성 강한 플라스틱의 발명
(d) 플라스틱 폐기물 재활용 촉구

해설 네 번째 문단 첫 줄에 19세기 후반에 과학자들은 더 많은 종류의 플라스틱과 훨씬 효율적인 생산방법을 개발하기 시작했다고 쓰여있다.

70
▶ 정답 ⓒ

Which type of plastic is used for the manufacture of telephone?
(a) acrylics
(b) natural resin
(c) phenolic resin
(d) shellac

해석
전화기를 만드는데 사용되는 플라스틱의 종류는 무엇입니까?
(a) 아크릴
(b) 천연 수지
(c) 페놀 수지
(d) 셸락

해설 Among the inventors who contributed to the development of plastics was Leo Baekeland, who created what is known today as "phenolic resin," also called Bakelite. It has been used to make telephones, pot handles, and many other products.를 통해 전화기에 사용된 플라스틱은 phenolic resin(페놀 수지)임을 알 수 있다.

71
▶ 정답 ⓑ

Based on the passage, why most likely are people being asked to lessen their use of plastic?
(a) It will conserve the animals plastics are made from.
(b) It will reduce the health dangers the material can cause.
(c) It will slow down society's rapid industrialization.
(d) It will control the consumers' dependence of plastic.

해석
글을 토대로, 왜 사람들은 플라스틱 사용을 줄여야 하나요?
(a) 플라스틱의 원료로 사용되는 동물들을 보호할 것이다.
(b) 그 물질이 유발할 수 있는 건강상의 위험을 줄일 것이다.
(c) 사회의 급진적인 산업화를 늦출 것이다.
(d) 소비자의 플라스틱 의존성을 억제할 것이다.

해설 플라스틱의 단점으로, 연소될 때 건강에 유해한 기체를 만들어낸다고 했으므로 건강상에 위협이 될 것이라는 내용을 담고 있는 (b)가 가장 적절하다.

72
▶ 정답 ⓓ

In the context of the passage, alloyed means _____.
(a) divided
(b) consumed
(c) hardened
(d) blended

해석
문맥상, alloyed은 _____을 의미한다.
(a) 나누다
(b) 소비하다
(c) 굳다, 단단해지다
(d) 섞다

해설 alloy 합금하다, 섞다

73
▶ 정답 ⓑ

In the context of the passage, noxious means _____.
(a) smelly
(b) harmful
(c) widespread
(d) powerful

해석

문맥상, noxious은 _____을 의미한다.

(a) 냄새 나는
(b) 해로운
(c) 널리 퍼진
(d) 강력한

해설 noxious 유독한, 유해한

Question 74-80

February 17, 2016

Ms. Adriana Kelly
General Manager
Kelly Design Studio
52 Sherman Avenue
Evanston, IL 60208

Dear Ms. Kelly:

The Chicago Architecture Foundation (CAF) is offering adult education classes for Spring 2016. 74) We invite you and the staff of Kelly Design Studio to enroll in any of the following courses:

Historic Western Architecture and Modern Chicago: 75) Students will discover how medieval France and Renaissance Italy 79) influenced the design of Chicago's civic commercial buildings, university campuses, and residential structures. The instructor is Prof. Nancy Cook from DePaul University's Art and Architecture Department.

Introduction to City Planning: 76) Students will explore issues of urbanism or city dwellers' lifestyles, including theories of city design and the history of city design in Rome, Paris, and Washington. The course will also examine recent trends in American and international city design. The instructor is Prof. Brent D. Ryan of the City Design Center, University of Illinois at Chicago.

Architectural Geology of the Chicago Region: 77) Students will learn the connection between natural elements and architecture and find out how city planners altered the Chicago coastline. This course includes two walking tours of Chicago's architectural landmarks. The instructor is Mr. Raymond Wiggers, an environmental geologist of the State of Illinois.

For course schedules, venues, and registration fees, please 80) refer to the attached sheet. 78-d) Your CAF membership entitles you and your employees to a 20% discount. 78-b) You may register in person at the CAF offices or online at www.architecture.org.

I hope to see you at the CAF soon. Thank you very much.

Sincerely,

Grant Moseley
78-c) Program Coordinator
Chicago Architecture Foundation
224 South Michigan Avenue, Chicago IL 60604
Tel: (312) 922-3432

Words

enroll 등록하다
civic 도시의
urbanism 도시화, 도시성
coastline 해안선
geologist 지질학자
entitle 자격을 주다
medieval 중세의
residential 주거의, 거주의
alter 바꾸다, 변경하다
landmark 역사적인 건물, 명소
venue 장소
register 등록하다

해석

켈리씨께:

시카고 건축 재단 (CAF)은 2016년 봄 성인 교육 강좌를 제공할 예정입니다. 74) 우리는 귀하와 Kellly Design Studio의 직원들이 다음 강좌들에 등록할 것을 권해드립니다.

역사적인 서양 건축 및 현대 시카고: 75) 학생들은 중세 프랑스와 르네상스 이탈리아가 어떻게 시카고의 상업 건물, 대학 캠퍼스 및 주거용 건물 설계에 영향을 미쳤는지 배우게 될 것입니다. 강사는 DePaul University의 Art and Architecture Department의 Nancy Cook 교수입니다.

도시 계획 입문: 76) 학생들은 로마, 파리, 워싱턴의 도시 디자인 이론과 도시 디자인 역사를 포함하는 도시화의 쟁점 또는 도시 거주자의 생활방식을 탐구할 것입니다. 이 과정은 또한 미국 및 국제 도시 디자인의 최근 동향도 살필 것입니다. 강사는 시카고에 있는 University of Illinois의 City Design Center의 Brent D. Ryan 교수입니다.

시카고 지역의 건축 지질학: 77) 학생들은 자연요소와 건축물 사이의 연결성을 배우고, 도시 계획자가 어떻게 시카고 해안선을 변경했는지 배우게 될 것입니다. 이 과정은 두 번의 시카고 건축명소들의 도보투어가 포함되어 있습니다. 강사는 Illinois주의 환경 지질학자 Raymond Wiggers입니다.

과정 스케줄, 장소 및 등록비는 첨부 서류를 참고하세요. 78-d) 귀하와 귀하의 직원은 CAF회원 자격으로 20% 할인을 받을 수 있습니다. 78-b) CAF 사무실이나 www.architecture.org에서 직접 등록하시면 됩니다.

CAF에서 곧 뵙길 바랍니다. 고맙습니다.

74 ▶ 정답 ⓒ

Why did Grant Moseley write Adriana Kelly the letter?
(a) to ask her to deliver a lecture on city planning
(b) to convince her to join an organization of architects
(c) to offer courses to her design company's workers
(d) to invite her to the inaugural of a building in Chicago

해석 그랜트 모슬 리가 아드리아나 켈리에게 편지를 쓴 이유는 무엇인가요?
(a) 그녀에게 도시계획과 관련된 강연을 요청하기 위해
(b) 그녀에게 건축가협회에 가입하도록 설득하기 위해
(c) 그녀의 디자인 회사 근로자들에게 강좌를 제안하기 위해
(d) 그녀를 시카고에 있는 건물 취임식에 초청하기 위해

해설 편지 첫 문단 마지막에 다음 강의에 등록할 것을 권한다는 내용이 나오므로 (c)가 가장 적절하다.

75 ▶ 정답 ⓓ

What will the first course of the adult classes be about?
(a) the history of Western architecture
(b) how Chicago's architecture was improved
(c) how Italy influenced French architecture
(d) European architecture's influence on Chicago

해석 성인강좌 첫 번째 과정은 무엇에 관한 것일까요?
(a) 서구 건축 역사
(b) 어떻게 시카고 건축이 향상했는지
(c) 어떻게 이탈리아가 프랑스 건축에 영향을 끼쳤는지
(d) 유럽 건축이 시카고에 끼친 영향

해설 Students will discover how medieval France and Renaissance Italy influenced the design of Chicago's civic commercial buildings, university campuses, and residential structures.를 통해 유럽 건축이 시카고에 끼친 영향에 관해 학습할 것임을 알 수 있다.

76 ▶ 정답 ⓑ

What is said about the Introduction to City Planning course?
(a) It will show how nature influences building design.
(b) It will discuss developments in worldwide city design.
(c) It will include a tour of major European and American cities.
(d) It will be handled by a well-known geologist.

해석 도시 계획 입문 과정에 관해 언급된 것은 무엇인가요?
(a) 어떻게 자연이 건축설계에 영향을 미치는지 보여줄 것이다.
(b) 전세계 도시 디자인의 발전에 대해 토의할 것이다.
(c) 유럽과 미국 주요 도시로의 여행을 포함할 것이다.
(d) 유명한 지질학자가 담당할 것이다.

해설 학생들은 다양한 국가의 도시 디자인 이론과 역사를 포함한 생활방식을 탐구하고 이 과정에서 최근 동향도 학습하게 될 것이라는 내용을 통해 (b)가 가장 적절하다.

77 ▶ 정답 ⓓ

Based on the letter, what is most likely the purpose of the walking tours during the last course?
(a) to know how Chicago's architecture can be improved
(b) to see how architecture will change Chicago coastline
(c) to give the students a break from the lessons
(d) to see how city planning influenced natural elements in Chicago

해석 편지에 따르면, 도보투어의 마지막 과정의 목표는 무엇인가요?
(a) 시카고 건축이 어떻게 향상될 수 있는지를 알기 위해서
(b) 어떻게 시카고 해안선을 변화시킬 것인지를 보기 위해서
(c) 학생들에게 수업에서 벗어나 휴식을 제공하기 위해서
(d) 어떻게 도시계획이 시카고의 자연 요소에 영향을 끼치는지를 보기 위해서

해설 Students will learn the connection between natural elements and architecture and find out how city planners altered the Chicago coastline. This course includes two walking tours of Chicago's architectural landmarks.을 통해 도시 계획이 시카고 자연 요소에 어떻게 영향을 끼쳤는지를 학습하게 될 것이라는 것을 알 수 있다.

78 ▶ 정답 ⓐ

What was not mentioned in the letter?
(a) the number of sessions for each course
(b) the ways for interested parties to register
(c) the official designation of the letter sender
(d) the discount being offered to CAF members

해석 편지에 언급되지 않은 내용은 무엇인가요?
(a) 각 과정의 세션 수
(b) 관심 있는 당들이 등록하는 방법들
(c) 편지 발신자의 공식적인 직함
(d) CAF 회원들에게 제공되는 할인

해설 마지막 단락에서 CAF회원은 20% 할인 받을 수 있으며 CAF 사무실이나 www.architecture.org를 통해서 접수할 수 있다고 언급했다. 편지 왼쪽 하단에 편지 쓴 사람에 대한 직책이 Program Coordinator임도 나와 있다. 반면, 각 과정의 세션 수는 편지글 전체 어디에도 언급되어 있지 않다.

79 ▶ 정답 ⓓ

In the context of the passage, influenced means _____.

(a) destroyed
(b) convinced
(c) designed
(d) affected

해석

문맥상, influenced는 _____을 의미한다.

(a) 파괴하다
(b) 설득하다, 확신시키다
(c) 만들다, 디자인하다
(d) 영향을 끼치다

해설 influence 영향을 끼치다

80 ▶ 정답 ⓓ

In the context of the passage, refer means _____.

(a) notice
(b) study
(c) ignore
(d) see

해석

문맥상, refer는 _____을 의미한다.

(a) 알아차리다
(b) 공부하다, 연구하다
(c) 무시하다
(d) 보다

해설 refer 참고하다, 참조하다

한 권에 끝내는
Level 2
G-TELP
실전모의고사

5회

초 판 1쇄 발행 2019년 1월 7일
　　2쇄 발행 2020년 3월 20일

출제 G-TELP KOREA 영어연구소 해설 이현아
발행인 이향준 발행처 (주)법률저널
등록일자 2008년 9월 26일 등록번호 제15-605호
주소 151-862 서울 관악구 복은4길 50 (서림동 120-32)
대표전화 02)874-1144 팩스 02)876-4312
홈페이지 www.lec.co.kr
ISBN 978-89-6336-365-3

정가 22,000원

도서소개

▌이현아 취향저격 한 권에 끝내는 G-TELP 32점
　정가 13,000원

▌이현아 취향저격 한 권에 끝내는 G-TELP 50점
　정가 17,000원

▌이현아 취향저격 한 권에 끝내는 G-TELP 65점
　정가 17,000원

▌이현아 취향저격 G-TELP 어휘 900
　정가 9,000원

한 권에 끝내는
Level 2
G-TELP
실전모의고사

5회

정가 22,000원

이현아 취향저격

지텔프코리아
공식
지정

한 권에 끝내는
Level 2
G-TELP
실전모의고사

5회

한 권에 끝내는
Level 2
G-TELP
실전모의고사

5회

이현아 취향저격
G - TELP